Architecture and Feminisms

Set against the background of a 'general crisis' that is environmental, political and social, this book examines a series of specific intersections between architecture and feminisms, understood in the plural. The collected essays and projects which make up the book follow transversal trajectories that criss-cross between ecologies, economies and technologies, exploring specific cases and positions in relation to the themes of the archive, control, work and milieu. This collective intellectual labour can be located amidst a worldwide depletion of material resources, a hollowing out of political power and the degradation of constructed and natural environments. Feminist positions suggest ways of ethically coping with a world that is becoming increasingly unstable and contested. The many voices gathered here are united by the task of putting critical concepts and feminist design tools to use in order to offer experimental approaches to the creation of a more habitable world. Drawing inspiration from the active archives of feminist precursors, existing and re-imagined, and by way of a re-engagement in the histories, theories and projected futures of critical feminist projects, the book presents a collection of twenty-three essays and eight projects, with the aim of taking stock of our current condition and re-engaging in our precarious environment-worlds.

Hélène Frichot is an Associate Professor and Docent in Critical Studies in Architecture, School of Architecture and the Built Environment, Royal Institute of Technology, KTH, Stockholm, Sweden, where she is the director of Critical Studies in Architecture. Her research examines the transdisciplinary field between architecture and philosophy; while her first discipline is architecture, she holds a PhD in philosophy from the University of Sydney (2004). Recent publications include: co-editor with Catharina Gabrielsson and Jonathan Metzger, *Deleuze and the City* (Edinburgh University Press, 2016); co-editor with Elizabeth Grierson and Harriet Edquist, *De-Signing Design: Cartographies of Theory and Practice* (Lexington Books, 2015).

Catharina Gabrielsson is Docent in Architecture and an Associate Professor in Urban Theory at the School of Architecture KTH, Stockholm. Her research employs writing as a means for exploration, bridging across aesthetics, politics and economics and combining fieldwork operations with archival studies to generate material for conceptual analysis. With Hélène Frichot and Jonathan Metzger, she is co-editor of *Deleuze and the City* (Edinburgh University Press, 2016), guest co-editor, with Helena Mattsson, of 'Architecture and Capitalism: Solids and Flows' (*Architecture and Culture* 5:2, 2017), and, with Helena Mattsson and Kenny Cupers, editor of the forthcoming volume *Neoliberalism: An Architectural History* (University of Pittsburgh Press). She is the director of the doctoral programme Art, Technology and Design.

Helen Runting is a an urban planner (B.UPD, University of Melbourne) and urban designer (PG.Dip UD, University of Melbourne; MSc.UPD, Royal Institute of Technology (KTH), Stockholm), and a PhD candidate within Critical Studies in Architecture at KTH. Her research is situated within the field of architectural theory and addresses the images, politics, property relations, and aesthetics of the 'unbuilt environment' of Sweden's architectural present. Helen is a founding member of the architecture collective Svensk Standard (2008–), and the architectural practice Secretary (2017–).

Critiques: Critical studies in architectural humanities
A project of the Architectural Humanities Research Association

Series Editor: Jonathan Hale (University of Nottingham)
Editorial Board:
Sarah Chaplin
Mark Dorrian (Newcastle University)
Murray Fraser (University of Westminster)
Hilde Heynen (Catholic University of Leuven)
Andrew Leach (University of Queensland)
Thomas Mical (Carleton University)
Jane Rendell (University College London)
Adam Sharr (Newcastle University)
Igea Troiani (Oxford Brookes University)

This original series of edited books contains selected papers from the AHRA Annual International Conferences. Each year the event has its own thematic focus while sharing an interest in new and emerging critical research in the areas of architectural history, theory, culture, design and urbanism.

Volume 1: Critical Architecture
Edited by: Jane Rendell, Jonathan Hill, Murray Fraser and Mark Dorrian

Volume 2: From Models to Drawings: Imagination and Representation in Architecture
Edited by: Marco Frascari, Jonathan Hale and Bradley Starkey

Volume 3: The Politics of Making
Edited by: Mark Swenarton, Igea Troiani and Helena Webster

Volume 4: Curating Architecture and the City
Edited by: Sarah Chaplin and Alexandra Stara

Volume 5: Agency: Working with Uncertain Architectures
Edited by: Florrian Kossak, Doina Petrescu, Tatjana Schneider, Renata Tyszczuk and Stephen Walker

Volume 6: Architecture and Field/Work
Edited by: Suzanne Ewing, Jérémie Michael McGowan, Chris Speed and Victoria Clare Bernie

Volume 7: Scale
Edited by: Gerald Adler, Timothy Brittain-Catlin and Gordana Fontana-Giusti

Volume 8: Peripheries
Edited by: Ruth Morrow and Mohamed Gamal Abdelmonem

Volume 9: Architecture and the Paradox of Dissidence
Edited by: Ines Weizman

Volume 10: Transgression: Towards an Expanded Field of Architecture
Edited by: Louis Rice and David Littlefield

Volume 11: Industries of Architecture
Edited by: Katie Lloyd Thomas, Tilo Amhoff and Nick Beech
Volume 12: This Thing Called Theory
Edited by: Teresa Stoppani, George Themistokleous and Giorgio Ponzo

Volume 13: Architecture and Feminisms: Ecologies, Economies, Technologies
Edited by: Hélène Frichot, Catharina Gabrielsson and Helen Runting

AHRA provides an inclusive and comprehensive support network for humanities researchers in architecture across the UK and beyond. It promotes, supports, develops and disseminates high-quality research in all areas of architectural humanities.

www.ahra-architecture.org

Architecture and Feminisms

Ecologies, Economies, Technologies

Edited by Hélène Frichot, Catharina Gabrielsson and Helen Runting

Routledge
Taylor & Francis Group

LONDON AND NEW YORK

First published 2018
by Routledge
2 Park Square, Milton Park, Abingdon, Oxon OX14 4RN

and by Routledge
711 Third Avenue, New York, NY 10017

Routledge is an imprint of the Taylor & Francis Group, an informa business

© 2018 selection and editorial matter, Hélène Frichot, Catharina Gabrielsson and Helen Runting; individual chapters, the contributors

The right of Hélène Frichot, Catharina Gabrielsson and Helen Runting to be identified as the authors of the editorial material, and of the authors for their individual chapters, has been asserted in accordance with sections 77 and 78 of the Copyright, Designs and Patents Act 1988.

All rights reserved. No part of this book may be reprinted or reproduced or utilised in any form or by any electronic, mechanical, or other means, now known or hereafter invented, including photocopying and recording, or in any information storage or retrieval system, without permission in writing from the publishers.

Trademark notice: Product or corporate names may be trademarks or registered trademarks, and are used only for identification and explanation without intent to infringe.

British Library Cataloguing-in-Publication Data
A catalogue record for this book is available from the British Library

Library of Congress Cataloging-in-Publication Data
Names: Frichot, Hélène, editor. | Gabrielsson, Catharina, editor. | Runting, Helen, editor.
Title: Architecture and feminisms : ecologies, economies, technologies / edited by Hélène Frichot, Catharina Gabrielsson and Helen Runting.
Description: New York : Routledge, 2017. | Series: Critiques : critical studies in architectural humanities ; volume 13 | Includes bibliographical references and index.
Identifiers: LCCN 2017021886 | ISBN 9781138304871 (hb : alk. paper) | ISBN 9781138304888 (pb : alk. paper) | ISBN 9780203729717 (ebook)
Subjects: LCSH: Feminism and architecture.
Classification: LCC NA2543.F45 A735 2017 | DDC 720.82—dc23
LC record available at https://lccn.loc.gov/2017021886

ISBN: 978-1-138-30487-1 (hbk)
ISBN: 978-1-138-30488-8 (pbk)
ISBN: 978-0-203-72971-7 (ebk)

Typeset in Univers
by Keystroke, Neville Lodge, Tettenhall, Wolverhampton

Contents

Contents

Contributors

Jos Boys is a tutor in interior architecture at Regents University London, as well as an independent scholar. She has a long background in feminism and architecture, as a co-founder of both Matrix in the 1980s and *taking place* more recently. Her research and creative practice focus on how to better understand everyday social and spatial practices and how to find ways to intervene creatively in altering inequitable practices. She is currently exploring intersections between architecture, dis/ability and gender, including in *Doing Disability Differently: An Alternative Handbook on Architecture, Dis/ability and Designing for Everyday Life* (Routledge, 2014) and *Disability, Space, Architecture: A Reader* (2017).

Lori A. Brown is a licensed architect in New York state and a Professor of Architecture at Syracuse University. Her research focuses on relationships between architecture and social justice with particular emphasis on gender. Her publications include *Contested Space: Abortion Clinics, Women's Shelters and Hospitals* (Ashgate 2013) and *Feminist Practices: Interdisciplinary Approaches to Women in Architecture* (Ashgate, 2011). She was awarded the American Institute of Architects Diversity Best Practice Honourable Mention (2008) and a commendation for the Milka Bliznakov Prize for the Feminist Practices exhibition (2008). In 2012, she co-launched *ArchiteXX*, a women and architecture group in New York City.

Alison Brunn is a Master of Architecture student at Iowa State University. Prior to studying architecture, she earned a B.A. in economics and German from CUNY Hunter College in New York City.

Karen Burns is Senior Lecturer in architectural design at the University of Melbourne. She is a critic and public commentator on issues in contemporary architecture and the co-editor of Parlour, a website building discussion and exchange on women, equity and architecture. Burns was an active researcher on the Australian Research Council funded project *Equity and Diversity in the Australian Architectural Profession: Women, Work and Leadership* (2011–2014). Her academic research focuses on three principal areas: Australian frontier housing and problems of interpretation, late-twentieth-century feminist architectural history and theory, and alliances between architects, aesthetics and manufacturers in mid-nineteenth-century Britain.

Emma Cheatle is a postdoctoral researcher at Newcastle University, UK, currently writing a creative-critical history of maternity spaces, *Spaces of (Modern) Maternity: Architecture, Literature and Birth, 1660–1880*. Emma's research uses different forms of text, both fictional and theoretical, combined with drawings and audio works to 'reconstruct' the past lives of buildings as sites of social history. Awarded 2014 RIBA President's Award for Outstanding PhD Thesis, her PhD is now published as the book *Part-architecture: The Maison de Verre, Duchamp, Domesticity and Desire in 1930s Paris* (Routledge, 2017).

Shelby Elizabeth Doyle, AIA, is an Assistant Professor of architecture and Daniel J. Huberty Faculty Fellow at the Iowa State University College of Design. Her scholarship is broadly focused on the intersection of computation and construction and specifically on the role of digital craft as both a social and political project. She holds a Master of Architecture degree from the Harvard Graduate School of Design and a Bachelor of Science in Architecture from the University of Virginia. Leslie Forehand and Doyle co-founded the ISU Computation + Construction Lab with their colleague Nick Senske: http://ccl.design.iastate.edu/.

Claudia Dutson recently completed an AHRC-funded PhD in architecture at the Royal College of Art. Her research investigates the politics of thermal management, extending a feminist critique, and using performative methods, to sustainability in architecture set within the organisational management and economic discourse of the new economy. Before training in architecture, she trained in media studies and worked in management consultancy in new media up until the dotcom crash. She teaches for the MArch at Canterbury School of Architecture, and for the MA of Information Experience Design at the Royal College of Art.

Leslie Forehand is a Lecturer in architecture at the Iowa State University College of Design and an internationally experienced architect/designer and researcher. Her research seeks to find new solutions in the digital processes, specifically advancing the materiality of additive manufacturing. Leslie holds a Master of Architecture from Pratt Institute and a Bachelor of Science in Architecture from the University of Virginia. Her personal and student work has been exhibited and published worldwide. Forehand and Doyle co-founded the ISU Computation + Construction Lab with their colleague Nick Senske: http://ccl.design.iastate.edu/.

Hélène Frichot is an Associate Professor and Docent in Critical Studies in Architecture, School of Architecture and the Built Environment, KTH, Stockholm, where she is the director of Critical Studies in Architecture. Her research examines the transdisciplinary field between architecture and philosophy. While her first discipline is architecture, she holds a PhD in philosophy from the University of Sydney (2004). Recent publications include: co-editor with Catharina Gabrielsson, Jonathan Metzger, *Deleuze and the City* (EUP, 2016); co-editor with Elizabeth Grierson, Harriet Edquist, *De-Signing Design: Cartographies of Theory and Practice* (Lexington Books, 2015).

Hannes Frykholm is an architect and PhD candidate at KTH School of Architecture. He has published projects and texts in *Nordic Journal of Architecture, Arkitektur, Soiled,* and *Future Arquitecturas*. He is partner of the speculative practice *Oh, architecture!* based in Stockholm.

Catharina Gabrielsson is Docent in Architecture and an Associate Professor in Urban Theory at the School of Architecture KTH, Stockholm. Her research employs writing as a means for exploration, bridging across aesthetics, politics and economics and combining fieldwork operations with archival studies to generate material for conceptual analysis. With Hélène Frichot and Jonathan Metzger, she is co-editor of *Deleuze and the City* (Edinburgh University Press 2016), guest co-editor, with Helena Mattsson, of 'Architecture and Capitalism: Solids and Flows' (*Architecture and Culture* 5:2, 2017), and, with Helena Mattsson and Kenny Cupers, editor of the forthcoming volume *Neoliberalism: An Architectural History* (University of Pittsburgh Press). She is the director of the doctoral programme Art, Technology and Design.

Katherine Gibson is an economic geographer with an international reputation for innovative research on economic transformation and working with communities to build resilient economies. As J.K. Gibson-Graham, the collective authorial presence she shares with the late Julie Graham (Professor of Geography, University of Massachusetts Amherst), her books include *The End of Capitalism (As We Knew It): A Feminist Critique of Political Economy* (Blackwell, 1996) and *A Postcapitalist Politics* (University of Minnesota Press, 2006). Her most recent books are *Take Back the Economy: An Ethical Guide for Transforming Our Communities*, co-authored with Jenny Cameron and Stephen Healy (University of Minnesota Press, 2013), *Making Other Worlds Possible: Performing Diverse Economies*, co-edited with Gerda Roelvink and Kevin St Martin (University of Minnesota Press, 2015) and *Manifesto for Living in the Anthropocene*, co-edited with Deborah Bird Rose and Ruth Fincher (Punctum Press, 2015).

Hilde Heynen's research focuses on issues of modernity, modernism and gender in architecture. She is the author of *Architecture and Modernity. A Critique* (MIT Press, 1999) and the co-editor of *Back from Utopia. The Challenge of the Modern Movement* (with Hubert-Jan Henket, 010, 2001), *Negotiating Domesticity. Spatial productions of gender in modern architecture* (with Gülsüm Baydar, Routledge, 2005) and *The SAGE Handbook Architectural Theory* (with Greig Crysler and Stephen Cairns, SAGE, 2012). She regularly publishes in journals such as *The Journal of Architecture* and *Home Cultures*.

Rixt Hoekstra is an architectural historian, who received her PhD in 2006. She is specialized in the fields of modern architectural theory, historiography and the development of architectural discourse in the twentieth century. In the past years she has published on the influence of poststructuralism in the work of Dutch architect-intellectuals for the journal *Archimeara: Architektur.Kultur.Kontext* (2013) and about the development of architectural discourse in the Communist GDR, in *The Journal of History & Theory of Architecture* (2014). The chapter included in this volume is part of her habilitation on the female actors within the CIAM.

Sandra Kaji-O'Grady has led the School of Architecture at the University of Queensland as its Head of School and Dean of Architecture since 2013. She led the transformation of the School of Architecture at UTS where she was Head (2005–2009) and her previous role was as Professor of Architecture at the University of Sydney (2010–2013). She has a Doctorate in Philosophy from Monash University (2001), a postgraduate diploma in women's studies, and professional architectural qualifications and experience. She researches in the architectural humanities, with a focus on the transfer – and translation – of ideas and techniques between architecture and the experimental sciences.

Nicole Kalms is a Senior Lecturer in the Department of Architecture at Monash University in Melbourne, Australia. Her recent book *Hypersexual City: The Provocation of Softcore Urbanism* (Routledge 2017) examines contemporary urbanism and sexualized representation. Nicole is the Founding Director of Monash University's XYX Laboratory, based in the Faculty of Art, Design and Architecture. In this role Nicole leads a team of interdisciplinary researchers examining the complex interaction of space, gender and communication in cities.

Daniel Koch is an architect and researcher at the KTH School of Architecture, whose research investigates spatial configuration, diagrams and abstractions, and processes of subjectification within the larger frame of architectural theory and urban design. Lately his research has focused a lot on the role of memory, projection and imagination within observation-based research and our understanding of relations between architecture and social structures.

Katie Lloyd Thomas is Professor of theory and history of architecture and Co-director of the Architectural Research Collaborative at Newcastle University, UK. She is an editor of *Architectural Research Quarterly* and a steering group member of the Architectural Humanities Research Association. Edited collections include *Industries of Architecture* with Tilo Amhoff and Nick Beech (Routledge, 2015) and *Material Matters: Architecture and Material Practice* (Routledge, 2007). Katie is a founder member of the feminist collective *taking place* (www.takingplace.org.uk). Recent publications on feminist theory and practice include: 'Between the Womb and the World' in *Architectural Relational Ecologies*, ed. Peg Rawes (Routledge, 2013) and 'Feminist Hydro-logics in Joan Slonczewski's *A Door Into Ocean* in *Landscript 5*. Much of her current research explores contexts where gender and technology intersect.

Janet McGaw is an architect and academic at the University of Melbourne with a PhD by Creative Works. Her research work, teaching and creative practice investigate ways to make urban space more equitable. In recent years she has contributed to the discourse on Indigenous placemaking practices and design research methods. Janet uses methods that are discursive, collaborative and sometimes ephemeral. Her collaborative installation with homeless women, 'Urban Threads', was exhibited in the international exhibition, *Feminist Practices*, curated by Lori A. Brown and the subsequent book *Feminist Practices: Interdisciplinary Approaches to Women in Architecture* (Farnham: Ashgate, 2011).

Aya Musmar is an Arabic-speaking feminist. She is a second-year PhD student at the University of Sheffield, where she has also finished her Master's degree in architectural design. Following a feminist approach, Aya's research aims at challenging the current western NGO intangible infrastructures in Za'atri refugee camp. She aspires to re-imagine such infrastructures by looking at the cultural context of the refugee community. Before her PhD, Aya worked as a community mobilizer in Za'atri refugee camp, Jordan, where she facilitated women's refugee committee meetings.

Janek Oźmin is an interdisciplinary architect, artist and doctoral candidate based at the School of Architecture, KTH where he undertakes research on the commodification of the home. In 2011 he established an interdisciplinary practice and was invited to present work at the Royal Hibernian Academy Gallery, Dublin. He has undertaken several commissions for landscape installations and sculptures and has exhibited work internationally. In 2011 he co-founded NAMAlab, a postgraduate architecture and urbanism research initiative investigating how the practice of architecture can contribute to the reimaging of the city in the aftermath of the 2009 financial crisis.

Christian Parreno is a Research Fellow and PhD candidate at the Oslo School of Architecture and Design, investigating the relation between boredom, space and modern architecture. He holds an MA in histories and theories from the Architectural Association, and an architectural degree from the Universidad San Francisco de Quito.

Doina Petrescu is Professor of Architecture and Design Activism at the University of Sheffield. She is co-founder, together with Constantin Petcou, of atelier d'architecture autogérée (aaa), a collective platform that conducts explorations, actions and research concerning participative architecture, resilience and cities' co-produced transformation. The most recent projects include R-URBAN, a participative strategy for local resilience, and Wiki Village Factory, a social and ecological innovation cluster in Paris. aaa's projects have received international recognition and numerous awards. Her publications include: *The Social (Re) Production of Architecture: Politics, Values and, Actions in Contemporary Practice* (2017), *R-URBAN Act: A Participative Strategy of Urban Resilience* (2015), *Trans-Local Act: Cultural Politics Within and Beyond* (2009), *Altering Practices: Feminist Politics and Poetics of Space* (2007).

Peg Rawes is Professor of Architecture and Philosophy, and Programme Director of the Masters in Architectural History at the Bartlett School of Architecture, UCL. Recent publications include: *Equal by Design* (co-authored with Beth Lord, in collaboration with Lone Star Productions, 2016); 'Humane and inhumane ratios' in The Architecture Lobby's *Asymmetric Labors* (2016); *Poetic Biopolitics: Practices of Relation in Architecture and the Arts* (co-ed., 2016); and *Relational Architectural Ecologies* (ed., 2013).

Sophie Read is a researcher and writer currently doing a PhD in architectural history and theory at the Bartlett. Her research examines unstudied lectures that the architect

John Soane delivered at the Royal Institution in 1817 and 1820. Previously she studied architectural history at the Bartlett and drawing at Camberwell College of Art; a trajectory which has informed her creative and scholarly approach to the reading and writing of architectural history. Often pursuing relationships between the drawn, written, built, spoken, performed and archival – Sophie's work makes the case for architectural history itself as a practice that is inherently live and performative. Sophie is a Teaching Fellow at the Bartlett.

Helen Runting is a an urban planner (B.UPD, University of Melbourne) and urban designer (PG.Dip UD, University of Melbourne; MSc.UPD, Royal Institute of Technology (KTH), Stockholm), and a PhD candidate within Critical Studies in Architecture at KTH. Her research is situated within the field of architectural theory and addresses the images, politics, property relations, and aesthetics of the 'unbuilt environment' of Sweden's architectural present. Helen is a founding member of the architecture collective Svensk Standard (2008–), and the architectural practice Secretary (2017–).

Karin Reisinger, postdoctoral researcher within Critical Studies in Architecture, School of Architecture, Royal Institute of Technology, KTH, Stockholm, Sweden, was a key organizer of the AHRA 2016 conference *Architecture and Feminism: Ecologies, Economies, Technologies*. She is currently working on a collection of small-scale narratives of large-scale environmental transformations, based on methodologies of feminist political ecology. Her PhD *Grass Without Roots–Towards Nature Becoming Spatial Practice* from the Visual Culture Unit at Vienna UT looks into genealogies of nature preservation areas. She is a lecturer at KTH Stockholm and at the Institute of Art and Design, Vienna UT, where she co-initiated the symposium *In Transitional Landscapes (work reports)*, held in 2015.

Elin Strand Ruin is an architect and an artist working within the field of feministic urban place making. Her work operates at the interface between performative art and architecture, exploring how to catalyse social and architectural change. Strand Ruin has exhibited at leading artistic, architectural and planning venues around Sweden and Europe during the last 15 years. Recent collaborative projects include *Knitting House (2010)*, *My Kitchen (2011)*, *The Heart of Darkness (2013)*, *An Animal Theatre with Feelings and Weather (2014–2017)*, *The Kitchen of Praxagora (2016)* and *The Feministic Recycling-Park (2016–21)* in collaboration with Spridd & Lovely Landskap. Strand Ruin teaches at the School of Architecture, Royal Institute of Technology, KTH, Stockholm, Sweden, and runs her own practice: Studio Elin Strand Ruin.

Douglas Spencer is the author of *The Architecture of Neoliberalism* (Bloomsbury, 2016). He teaches and writes on critical theories of architecture, landscape and urbanism at the AA's Graduate School of Design at the Architectural Association and at the University of Westminster, London. A regular contributor to *Radical Philosophy*, he has also written chapters for collections such as *Architecture Against the Post-Political* ed. Nadir Lahiji (Routledge, 2014), and *This Thing Called Theory*, eds. Teresa Stoppani, Giorgio Ponzo and George Themistokleous (Routledge, November 2016), and published numerous essays in journals such as *The Journal of Architecture, AD, AA Files, New Geographies, Volume* and *Praznine.*

Despina Stratigakos is Professor of Architecture at the University at Buffalo. She is the author of three books that explore the intersections of power and architecture. Her most recent book, *Where Are the Women Architects?* (2016), confronts the challenges women face in the architectural profession. *Hitler at Home* (2015) investigates the architectural and ideological construction of the Führer's domesticity, and *A Women's Berlin: Building the Modern City* (2008) traces the history of a forgotten female metropolis. She has served as a Director of the Society of Architectural Historians, an Advisor of the International Archive of Women in Architecture at Virginia Tech, a Trustee of the Beverly Willis Architecture Foundation, and Deputy Director of the Gender Institute at the University at Buffalo.

Tijana Stevanović is a Lecturer at the School of Architecture, UCA. She also leads MArch History and Theory unit 'Flexible Bodies, Flexible Selves' at the Bartlett. Tijana is currently writing her PhD thesis in Architectural Theory and Criticism (University of Newcastle). It explores the conditions of architectural production and social property within the culture of self-management in New Belgrade. Tijana studied architecture (University of Belgrade) and culture theory (UCL). Her practice also includes collaborative art projects, which question systems of knowledge-classification, feminist economies and flexible working conditions. Tijana's most recent publications are chapters in edited volumes: *Architecture's Turn to History 1970–1990* (Birkhäuser, 2016) and *Industries of Architecture* (Routledge, 2015).

Igea Troiani (PhD) researches architectural production and culture from sociological, political, economic and gender perspectives. She is a partner in the architectural firm, Original Field of Architecture Ltd. and founder of the architecture research company, Caryatid Films. She is co-editor of *The Politics of Making* (2007) and *Transdisciplinary Urbanism and Culture* (2017) and founder and editor-in-chief of the international interdisciplinary award-winning journal, *Architecture and Culture* (Taylor & Francis). She is currently writing a manuscript entitled *Work-life Balance in Architecture* (Routledge, due 2018).

Huda Tayob is an architect, researcher and educator. She practiced as an architect in Cape Town, Mumbai and Tokyo prior to starting her PhD at the Bartlett School of Architecture, UCL, where she is currently a doctoral candidate. Her doctoral research draws on postcolonial theories, the politics of invisibility and the notion of everyday and minor architectures to research Pan-African shopping arcades and refugee markets in Cape Town. In addition, her PhD engages with the potential of drawing as a form of research.

Olga Tengvall is a practicing architect with a master's degree from School of Architecture, Royal Institute of Technology, KTH, Stockholm, Sweden.

Julia Wieger is an architect and researcher. She is working as a senior scientist at the architecture department at the Academy of Fine Arts Vienna where she was part of the research project Spaces of Commoning (2014–16). She is a member of the board of VBKÖ – an artist-run queer feminist art space in Vienna. Her work is concerned with queer feminist productions of space, archive politics and history writing, as well as collective approaches to research, knowledge production and design.

Malin Zimm is an architect with a PhD, and currently a research and analysis strategist at White arkitekter. Zimm has previously been employed as Senior Advisor in Architecture at ArkDes (Swedish Centre for Architecture and Design), editor-in-chief of the architecture magazine *Rum* and teaching assignments at Royal Institute of Technology, KTH, School of Architecture and Konstfack. Zimm completed her doctorate studies at KTH School of Architecture in 2005 with the thesis 'Losing the Plot – Architecture and Narrativity in Fin-de-Siècle Media Cultures, investigating pre-digital virtual architecture.' Zimm is a contributor to Swedish and international architecture magazines and publications since 1999.

Maria Ärlemo is an architect and PhD candidate in Critical Studies in Architecture, School of Architecture, Royal Institute of Technology, KTH, Stockholm. She holds a Master degree in Architecture from KTH and has qualifications in ethnology from the University of Stockholm and urban sociology from Berkeley, University of California. Her PhD research explores contemporary discourses on justice that have emerged within and in relation to large-scale postwar housing areas in Sweden marked by economic disadvantage and racial segregation. The research aims to contribute to the development of justice perspectives on architectural practices, and to inform critically engaged architectural practices.

Acknowledgements

The essays collected in this volume were first presented as papers at the thirteenth international Architectural Humanities Research Association (AHRA) conference, hosted by the School of Architecture, Royal Institute of Technology, KTH, Stockholm. We want to thank the steering group of the AHRA for their advice during the process of organizing the conference and editing this book. We are grateful to our colleagues, students and administrative staff for making this event possible through their tireless, mostly unpaid labour. We especially acknowledge the indispensable work of Karin Reisinger in coordinating the conference, and wish to thank Meike Schalk and the collective MYCKET for curating contributions and staging events at the conference. We are grateful to our authors for their expedited responses to our editorial comments, and their willingness to work with us over the brief editorial production period. We acknowledge the financial support we have received from a Formas Swedish research council grant, and from the Formas funded Strong Research Environment, Architecture in Effect.

Introduction

Architecture and feminisms

Ecologies, economies, technologies

*Hélène Frichot, Catharina Gabrielsson
and Helen Runting*

The disciplinary practices and the products of architecture, thought and drawn and made, produce and reproduce material and spatial relations of power in designed environments. It is for this reason that architecture forms both a critical object of analysis and a highly effective technology for advancing the diverse projects of contemporary feminism. This book offers a diffracting collection of practical and intellectual resources for thinking feminism in architecture and for practicing a feminist architecture in the twenty-first century. It brings together a range of thinkers and practitioners who were first united at the KTH School of Architecture at the Royal Institute of Technology in Stockholm, in November 2016, at the thirteenth AHRA conference *Architecture and Feminisms: Ecologies, Economies, Technologies.*

Situated at the nexus between architecture and feminisms, the intellectual outset for this book shares the ethos of the conference. Interweaving the strands of connection between spaces, means and formations of power, we implicitly address what feminist philosopher Nancy Fraser sums up as 'the general crisis' of 'global warming', 'care deficiencies' and 'the hollowing out of political power at every scale'.[1] Architecture has fully participated in the processes leading to this crisis, and with this book we hope to contribute, however humbly, to the urgent project of shifting the values and habits that produce our near exhausted existential territories. In adopting a transversal approach, emphasising the complex weaving together of strands that intersect with and exacerbate one another, we also draw on Félix Guattari and his essay *The Three Ecologies.*[2] Calling for the need to think across the categories of nature, culture and the human subject, the importance of Guattari's imperative has only increased and is echoed by Nancy Fraser's emphasis on the border struggles between capitalist production and the political, natural and social resources it exploits. If Guattari's work centred on the formation of human subjectivity, urging us to 'rethink ourselves' if we are to save the planet, the challenges implicit in such a project are further accentuated by the controversial term 'Anthropocene'. In calling for the recognition of the formation of a new geologic age induced by industrialisation, it identifies the 'human' (*Anthropos*) as a blind natural force. The French philosopher Catherine Malabou has recently pointed to the conflicting human identities presupposed by the term. How can we understand this 'human', she asks, that acts unthinkingly, 'like a glacier', yet is endowed with rationality, and supposedly has the ability to take responsibility over these processes that threaten to destroy the habitat of living creatures (including our own)?[3] Confronted with capitalism as 'an institutionalised social order', expanding across every sphere of the life-world, overcoming 'the general crisis' would thus also, as Malabou explains, take nothing less than a new consciousness, a non-consciousness, yet one different from that of denial.

From the outset of this deeply troubling and complex scenario, questions of the subject in formation and the (natural) body in relation to the (gendered) terms of rationality and agency rise to the fore as matters of urgent concern. Rather than speaking from the margins of academia, industry and patriarchal society, feminist scholarship within architecture thus raises issues and evinces insights that are central for dealing with this 'general crisis'. Economies, ecologies and technologies (the sub-title of this book) are adopted here as figures for the forces and means influencing, organising and even making architecture. Enfolding archives of knowledge, assemblages of labouring bodies, practices of environmental production and critiques of power and control, they contribute to forming complex 'string figures', to borrow a material thought-figure from Donna Haraway's most recent book, *Staying with the Trouble: Making Kin in the Chthulucene*. Composing string figures (also called 'cat's cradle') from a simple loop of yarn is one of 'humanity's oldest games', the manipulation of the yarn between one, two or more sets of hands manifests multiple patterns and connections.[4] In casting such connective threads across the registers of economies, ecologies and technologies, we hope to facilitate understandings of how architecture – through its many complex modalities – operates and is maintained through its relations to normative power and capital. Such relations are unveiled, we suggest, by a critical feminist approach that also holds the power to intervene in these constructs. Thinking economies, ecologies and technologies through each other produces a woven grid of reference that unites the diverse thinking brought together in this anthology. At the same time, we suggest, these conceptual figures constitute lines of solidarity.

This book considers the diversity of feminisms that runs across, and at times produces contradictions between ways of thinking and practicing a feminist architecture. While acknowledging feminism as a plural, dynamic and multiple movement, rather than one coherent 'ism', the common denominator for the diversity of approaches presented in this book is a desire for political transformation.[5] Feminism as a broadly defined sociopolitical and theoretical formation tends to be characterised as proceeding in waves, commencing from a basic demand for emancipation. Departing from a 'first-wave' search for equality within patriarchal societal constructs, second-wave feminism advances an acknowledgement of difference, and the transformation of socio-cultural and political conditions via a plural agenda that includes questions addressed to the built environment. In acknowledging how the category of 'woman' constitutes a diverse and complex cohort, concrete specificity cannot be overlooked. In the light of this understanding, third and even fourth-wave feminisms splinter across an array of trajectories marked by 'intersectionality', and are thus articulated by myriad nodes wherein issues of race, ethnicity, class, cultural location, sex, embodied capacity and dis/ability clash and intersect. Nevertheless, as Judy Wajchman explains: 'While standard accounts of feminist thought tend to present liberal, socialist and postmodern feminisms as distinct perspectives, in reality they did not develop as independent strands or in a simple chronological order.'[6] We too wish to advance an understanding of the combined feminist project as temporally complex and non-linear, operating according to a fluid dynamics, wherein ripples and waves necessarily diffract, creating cross-flows, resonances and dissonances.[7] As more than one million people marched across the world on 21 January 2017 to protest against racism, injustice and the dismantling of institutions of emancipation and transparency, it seems that feminism has the power to unite in a political struggle that forefronts the similarities, rather than the differences, amongst us. Therefore, while the aim of this book is to accommodate more voices rather than less, and to allow space for different positions, we also acknowledge how 'feminism' today operates as a banner heading, and a bulwark, against injustice and oppression of all kinds. This is a task where architecture's archives of knowledge, critiques of power, techniques of environmental production and labouring bodies can assist us in imagining, thinking and even undertaking.

Given an understanding of the present moment as structured by history – and of how the future relies on our ability to understand and if necessary re-read that history – *Architecture and Feminisms: Ecologies, Economies, Technologies* commences in the archive, progresses into questions of security and control, traverses social and natural environments, and concludes with considerations of work. The four sections that organise the chapters of the book form knotted assemblages where specific conditions, conceptual frameworks or material sources come forth as shared concerns. The 'archive', in these readings, turns out to be lively; bodies and spaces are managed through circuits within which power sometimes gets stuck; the 'milieu' is witnessed as a complex entanglement of environmental, economic and technological factors; and the act of situating labouring bodies helps to illuminate the overlooked and devalued locations in which bodies meet, produce and maintain architecture. Running across the four sections of the book, a series of 'projects' offer glimpses of ways of working with feminist ecologies, economies and technologies through, within, and in relation to architecture.

Archive

The task of bringing together diverse thoughts on the feminist project and its, at times, troubled relation to architecture is neither easy nor new. Difficult battles have been won and lost, diverse disciplinary and epistemological ground have been introduced and abandoned. There is no simple storyline, but a complex matrix of concerns, which counters attempts at offering decisive historiographical accounts. Furthermore, we remain at risk of forgetting what we have learnt, whether that pertains to our practices or our theories. As Karen Burn's opening essay explains, while the archive reveals a history of scholarship dedicated to articulating the relationship between architecture, gender and feminist theories and practices, a great deal more work needs to be done to address the important connection between feminist action and theory. She also argues that we are in urgent need of more strategic accounts of subjectivity and identity in relation to the public sphere. With Project 1, Shelby Doyle and Leslie Forehand also point to the library shelf, alerting us to the proximities between the past and the future in how advanced digital technologies and feminist theory can be brought together. With Rixt Hoekstra's chapter, we turn to the women of CIAM (International Congress of Modern Architecture) operating in the background of famous male figures. Using historiographic material such as magazine cuttings and love letters, Hoekstra demonstrates these women's influence on the modernist movement. Hilde Heynen, well known for her research on modernism and modernity, resituates the work of the architectural critic Sibyl Moholy-Nagy as an early eco-feminist, and deliberates on the deep ambivalences in how and on what grounds feminism can be based. In Project 2, Sophie Read and Tijana Stevanović argue that history can be embodied and performed. To make their point, they collage images that allude to Victorian drag practices from the late nineteenth century. Using a mix of fact and fiction, Katie Lloyd Thomas studies the role taken by women during the post-war years amidst what she identifies as the proprietorial turn, wherein women became shoppers of architectural products, as well as salespersons of these services. Continuing this creative turn, Emma Cheatle sends a series of postcards to Mary Wollstonecraft, a well-known and vocal advocate for women's rights from the eighteenth century. Cheatle explores how Wollstonecraft's poetics were bound up with her politics, and how her interest in intimacy and care went hand in hand with a demand for equal rights.

Control

Across our increasingly mediatised control societies, power is diffuse and operates in complex relays. The control of our embodied minds, as individual units ('dividuals'), and at the scale of populations, is insidious. While the spatial segregations of disciplinary societies have increased in sophistication, in control societies behavioural correction has become further internalised, and augmented through complex media technologies.[8] In her chapter, which addresses how regimes of control are enabled through media imagery, Despina Stratigakos presents the unsettling scene of Hitler at home, in part achieved through the skills of architect Gerdy Troost. Also looking to the past through the lens of control, Christian Parreno deliberates on the ambivalent effect of boredom and the labour of preservation in the American Museum of Natural History, arguing that preservation – what is preserved, and for whom, and with what future in mind – is never gender neutral. Remaining in the space of the museum, in Project 3, Daniel Koch compellingly explores how subjectivity is constructed and projected onto the screen that is the mannequin.

Alison Brunn addresses the role of digital data in how subjects sense and are sensed in contemporary urban environments. Further to the issue of the role of digital and Web 2.0 technologies, Nicole Kalms' chapter demonstrates the real and perceived safety of women and girls in urban environments, mediated through the design and use of 'apps' intended to placate their anxieties. While the 'apps' Kalms discusses are aimed at the security of women and girls, at the same time they paradoxically reproduce the assumption that urban environments will remain unsafe places for such subjects. Janet McGaw turns to yet another domain where women are at risk of remaining marginalised – computational architectures – in order to reinsert a feminist legacy into this techno-architectural domain. In Project 4, Sandra Kaji-O'Grady demonstrates the position of women in academic publishing, using statistics to reveal how practices of peer reviewing in fact promise a better representation of gender. To close this section on control, Hélène Frichot and Helen Runting address the problems of real estate through the created communities of the 'co-living' model, arguing that they only serve to further control the formation of post-millennial subjectivities.

Milieu

The built environment is a facilitative milieu in which events unfold, things take place, and relations are formed. Made up of natural, cultural and imaginary components, we understand architecture as embedded in this milieu with its objects, subjects and systems of thought. We must think 'by the milieu', Isabelle Stengers insists,[9] and acknowledge our material situation. Peg Rawes, known for her work on relational architectural ecologies, and Douglas Spencer, who takes his point of departure from material dialectics and Marxist critique, open this section with a conversation on our intellectual milieu. They reverse a long-standing feminist as well as postmodernist critique in suggesting that we must be wary of an uncritical celebration of effect, feeling and emotion, and instead venture a new approach to rationality. In Project 5, Malin Zimm adopts the perspective of a post-human other, alerting us to the ubiquity of technologies of biopolitical surveillance and control. Addressing how capitalism now shapes universities, in her chapter Igea Troiani argues that we are at risk of being overwhelmed by a mounting pressure to perform, to produce, to disseminate. Venturing into the milieu of a refugee camp, Aya Musmar addresses how subjectivities are forged and agency is denied in the architecture of the humanitarian camp and in relation to the institutional manoeuvres of NGOs. As Maria Ärlemo's chapter shows, the participation Musmar calls for can also devolve into spaces of exclusion. Drawing on an ethnographic study of the Swedish suburb of Husby, which is soon to undergo renovation, she unpacks the underlying assumptions and conflicts surrounding a 'feminist' urban planning project. Composing a feminist political and ecological narrative for three sites, Karin Reisinger suggests that a feminist ethos allows us to consider human *and* non-human relations amidst abandoned architectures. In Project 6, dilapidated infrastructures are revived with a modicum of love, as Olga Tengvall and Hannes Frykholm insert a speculative series of interventions along an old rail line. Doina Petrescu and Katherine Gibson conclude this section with a dialogue on diverse economies entangled amidst ecologies, and implicitly question human exceptionalism. The focus of their discussion is atelier d'architecture autogérée's R-URBAN project in France, presented as a manifestation of urban commoning.

Work

In recognising the system of valorisation and localisation implicit in 'work' and its bifurcating meanings, questions of gender partake in organising the conditions for architectural practice and what finally counts as its outcome. In the present era of financialised capitalism, the significance of work has mutated along with the spaces, commodities and subjectivities it generates. Making reference to the work of J.K. Gibson Graham, Julia Wieger brings up the question of domestic work in her case study, where the kitchen emerges as one of many 'places' in which the collective struggle over reproduction continues to be waged. In Project 7, Elin Strand Ruin draws upon Greek myth in displacing the kitchen from the private interior of the apartment and making cooking public. Framing 'housework' as a series of non-representational practices engaged with the sensibilities, maintenance and care of buildings, in her chapter Catharina Gabrielsson argues that housework carries a critical potential for re-thinking architecture within a political ethos of care. The topic of maintenance is continued in Janek Oźmin's chapter where by combining historiography with film analysis, he looks at the significance of the garage as informed by masculinist theory. In Project 8, Huda Tayob uses drawings to describe home-making in the contested markets of Cape Town, South Africa. Jos Boys' chapter draws our attention to the need to address dis/ability, and how embodiment in its relation to architectural and urban space is varied and nuanced. Having edited the anthology *Feminist Practices* in 2011, Lori A. Brown's chapter presents her recent work on abortion clinics, an issue that has become even more fraught in the American context in terms of the control of women's right to make decisions about their own bodies. We conclude with Claudia Dutson's chapter, which is dedicated to the rise of the entrepreneurial subject; here, the illusion of a self-employed and sovereign life sinks into exhausting and untenably precarious work/life situations.

These twenty-three chapters and eight projects do not compose one cohesive and consistent feminist project for architecture. Rather, they expose how feminism operates as a lens for a more complex and multi-stranded critique. Much as the general crisis – environmental, political and social – cannot be grasped within the categories in which it occurs, this critique cannot be encompassed within the boundaries of individual chapters, but emerges in, over and across the different chapters of the book. Beyond the celebration of diverse positions, what emerges, we argue, is a clear and prescient need, historically situated by those who continue to relate stories of struggle and relevant to our contemporary moment, to locate solidarities between diverse voices and bodies. Collective action is only possible if a shared 'orientation' towards radical political transformation can be located. In a moment coloured by the threat of a return to and solidification of patriarchy, and its closure of alternate modes of subjectification, the question of how subjectivities come to be formed in relation to spaces, places and material relations that are entangled with ecologies, economies and technologies, *matters*. Developing in unison this multi-stranded and complex critique is a project for the future that depends on the agency of the reader and their willingness to explore different relations and connections as they occur in this book. In setting forth feminisms as ongoing processes of transformation, we situate them as critical for the development of an architecture beyond patriarchy. We also wish to bring forth the neglected, suppressed and unexploited potential carried by architectures – resituated now in the plural – for intervening in the world. In pointing to the critical tools that a feminist approach can avail us of, we hope that some of what is on the table here creates the possibility of a politics that puts the intellectual and embodied 'resources' of architecture – its histories, its bodies, its theories, its works (material and immaterial) – in motion.

Notes

1   Nancy Fraser, 'Behind Marx's Hidden Abode: For an Expanded Conception of Capitalism', *New Left Review*, 86 (2014): 56.
2   Félix Guattari, *The Three Ecologies*, trans. Ian Pindar and Paul Sutton (London: The Athlone Press, 2000).
3   Catherine Malabou, 'The Brain of History and the Mentality of the Anthropocene', public lecture held at Moderna Museet, Stockholm, January 21, 2017.
4   For Haraway the string figure (SF) relates to science fiction, science fabulation and speculative fiction, which open up processes of 'becoming-with' and how we 'conjugate' with worlds. Donna Haraway, *Staying with the Trouble: Making Kin in the Chthulucence* (Durham and London: Duke University Press, 2016), 12–13.
5   We agree with Judy Wajchman who argues that 'Rather than thinking of feminism, we need to think of feminisms as multiple and dynamic, and in the process of ongoing transformation.' Judy Wajchman, 'Feminist Theories of Technology' in *Cambridge Journal of Economics*, 34 (2000), 143–152; 147.
6   Wajchman, 143.
7   Barad, who took on the chair of the History of Consciousness program at the University of California Santa Cruz after Donna Haraway's retirement, is a theoretical physicist who explains the usefulness of the 'material semiotic' concept of diffraction, that is, how complex patterns (such as ripples on the surface of water) entangle matter with meaning. Karen Barad, *Meeting the Universe Halfway: Quantum Physics and the Entanglement of Matter and Meaning* (Durham: Duke University Press, 2007).
8   Gilles Deleuze, 'Control and Becoming' and 'Postscript on Societies of Control' in *Negotiations: 1972–1990*, trans. Martin Joughin (New York: Columbia University Press, 1995), 167–168; 169–182.
9   Stengers is making reference to Gilles Deleuze and Félix Guattari's well known imperative to think by the milieu. See Isabelle Stengers, *In Catastrophic Times: Resisting the Coming Barbarism* (Ann Arbor, MI: Open Humanities Press, 2015), 103, accessed April 12, 2017. http://openhumanitiespress.org/books/download/Stengers_2015_In-Catastrophic-Times.pdf.

Archive

Chapter 1

Feminist theory and praxis, 1991–2003

Questions from the archive

Karen Burns

. . . my choice of a nomadic style is intended as a gesture of rejection of the competitive, judgemental, moralizing high tone that so much feminist theory has come to share with traditional academic writing . . . the assumption of the critical thinker as judge, moral arbiter or high priest(ess) . . . (is) a reactive deployment of protocols of institutional reason.

Rosi Braidotti[1]

These days, as I am increasingly asked to write and speak on women and architecture, I find myself revisiting one small shelf in the open access stacks of our architecture library. The books on this shelf are labelled with Dewey decimal call number 720.82: a non-descript label for a set of books from a decade of insurgent 1990s thinking on feminism, gender, theory and architecture. Not all of the relevant material from this decade is housed at 720.82. The anthology *Sexuality & Space* (conference 1991, publication 1992) which helped set the agenda for the decade – gender not women, interdisciplinarity not architecture, poststructuralist theory not second wave feminism – is far from its feminist comrades at shelf number 720.1. The bulk of books at 720.82 are my foundational archive for thinking about feminist theory and feminist praxis in architecture. Hovering over the shelf I experience the 'strong archival impulse' of desire and longing, and admiration and frustration; for this archive of feminist theory remains informal.[2] We lack histories of feminist architectural theory in either paper or analog form.[3] Public and private libraries house this uncollected history. In today's era of feminist renewal in architecture and broader social actions, conversations about feminist praxis and the role of feminist theory are usefully grounded in historical knowledge. In this chapter I retrieve the fractious theory/practice exchanges of 1990s feminism to ask questions about the role of theory and public scholarship in fostering gender literacy and feminist activism.

Feminist theory, 1990–2003

In the 1990s women academics in architecture gained a brief, although impermanent, place in the discipline's mainstream. High profile conferences and anthologies were issued from North America and a few emerged from Britain. In 1996 Mark Wigley quipped that most (poststructuralist) theorists were women.[4] For some feminists this new female-dominated theory formation was actually a problem; it seemed to represent a historical break with a tradition of activism, as women moved into the 'ivory tower' of academe. Since the 1970s however, feminist architects, scholars and activists have grappled with questions about the most effective sites for feminist action. In particular we struggle with the dilemma of the mainstream, wondering if we should work within existing institutions or operate outside established structures in new, alternate, parallel or community organisations.[5]

The 1990s exchanges on the role of theory and praxis revisited the problem of sites of feminist action and added new questions about the role of specialist language and audience. Many of these writings however, are abrasive and openly hostile to 'theory'. Yet, following Meaghan Morris, we can read these texts sympathetically: to understand works that interrupt answers automatically provided by poststructuralist feminism.[6] These voices help revive important debates about the role of theory in feminist action.

By the mid 1990s North American feminist architect-activists were increasingly characterising new inter-disciplinary feminist theory with terms previously used to negatively describe the 'masculine' and 'patriarchal' profession. Now feminist theory was, 'oppressive(ly)', 'exclusive', 'exclusionary' and 'intimidating'. A call to practice – 'it is now time to put down the books' – was declared.[7] Writers argued over the course of action for transformative feminist politics. In 1996 Debra Coleman introduced the anthology *Architecture and Feminism* as a text that would prompt debate about a future course of feminist practice in a time of theory. The book would:

> reanimate questions about the limits of architectural discourse in the expression of sociocultural and political critique . . . at a time when the discourse of feminism and architecture are suffused with uncertainty . . . it is tempting to favour the search for 'better' theories over interventions that – with all their unpredictability – seem to transform current social, cultural and political conditions.[8]

Feminism, like the discipline at large, was the site of a theory/praxis stand-off in the late 1990s. Through the 1990s, twelve feminist anthology collections (four based on conferences) were published in the Global North (North America and Britain).[9] In America, the feminist debate and the discipline's mainstream were overshadowed by the culture wars, and increasingly a theory backlash gripped the North American academy.[10] The feminist attacks on theory were abrasive and perhaps unhelpful to feminism's long-term survival, but neither the advocates of theory nor their opponents knew that feminism's place in the architectural mainstream was drawing to an end. In 2000 the theory journal *Assemblage* published its last issue, and feminist discourse disappeared from its decade-long spotlight. This silencing was echoed in the rush of theory anthologies published in 1998 and in the following years. Although seven theory anthologies were published only six feminist essays were included overall.[11] And all anthologies, even those trumpeting the post-theory turn, ignored the 'anti-theory' feminist critique.

Architecture's sophisticated feminist discourse and the anthology's documentary spread were diminished by these silences. From 1991 to 2003 a significant discourse of feminist dissent had developed around the feminist theory characterised as 'post-modern', 'poststructuralist' or 'decon'. Sherry Ahrentzen, Diane Ghirardo, Pat Morton, Mary McLeod, Margaret Crawford, Andrea Kahn and Lois Nesbitt were the leading voices of this opposition. Like the feminists whose practices they contested, this generation of architectural academics did not belong to the cohort of American feminists of the 1970s and early 1980s, whose ranks included Dolores Hayden, Ellen Perry Berkeley, Susana Torre and Doris Cole. The new cohort was antagonistic to a wave of theory that seemed to fracture feminism's unitary identity. For the outspoken commentator Sherry Ahrentzen, the 1970s and early 1980s had twin 'concomitant and compatible realms' of investigation: 'her stories' – an alternative history of women's contribution to architecture – and 'designing for diversity' – a focus on the contemporary situation of women in architecture offices and architectural education. Dissenters cast the feminist work 'produced in the late 1980s and 1990s' as sharply different.[12] They evoked the long 1970s as an age of feminist unity, cohesive identity and shared goals.

Over the 1990s decade the seven feminist authors who dominated opposition to the new theoretical turn (Ahrentzen, Ghirardo, Morton, McLeod, Crawford, Kahn and Nesbitt) shared three broad suppositions. First, their positions were stated in opposition to a certain kind of language and 'discourse'. This was a strong thread across all the voices of protest. As first announced in 1991 this argument concerned both the nature of theoretical language and the role of language in fostering transformation. In a post-script to Andrea Kahn's *Drawing, Building, Text*, Lois Nesbitt described many of the anthology's essays as 'oppressively allusive texts', 'revealing an impressive and intimidating erudition.'[13] In her introduction to this volume Kahn had posed the slanted questions: 'do they engender exclusive realms of discourse, Do they lead to exclusionary audiences and constituencies?'[14]

By 1997 theory's opponents began to mimic terms used by poststructuralism. They cleverly turned key poststructuralist words into negatives. Diane Ghirardo would describe poststructuralist feminist writing as 'spacey' with a 'circular indecipherability' (indecipherability being a key Derridean word).[15] Sherry Ahrentzen, writing in 1996, characterised the theory formation as an engagement that 'is primarily formal and philosophical' with 'textual devices of etymology, linguistic conundrums, and semiotic meanings'.[16] The most serious charge concerned the alignment of feminist theory work with patriarchy. Ahrentzen argued that this highly theoretical form of feminist knowledge production continued the Western patriarchal project by its 'separateness and control through abstraction' and its lack of accessibility, directed to: 'a specialized audience that shares a language or a coded familiarity . . . rooted in the very master narratives it claims to challenge.'[17] I will return in the next section to these important comments on the nature of specialized language and the notion that expert and technical languages are gendered.

Second, many voiced a discontent with feminist poststructuralist theory's failure to deal with what's going on 'out there'; a space defined by topics and sites. 'Out in the field' is where 'new structures' are erected (Nesbitt), it is design not discourse (Agrest, Conway, Weisman) and intervention not theory (Coleman), it is the 'fringe' with 'non-traditional clients' and 'new modes of practice' (Crawford), 'the social' (Morton), 'actual person's lives and lived experiences (Ahrentzen), it is the 'political realities or the landscapes that hold the problems and experiences of everyday life' (Ahrentzen), it is 'consumption, mass culture and popular taste' (McLeod).[18] Feminist opponents of the theory turn were not advocating an embrace of practice in the marketplace, however. Rather they pressed for a return to the alternative modes of community-based practice and a commitment to developing alternative forms of architectural production. These were key strands of 1970s feminism.

In broader historical terms poststructuralist theory was seen as a replacement for a mode of action; 'the search for better theories over intervention' (*Architecture and Feminism*, 1996) a situation of 'discourse versus design' in which 'discourse is more important' (*The Sex of Architecture*, 1996).[19] Key writers framed these disciplinary choices as evidence of a significant historical transition in which activism was replaced by texts and work on architecture's symbolic realms. Patricia Morton put this succinctly in 2003 when she organised feminist practices into a poetics/politics binary and declared: 'Their emphasis on the "poetics" of architecture and its gendered representational systems has replaced the socially engaged work of an earlier generation, exemplified by Matrix.'[20] A sense of epochal change was declared in the introduction to another 1996 anthology collection *The Sex of Architecture*: 'We are in an era where discourse is as important as design, often more important.'[21]

The third point that united many of the voices of the opposition was the belief in the 'real' or other landscapes outside theory as the place for enacting social agency. Sherry Ahrentzen was the most persistent critic of the 1990s theory formation. In 1996 she published a lengthy summary of architectural feminism's historical development and goals. Analysing her opponents in coruscating language, she declared that an alternative to new feminist theory was offered by the role of architects as social advocate. Drawing on the advocacy work that had developed out of the 1970s and flourished in the 1980s she pronounced on the particular ethical responsibilities of the architect: the 'professional is responsible . . . for the creation of the environmental conditions that facilitate the realization of the empowerment potential within the individual and the community.'[22]

What then were theoretical architectural feminists doing? Many opponents implied that architectural theory had become lost in an internal academic world.

'Criticism here is a self-justifying end,' declared Ahrentzen.[23] Other writers continued this theme of misguided goals; Debra Coleman declared that a number of theorists were engaged in, 'the search for "better" theories over intervention'.[24] As noted earlier, Ahrentzen elevated these problems into a familiar feminist framework when she aligned the 'separateness and control through abstraction' of theory to familiar (patriarchal) professional practices. This binary echoes an earlier voice in the landmark 1977 *Women in American Architecture* exhibition when one woman declared, 'Architecture, is, next to men, the most oppressive force in our society' in a section headed 'Architecture is for the People'.[25]

In the early years of the twenty-first century, writers Pat Morton and Sherry Ahrentzen would use the work of the British feminist collective Matrix to bolster their social agency argument, but Matrix had in fact developed a different line of critique; one that refuted the conspiracy narratives of patriarchy and professionalism. In their 1984 book *Making Space*, Matrix had declared: 'We do not believe that the buildings around us are part of a conspiracy to oppress women. They have developed from other priorities, notably the profit motive. . . . Buildings do not control our lives. They reflect the dominant values in our society . . . but we can live in them in different ways from those originally intended.'[26] Matrix were also clear that the acquisition of professional codes and training involved the absorption of (white) middle-class values and the defensive systems produced by the studio jury education system.[27] Professionalism was seen as a form of class privilege.

If Matrix's work was formed within the consciousness of the British class system, the 1990s anti-theory feminism of the United States was informed by geographically specific histories. In 2003, Sherry Ahrentzen would firm up her continuing opposition to poststructuralist theory by advocating the philosophy and practices of a North American pragmatist tradition developed in the writings of Richard Rorty. Summarising Rorty's invocation of a John Dewey school of pragmatism, Ahrentzen declared, 'They aimed at democratic exclusiveness and, for the most part, fought the development of a specialized disciplinary jargon inaccessible to a specialized elite.'[28]

In this 2003 essay, Ahrentzen acknowledged that poststructuralist theory was a form of praxis, as 'change (is) instigated from transformed consciousness and awareness'.[29] Theory's impact however was minimal, for:

> the audience who can capitalize on such writings to challenge and subvert their thinking is a very limited, elite one. The sense of distance or abstract theorizing in these analyses may not be very empowering or enabling for many women, their approaches may be far too removed from reality and real needs, and their language may be inaccessible and difficult to understand – all claims that make one question whether such feminist suspicion is simply an intellectual indulgence.'[30]

Yet not all feminist thinkers through the 1990s who held different ideological positions from poststructuralism defined their goals abrasively in binary opposition to the new theory formation. Sharon E. Sutton, a long-standing practitioner of social advocacy and the younger Leslie Kanes Weisman, presented advocacy agendas for architectural education and ideals of architecture as social agency, social justice and community oriented architectural design in their individual chapter contributions to the 1996 collection, *The Sex of Architecture*. Aherentzen's combative language is undergirded by the 'school of suspicion' approach – unmasking the lies and illusion of consciousness that critics would later query as a default approach of criticism.[31] As one feminist historian working outside architecture has observed, a 'sense of power and agency' can be 'achieved through a kind of scapegoating' but this mode of speech may in fact, as Braidotti asserts, reinforce traditional norms of academic practice.[32]

The characterisation of the content of poststructuralist work reprised in this chapter does not adequately describe the dazzling work of the new theory turn.[33] A history of this period would uncover continuities between the second wave feminist project adhered to by Ahrentzen, and at least one feature of poststructuralist feminist writing practice: its emphasis on autobiography. Evocations of personal memory connected structural political issues to individual experiences of subjectivity. This interweaving was evident for example, in Jennifer Bloomer's fine piece on growing up in the racialised spaces of America's South.[34] This mode of writing speaks directly to the issue that Ahrentzen laments – the intersection between the personal and a greater social project. Autobiography was a striking feature of third wave feminism in the United States, as writers asserted the distinctiveness of their lives and identity, as a counter to the essentialising modes of second wave feminism.[35]

A complex historical account will need to move beyond the architectural arena and its focus on the agency of individual academics and their ideologies and biographies; to consider the distinctive features of this historical period. The fracture lines in 1990s architecture between established feminist scholarship and new theoretical modes, between university and community based knowledge, and the decline of feminism as a mass movement in the United States – while it grew in the Global South – are fault lines common to numerous academic disciplines in this period. Larger social and political forces framed the theory turn; as the mass feminist movements of the 1970s increasingly faced a strong backlash from conservatives and the 'interweaving of gender and race' with the relations of late capital contributed too, to the flat lining of feminism.[36] Opponents of the theory turn depicted theory as an historical agent of feminist activist decline. Despite the polemic this archive remains relevant for some of the tough questions it asked about theory and practice and it is to these I now turn.

On-going questions

The creation of a discourse is fundamental for changing a discipline.

Susana Torre[37]

Feminism transforms the discipline by critically addressing its problematics from the perspective of gender and power.

Joan Scott[38]

Architectural theorists inherit a historical tradition in which the term 'theory' is often coupled to 'practice', with theory configured as the negative other. In the late 1990s the binary was strongly at work and practice asserted its superior identity over theory.[39] The binary is not simple or tenable, but because of this inheritance I prefer to use the word action rather than practice. Theory and action can interact in productive ways. Theorists have spent much time developing and refining key skills with language, representation and conceptual thinking. Theory can be a form of action when it is deployed in a concrete situation. Our skills in concept branding and thinking outside the box – otherwise known as creativity – can set the agenda for public essays, public panels, protests, petitions, digital platforms, policy and fundraising campaigns. Each of these actions may not be the equivalent of passing a resolution at the UN, but these 'thought actions' shape ideas, discourse, public debate and group and individual consciousness.

Feminist thought in the public sphere

Particularly outside architecture, feminist thought has developed a sophisticated body of work on identity that often doesn't circulate beyond those schooled in feminist theory. It has barely made an imprint on architecture and we urgently need more sophisticated accounts of subjectivity and identity in architecture's public sphere. The inadequacy of current conceptual tools is manifest when the fraught term 'woman architect' is introduced into public conversations. Our discipline's mainstream account of subjectivity is organised around a notion of supreme individual agency and a notion of the profession's disempowerment in the world. Neither of these frames reveals the discipline's construction of subject positions. Unhelpful binaries are used to address the question of those who do identify with the term 'woman architect' and those who don't; for many assert their claim to be judged on their competency as architects. Structural accounts of discrimination are difficult to present in this thought sphere since the conversation often devolves to the question of whether the individual has experienced discrimination. Many individuals have little agency – whatever their personal declaration – over who will unconsciously or consciously regard them as women architects rather than architects.

There persists a poor understanding that the term 'woman architect' has to be a universal, stable biological category, where instead it can be a conceptual, temporary tool.[40] 'Woman architect' is a useful category to recognise and organise marginalised groups 'in order to critique, to speak back to a centred subjectivity that does not need an "identity politics" because they have not had an identity imposed upon them'.[41] Understanding the strategic potential of an identity term can undermine assumptions of identity as a universal category that is either claimed or refuted for life. The mutability of identity and the strategic value of identity claims are ideas that need to be continually restated in everyday language. These ideas give people more enhanced understandings of identity categories.[42] When identity terms are exercised in strategic ways they can contest 'institutional forms of knowledge that oppress certain communities or social groups.'[43]

Language

We are living in a time when representation and language have charged to the fore and asserted themselves as forceful political agents. Those of us who've worked on language and power for many years know this in our intellectual DNA, but this observation has now achieved mainstream visibility with media reports dissecting new neologisms: alternate facts, scare quotes as a form of deniability for evidence-free assertions, etc. Timothy Snyder's recently published *On Tyranny: Twenty Lessons From the Twentieth Century*,[44] has a strong focus on the way in which authoritarian leaders and autocratic states use symbols, language and (media) propaganda as tactical strategies for eroding democratic, civic values.

After the second Iraq war writer John Berger claimed one of the war's effects was 'collateral damage to language'.[45] Understanding how language becomes damaged requires skills in careful listening and reading. Dominant elites and media conservatives strategically use language. They have deployed strategies of mimicry and appropriation to repurpose terms once used to describe subjugated identities. We see this in the emergence of terms like 'reverse racism' and 'all lives matter'. Moreover contemporary identity categories are often cast in spatial metaphors. A topography of inside and outside maps exclusionary identities between citizen and non-citizen, nation state and world. Architectural theory's spatial skills can analyse these formations and the complex inhabitation and border crossings of contemporary geography.

If one tactic is the picking apart of linguistic appropriations, another tactic is to brand concepts in concrete ways. My knowledge of feminist history and poststructuralist theory helped me invent the name 'Parlour' for our web platform and NGO. The term refers to the domestic sites of women's political organising in the nineteenth and twentieth centuries, to an older tradition of the parlour as a reception hall for guests, and as a pun on 'parler', a critical French feminist formation centred around the question of who speaks and who is allowed to speak. Along the way I've come up with titles for a major workshop entwining gender inclusivity and the future of the profession ('Transform') or a regular conversation series (Seasonal Salons) and named categories for various levels of sponsorship that could twist the normative corporate language of 'friends' and 'institutional sponsors' into new categories for a gender mobilised community. So we have the Parlour aficionado, provocateur and partisan. No I haven't invented a cure for cancer. But I have shaped a new community and given form to collective identity through names. The symbols of social movements are important for forging shared objects of identity.

Theory and specialist language

The most serious charge of the 1990s against theory denounced theory as a specialised language; and this accusation needs to be taken seriously. The technical language of theory is not inherently an elite tactic, nor is theory's expertise gendered male or patriarchal. In fact poststructuralism developed modes of writing to undermine claims of mastery and objectivity and these practices resonated strongly with feminists. This way of writing can be a strategic form; usefully exercised in specific situations. The critique of elitist language assumes a universal speech situation that requires all participants at all times to speak plainly in a non-technical way. But as Meaghan Morris once brilliantly observed, specialist language is everywhere in daily life; try reading the cricket reports in sports pages or knitting patterns without expert knowledge of these activities. It's not helpful to conflate speaking at an academic conference with a generalised ideal speech situation. Scholarly books and journals have their role. The portrait of an academic as someone who only speaks within the academic world without moving through other worlds and situations is mono-dimensional. It certainly doesn't reflect my life.

Academics speak and write in different places. I agree with Ahrentzen that we need to be able to address the results of our research to different audiences. We do this already inside the classroom when introducing unfamiliar theory material to students; we communicate with them in less technically expert ways. New online venues, like *Places* journal, aim to present public scholarship in well-turned prose and *Places* journal – or Parlour, the platform with which I am affiliated – is also a good venue for engaging broader publics with theoretically informed, not theoretically dominated, essays. New genres of small essay-length books and blog posts are also useful forms for scholarly ideas embedded in less technical writing forms. Theoretical and historical scholarship can benefit from intersections of formal and informal knowledge, or vernacular and disciplinary knowledge as one identity scholar has described the pairing.[46] The context-embedded vernacular knowledge of life in architectural offices has been critical in shaping the goals and sites of practice for Parlour, the Australian based gender equity NGO. This research also extended beyond the usual terrain of feminist architectural theory by re-connecting research on women to the sociology of work and studies of organisations. New digital platforms and live public panels provide places for different forms of knowledge to overlap. Public spheres for diverse architectural audiences can bring community and academic intellectuals together.[47]

The category of the everyday so often brandished in opposition to poststructuralist feminism is also a useful trope for situating the everyday lives of poststructuralist scholars. I am asked by people in the different spheres in which I live (local neighbourhood, school parent community and friends) for thoughts on architecture, spatial politics and feminism. In the last year three women architects who were educated in the early 1990s have separately reflected to me on the usefulness of the conceptual tools provided by their university training. We underestimate the long-term effects of theory acquisition on graduates as they carry these skills forward over their lives. Theory isn't a quarantined commodity, but circulates in afterlives and outside the academy.

Feminist life cycles

Studies of feminism as a social movement have identified life-long feminists as a distinct group; people whose commitment is maintained in periods of scarcity and abundance.[48] Feminism becomes a mass movement only in certain historical moments. Outside these brief periods, life-long feminists can experience their own values in discord with the mainstream. As a life-long feminist I have cycled in and out of different modes of feminist activism. Historically contingent conditions structure and shape our agency. I have lived out various feminist projects, starting at 16 when I went to work as a volunteer for a local women's shelter for women and children who were survivors of domestic violence. At university I worked on greens environmental campaigns and since moving into academia, I have worked on a variety of theoretical projects – from large-scale installations with work on gentrification and symbolic representation – as well as publishing a journal that was addressed to broader publics, co-founded a women-only architectural collaborative called E1027, and in the last five years worked with Parlour, a web platform and NGO. I agree with Ahrentzen that a theorist (if they can) should move beyond their own sphere of knowledge production, but we should be mindful of mandating what the sphere of action should be, or judging one critical essay or a five-year career period as the summation of a feminist life. Finding connections and common ground across different projects and life moments provides a less abrasive, conflict ridden or binary frame for the varieties of feminism. This is a strategy of feminist critique at work in this essay.[49] We can work in dialogue rather than dialectic.

Difference in feminism

In her introduction to the last of the great 1990s feminist theory conferences in the Global North, *Altering Practices: Feminist Politics and Poetics of Space,* convenor Doina Petrescu argued for a situational account of knowledge production.[50] She was arguing against normative foundational gestures and for 'alterities' or 'codes of conduct, (a) heterogeneous spectrum'.[51] The conference and the anthology published eight years later deliberately brought together different feminist 'genealogies'. The constellation included Matrix and other British feminist collectives founded after Matrix in the 1990s/2000 whose work included a different range of spatial practices such as installation and performance work. Like *Alterities*, I would champion many feminist practices across a very broad range of sites and modes, including direct action and community genres.

New directions for feminist scholarship will come about through greater recognition of differences – amongst women and feminism. I believe this will happen as a result of architectural scholarship finally entering transnational arenas. Laila Farah, a Lebanese-American feminist, performer scholar, commented recently that feminism could relocate 'what is considered knowledge and resistance outside of academe and US-based activist circles'.[52] This comment reflects a transnational push for mappings of location-specific feminist knowledge, organising and struggle. Any binary paradigm of the 1990s as a US-based feminist theory war is collapsed by global documentation of the varieties of feminist praxis down on the ground. Other disciplines are well advanced in this project, most evident in the new *Oxford Handbook of Transnational Feminist Movements*.

Rethinking architecture's key feminist exemplars in a global frame helps us to understand modes of feminist action in their geographic specificity. The Matrix building for the *East London Jagonari Educational Resource Centre* (completed 1987) was proffered as a key historical example for feminist practice in the community/advocacy model pushed hard by Ahrentzen in the mid 1990s.[53] The design process and building have been described as modes that do not impose 'Eurocentric' values, as well as foregrounding a consultative approach to users.[54] Examining the building from a larger global perspective, we could usefully compare it to the stylistically similar *ASR Resource Centre*, Lahore (completed before 2000), a building designed by architect Fauzia Qureshi for an NGO devoted to feminism, women's issues and activism. Qureshi does not describe the project in consultative and advocacy terms, but in the more familiar mainstream terms of a design brief given to an architect by a client.[55] The comparison – rather than the continuing repetition of the *Jagonari* example – helps dislodge underlying stereotypes of what constitutes a feminist mode of action. This pairing counters the image of Western feminism as liberating an Eastern femininity that is passive or oppressed.[56] Modes of feminist practice vary across geographies and better transnational comparisons will enlarge the terms for architectural feminism.

Feminism: A transformative politics

The goal of all feminism is a transformative politics. The imperative is to change patriarchal institutions, including universities.[57] Social change processes work 'simultaneously within and outside institutions' and feminists should be allowed to choose their sites of political struggle.[58] Revisiting the battles of the 1990s and the ensuing architectural blindness to feminist work in the decade that followed, encourages me to take the long view, to always look beyond the immediate politics of our own historical moment. Feminism – even now when it is once more widespread and has a large voice – will experience some gains and probable reversals and backlashes in the future. We are at a rare historical conjuncture in 2017 when feminist and gender issues have some purchase on the discipline's mainstream stage. It's not big and flares up around particular events, such as the Pritzker Prize petition for Denise Scott Brown or the death of Zaha Hadid, the AJ Annual survey of women in architecture and women-only prizes. We need strong feminist thought in the public sphere to increase the discipline's gender literacy. Decades of sophisticated feminist thought needs to be retrieved in order to move public conversation beyond media stereotypes of 1970s feminism and 'feminine' buildings. Structural analysis is needed to repeatedly contest the claims of neutral, unbiased merit underlying appointments to public lecture series, jury panels and employment. Feminism's paper archive is crucial because the digital genealogies of feminist architectural thinking are sparse. Too frequently gender is presented as a personal form of lived knowledge – which it is – but without history and theory the personal is disconnected from a long discourse.

Theory uses abstractions to make claims about gender, discourse, architecture, power, knowledge and other topics. Abstractions are reconfigured when deployed in specific situations, and it is here that theory informs political action. I have given some examples already of public events and campaigns. Our theoretically informed speech also circulates in new ways. Language is a key activist tool, at work in hash tags and Instagram posts and tweets. Theorists can be active in these public sphere campaigns.

The new digital public sphere and the analog public sphere are places where different kinds of knowledge – academic, informal, community and personal – can be presented. Websites have enabled geographically and culturally diverse knowledge producers from various parts of the globe to reshape the map of feminist knowledge and praxis. These digital technologies can foster powerful transnational alliances, such as the WIKID project to write more women architects into Wikipedia. New connections and coalitions conjoin varied feminisms. Different feminist voices break the myopia of conversations forged only in metropolitan locations.

The neglected archive retrieved by this paper testifies to the long-term inability of mainstream architectural theory to engage with the feminist theory turn or with its feminist opponents. Both of these 1990s formations held very different positions on language. Yet in the end the library as an archive overruled these distinctions and shelved the 1990s anthologies together at call number code 720.82. I have been retrieving material from the feminist archive for six years now. This project takes on renewed urgency when feminist ideas have an increasing place in the spotlight. The archive collects those years of hard thinking and varied actions; it is an archaeology of feminist knowledge and informs our toolkits for action now.

Notes

1   Rosi Braidotti, *Metamorphoses: Towards A Materialist Theory of Becoming* (Cambridge: Polity Press, 2002), 9.
2   Hammad Nasar, 'Intensive Geographies of the Archive' in *Fantasies of the Library*, eds. Anna-Sophie Springer and Etienne Turpin (Cambridge, Massachusetts: The MIT Press, 2016), 34.
3   For example, there is no Wikipedia entry for feminist architectural theory and there are no histories of feminist architectural thought from post-1970, although footnote 9 of this essay references one interdisciplinary volume on gender and space.
4   Mark Wigley, 'Story-time' in *Assemblage*, 30 (August 1996), 91.
5   The trope of being inside or outside existing institutions is used to organise material in *Women in American Architecture: A Historic and Contemporary Perspective,* ed. Susana Torre (New York: Whitney Library of Design, 1977), 149–151; 157–161.
6   Meaghan Morris, *The Pirate's Fiancee* (London: Verso, 1988), 6.
7   Questions from Andrea Kahn, 'Foreword', and quotations from Lois E. Nesbitt 'Postscript' in *Drawing Building Text*, ed. Andrea Kahn (New York: Princeton, 1991), 7: 168.
8   Debra Coleman, 'Introduction' in *Architecture and Feminism Yale Publications on Architecture*, eds. Debra Coleman, Elizabeth Danze and Carol Henderson (New York: Princeton Architectural Press, 1996), xv.
9   *Architecture A Place for Women*, eds. Ellen Perry Berkeley and Matilda McQuaid (Washington and London: Smithsonian Institution Press, 1989); Andrea Kahn, 'Foreword', *Drawing Building Text,* ed. Andrea Kahn (New York: Princeton, 1991), 5–7; *Cracks in the Pavement: Gender, Fashion, Architecture,* ed. Lynne Walker (London: Sorella Press, 1992); *Women and the Environment*, eds. Irwin Altman and Azra Churchman (New York: Plenum, 1994); Debra Coleman, 'Introduction' in *Architecture and Feminism Yale Publications on Architecture*, eds. Debra Coleman, Elizabeth Danze and Carol Henderson (New York: Princeton Architectural Press, 1996), ix–xvi; *The Architect Reconstructing Her Practice*, ed. Francesca Hughes (Cambridge, Massachusetts: The MIT Press, 1996); Diane Agrest, Patricia Conway and Leslie Kanes Weisman, 'Introduction' in *The Sex of Architecture*, eds. Diane Agrest, Patricia Conway and Leslie Kanes Weisman (New York: Harry N. Abrams, 1996), 11–13; *Desiring Practices: Architecture, Gender and the Interdisciplinary*, eds. Katerina Ruedi, Sarah Wiggglesworth and Duncan McCorquodale (London: Black Dog Publishing, 1996); *Design and Feminism: Re-envisioning Spaces, Places, and Everyday Things*, ed. Joan Rothschild (New Brunswick, New Jersey: Rutgers University Press, 1999); *Gender & Architecture*, eds. Louise Durning and Richard Wrigley (Chichester: John Wiley and Sons, 2000). *Gender, Space, Architecture: An Interdisciplinary Introduction*, eds. Jane Rendell, Barbara Penner and Iain Borden (London and New York: Routledge, 2000); Doina Petrescu, 'Altering Practices' in *Altering Practices: Feminist Politics and Poetics of Space*, ed. Doina Petrescu (London and New York: Routledge, 2007), xv–xx. See Footnote 55 for the Global South.

10 'Culture Wars' refers to conservative contestations over American 'values', minorities and progressive breakthroughs. Andrew Hartman, *A War for the Soul of America: A History of the Culture Wars* (Chicago: University of Chicago Press, 2015).

11 Karen Burns, 'A Girl's Own Adventure: gender in the contemporary architectural theory anthology', *The Journal of Architectural Education*, 65, no. 2 (2012): 127.

12 Sherry Ahrentzen, 'The Space Between the Studs: Feminism and Architecture', *Signs*, 29, no. 1 (Autumn 2003): 184.

13 Nesbitt, 'Postscript', 170–171.

14 Kahn, 'Foreword', 7.

15 Nesbitt, 'Postscript', 170; Diane Ghirardo, 'Review of *Space, Place and Gender*, by Doreen Massey' and *Architecture and Feminism*. eds. Debra Coleman, Elizabeth Danze, and Carol Henderson', *Harvard Design Magazine*, (Winter/Spring 1997): 77.

16 Sherry Ahrentzen, 'The F Word in Architecture: Feminist Analyses in/of/for Architecture' in *Reconstructing Architecture*, eds. Thomas A. Dutton and Lian Hurst Mann (Minnesota: University of Minnesota Press, 1996), 92.

17 Ahrentzen, 'The F Word in Architecture', 92–93.

18 Nesbitt, 'Postscript', 171; Agrest, Conway and Weisman, 'Introduction', 11; Coleman, 'Introduction', xv; Ahrentzen, 'The F Word', 92; Margaret Crawford, 'In Favour of the Fringe', *Progressive Architecture*, 74, no. 3 (1983): 116; Patricia Morton, 'The Social and the Poetic' in *The Feminism and Visual Culture Reader*, ed. Amelia Jones (London and New York: Routledge, 2003), 278; Mary McLeod, 'Everyday and "Other" Spaces' in *Architecture and Feminism*, 27 notes:' "Politics" – feminism, issues of gay and lesbian identity, race, ethnicity – have themselves begun to gain a certain fashionability in academic circles, though often in the framework of previous Derridean currents.

19 Agrest, Conway and Weisman, 'Introduction', 11.

20 Morton, 'The Social and the Poetic', 279.

21 Agrest, Conway and Weisman, 'Introduction', 11.

22 Ahrentzen, 'The F Word', 96.

23 Ahrentzen, 'The F Word', 92.

24 Coleman, 'Introduction', 12.

25 Unsourced quotation in *Women in American Architecture*, ed. Susana Torre, 166.

26 Matrix, *Making Space: Women and the Man Made Environment* (London: Pluto Press, 1984), 9–10.

27 Matrix, *Making Space*, 13.

28 Ahrentzen, 'The Space Between the Studs', 188.

29 Ahrentzen, 'The Space Between the Studs', 194.

30 Ahrentzen, 'The Space Between the Studs', 194–195.

31 Rita Felski, 'Critique and the Hermeneutics of Suspicion', *M/C Journal*, 15, no. 1 (November 2011). Available at: http://journal.media-culture.org.au/index.php/mcjournal/article/view/431. Date accessed: March 20, 2017.

32 Mary M. Childers, 'The Parrot or the Pit Bull: Trying to Explain Working-Class Life', *Signs*, 28, no. 1 (Autumn 1992): 210.

33 Burns, 'A Girl's Own Adventure', 127–136 and Karen Burns, 'Ex Libris: Archaeologies of Feminism, Architecture and Deconstruction', *Architectural Theory Review*, 15, no. 3 (2010): 242–265.

34 Jennifer Bloomer, 'Pale Houses, Silenced Shadows', *Assemblage*, no. 37 (December 1998): 46–67.

35 R. Claire Snyder, 'What is Third-Wave Feminism? A New Directions Essay', *Signs*, 34, no. 1 (Autumn 2008): 175–196.

36 Joan W. Scott and Joan Acker, 'Correspondence', *Monthly Review*, 53, no. 5 (2001). http//monthlyreview.org/

37 Susana Torre, 'Feminism and Architecture Part 3: Where To Next?' August 21, 2014, www.archiparlour.org.

38 Joan W. Scott, 'Feminism's History', *Journal of Women's History*, 16, no. 2 (2004): 25.

39 See the documents in *Constructing A New Agenda: Architectural Theory 1993 – 2009*, ed. A. Krista Sykes (New York: Princeton Architectural Press), 210.

40 This is particularly important given feminist transphobia and essentialist accounts of women's identity.

41 Jeffrey Allen Tucker, *A Sense of Wonder: Samuel R. Delany, Race, Identity and Difference* (Middletown, CT: Wesleyan University Press, 2004), 8.

42 Karen Burns, 'Who Wants To Be A Woman Architect', May 1, 2012, www.archiparlour.org.

43 Jeffrey Escoffier, 'Community and Academic Intellectuals: The Contest for Cultural Authority' in *Cultural Politics*, eds. Marcy Darnovsky, Barbara Epstein and Richard Flacks (Temple University Press, 1995), 21.

44 Timothy Snyder, *On Tyranny: Twenty Lessons From the Twentieth Century* (New York: Tim Duggan Books, 2017).

45 Quoted by Linda Carty and Chandra Talpade Mohanty, 'Mapping Transnational Feminist Engagements: Neoliberalism and the Politics of Solidarity' in *The Oxford Handbook of Transnational Feminist Movements*, eds. Rawwida Bakash and Wendy Harcourt (Oxford Handbooks online, Oxford University Press, March 2015), 16.

46 Escoffier, 'Community and Academic Intellectuals', 20–34.

47   Escoffier, 'Community and Academic Intellectuals', 30.

48   Verta Taylor, 'Social Movement Continuity: The Women's Movement in Abeyance', *American Sociological Review*, 54, no. 5 (1989): 761–762.

49   Thanks to Hélène Frichot for observing that my dialogue with Ahrentzen could be read this way.

50   Petrescu, 'Altering Practices', xx.

51   Petrescu, 'Altering Practices', xvii.

52   Carty and Talpade Mohanty, 'Mapping Transnational Feminist Engagements', 14.

53   Ahrentzen, 'The F Word', 96.

54   Janie Grote, 'Matrix: A radical approach to architecture', *Journal of Architecture and Planning Research*, 9, no. 2 (Summer 1992): 164.

55   Fauzia Qureshi, 'Fauzia Qureshi – Pakistan' in *An Emancipated Place 2000 Plus Women in Architecture a conference on the work of women architects – focus south asia,* eds. Brinda Somaya and Urvashi Mehta (Mumbai: The Hectar Foundation, 2000), 43; 45. Thanks to my colleague Anoma Pieris for alerting me to the book.

56   This binary is one of many summarised by Rawwida Bakash and Wendy Harcourt, 'Introduction: Rethinking Knowledge, Power, and Social Change' in *The Oxford Handbook of Transnational Feminist Movement*, 54.

57   Bakash and Harcourt, 'Introduction', 33.

58   Bakash and Harcourt, 'Introduction', 15.

Project 1

Searching for cyborgs

Shelby Doyle and Leslie Forehand

One of the impossibilities of library categorization is the premise of fixing knowledge in place by naming and stabilizing ideas, then locating them in space. The lower level of Parks Library at Iowa State University houses 'Architecture' (NA1-9428) – the annotated photo on the following pages is of the shelf where 'Technology' (NA2543.T43) and 'Women' (NA2543.W65) coexist. If we accept the premise that the library is a codification of knowledge, then there is a gap, physically and theoretically, between 'Technology' and 'Women'.[1] The space in-between has a name – *cyborg* – though not a call number to locate it. Cyborgs defy easy categorization, they are hybrid creatures, composed of organism and machine. Simultaneously gendered and genderless, cyborgs have a legacy of destabilizing the great Western evolutionary, technological, and biological narratives, and embody the ambiguities of 'nature' and 'experience'.[2] In Donna Haraway's *A Cyborg Manifesto* the cyborg is the 'illegitimate child' of every binary: dominant society and oppositional social movements, users and used, human and machine, subject and object, 'first' and 'third' worlds, male and female.[3] Cyborgs, like other nonhuman subjectivities (or *zoes*), already exist, but are not legitimized by neoliberal society. They are named but they do not have space 'on the shelf' or in our culture.[4] They impatiently wait for their turn in the architectural canon: their history to be written, their contributions to be recognized, and their power to be emancipated.

This is a call for the development of a more robust theoretical position about the gender implications of advanced parametric design and the use of machines to design and fabricate architecture. As digital fabrication has made material the network conditions of cyberfeminism it is time to revisit the relationships between feminism, architecture, and technology. We propose a framework that relies upon intellectual traditions of feminism and deliberately focuses on developing technologies as a locus of power and influence in architecture. It is well established that architecture has been slow to fully acknowledge, incorporate, and integrate women into its architectural practices.[5] Within the building profession, digital technology is an emerging site of architectural influence: those who control the process of design through technology control architecture. Technologies such as digital fabrication and robotic construction cultivate a new culture of digital craft, which simultaneously recall a long history of craft and feminine labour and presents future opportunities. Acknowledging these contributions and revealing their influence upon current digital practices is a means for subverting existing architectural origin stories.

Advanced parametric design and fabrication recall historical methods typically associated with domestic labour, such as weaving, ceramics, and embroidery. Architecture can learn much from this shadow history.[6] The cyborg is central to this narrative. Once considered a fictional entity occupying a visionary part of our cultural imagination, cyborgs are revived as vital participants in the history of technology:[7] witnesses to crucial moments in what Manuel DeLanda defines as the 'migration of control' from human hands to software systems or in this case the *migration of control* from female and domestic *craft* to the masculine and industrial *digital*.[8] The cyborg embodies Haraway's 'ironic dream of a common language for women in the integrated circuit': Rachel Grossman's image of women in a world fundamentally restructured through the social relations of science and technology.[9] [10] Not always visible or legitimized, cyborgs are present within current and past technologies providing 'spaces for disguise, concealment, and masquerade'.[11] Making their contributions evident is a subversive, disruptive, and powerful force in architecture: a skill required for survival under increasingly techno-human conditions.[12] What is at risk is nothing less than the continuation of past hierarchies via technological ownership of both technology and technology's narratives. In defiance, the cyborg (woman-as-technologist) must reveal her history, build her technology, code her world, write her scripts, distribute her tools, and methodically disrupt the systems of those constructing, documenting, and disseminating 'the integrated circuit'.[13]

Notes

1   In the LCC between Technology and Women are 2543.T68 Tourism and 2543.W37 War. Library of Congress, 'Library of Congress Classification PDF Files,' retrieved January 2017 from www.loc.gov/aba/publications/FreeLCC/freelcc.html.
2   Donna Haraway, *A Cyborg Manifesto: Science, Technology, and Socialist-Feminism in the Late Twentieth Century* (New York: Routledge, 1991).
3   Donna Haraway, 'A Cyborg Manifesto: Science, Technology, and Socialist-Feminism in the Late Twentieth Century' in Donna Haraway, *Simians, Cyborgs, and Women: The Reinvention of Nature* (London: Free Association Books, 1991), 149–182. See also Chela Sandoval, 'New Sciences Cyborg Feminism and the Methodology of the Oppressed' in *The Cybercultures Reader* (London: Routledge, 2000).
4   Peg Rawes, 'Spinoza's Geometric and Ecological Ratios' in *The Politics of Parametricism: Digital Technologies in Architecture*, Matthew Poole and Manuel Shvartzberg, eds. (London: Bloomsbury, 2015).
5   L. C. Chang, 'Where Are the Women? Measuring Progress on Gender in Architecture. Association of Collegiate Schools of Architecture' (2014), retrieved February 1, 2017, from www.acsa-arch.org/resources/data-resources/women

6   Patricia Morton, 'The Social and Poetic: Feminist Practices in Architecture, 1970–2000' in *Feminism and Visual Culture Reader*, Amelia Jones, ed. (London: Routledge, 2003).

7   Fiona Hovenden, Linda Janes, Gill Kirkup, and Kathryn Woodward, eds., *The Gendered Cyborg: A Reader* (London: Routledge, 2013).

8   Manuel De Landa, *War in the Age of Intelligent Machines* (New York: Zone Books, 1991).

9   Morton, 'The Social and Poetic.'

10   Haraway, *A Cyborg Manifesto*.

11   Sadie Plant, *Zeroes + Ones: Digital Women + The New Technoculture*, 1st ed. (New York: Doubleday, 1997).

12   Chela Sandoval, *Methodology of the Oppressed* (Minneapolis, Minn.: Univ. of Minnesota Press, 2000).

13   Rachael Grossman, *Women's Place in the Integrated Circuit* (Somerville, Mass.: New England Free Press, 1979).

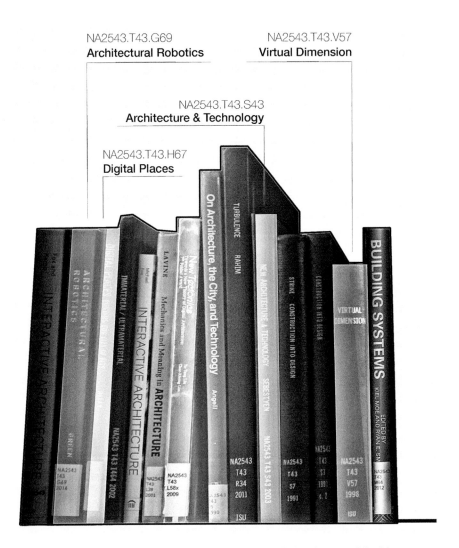

NA2543.T43.G69
Architectural Robotics

NA2543.T43.V57
Virtual Dimension

NA2543.T43.S43
Architecture & Technology

NA2543.T43.H67
Digital Places

Project 1 Fine Arts: NA; Architecture: NA2500-2599; Technology and Architecture: NA2543.T43; Women and Architecture: NA2543.W65; Parks Library, Iowa State University, Ames, Iowa, USA, 2016. These call numbers locate topics within the Library of Congress Classification (LCC) system. The LCC was first developed in the late nineteenth and early twentieth centuries to organize and arrange the book collections of the Library of Congress. The system divides all knowledge into twenty-one basic classes, each identified by a single letter of the alphabet. Photo and illustration by Shelby Doyle and Leslie Forehand.

NA2543.W65.A11.D68x
Architecture & Women

NA2543.W65.G455
Gender & Architecture

NA2543.W65.G46
Gender Space Architecture

NA2543.W65.S48
Sex of Architecture

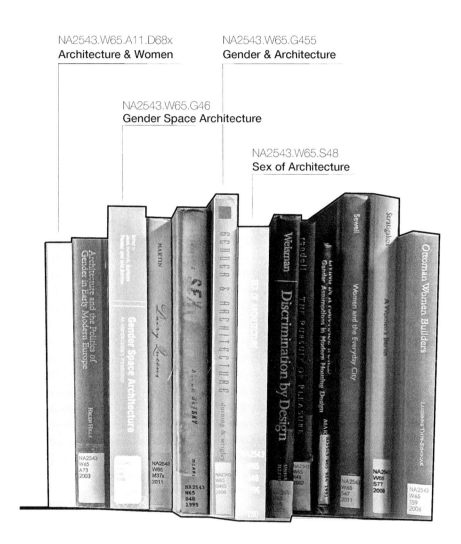

Chapter 2

The role played by women linked to the CIAM

The case of Frieda Fluck, 1897–1974

Rixt Hoekstra

Introduction: the CIAM and feminist historiography

Until well into the 1980s, the Congrès internationaux d'architecture moderne (CIAM) was viewed negatively in both the popular media and scholarly publications. The CIAM congresses were seen as having delivered the ideology that eventually led to the failed practice of post-war urban planning; moreover, the CIAM was identified with Le Corbusier's radical modernist city planning.[1] Influenced by the sociologically minded protests of such thinkers as Jane Jacobs, Alexander Mitscherlich and Hans-Paul Bahrdt, the CIAM program was held responsible for the lack of humanity in post-war city development in the Western world. A first re-evaluation occurred at the end of the 1970s, following the publication of the original documents of the CIAM congresses.[2] The 1980s were marked by a series of critical studies of the CIAM, which were written while maintaining a distance from the writings of the CIAM members themselves.[3] While recent scholarship has continued to distance itself from the self-promotion of its major protagonists – as well as the functionalist turn in urban planning which CIAM stood for – CIAM's history remains focused on the male architect, with little or no discussion being had about such protagonists as, for example, Margrit Wyss-Vögtlin or Helena Syrkus.[4]

The legacy of second-wave feminism was such that it led to a focus on women as intentionally forgotten protagonists or as actors who had been rendered silent by their male environment. As a consequence, the aim of feminist scholarship since the 1960s and 1970s has been to retrieve female actors excluded from the accepted canon of architectural history.[5] This attempt fits within a larger ideological framework in which feminist authors saw it as their task to end women's subordination, which in the past implied a harsh confrontation with male-designed institutions and well-defended patriarchal structures. Through the recuperation of women's 'lost' histories, feminist scholarship aimed not only at giving individual actors a place in history, but also at showing how the editing out of women from the historical accounts could itself be seen as an example of male domination, an idea that is still very much present in feminist literature today.[6] However, this stress on domination and subordination risks eclipsing the way in which women also managed to achieve success in these male-defined environments.

It is well known that women faced a long struggle to become accepted as professional architects in the nineteenth and twentieth centuries.[7] It is also the case that the arrival of women in the architectural profession should not be regarded as an absolute break-through. During the 'enlightened' twentieth century, gender inequality remained particularly tenacious, at least in the architectural world. The progressive, enlightened work environment aspired to within architecture – a work environment that was open to the idea of women's emancipation – did not guarantee the professional success of women. Some women were able to obtain positions of power and influence while others were not. At the same time, a traditional work environment did not automatically imply that women could not have a career or gain a position of influence. Writing about CIAM from a gender perspective thus implies that we must analyse the mechanisms that decide a career.[8] With this task in mind, the history of CIAM provides us with an example of the extent to which women were able to gain influential positions, while not being counted among the major protagonists and not always being, or remaining, visible.

The CIAM women

Who were the women involved in the CIAM? According to the official CIAM documents, only a few women played a role as delegates or as members of Comité international pour la résolution des problèmes de l'architecture contemporaine (CIRPAC), which was the steering committee for the CIAM congresses. The role played by the Swiss aristocrat and 'founding mother' Hélène de Mandrot (1867–1948), for instance, is well known; but the efforts of many other women – architects like Lotte Stam-Beese (1903–1988), Charlotte Perriand (1903–1999) and Margarethe Schütte-Lihotzky (1987–2000), as well as women who played a more managerial role such as Jacqueline Tyrwitt (1905–1983) or Margrit Wyss-Vögtlin – remain undocumented.[9] Likewise, the role played by the spouses of CIAM members, who often stood in the shadows of their husbands, often without a clear professional identity themselves, has been largely occluded from existing scholarship. In this paper I will focus upon one of these women: Frieda Fluck (1897–1974), the wife of Cornelis Van Eesteren (1897–1988), the celebrated Dutch urban planner who was the chairman of the CIAM for many years.[10]

Frieda Fluck was born in 1897 in Bulach, a German village near Karlsruhe. In 1922, she met Cornelis Van Eesteren, who was by then a modern architect-in-the making with a great love for travelling. With the help of a Prix-de-Rome fellowship, he travelled

Figure 2.1 Frieda Fluck and Cornelis Van Eesteren on the occasion of his retirement from the Town Planning Department of Amsterdam, 1963. Copyrights Het Nieuwe Instituut Rotterdam, Eesteren C. van/archief, 101360.

extensively in Central Europe, familiarising himself with a myriad of interesting architects and movements. Whilst on a train from Munich to Zürich, he sat opposite a young woman; it was love at first sight, as he later related the experience in Franziska Bollerey's book about him – one of the few publications, alongside the monography by Bock, van Rossem and Somer, that mention Fluck at all.[11] Frieda Fluck remains today a somewhat enigmatic figure in the margins of the biography of Van Eesteren, despite various efforts by him to accord her recognition. For example, in 1975 Van Eesteren founded the Van Eesteren-Fluck and Van Lohuizen Foundation, with the aim of managing his own intellectual heritage and that of his colleague Karel Van Lohuizen (1890–1956). Van Eesteren intentionally added the name of his wife to that of the Foundation in acknowledgement of the role she played in his professional life. However, while the website of the foundation provides us with ample information about both Van Eesteren and Van Lohuizen, there is nothing on Frieda Fluck.[12] Photographs of Van Eesteren also attest to her importance: several pictures exist in Van Eesteren's archive that clearly show the architect in his study with a large photograph of Frieda Fluck on the wall behind him. That photo was already there at the start of his career in 1924, and the records indicate it would remain on the wall for the rest of his life.[13]

The Fluck and Van Eesteren correspondence

Van Eesteren was almost obsessive about collecting every little detail of his life and giving it a place in his archive. It contains not only correspondence with the members of the CIAM but also records of seemingly trivial matters such as packing lists for his holidays and lists of gymnastic exercises prescribed to him by doctors.[14] Importantly, the archive preserves his diary and love letters sent to Fluck at the beginning of their relationship, the first of which is dated one year after his meeting with his future wife.[15] The encounter with Fluck coincided with the start of Van Eesteren's career, a period in which he developed his identity as an avant-garde, travelling architect. In 1922 he started to collaborate with the Dutch avant-garde artist Theo van Doesburg, and became a member of the 'De Stijl' movement in the following year. Together with van Doesburg he prepared sketches and scale models for three dwellings to be presented at the first 'De Stijl' exhibition in the Léonce Rosenberg gallery in Paris in 1923. In 1924, Van Eesteren designed a number of dwellings for his home town of Alblasserdam and began studying urban planning at the Institut des Hautes Études Urbaines in Paris, while also participating in a competition to re-design the Rokin, a major street in the city centre of Amsterdam.[16] In the midst of this busy, international life, Fluck and Van Eesteren engaged in intense, indeed passionate, correspondence. Their letters appear to be the main medium through which they exchanged their feelings for each other.

This seems logical in view of Van Eesteren's lifestyle, but there was another reason why these letters were so important for them: when Van Eesteren first met Fluck on the train to Munich, she was still a married woman. Frieda Fluck was married to Johann Schwendimann; together with her husband, she had a shop in 'Feiner Lederwaren' – quality leather goods – on Seefeldstrasse in Zürich. There is no information on whether their marriage was unhappy, or her reasons for falling in love with the Dutch architect. During the years in which they corresponded, Fluck was not free to marry Van Eesteren – she did not divorce Schwendimann until 1929, marrying Van Eesteren the following year.[17] In their correspondence, Van Eesteren never explicitly mentioned Frieda's situation nor any negative reactions from his social circle, provided they were aware of her existence. What can be deduced from his correspondence – not only to Frieda but to a wide array of people – is that in 1924 Van Eesteren had a dispute with his father, who tried to persuade him to finally start leading an orderly bourgeois life. However, as Van Eesteren confessed in a letter to the architect Lonberg-Holm, he feared the loss of his freedom and the absence of personal growth. As a consequence, from 1925 onwards Van Eesteren's father was no longer prepared to support him financially.[18]

In general, Van Eesteren's start in the world of avant-garde architecture was difficult and tainted by insecurity: his overture to the avant-garde – a movement he experienced as rich and full of ideas, but also chaotic and incoherent – was hesitant and full of suspicion. Most of all, he feared that the avant-garde's stress on collectivity might damage his chances to make a name for himself and to establish a reputation. He yearned for recognition and a position of equality within the avant-garde circles.[19] During this difficult first period of his career, Fluck was of great importance to him: she was his companion during lonely periods and supporter in his fight for recognition. Van Eesteren closely intertwined his private and professional life, asking of Frieda that she act as a companion in both spheres.[20] However, while Van Eesteren frequently expressed his love for Fluck, many doubts and insecurities existed for both parties. From Van Eesteren's letters we may deduce that Frieda experiences both solitude and a feeling of being peripheral to her partner's life. Van Eesteren too has many doubts. As he writes in 1923: 'But why do you love me Fritzi [Van Eesteren's nickname for Fluck] since I cannot offer you anything but my love? I have my plans for the future which offer nothing to a wife.'[21] However, Van Eesteren's passionate desire for his girlfriend is clear in his correspondence to her, and she is also professionally relevant to him, which becomes evident from the

Figure 2.2 Cutting from a fashion journal included in a letter from Van Eesteren to Fluck, 01-31-1925. Copyrights Het Nieuw Instituut Rotterdam Eesteren C. Van/Archief (EEST), X1010.

constant debates they have about the people around them, from Adolf Loos to Paul Schultze-Naumburg and many more.

A frequently recurring element in their correspondence is their shared interest in fashion and matters of styling. In fact, Van Eesteren was a carefully dressed man who chose his outfits with an eye for both their practical suitability (for example, on journeys) and style.[22] In his letters to Frieda he often sent pages of fashion journals with his comments written in the margins.[23] As a leatherwear vendor, Frieda was a well-groomed woman with a taste for fashion and styling – and Van Eesteren greatly appreciated this in her. These exchanges in the field of fashion and styling also had an influence upon Van Eesteren's professional work: for example, in 1924, he participated in a competition to design a façade for a gallery of shops with a restaurant in the Laan van Meerdervoort in The Hague. The plan contains a colourful horizontal block – the colours of which were designed by van Doesburg – that ends in a large, tower-like vertical volume on the street corner. It is here, in front of the building, that Van Eesteren had cut out and pasted a fashionable gentleman onto the drawing.[24]

Frieda Fluck herself was convinced that she had stumbled upon a 'truly peculiar man', as she wrote.[25] Of course, Van Eesteren was a peculiar man indeed. At the start of the 1920s, he was every inch the progressive architect, working in a revolutionary environment of avant-garde artists and anarchists. Importantly, as a humanist intellectual, Van Eesteren's mental universe not only encompassed ideas about a radical new type of city; he also developed his own ideas about the role of men and women in a modern society. In diary entries from between 1922 and 1926, he writes about modern women: 'All sound and firm wives have something against childbirth, because they feel they are hindered by children.'[26] Van Eesteren cherished the ideal of the free development of each individual and felt that the care of children hampered that process. According to him, weak persons gave in because of lack of determination; this category included both men and women. The houses of his day, he added to this lament, were also unfit for the task

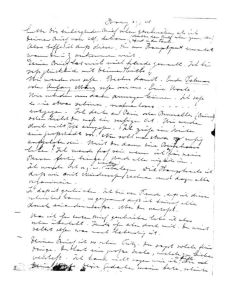

Figure 2.3 Letter from Cornelis Van Eesteren to Frieda Fluck dated 01-31-1925. Copyrights Het Nieuwe Instituut Rotterdam Eesteren C. Van/archief (EEST) X1010.

of caring for children. Instead of family houses, he argued, houses should be built for single occupancy, thereby fostering the development of each individual.[27] In addressing his relationship with Fluck, Van Eesteren stressed the necessity of free choices: 'our contact should give you a sense of liberation', he writes in 1924; 'only then one is really a free individual, a personality'.[28] In this spirit, he also advised her to read Nietzsche. However, this progressive outlook on life is mixed with traditional undertones. For example, in the following year he told her that he wanted to have a child with her and that he would prefer a boy. Whilst conceding that a child should only be 'created' out of one's own free will, he also writes: 'When a woman has given birth to a child her mission is accomplished.'[29] He also praised Frieda for being a 'real woman': simple, but cut of fine cloth; with a zest for life that he himself lacks.[30] In 1925, he expressed his doubts about traditional patterns, asking her, 'should we get married as everyone does?'[31] Cornelis Van Eesteren was clearly looking for independence in a woman, but in a form that closely mirrored traditional roles and patterns.

Frieda Fluck as wife of Van Eesteren

Cornelis Van Eesteren and Frieda Fluck married in 1930. It seemed like Frieda was destined to play a range of disparate roles, going beyond the traditional role of the supportive woman in the background. As their correspondence suggests, from this position she was able to exert influence. Fluck was an important sparring partner for her husband, and they constantly discussed professional matters. For example, in 1930 Van Eesteren was proposed as a candidate for the chairmanship of CIAM. He confessed his doubts to Frieda about the whole enterprise. As he wrote: 'I do not know whether it is just me, but

. . . the whole congress gives me a vague feeling of mistrust.' He then forced himself, he wrote, to think about the whole matter in a more positive way.[32] Interestingly, the Van Eesteren archive contains several letters that the 'CIAM women' wrote to each other.[33] For example, Helena Syrkus often wrote to Frieda and Cornelis. The letters are emphatically addressed to both of them and the tone is informal: Syrkus is clearly writing to friends.[34] At the start of the war, in 1940, Frieda Fluck even tried to organize the emigration of the Syrkuses to Argentina – she had the address of a friend who lived there and who was willing to help the couple.[35] In 1945, Fluck wrote to Nelly van Doesburg, relaying the first messages received from those CIAM members they lost sight of during the war: Sert, Giedion and Moser in Zürich, and Helena Syrkus in Paris, amongst others.[36] She also told Nelly about a recent telephone call from Ida Falkenburg-Liefrinck, who was working at that moment at the architectural office of Merkelbach and Karsten in Amsterdam. In reaction to what Falkenburg-Liefrinck told her, Fluck took a clear stand that in fact contradicted Dutch policy after the armistice in 1945. Immediately after the war, Merkelbach and Karsten was one of the architectural offices confronted with the 'cleansing' actions of the Dutch government – the actions undertaken to punish the people that had collaborated with the Nazis. In these first post-war years, the definition of right and wrong actions strongly influenced the architectural profession. A so-called 'Honourable Council for Architecture and the Applied Arts' was established to bring the 'wrong', collaborating architects to justice. The problem with the Merkelbach and Karsten office was that they had continued to work for a number of companies that were owned by the Germans during the war: the Fokker aircraft company, the Cinetone film studio and the broadcasting company AVRO. After the war, they were punished for this by having to appear in front of a tribunal.[37] Frieda Fluck condemned cleansing actions like this as unjust, and expressed fear that they might damage the reputation of the architects implicated for years to come.[38]

Conclusion

What reasons might we have to include a woman like Frieda Fluck in the history of the CIAM? It makes little sense to write her into a history that understands the organization to consist solely of architects and urban planners. Her story also holds little apparent weight in a history of the CIAM told in terms of the mythic narratives of the Modern Movement. However, Frieda Fluck gains importance if the CIAM is regarded as a professional network that aimed to exert influence on terms dictated by a complex internal chemistry of power and influence. Fluck in many ways exemplified the stereotype of the female partner who provided an unconditional support system for her husband. However, true as this may be, at the same time the relationship entailed a complex psychological interplay between two partners that both stood to gain from standing by the arrangement they had established. Cornelis Van Eesteren seems to be an example of the rule that says the bigger the ego, the heavier the burden and the more intense the longing for love and recognition. This orientation made him emotionally dependent upon the intimate support of his wife, which in turn gave Frieda the possibility to exert influence over him. The scarce information we have about Frieda Fluck suggests that she was more than just a silent figure in the background. She enthusiastically accompanied her husband to congresses and was intimately familiar with the Dutch and international avant-garde scene. His mission was her mission. As their correspondence stops in 1930, the exact nature of the influence that she had remains difficult to define; however, it can be argued that Fluck is representative of the kind of informal power that women in her position were able to obtain, both as a result of their position in the life of their partners but also because of their position in a much broader network of friends and relationships. In this way, Fluck is an example of a female actor who has remained almost totally invisible, yet has played a background role within CIAM and within the architectural avant-garde of Europe in the twentieth century. It is time we started writing the history of women like Frieda Fluck.

Notes

1 Eric Mumford, *The CIAM Discourse on Urbanism 1928–1960* (Cambridge MA: MIT Press, 2000), xi.
2 Martin Steinmann, comp., *CIAM Internationale Kongresse für das Neue Bauen, Dokumente 1928–1939* (Basel, Stuttgart: Birkhäuser Verlag, 1979).
3 Giorgio Ciucci, 'The Invention of the Modern Movement', *Oppositions* 24 (1982): 69–89; Auke van der Woud, *Het Nieuwe Bouwen internationaal/International: CIAM volkshuisvesting stedebouw/Housing Town Planning* (Delft and Otterloo: Delft University Press, 1983).
4 An example of this recent scholarship is Martin Kohlrausch and Helmut Trischler, *Building Europe on Expertise: Innovators, Organizers, Networkers* (London: Palgrave Macmillan, 2014).
5 Susana Torre, ed., *Women in American Architecture: A Historic and Contemporary Perspective* (New York: Whitney Library of Design, 1977); Gwendolyn Wright, 'On the Fringe of the Profession', in *The Architect: Chapters in the History of a Profession*, ed. S. Kostof (Oxford: Oxford University Press, 1977), 280–309.
6 Dörthe Kuhlmann, *Gender Studies in Architecture: Space, Power and Difference* (Abingdon: Routledge, 2013).
7 Lynne Walker, 'Bricks and Daughters: British Women and Architecture 1835–1938', in *The Wise Woman Buildeth Her House: Architecture, History and Women's Studies*, Margrith Wilke et al. (Groningen: stichting Uitgeverij Xeno, 1992), 8–13.
8 Regina Göckede and Gabriele Diana Grawe, 'Das Geschlecht des Neuen Bauens – Genderrollen und geschlechtliche Kodifizierung im Diskurs des CIAM II', in *Neues Wohnen 1929/2009, Frankfurt und der 2. Congrès International d'Architecture Moderne*, ed. Helen Barr (Berlin: Jovis Verlag, 2011), 39–54.
9 Regarding Tyrwitt, see Ellen Shoskes, *Jacqueline Tyrwitt: A Transnational Life in Urban Planning and Design* (Farnham: Ashgate, 2013). Although we know little about Margrit Wyss-Vögtlin, there is information on the life of her husband that also sheds some light on hers. Wyss-Vögtlin was married to Otto Wyss (1889–1960) a Swiss lawyer and legal scholar and a Communist. In 1930 he moved to Moscow with his wife and took up a position in the legal department of the Communist Academy in Moscow. In 1937 Otto Wyss barely escaped execution by the Stalinist regime and returned to Zürich with his wife. In the following year they moved to Bern, where Wyss opened a legal office. Otto Wyss married Margrit Vögtlin in 1916; in that same year she gave birth to a daughter Julia (von) Wyss (1916–1990). In 1939 Wyss married his second wife, which suggests either that Vögtlin had died around that time or that they divorced. Archival material about Otto Wyss and his family can be found at the Schweizerisches Sozialarchiv in Zürich.
10 Van Eesteren was the chairman of the CIAM from 1930–1947. From 1947 Van Eesteren became the honorary chairman of the CIAM. See R. Blijstra, *C. Van Eesteren* (Beeldende Kunst en bouwkunst in Nederland) (Amsterdam: Meulenhoff, 1968), 49.
11 The first monograph about Van Eesteren, written by the Dutch architectural critic Reinder Blijstra, does not mention Fluck. For the role of Fluck, see Franziska Bollerey, *Cornelis van Eesteren, Urbanismus zwischen 'De Stijl' und CIAM* (Wiesbaden: Vieweg Verlag, 1999), 25; and Manfred Bock, ed., *Cornelis Van Eesteren Architect Urbanist, deel I: Bouwkunst Stijl, Stedebouw Van Eesteren en de Avant-garde* (Rotterdam: NAI Uitgevers, 2001).
12 See www.http://efl-stichting.nl (accessed 27 October 2016).
13 Bollerey, *Cornelis van Eesteren*, 13.
14 Ibid., 9.

15 Het Nieuwe Instituut Rotterdam, Rijksarchief voor Nederlandse Architectuur en Stedebouw, Van Eesteren archief. The diary of Van Eesteren: 110440488 Eest X 1055; the letters to Fluck1 1044694 EEST X 1008–1016.

16 Bollerey, *Cornelis van Eesteren*, 250–53.

17 Het Nieuwe Instituut Rotterdam, EEST X1016. The archive contains the marriage certificate of Van Eesteren and Fluck and mentions the previous divorce.

18 Bock, *Cornelis Van Eesteren*, 331.

19 Ibid., 11.

20 Ibid., 103.

21 Letter of Cornelis Van Eesteren to Fluck, 11 July 1923; Het Nieuwe Instituut Rotterdam, EEST X1008.

22 Bollerey, *Cornelis van Eesteren*, 39.

23 For example, in his letter to Fluck dated 8 January 1927; Het Nieuwe Instituut Rotterdam, EEST X1012.

24 Bock, *Cornelis Van Eesteren*, 199; Blijstra. *C. Van Eesteren*, 20.

25 The archive of Van Eesteren contains one letter written by Fluck herself; it was addressed to Nelly van Doesburg dated 17 September 1945. Het Nieuwe Instituut Rotterdam, EEST X 1016.

26 Diary of Cornelis Van Eesteren, 17 July 1923: 'Alle gezonde en flinke vrouwen hebben iets tegen kinderen krijgen omdat deze ze belemmeren.' Het Nieuwe Instituut Rotterdam EEST X1008.

27 Diary of Cornelis Van Eesteren, 17 July 1923.

28 'Das muss ein Gefühl von Befreiung geben. Nur dann ist man völlig Individu. Persönlichkeit.' Letter of Cornelis Van Eesteren to Fluck, 29 November 1924; Het Nieuwe Instituut Rotterdam EEST X 1009.

29 'Wenn ein Frau ein Kind hat, hat Sie ihre Zweck erfüllt.' Letter of Cornelis Van Eesteren to Fluck, 8 August 1925; Het Nieuwe Instituut Rotterdam EEST X 1010.

30 '. . . du bist viel munterer und lebensfreudiger wie ich'. Letter of Cornelis Van Eesteren to Fluck, 8 August 1925.

31 Letter of Cornelis Van Eesteren to Fluck, 15 September 1925; Het Nieuwe Instituut Rotterdam EEST X 1010.

32 'Anderseits habe ich aber gegen den ganzen Kongress einen unbestimmten Gefühl von Misstrauen.' Letter of Cornelis Van Eesteren to Fluck, 20 January 1929; Het Nieuwe Instituut Rotterdam, EEST X 1019.

33 These letters are present in, among other places, the correspondence of Van Eesteren with Nelly van Doesburg, Het Nieuwe Instituut Rotterdam, EEST X1005, and the correspondence with Ida Falkenburg-Liefrinck, EEST X 1007.

34 For the extensive correspondence between Helena Syrkus and Van Eesteren among others, see Het Nieuwe Instituut Rotterdam, EEST X1048 and EEST X 997–999.

35 This is mentioned in a letter written by Helena Syrkus to Frieda Fluck dated 7 October 1945; Het Nieuwe Instituut Rotterdam, EEST X1048.

36 Letter from Frieda Fluck to Nelly van Doesburg, 17 September 1945, Het Nieuwe Instituut Rotterdam, EEST X 1005.

37 Ben Rebel, *Ben Merkelbach: Architect en stadsbouwmeester* (Amsterdam: Architectura et Natura Pers, 1994).

38 Reflections like these were intertwined with fashion photographs and advice on how a lady should dye her hair. See letter from Frieda Fluck to Nelly van Doesburg, 17 September 1945, Het Nieuwe Instituut Rotterdam, EEST X 1005.

Chapter 3

A feminist in disguise?

Sibyl Moholy-Nagy's histories of architecture and the environment

Hilde Heynen

Sibyl Moholy-Nagy and Paolo Soleri

Arcosanti today is a somewhat dusty and derelict ecological megastructure in the desert some 70 km from Phoenix, Arizona. Started in 1970, Acrosanti is built and inhabited by volunteers following the teachings of Paolo Soleri (1919–2013), an Italian-American architect with big dreams and utopian projects. To this day, it is fondly remembered at Arcosanti that Sibyl Moholy-Nagy (1903–1971) was the first critic to write a major piece on Paolo Soleri's work. One of her last contributions in the journal *Architectural Forum* was indeed a six-page spread on 'The Arcology of Paolo Soleri', published in May 1970.[1] It reviewed the large exhibition of his work that had just taken place in the Corcoran Gallery in Washington.

For Soleri and his group it was very significant that Sibyl Moholy-Nagy deemed their work worthy of praise. Moholy-Nagy – although now somewhat forgotten – was at that time quite a voice in American architectural culture. She had come to America with her husband Laszlo Moholy-Nagy, when he took up a position in Chicago in 1937. After he passed away in 1946, she wrote his biography and later turned herself into an architectural historian and critic.[2] She became a professor of architecture at Pratt Institute in New York and wrote several books on architecture and on the history of the city.[3] She was a regular contributor to both *Architectural Forum* and *Progressive Architecture*, the two major architectural journals in the United States at that moment. She was known to be a tough critic, witty and polemical, who used words as weapons and often went in for the kill. Not this time, however. Although the article on Soleri doesn't shy away from critical remarks, these are reserved for only a few projects, and the general tone of the article is definitely positive – positive enough, in fact, for the Arcosanti website to display an excerpt from it to this day:

> Soleri bases his entire arcology neither on economic, social, or industrial considerations but on a philosophical system. It is so all-embracing in its scope that it relates the arcological city unity to the entire evolution of organic life, from the proto-biological primordial ooze to an as yet unevolved Neo-Matter . . . Insisting that nature and human evolution work as vectors or parallel progressions, he ties the future fate of mankind to the same increasing complexification that has marked the rise of our organism from the amoeba.[4]

Soleri's concept of arcology (formed from 'architecture' and 'ecology') refers to vast three-dimensional environmental structures that house urban men in an ecologically sound way. They minimize their residents' ecological footprint by providing compact and concentrated housing together with a lot of shared infrastructures and amenities. Soleri was very inventive in imagining different versions of these structures. Mesa City 'rose like gigantic plants from the landscape, parts sunk into canyons, and residential "villages" sprouting like mushrooms from vertical communication and utility stems.'[5] Babeldiga, which was meant for a population of 1,200,000, was to be built as an extension of a hydraulic dam site (Figure 3.1). It concentrated all these people in two gigantic structures whose height can be gaged from the Empire State symbol on the drawing. The density was supposed to be 665 people per acre in terraced layers rising from an aqueduct. Other arcologies, like Hexahedron, are adaptable to any topography.

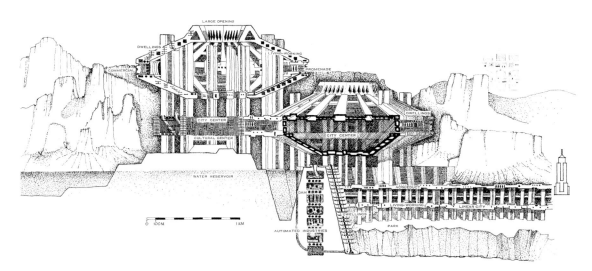

Figure 3.1 **Babeldiga. Arcology Design from 'City in the Image of Man' by Paolo Soleri, first published by M.I.T. Press in 1969. From an original drawing in black ink on paper, 1968–1969, Copyright Cosanti Foundation.**

Two inverted pyramids of dynamic asymmetry are supported by communication columns and carry on their outside an infinite variety of dwellings that can be plugged in in the loadbearing structure that is first constructed. Babel IID houses a population of 550,000 in several massive towers, the light conditions of which might be slightly less attractive than that of the Hexahedron.

Moholy-Nagy was quite appreciative of Soleri's ideas and proposals, which is somewhat unexpected since she was often very critical of technocratic approaches to architecture and urbanism. In Soleri's case however she accepted his logic because she recognized vitalism and utopianism as the strongest driving forces in his work. She respected his imagined megastructures because, as she claimed, Soleri postulated aesthetics over structure and technology, thus rightly prioritizing creativity, culture and organic relationships over rationality and efficiency. She also liked his philosophical system, which she saw as a compilation of Henri Bergson's Vitalism and Teilhard de Chardin's Teleology.[6] The ecological dimension in Soleri's work was thus understood by her as part of an outlook on life and the human environment that respected organic and natural life forces as more important than rationality and scientific efficiency.

This understanding, I argue, is where her feminism-in-disguise resides. According to her daughter, Hattula Moholy-Nagy, Sibyl Moholy-Nagy was not really sympathetic towards the women's movement of her day.[7] Notes from her diaries and some of her published work confirm that she thought that women first of all had responsibilities towards their children, and that most women were not made out to aim for a career. Her attitude and self-understanding seemed to have been that of a queen bee: she thought of herself as exceptional among women, because she very much desired an intellectual life and she really wanted to accomplish something worthwhile in the cultural sphere. She did not, however, generalize her personal sense of frustration in this respect as something that many women would experience. She was not active in the women's movement, nor did she seek out other women as friends or as a support system. She thus certainly did not fit the mold of a 1960s feminist. Apart from some odd references to women such as Hannah Arendt or Helena Syrkus,[8] there are few indications in her work that she was especially inspired by fellow women intellectuals.

Nevertheless, there are some tendencies in her work that bring her close to a form of feminism, even if it is not the activist version based upon principles of solidarity and struggle. Moholy-Nagy's feminism rather resided in the way she aligned the overemphasis on rationality and efficiency with masculinity, and the forces of vitality and respect for nature with femininity.

The four environments of men

In general Sibyl Moholy-Nagy was very critical of technologically based dream images of future cities. Her 1968 book *Matrix of Man* opened with an introduction that sharply condemned the likes of engineers and architects such as Doxiades or Buckminster Fuller who thought they could re-invent the human environment on the basis of science and technology and nothing else. She lashed out especially against Archigram's Plug-In City (1964), which she acerbically described as follows:

> Plug-in City, developed by Chalk and Herron of the British Archigram group. The similarity between fascist systems – which subject each individual to the brutalizing regimentation of centralized dictatorship – and a computer-controlled environment system makes Orwell's 1984 look positively humanistic.[9]

In her 1970 piece on Soleri, Archigram's Plug-in City was again singled out, this time in order to compare it negatively with Soleri's megastructures. Whereas both Soleri and Archigram operated as utopianists, she thought Soleri's work made much more sense because he had a much broader understanding of what human environments were all about.

Soleri's ideas were indeed closer to Moholy-Nagy's own conceptualization of the human environment, which she elaborated in *Matrix of Man*. These ideas were first formulated in two earlier articles, where she took an outspokenly gendered position.[10] Significantly these articles were published in *Landscape. Magazine of Human Geography,* a journal started in 1951 by John Brinckerhoff Jackson, who remained its editor-in-chief until 1968.[11] *Landscape* was seen by Jackson as a human artifact, as the product of humankind's effort to shape the earth's surface according to his ideals. With his interest in vernacular landscapes and ordinary buildings, Jackson was a keen critic of the Modern Movement in architecture. He gathered around him many talented authors, who shared his sensibilities – among them other critics of modern architecture such as Lewis Mumford and Sibyl Moholy-Nagy.

Moholy-Nagy's first *Landscape* article, 'The Four Environments of Man', discussed four basic categories of man-made environments, distinguished according to their physical shape. Geomorphic communities, the first category, were determined by their position in the landscape. They had an organic structure and were based upon an interaction with the topography and the climatic conditions of the site. They were typical for rural environments, where the interaction with nature was paramount. 'Seeding, harvesting, storing, preserving are part of an organic cycle that is invariable and endlessly repetitive. . . . geomorphic environment is static, uniform, and non-hierarchical.'[12]

The second category she mentioned was concentric settlements. They came forth from a different lineage, since they fostered individualism rather than collectivism. The concentric plan was based upon the symbolic identification of each citizen with the *temenos,* the sacred center devoted to the gods. Moholy-Nagy contrasted organic village society, which 'had celebrated its own power to force nature into human sustenance by worshipping its sources of supply' to the concentric city, which spoke of 'a single-focused urban society', which 'invented the invisible arbitrator, hovering axially above his own territorial realm whose destiny was unrelated to other realms claiming different leadership prototypes for cosmological protection.'[13]

The third type of environment in her scheme was orthogonal. In *Matrix of Man* she would later differentiate between an orthogonal-connective and an orthogonal-modular patterns. Here she did not yet make this distinction, but she already stressed how the orthogonal city derived from a shift in focus: the monumental building in the center of concentric settlements gave way to the monumental road which had to be fed by a network of access roads. The orthogonal city was thus the city of merchants, where lines of communication and trade were the most important elements. Some versions of the orthogonal city, such as the Roman cities, were based on modules and grids, and those spoke of coercive powers. In general she saw the orthogonal city as balanced, shaped by an alliance between imperialistic forces and the merchant classes.

The final category was that of clustered environments. She introduced these ex-urban and regional environments by referring to Brasília, which, according to her, was a failed orthogonal city, formed of only splinters of the urban unit, without contributing to its environmental order. Clustered environments, she claimed, were dependent upon a city for all aspects of existence, but did not contribute to its vitality. In the 20th century they unfortunately started to gain an importance that might be decisive for the death or life of great cities: 'The cluster invaded the urban body like a cancer disrupting the continuity of street elevations and plazas with welfare housing ghettos which turn their bare backsides to the community and hold a piece of tattered lawn in front to hide their ugliness.'[14]

She concluded the article by calling for a potential synthesis of the four environments of man, as the task awaiting architects and urban designers. They should understand that 'modern life is urban, and only tightly maintained urban contact can save half our population from turning into sub-urban village idiots.'[15] They should therefore respect the importance of roads, rather than highways, as lines of communication that allow for the transition between the individual and the collective. The factors that determine man's relation with his environment did not fundamentally change during the last century – hence historical continuity in city shaping is much more crucial than any technocratic progress in mechanical equipment.

Moholy-Nagy understood 'environment' not in the ecological sense that is dominant today. For her, as for Jackson, 'human environment' was per definition an artifact, generated by the human desire to carve out his existence from the earth. There is a clear sense in 'The Four Environments of Man' that she considered respect for the organic qualities of nature and of life absolutely necessary, and that this should be the basis of the further development of human settlements. This conviction informed her anti-technocratic position, which also came to the fore in *Matrix of Man*:

> In city planning and architecture, the 'scientific outlook' still has the romantic glow of the untried dream. The technocratic illusion that man-made environ-ment can ever be the image of a permanent scientific order is blind to the historical evidence that cities are governed by tacit agreement on multiplicity, contradiction, tenacious tradition, reckless progress and a limitless tolerance for individual values.[16]

Critique of science and technology

Moholy-Nagy's anti-technocratic outlook was firmly established in the second article in *Landscape*, entitled 'On the Environmental Brink' (1968).[17] The article started with a diatribe against the computer, and against Warren M. Brodey, an MIT based psychiatrist and sociologist who had written an article on 'Soft Architecture' in a previous issue of *Landscape*.[18] This article, which is still occasionally referenced in essays on domotica or smart architecture, presented a thought experiment in which cybernetics and feedback loops would have been developed to such an extent that man's environment would respond in an intelligent way to its occupants' individual and momentous needs. Humans would thus, thanks to the computer, be surrounded by pliable, intelligent, self-organizing and evolutionary systems, which would be connected to their occupants in an artificial, continuous-feedback-generating man-machine loop, which Brodey dubbed 'soft architecture'.

Apparently, the very idea of 'soft architecture' was absolute horror to Sibyl Moholy-Nagy. She called the computer America's *deus ex machina*, which was believed to be the final trump card in the country's competition with the old world. The effects of it, when applied to architecture and planning, would be disastrous, she believed. It would make humans part of a system the only teleology of which would be utter efficiency. She saw this attempt to technologize the home and the city as part of a systematic destruction of the man-made environment understood as architecture. This destruction started, according to her, with industrialized building in the 19th century, was proliferated by 'Bauhaus Functionalism' in the first half of the 20th century and was now reaching an apogee with the calls for a post-architectural perfect environment. That was the point at which a destructive analogy was useful:

> The destructive analogy of a computer-controlled environment is with the Fascist systems many of us have observed in full action. It is the same raw drive for power over the lives of the multitude that produces the political dictator and the environmental system-maker. It makes no difference whether the Central Control is called Gestapo, Central Intelligence Agency, or Self-organizing, Computer-based Man-Machine System. The common denominator is the reduction of personality to 'a stabilized input-output pattern' that erodes vitality . . . [19]

The hopeful obstacle, she claimed in the concluding section of the essay, to this disastrous evolution was 'woman'. Women would continue to give birth to children with unaltered biological and psychological characteristics, which would learn the path to self-realization in designed environments made by them. They would continue to play the fostering and protecting role of the old goddesses. She recalled a couple of these. First there was the Paleolithic mother goddess of the earth, idol of chthonic fecundity and represented by the Greek goddess Demeter. After her deposition she was replaced by 'Tyche, the Fortuna Redux of safe return', at whose feet the Greek put the spoils of conquest and whose head they crowned with a mural crown representing urban success (Figure 3.2). These goddesses stood in for a long lineage of women who resisted the reduction of city life to efficiency.

> [For] woman is an old practitioner of 'relative unformalized synthetic reasoning and stimulation' by which to maintain her supremacy as the maker of the

The Tyche of Antioch, idol of urban success, seen
against a paleolithic Demeter, idol of chthonic fecundity. They are one in absolute domination over
the world of man.

Figure 3.2 Image of goddesses, with original caption, as published in Sibyl Moholy-Nagy, 'On the Environmental Brink'. *Landscape* 17, no. 3 (Spring 1968): 3–6, p. 6.

individualized environment – for loving, working, learning, playing, healing. It is she for whom the architectural matrix of the human collective has been designed. . . . Only her staying power can prevent the turn of the screw that programs men into morons, and a national symbol – the computer- into a world menace.[20]

The metaphor of the matrix

The word 'matrix', according to the dictionary, means several things, 'something that constitutes the place or point from which something else originates', 'a formative tissue', 'a mold for casting type faces'. The Latin *matrix* means womb. By using matrix, Moholy-Nagy gendered the city, qualifying it as a maternal body, giving life and nurturing man (*Matrix of Man*), while at the same time molding his form.

Moholy-Nagy clearly had a predilection for the term 'matrix', a word that is not so commonly used in everyday language, nor among architectural historians. The term appeared in her 1945 novel *Children's Children*,[21] and again in 1958, in the article 'Steel, Stocks, and Private Man'. In this article she asserted that there was a profound difference between public and private buildings, since public buildings expressed common achievements such as technological progress, whereas private buildings responded to hidden personal and family needs. She argued that the need for privacy was at odds with modern architecture's tendency towards transparency and technological unity, since it rested upon the workings of an 'enclosing form that forms man'. Moholy-Nagy thus argued against the open plan, with its uniform, indifferent, or neutral space, stating that the abolition of the 'subdivision of space' had 'deprived the family group of the creative stimulus of independent personalities'. It was therefore important that architects designed many different spaces that could be personalized. It was 'the obligation of the architect . . . to see himself not only as the builder of technological monuments but [also] as the keeper of the matrix in which each individual being is cast'.[22]

A few years later Moholy-Nagy repeated this argument, outlining the task of the architect as different from that of the planner. Whereas it was 'the task of the planner to supply the collective groundwork for society' (i.e. to think in terms of land use and density), it was 'the destiny of the architect to protect and enhance the singularity of each citizen through the walled-in matrix against the executive pressure of the community'.[23] She thus implied that it was the task of architecture to counteract the leveling and homogenizing forces that resulted from dominant social conventions. In *Matrix of Man,* Moholy-Nagy extended the metaphor of the matrix to comprise not only individual buildings but also complete urban settlements. The title was chosen in a rather late stage in the development of the manuscript; its first title was *A History of Urban Origins.*[24] *Matrix* is appropriate since she treats the city as a generative force, capable of molding people and civilizations, bringing forth creative energies and interconnectedness, with Rome as the utmost example: 'the city above other cities, the primordial urban matrix upon which all civilization had to shape itself'.[25]

The term 'matrix' has since also been used by others, often with explicitly feminist overtones. It was e.g. the name of an architectural collective design practice, which operated in London from 1980 untill the mid 1990s.[26] Matrix is also a core notion for Brachta Lichtenberg Ettinger, the artist and psychiatrist, who uses it to describe her specifically female approach to art and to the psyche, trying to get hold of this special relationship between I and non-I that occurs in the womb.[27] The metaphor of the environment as matrix is moreover key to the thinking of some ecofeminists. Ecofeminism as a movement did not yet exist at the moment Sibyl Moholy-Nagy was writing, but there are clear parallels with her thinking. The origin of ecofeminism is usually traced back to French feminist and writer Françoise d'Eaubonne, who in 1972 set up a group called Ecologie-Féminisme, arguing that 'the destruction of the planet is due to the profit motive inherent in male power'.[28] She introduced the term ecofeminism two years later, in her book *Le féminisme ou la mort.*[29] The ensuing decades have seen the development of many strands of ecofeminism, but they all shared 'the assumption that there is a connection between the patriarchal oppression of women and the destruction and exploitation of the natural world by capitalist, male-dominated, modern society'.[30] Among ecofeminists, it is especially Rosemary Radford Ruether who relied upon the matrix metaphor. She argued that 'We need to recognize our utter dependence on the great life-producing matrix of the planet in order to learn to reintegrate our human systems of production, consumption, and waste into the ecological patterns by which nature sustains life'.[31] This comes very close indeed to Sibyl Moholy-Nagy's argument, even though the latter would not use the word 'ecology', nor the term 'feminism'.

Sibyl Moholy-Nagy as proto-ecofeminist?

Although Sibyl Moholy-Nagy did go through life without an explicit alliance to the feminist movement and although it is hard to detect in her work explicit traces of feminist solidarity, the analysis above shows how she implicitly relied upon a gendered awareness in her understanding of the city and the human environment and how she used this gendered awareness to advocate the balancing out of masculine and feminine values. In some of her texts she clearly positioned science and technology as based on masculine values that were imperialist, coercive and dominating, contrasting them with life-giving and nurturing forces associated with women and femininity. She insisted on the quality of the human environment as 'matrix of man', stressing how the city as well as the broader human environment encompassed generative and organic forces of life, which alone could ensure the vitality of human culture. She positioned women and femininity as counterbalancing forces to technocratic desires for control and mastery, purely based upon rationality, functionalism and computerized management.

Sibyl Moholy-Nagy's lectures and writings were theatrical and sharp, but not always scholarly and sophisticated. She did not have a formal academic education, and that shows in her work. Her arguments are often somewhat rough around the edges, and deliberately provocative rather than fine-tuned or subtle. The way she referred to men and women is certainly essentialist: she was inclined to think of them in terms of innate characteristics that set them apart as opposing sexes. Many passages in her diaries and elsewhere also show the influence of the essentialist discourse on masculinity and femininity that was current in the Germany of her youth, where for example Otto Weininger's misogynist *Geschlecht und Charakter* was a bestseller.[32] It remains remarkable, however, to see how she, while continuing to admire and respect patriarchal cultural patterns, also came to identify, in her *Landscape* articles and in the subsequent book *Matrix of Man,* feminine forces as absolutely crucial for the well-being of humankind and its environment. Without articulating an explicitly ecofeminist position, she certainly came close to some of the arguments that later ecofeminists elaborated.[33] She thus offered a very significant contribution to the downfall of modernism in architecture, criticizing its technocratic tendencies from a gendered perspective and insisting on the value of the historical city, which embodied in her eyes, feminine qualities of nurturing and care.[34]

Notes

1   Sibyl Moholy-Nagy, 'The Arcology of Paolo Soleri', *Architectural Forum* 132, no. 4 (May 1970): 70–75.
2   Sibyl Moholy-Nagy, *Moholy-Nagy. Experiment in Totality* (New York: Harper, 1950).
3   Sibyl Moholy-Nagy, *Native Genius in Anonymous Architecture* (New York: Horizon, 1957); Sibyl Moholy-Nagy, *Matrix of Man. An Illustrated History of Urban Environment* (New York: Praeger, 1968).
4   https://arcosanti.org/node/7331, consulted March 20, 2017.
5   Moholy-Nagy, 'The Arcology of Paolo Soleri', 70.
6   See also Larry Busbea, 'Paolo Soleri and the Aesthetics of Irreversibility', *The Journal of Architecture* 18, no. 6 (2013): 781–808, doi:10.1080/13602365.2013.858271.
7   Interview of Hattula Moholy-Nagy by Hilde Heynen, Ann Arbor, April 28–29, 2003.
8   The reference to Helena Syrkus is in Sibyl Moholy-Nagy, 'The Diaspora', *Journal of the Society of Architectural Historians* 24 (March 1965): 25. Hannah Arendt is not explicitly referred to, but in a personal letter to Hannah Arendt dated November 23, 1968 Sibyl Moholy-Nagy described her book *Matrix of Man*, which she was sending Arendt as a gift, as a long fan letter about the philosopher's work (AAA944 – see pdf in AAA944-5 / 184/194). This connection is also commented upon by Jeffrey Lieber. See Jeffrey Lieber, 'Knowledge in the Making', *Cuadernos Del Centro de Estudios En Diseño Y Comunicación. Ensayos*, no. 53 (July 2015): 231–42.
9   Moholy-Nagy, *Matrix of Man. An Illustrated History of Urban Environment*, 15.
10 Sibyl Moholy-Nagy, 'The Four Environments of Man', *Landscape* 16, no. 2 (Winter 1967): 3–9; Sibyl Moholy-Nagy, 'On the Environmental Brink', *Landscape* 17, no. 3 (Spring 1968): 3–6.

11 On Jackson, see Helen Lefkowitz Horowitz, 'J. B. Jackson as a Critic of Modern Architecture', *Geographical Review* 88, no. 4 (1998): 465–473; Marc Treib, 'The Measure of Wisdom: John Brinckerhoff Jackson (1909–1996)', *Journal of the Society of Architectural Historians* 55, no. 4 (1996): 380–491, doi:10.2307/991179. Symptomatically Treib mentions Laszlo Moholy-Nagy as a contributor to *Landscape*, which was a mistake, since Sibyl was the only author of that name contributing to it.

12 Moholy-Nagy, 'The Four Environments of Man', 4.

13 Ibid., 5.

14 Moholy-Nagy, 'The Four Environments of Man', 8.

15 Ibid., 9.

16 Moholy-Nagy, *Matrix of Man. An Illustrated History of Urban Environment*, 12.

17 Moholy-Nagy, 'On the Environmental Brink'. The title contained a double-entendre, since John Brinckerhoff Jackson himself was known in daily life as 'Brinck'.

18 Warren M. Brodey, 'Soft Architecture. The Design of Intelligent Environments', *Landscape* 17, no. 1 (Autumn 1967): 8–12.

19 Moholy-Nagy, 'On the Environmental Brink', 6.

20 Ibid. The quoted fragment is taken from Brodey's article, which claimed that analytic logic fails when complexity increases, leaving us 'with the relatively unformalized power of synthetic reasoning and simulation' (p. 10).

21 S.D. Peech (Sibyl Moholy-Nagy), *Children's Children* (New York: Bittner, 1945), 70.

22 All quotes from Sibyl Moholy-Nagy, 'Steel, Stocks, and Private Man' *in Progressive Architecture*, January 1958, 128–129, 192.

23 Sibyl Moholy-Nagy, 'Of Planners and Primadonnas' in *Journal of the American Institute of Architects*, March 1961, 59–63.

24 Letter of Sibyl Moholy-Nagy to the publisher Frederick A. Praeger, dated January 8, 1967, *Papers of Sibyl Moholy-Nagy*, roll 945.

25 Moholy-Nagy, *Matrix of Man. An Illustrated History of Urban Environment*, 123.

26 Julia Dwyer and Anne Thorne, 'Evaluating Matrix: Notes from inside the Collective' in *Altering Practices. Feminist Politics and Poetcis of Space*, ed. Doina Petrescu (London: Routledge, 2007), 39–56.

27 Bracha Lichtenberg-Ettinger et al., *Bracha Lichtenberg Ettinger Artworking, 1985–1999: [exposition, Palais Des Beaux-Arts, Brussels, from February 25th till May 21th, 2000]*(Brussels; Ghent: Palais des Beaux-Arts ; Ludion, 2000).

28 Quoted in Carol J. Adams, ed., *Ecofeminism and the Sacred* (New York, N.Y.: Continuum, 1993), xi.

29 Françoise d'Eaubonne, *Le féminisme ou la mort*, Femmes en mouvement 2 (Paris: Horay, 1974).

30 Beate Littig, *Feminist Perspectives on Environment and Society*, Feminist Perspectives Series (Harlow: Prentice Hall, 2001), 9.

31 Rosemary Radford Ruether, 'Ecofeminism' in *Ecofeminism and the Sacred*, ed. Carol J. Adams (New York: Continuum, 1995), 21.

32 Otto Weininger, *Geschlecht und Charakter: eine prinzipielle Untersuchung* (Wien: Braumüller, 1903).

33 Also ecofeminism sometimes comes close to an essentialist position. For a critique of essentialism in ecofeminism, see Val Plumwood, *Feminism and the Mastery of Nature*, Opening out: Feminism for Today (London: Routledge, 1993).

34 She played e.g. an important role in the critical onslaught on Walter Gropius's PanAm bulding. See Meredith L. Clausen, *The Pan Am Building and the Shattering of the Modernist Dream* (Cambridge, Massachusetts, London: The MIT Press, 2005).

Project 2

Overpainting that jostles

Tijana Stevanović and Sophie Read

As soon as knowledge is seen as purely conceptual, its relation to bodies, the corporeality of both knowers and texts, and the ways these materialities interact, must become obscure.

Elizabeth Grosz[1]

Here many representations and images jostle in an expanded archive across time and space, prompting other resonances and opening out unexpected pathways through an archive of the image in time and space . . . The Virtual Feminist Museum is not, like the modernist museum, about mastery, classification, definition. It is about argued responses, grounded speculations, exploratory relations, that tell us new things about femininity, modernity and representation.

Griselda Pollock[2]

Feminist methodologies that aim to shift habits of architectural discourse might, we suggest, inquire into the practices of the architectural historian. Inspired by feminist thinkers such as Elizabeth Grosz and Griselda Pollock, we here explore the question and implications of approaching architectural history not only as a conceptual and intellectual endeavour but one that also involves performed and embodied actions of reading, improvising and intervening with the past.

'Overpainting that jostles' was first shown at the Architecture Humanities Research Association conference, 'Architecture and Feminisms,' in Stockholm in 2016. The installation comprised of a series of enlarged archival photographs of Victorian drag practices from the late nineteenth century, found in the papers and case notes of the

Viennese sexologist Richard von Krafft-Ebing (1840–1902). Through the act of enlarging these images – from their original, pocket-sized, carte-de-visite format to life-size – we sought to draw attention not only to the subjects and practices photographed but to the overpainting technique used later to amend the representations of their bodies.

We also attempted to read the more invisible social relations suggested by the labour of overpainting itself. Through digitally and physically re-colouring, framing, filtering and pointing to different dimensions of these images we emphasised: finger prints; details of the staged built environment of the photographer's studio; particular patterns and regions of colour use and application; differing degrees and qualities of artfulness of line; as well as the collaboration between drawn/painted colour, live staging and photographic lens. Here, we pursued the critical and creative potential of playing with and working through digital and physical copies of the photographs – obliquely inspired by what Walter Benjamin described in 1931 as a gaining access to the 'optical unconscious' of the photograph afforded through technologies of enlargement (albeit eighty years later and through digital means).[3] During the course of this enquiry, we became interested in the ways in which the material applications of paint, colour and line which were added later to prints' surfaces in differing ways (to add, to clothe, to deface, to contour, etc.), thereby seemed to theatrically participate in the nineteenth-century performance of gender being both recorded and enacted through the photographs.

The emergence of photography in the nineteenth century as the first mass media is usually situated through the codified reading of the individualised, clear-cut subjects of the author/producer and the model/consumer. Can our re-staging of this archival record contest the limitations of the emerging urban condition, beyond the grouping of individual bodies? Read in this way, the act of overpainting does not constitute the addition of a secondary, decorative layer to the primary surface. Rather, the manual intervention corrupts the realistic capacity of the photographic medium.

Our methods of framing and intervening in these historical instances of overpainting aim to highlight the work and social relations that were either absent or not yet acknowledged by the professionalised photography of the time. 'Overpainting that jostles' strips the photographers of their production field. We use the act of enlargement to practically awaken the elements of architectural history work *at scale*, alongside more conventional acts of reading and writing. How can the overpainted photograph that documented the emerging subjectivities of the nineteenth century be re-animated to evoke the social relations it depicts? Can it do so on its own, that is, without complementing it with individual testimony? Could the photograph itself be rendered in such a way as to invite the transpersonal reading of the social body it addresses?

Notes

1   Elizabeth Grosz, *Volatile Bodies: Toward a Corporeal Feminism* (Bloomington and Indianapolis: Indiana University Press, 1994), 4.
2   Griselda Pollock, *Encounters in the Virtual Feminist Museum: Time, Space and the Archive* (London: Routledge, 2007), 9–11.
3   Walter Benjamin, 'A Short History of Photography', *Screen* 13, no. 1 (1972): 7.

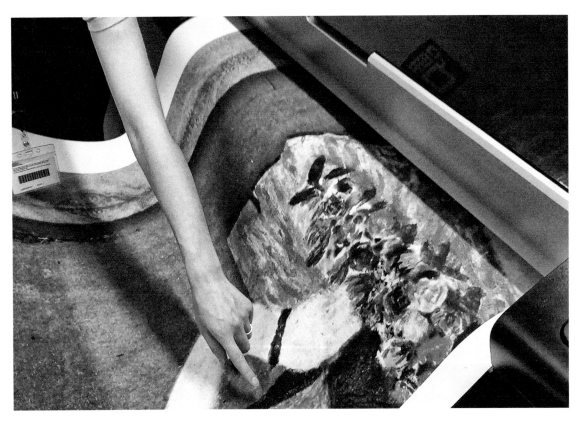

Project 2 Process of printing enlarged copy of 'Man seated wearing a pink tutu and shoes, black face mask and tiara with large star on top', Wellcome Library, London. Photograph by Sophie Read and Tijana Stevanović.

Project 2 Installation at KTH Stockholm, including modified photographs from Professor Richard Freiherr von Krafft-Ebing's case notes, c. 1890s, Wellcome Library, London, and screen-capture of the digital archive record, showing four photographs from the same collection. Image by Sophie Read and Tijana Stevanović.

Chapter 4

The architect as shopper

Women, electricity, building products and the interwar 'proprietary turn' in the UK

Katie Lloyd Thomas

This chapter looks at a moment in the UK in the 1930s when the vast expansion of the manufacture and the marketing of building products transformed the role of architects and their relationship to industry, and argues that these developments also provided conditions which facilitated the entry, in any number, of women into the architectural profession. To make this case I look in particular at The Building Centre, which opened in New Bond Street, London in 1932 to showcase new products, and then draw parallels with the work of the Electrical Association for Women who saw in the expansion of electrification real potentials for women's emancipation, and mobilised female electrical demonstrators, 'housecraft' educators, technicians and product specialists who were recruited into the industry for their ability to communicate with the newly-targeted female market.

      The chapter is organized around five women involved in this 'proprietary turn'; a practicing architect, an architect employed at The Building Centre, and one of its many visitors (and her friends); the president of the EAW and an electrical technician who trained with them. Three of these women are real individuals whose biographies we know something about, whilst the names of two are invented and based on anonymous portraits in photographs. By giving space to the wide range of roles women played, I aim to show that there was no single monolithic category of women affected by these developments. And even in the 1930s, as today, there are more ways in which women engaged with the production of the built environment than as architects, or as clients.[1]

Figure 4.1. From left to right: Miss Elisabeth Benjamin (family photograph of Lucy White née Nagelschmidt). Miss Alma Dicker (perhaps?) in the shadows of The Building Centre lobby (Architectural Association Archive) and Mrs. Venesta Ripolin and 'friends' admiring a 'washstand for 3' at The Building Centre (Architectural Association Archive).

Miss Elisabeth Benjamin: Architect

3.10.36

Dear Betty,

I understand from our phone conversation that it is not your intention to remove the false ceiling in the hall and entirely lag the domestic hot water pipes at East Wall.

I feel I must write you that clause H27 was inserted in the specification after taking the advice of several persons who had special knowledge of ELECTRIC water heating and in view of our rather excessive sum for this type of heating.

[Various other . . .]

Yours Sincerely,

A. Colaço Osario

P.S. Have you been in touch with Crabtree. My catalogue shows the switch covers we want.[2]

With its references to Crabtree switch covers and the specification for electric water heating, this letter from Arnold Colaço Osorio to his architect Elisabeth 'Betty' Benjamin, concerning the modernist house she was designing for him, is one of a number of documents in a remarkably complete job file which demonstrate the degree to which the specification of proprietary products had started to play a key role in architectural practice in the interwar period in the UK. The file is bursting with Benjamin's collection of trade brochures and catalogues; her correspondence with manufacturers and their letters demanding she returns samples she has been hoarding for many months; and with Colaço Osorio's letters like the one above, insisting she consider yet another self-feeding boiler or electric clock that he has come across in his perusal of trade literature and advertisements.

East Wall was built in Gerrards Cross in 1936. Its designer Elisabeth Benjamin[3] was recently graduated from the Architectural Association (AA) in London, and her client Arnold Colaço Osorio was the director of the UK arm of the paint company made so famous by Le Corbusier's 'Law of Ripolin'.[4] When interviewed for a short documentary about East Wall (1997) Benjamin recalled that Colaço Osorio gave her 'absolute carte blanche' with the design of the house.[5] His correspondence in the job file suggests this was true in terms of the general design, but when it came to specifying the products, fixtures and fittings for East Wall, Colaço Osorio was very much involved. Below, for example, is the clause he wrote out in full for Benjamin to insert into her specification for the contractor, and of course he specifies his own company's paint:

PAINTER.

M 1.   GENERAL.

All materials to be bought direct the manufacturers Ripolin Ltd. at 3 Drury Lane, WC2

M 1.A   DISTEMPER.

Distemper where used to be Duresco and to be applied strictly in accordance with the manufacturers instructions and obtained direct from Messers. John Lines.

M 1.B   USE.

All undercoatings and finishings to be obtained ready for use both in respect of body and colour. No tinting, thinning, or intermixing except on the specific instructions of the architect.

M 1.C   APPLY.

At least one day is to be allowed between application of each coat.[6]

The correspondence between Colaço Osorio and Benjamin can read like a contest over expertise, as a young, inexperienced architect tries to hold her own against a technocrat working in the building industry, obsessed with the latest technical and material advances and keen to include them in his new house. I was fascinated by Benjamin's intense navigation through these products and at first put it down to inexperience and a demanding client, before discovering that this was in fact a new aspect of the client/architect relationship that was only just developing in the interwar years. On the one hand there was a vast acceleration in the number and variety of building products available. Architects engaged closely with the manufacturers. For example, the modernist stands they designed for product manufacturers at the popular annual Building Trades Exhibitions were much admired in the trade press and visited by thousands of lay people. Commentators at the time recognised this as a general sea change from, 'a predominantly traditional industry' in which both builders and architects underwent long trainings by apprenticeship to one with a focus on the invention of new materials and systems,[7] and the architect was described as 'the synthesist' between art, science and industry.[8] On the other hand, a new form of specification – the proprietary clause – emerged at the time that would transform the architect's role. Whilst previously, with only a few exceptions, architects had specified building materials by generic names – brick, plaster, glass and so on – by the mid 1930s they were selecting and naming *specific products* and *brands* for their contractors, and it was this shift I had noticed in Benjamin's specification for East Wall.

We can date the formalisation of this change to 1935 when F.R.S Yorke,[9] the newly appointed editor of *Specification* – an annual publication that gave guidance on best practice for specification writing – formally introduced 'proprietary' or branded specification into the main body of his guide document. Introducing the new edition, he wrote:

> Proprietary materials are playing a more and more important part in building construction. The early editions of *Specification* ignored them, as architects were inclined to ignore them . . . Today it is impossible to ignore proprietary building products and to continue to practise as an architect.[10]

Yorke's significant innovation was to move the proprietary information from the back of his guide – where it was included in an advertisers' appendix – into the main body of the specification itself. This meant that architects' product selections were no longer to be simply recommendations outside the main body of the specification; they were now named within the legally binding contractual document. As a result, if manufacturers could persuade architects to select *their* products within the specification, they could guarantee sales. For the first time in the UK, the selection of one product over another became part of the architect's job. Architects became *shoppers* on behalf of their clients, just as I had observed in Benjamin's job file. Today this role is so ubiquitous for architects that we neither imagine it had ever been otherwise, nor stop to ask what the implications might be of architects being product-brokers for industry.

Miss Alma Dicker: Employee at The Building Centre, London

THE CENTRE

> For the mutual benefit of architects and manufacturers of materials and equipment, and all those engaged in the building industry, and to stimulate public interest in building.[11]

Whilst Colaço Osorio and Benjamin managed the selection of building products for East Wall through a protracted correspondence, another more direct approach to the facilitation of this new aspect of the architect/client relationship was the opening in September 1932 of The Building Centre at 158 New Bond Street in the heart of the London's fashionable shopping district, the West End. There, four storeys of the latest building products – from sanitary appliances, electrical fixtures and fittings to bricks, tiles and paints – were on display to the general public, with the express intention that an architect could visit with 'his' client and, 'during his visit be able to settle with his client practically the whole of the materials and equipment to be used in this building.'[12] The

Centre carefully distinguished itself from a showroom; whilst manufacturers applied and paid to have their products on display, goods were not on sale to visitors. They could request information sheets from the Centre and 'retain these as a complete catalogue of all the materials or firms to be used on one particular job,' but no money was to change hands.[13] As we saw in Yorke's 1935 edition of *Specification*, the supplying of proprietary information was precariously close to advertising, and the boundary between the two was carefully negotiated.

The Building Centre was the brainchild of Frank Yerbury, secretary of the AA, but much better known today for his groundbreaking and widely published photographs of modernist architecture across Europe.[14] He had already set up the Materials Bureau inside the AA school, where students and members could peruse samples of the latest building products, but his mission was to bring these new products and technologies – paints, concrete finishes, sealants, roofing asphalts, bricks, glass bricks, plumbing, electrical appliances and fittings – to a wider public. Benjamin would have made use of the product library, as well as Alma Dicker, another pioneering female student who began her studies at the AA in 1922[15] and started working at the Building Centre when it opened, eventually becoming general manager. At first Dicker managed just one floor of The Building Centre, but she also took part in organising in the temporary exhibitions at the Centre,[16] and, as the *Morning Post* reported, in designing the Centre's extension in 1936:

> Mr. Yerbury and Miss Alma Dicker are responsible for the redecoration of the roofs and walls and this has been effected in delightful fashion wholly by means of colour values of artistic nuances. The blackening of the dome of the octagon room was a daring idea, justified by the forceful concentration of the lift from the glazed panels.[17]

Like Benjamin, Dicker's architectural training led her into the almost entirely male sphere of the building industry in the 1930s. Her role at The Building Centre demanded technical and practical understanding of the building products on display, in addition to design skills. But Dicker's gender may also have been a particular advantage in her work since, as the press coverage of the Centre would frequently report, this beautifully designed products exhibition actively developed a new market for building products – women.

Mrs Venesta Ripolin (and friends): Visitors to The Building Centre

> Though the Building Centre, as a recently-opened exhibition in New Bond Street is called, is primarily intended to be of assistance to architects and builders in the selection of their materials, I think it is likely to prove of equal use and value to housewives. Certainly, would-be home-makers, whether they are contemplating the building of a house or merely the interior decoration of one already built, would do well to pay a visit to the Centre. All the latest ideas in building construction, heating, lighting, sanitation and structural decoration are exhibited in a way which requires no technical knowledge to appreciate their conveniences and artistic merits.[18]

Yerbury's stated intention for the Centre in its pre-launch promotional materials was to educate the public into understanding and choosing new high quality products with their architects. There is no explicit evidence to prior to the Centre's opening to suggest that women were a target audience, but reviews in the extensive national and trade press coverage of its opening in 1932 and continuing activities often feature photographs of women visitors. For example, a delightful photograph the *Daily Sketch* shows a group of smiling women, Mrs. Venesta Ripolin and 'friends', gathered around a freestanding, pedestal 'washstand for three' in its news item on the opening of the Centre's extension in 1936.[19] To many journalists it seemed surprising that women (assumed, of course, to be non-professionals) should want to engage with the masculine world of building products:

> In less than a month, I hear, nearly 20,000 people have visited [The Building Centre], most of them being architects and builders, of course, but a surprising proportion being people with no professional interest in the exhibition. Very curiously, too, women have predominated amongst these "outsiders."[20]

Others recognised that The Building Centre's location on New Bond Street set it amongst the department stores, jewellery shops and boutiques where wealthy women already shopped, although it was a 'strange interloper':

> We thought Bond Street, the world's most exclusive shopping centre, was a place to buy Rolls' cars and diamond pendants, not to exhibit bricks and slates and patent floors. As we entered, we noted an aristocratic lady looking at the cartoons of building activities in the window and then with a look of determination, she entered, evidently intent on finding out what this strange interloper was doing in Bond Street. We do not think she was disappointed. There are more ideas in this free exhibition than in any shop in this famous thoroughfare.[21]

The design of The Centre was seen as playing a key role in its appeal to women and other 'outsiders'. Mrs. Ripolin could simply browse the changing displays in the shop window, just as with any other shop on New Bond Street. If she decided to enter, a statue of a reclining nude at the centre the opulent art deco foyer would greet her, with temporary exhibition spaces to either side, directly behind the display windows. A grand panelled corridor, illuminated with the latest neon fittings, led visitors to the library-style Enquiries desk on the left, past smaller semi-enclosed display areas for each of the categories of products on display, and on, to the stairs to further floors of exhibits. Reviewers noted the 'artistic' nature of the displays and that products were placed in situ, enabling visitors to imagine easily where products would be used in their own homes. Brick panels were mounted on the walls as they would appear in a finished building; tiles were laid on to small sections of roof and bathroom and lighting fittings were arranged on the walls in graphically arresting compositions. The Centre's design elevated an otherwise dreary library of building products to department store or art gallery; as the *Sheffield Daily*

Figure 4.2. **From left to right: Portrait of Dame Caroline Haslett in the Club Room at the EAW headquarters (reprinted from *An Electrical Adventure,* Hodder & Stoughton, 1936). Miss Electra Spark (reprinted from *The Electrical Handbook for Women,* Hodder & Stoughton, 1934).**

Telegraph noted, the new Centre opened with a private view, 'like painters do for their pictures.'[22]

Clearly the Centre proved a draw to the female consumer, but the press' emphasis on gender in its coverage may have been in part a response to what was perceived as a certain 'feminising' of the hitherto masculine realm of building products, so that it required 'no technical knowledge to appreciate their conveniences and artistic merits.'[23] The marketing of building products to women was certainly one of the ways the industry sought to expand its market, but it was also part of a discourse prevalent at the time that saw consumption of domestic products and appliances in terms of women's emancipation.

Dame Caroline Haslett: Director of the Electrical Association for Women

> The British housewife must not undertake the drudgery that she did generations ago . . . Our girls are better educated. They have been promised a higher standard of life and when they come home from their day's work in the factory, office or shop, things must be made easier for them. Only the work of the architects' centre will bring that task nearer to completion.[24]

It seems at first an unlikely claim from the General Electrical Company executive Sir Hugo Hirst in a public lecture at The Building Centre 1932, that by encouraging women to become consumers of the products on display, the Centre could play a part in freeing women from their domestic drudgery for more rewarding pursuits. But since the 1920s women's emancipation had been a cornerstone of the electrical industry's campaign for widespread domestic electrification. Moreover, women's organisations and suffragists also saw the potential of electrification for the improvement of women's lives, and were passionate advocates for the new domestic products – from light fittings to irons to toasters and washing machines – that could mechanise many of the chores that had been previously done by hand.

The most important of these organisations was the Electrical Association for Women (EAW), an offshoot of the Women's Engineering Society (founded in 1919) that was proposed in 1924 and officially named in 1925, with Caroline Haslett appointed its secretary. Her address (n.d.) is very similar to Hirst's, who was an active supporter and benefactor of the EAW and might have influenced his own choice of words:[25]

> Way is being made by Electricity for a higher order of women – women set free from drudgery, who have time for reflection; for self-respect. We are coming to an Age when the spiritual and higher state of life will have freer development, and this is only possible when women are liberated from soul-destroying drudgery . . . I want her to have leisure to acquaint herself more profoundly with the topics of the day.[26]

One of the EAW's central missions was to introduce electrification to the domestic environment thus liberating housewives 'from soul-destroying drudgery'. In line with the expansionist electrical industry, this involved campaigning for the extension of electrical infrastructure to the home (where the EAW focused their efforts), and encouraging women to feel comfortable with electricity and to become familiar with and purchase the vast range of electrified commodities already available – cookers, toasters, hair dryers, washing machines and so on. They saw themselves as first and foremost a women's organisation.[27] Indeed one of their most well-known members, vice-president of the EAW,[28] and the first president of its Manchester branch,[29] was the labour MP and suffragist Ellen Wilkinson, who was reported to have 'believed that the twin keys to women's earthly paradise were the Vote and Electricity.'[30]

Wilkinson's passion lay 'in pressing for schemes which will enable the poorer working families to have the benefits of electric help in their homes,' towards reducing the toil of domestic labour and the ailments and dangers of smoke in the home.[31] But although Haslett reportedly was much pleased by the tale of 'an old woman who takes in washing in Norfolk' who on the advice of an electrical demonstrator took out a hire-purchase on a washing machine and increased her income,[32] the work of the EAW was aimed largely at middle class women. During the 1920s and 30s domestic service was coming to an end, and middle class women found themselves with new responsibilities for the same household chores that could be alleviated by electrical domestic appliances. For example, East Wall still had a bed and sitting room for the nanny but was otherwise a house to be serviced by the housewife.

As at The Building Centre, the EAW found ways to present the new products in situ, and often made use of modernist design. When they moved into their new Headquarters at 20 Regent Street in 1933, another AA trained architect Edna Mosely, designed an elegant Club Room with the latest tubular steel chairs and Bauhaus-inspired rugs, watched over by a portrait of Haslett.[33] Mosely's sleek, streamlined modernist design for the EAW's own 'Electrical Housecraft' kitchen where demonstrators trained women in how to use the latest appliances, was later featured in The Building Centre's groundbreaking 'Work of Women Architects' exhibition in 1936. In 1935, the Bristol Branch of the EAW commissioned Adrian Powell to design an 'all-electrical' show home, which featured all the latest appliances. Electric heaters replaced coal fires, telephones, cookers and clocks were all fitted carefully into the clean white lines of a modernist flat-roofed villa.[34] If these initiatives were intended to educate women consumers, the EAW's mission was also to train women in electrical careers, and it was in mobilising large numbers of women – paid and unpaid – to become skilled in electrical housecraft that the EAW had its greatest impact.

Miss Electra Spark: Electrical technician

> I do not think the woman's world has yet realized that the machine has really given women complete emancipation. With the touch of a switch she can have five or six house-power at her disposal; in an aeroplane she has the same power as a man. I do not want all women to be engineers, but I want them to have a chance of electrical knowledge; to have time to follow their own interests; to be able to work in the easiest way; and to live in beautiful surroundings. No other material force has such power as electricity to help women.[35]

With these sentiments, which seem to anticipate Donna Haraway's *Cyborg Manifesto*,[36] Dame Caroline Haslett saw in the electrified machine the potential for women to have 'the same power as man.' But women needed first to be persuaded of the benefits of electricity and to overcome their fear of this mysterious new power. In an address at the founding assembly of the EAW in 1924, entitled 'The Development of Women's Interest in the Domestic Uses of Electricity', the electrical engineer Mabel Matthews proposed that the industry would 'need the help of women, however, in order to help all women to the thrift and gift of electricity.'[37] Who better to render electrification acceptable and desirable to women than women?

Towards this end, the EAW set up courses in Electrical Housecraft where female electrical demonstrators, trained by them, taught other women to become adept in the use of electrical appliances. They established more than 50 branches of the Association across England, Scotland and Wales, each of which had an independent president and arranged their own programme of activities, including Electrical Housecraft classes.[38] *An Electrical Adventure* narrates numerous ways in which its members and affiliates took up the cause of electrification, from working as administrators in the Association, to making innovations in their own homes and businesses, and even becoming electrical contractors themselves.

In 1934 the Association published *The Electrical Handbook for Women*, which would be updated and reprinted many times.[39] The book offered an accessible grounding in electrical engineering and its basic physics, as well as detailed guidance on the practices of wiring, repairs and use of appliances in the home, and advice on sales techniques and the proper comportment of demonstrators. A particularly charming illustration shows one of the EAW's trained technicians, Miss Electra Spark, deep in concentration, her face framed by a floppy hat, her dainty fingers fixing a fuseboard. Women were especially suitable, the argument went, because of their nimble fingers; but as Deidre Beddoe points out, their suitability may in fact have related to the fact that they could be paid much lower wages.[40] Nevertheless, mobilised to bring about emancipation for other women, these engineers, technicians and demonstrators themselves experienced some of those same benefits of skilled work and income, and at the same time had the means to furnish their own homes with the very appliances they were promoting.

'Work of Women Architects'

In 1936 The Building Centre mounted a groundbeaking exhibition of the 'Work of Women Architects'. No exhibition catalogue has yet been found and only two original photographs remain to give us any sense of what the exhibition was like.[41] In each image we see the face of a woman peering at a model. She is not a visitor or an 'outsider', but one of the exhibitors, the architect Mary Medd.[42] From the extensive press coverage of the exhibition, we can piece together a list of most of the 30 or so exhibitors, who had been selected from a call for contributions set up by Alma Dicker. Neither of Elisabeth Benjamin's two house designs featured, but Edna Mosely's work for the EAW was on show and one journalist mentioned Dicker's setting out of 'the building materials and fittings displayed,' as a 'novel type of work' alongside the more conventional forms of architectural work exhibited.[43]

It's easy to imagine that women's entry into the profession, and this celebration of their new contributions, arose from the egalitarian ideals of architectural educators and practitioners, but in fact coverage in the architectural press is scant, and limited to tiny paragraphs in the journals' news and events sections,[44] where comments are often disparaging. The only comment recorded from inside the profession – a professor at a leading school of architecture – claimed that women were not likely to be as first rate or as creative as men.[45]

Instead the 'proprietary turn' and the recruitment of women as consumers of building products and of electrical appliances, established conditions in which women became active in the design and fitting out of the built environment in the interwar period. Despite there being no equivalent to the EAW for the promotion of building products, similar trends can be observed, albeit at smaller scale; the recruitment of women such as Dicker as technical experts to facilitate women's introduction to building products; the use of modernist design, the 'artistic' placing of products in situ and the feminizing of technical information to appeal to a female market. In their many new professional roles women became the handmaidens of industry, but they were also householders and the new consumers of the products they worked to promote. In this sense, women were doubly recruited, as architects *and* as shoppers.

Notes

1   An important influence here is Alice T. Friedman's groundbreaking *Women and the Making of the Modern House: A Social and Architectural History* (New York: Harry N. Abrams, 1998), which *both* establishes the significance of women's contribution to modern architecture as clients, and in turn, challenges conceptions of architectural production that focus only on the designer.

2   Client/architect correspondence from job file for East Wall, Gerrards Cross, Bucks, (1936), RIBA Archives, SaG/9/4.

3   For the only account of Elisabeth Benjamin's work see, Lynne Walker, 'Interview with Elisabeth Benjamin' in *Twentieth Century Architecture*, *Vol.2*, 1996: 74–84.

4   Le Corbusier, *The Decorative Art of Today*, trans. James Dunnett (London: The Architectural Press, 1987):192.

5   *Light, Air and Simplicity: House at Gerrards Cross [1936]*, produced and directed by Angela Daniell (London: Momentum, 1997).

6   Specification for house at Hedgerley Lane, Gerrards Cross, Bucks, (1936), RIBA Archives, SaG/9/4.

7   'A First Review of the Building Trades Exhibition, Olympia, 1936' in *The Architect and Building News*, September 18 1936: 350. All newspaper and magazine articles cited in this chapter are from The Building Centre press-cutting books in the Architectural Association (AA) Archives, and hence they have no page numbers. I am grateful to the archivist Ed Bottoms for introducing me to this treasure trove.

8   'Olympia, 1936' in *The Builder,* September 4, 1936: 296, AA Archives.

9   F.R.S. Yorke is better known today as designer and publicist of modern architecture. His seminal book *The Modern House in England* (Cheam: Architectural Press, 1937) featured East Wall.

10   F.R.S. Yorke, 'Preface' in *Specification 1935* (London: Architectural Press, 1935): iii.

11   Prospectus for The Building Centre Ltd., n.d., front cover, AA Archives.

12   Ibid., 'The Scheme in Practice'.

13   Ibid.

14   See Ian Jeffrey and Andrew Higgott, *Frank Yerbury: Itinerant Cameraman – Architectural Photographs 1920–35* (London: Architectural Association Publications, 1987).

15   AA student register (1924–33), AA Archives.

16   Both *The Builder* and *Architect & Builder* 20 December 1935 carried ads looking for contributions to an 'Exhibition of Work Executed by Women Architects' that opened at The Building Centre in 1936. Potential contributors are asked to send preliminary prints to 'Miss Alma Dicker, FRIBA, Honorary Secretary', AA Archives.

17   'Building Centre's New Home' in *Morning Post*, January 9, 1936, AA Archives.

18   Review of the opening of The Building Centre in the *Nottingham Evening Post,* 9 September 1932, AA Archives.

19   *Daily Sketch*, January 10, 1936, AA Archives.

20   Review of the opening of The Building Centre in the *Edinburgh Evening News*, 15 October 1932, AA Archives.

21   *The Builder*, n.d., ca. October 15, 1932, AA Archives.

22   *Sheffield Daily* Telegraph, September 3, 1932, AA Archives.

23   Review of the opening of The Building Centre in the *Nottingham Evening Post,* 9 September 1932, AA Archives.

24   Report of Sir Hugo Hirst's lecture at The Building Centre in the *Birmingham Post*, October 28, 1932, AA archives.

25   Hirst's contributions to the EAW's activities are in a history of its first 10 years; Peggy Scott, *An Electrical Adventure* (London: Hodder and Stoughton,1934), 102, 61–62. For his financial support of the Association see https://sites.google.com/a/staff.westminster.ac.uk/electricity-for-women/home/electrical-promotion-between-the-wars, (accessed 24 April 2017).

26   Reprinted in Scott, *An Electrical Adventure*, 108.

27   Carroll Pursell, 'Domesticating Modernity: the Electrical Association for Women, 1924–86', *British Journal for the History of Science*, 32 (1999) 47–67: 47.

28   Scott, *An Electrical Adventure*: 100.

29   Ibid., 17.

30   Introduction to Ellen Wilkinson's annual EAW address in 1934. As reported in *Electrical Age for Women*, no.2, 1934: 653.

31   Ibid.

32   Scott, *An Electrical Adventure*: 72.

33   Ibid., 96.

34   For plans, photographs and description of the show home, see R. Randall Philips, *Houses for Moderate Means* (London: Country Life Ltd., 1936): 50–52.

35   Haslett's words, as reported in Scott, *An Electrical Adventure*: 12.

36   Donna Haraway, 'A Cyborg Manifesto: Science, Technology, and Socialist-Feminism in the Late Twentieth Century' in *Simians, Cyborgs and Women: The Reinvention of Nature* (London: Routledge, 1991).

37 Scott, *An Electrical Adventure*: 3.

38 Ibid., 113–9.

39 Caroline Haslett (ed.), *The Electrical Handbook for Women* (London: Hodder & Stoughton, 1934).

40 Deidre Beddoe, *Back to Home and Duty: Women Between the Wars, 1918–1939* (London: Rivers Oram Press, 1989).

41 These photographs are in the stores of The Building Centre, as it exists today, much changed, Store Street, London (and only a stone's throw from the AA). I am grateful to Colin Tweedy, director of the Centre, for enabling me to see the collection.

42 I am grateful to Elizabeth Darling for identifying the face in the picture.

43 'Women Build New Reputation in Reinforced Concrete' in *News Chronicle,* February 11, 1936.

44 For example, there are no mentions of the exhibition in *Journal of the RIBA* (8 & 22 February 1936) or *Architectural Review* (February 1936); and brief entries 'Building Centre Exhibition' under 'News and Notes' in *Architectural Design and Construction* (Vol VI.4, February 1936, p.110) and 'Work of Women Architects' under 'General News' in *The Builder* (21 February 1936, p.378), AA Archives.

45 'Women as Architects What they are Doing Today' in *Homes and Gardens*, April 1936.

Chapter 5

Between landscape and confinement

Situating the writings of Mary Wollstonecraft

Emma Cheatle

9 September 1977,

and I write to you that I love the delicate levers which pass between the legs of a word and itself.

Jacques Derrida[1]

This chapter speculates on the importance of spatial and material references to the eighteenth-century feminist Mary Wollstonecraft (1759–1797). Elsewhere, my research on the history of maternity spaces evaluates Wollstonecraft's attitudes to hospitals and midwifery.[2] These, and her tragic biography, neatly intersect the eighteenth-century debates on spatial practices in maternity. Whilst I return to this context later in the chapter, overall I present the way in which Wollstonecraft's feminism developed through references to landscape, domestic objects, and interior space. There are two sections. First, 'Landscape' sets out the way that Wollstonecraft used the material motifs of place, air, and built structure to repudiate Edmund Burke's condemnation of the French Revolution and, continuing to be inspired by the same, presented her treatise for a feminist revolution.[3] Her subsequent book, on the natural landscape of Scandinavia, dwells on the detailed materiality of place to argue that Burke's gendered tropes of 'sublime' and 'beautiful' are interdependent and grounding rather than in terrifying opposition.[4] Second, 'Confinement' draws out Wollstonecraft's seemingly contradictory positions towards domesticity: on the one hand, she was known for her caustic rejection of the conventions of Georgian marriage, domesticity, and property, and their ensuing confinement of women; on the other hand, she carefully positioned the objects of domesticity at the centre of family life. This section moves to Wollstonecraft's maternal 'confinement' in her home, the Polygon, Somers Town, North London, resulting in the birth of her second child – the future Mary Shelley – and her own death eleven days later.

Wollstonecraft resisted the gendered separation of 'external' public space from 'internal' household space. 'Landscape' and 'Confinement' track her politicisation of the private, outlining her feminism as it developed through both intellectual analysis and personal experience.[5] If this combination was contentious in her lifetime, the memoir revealing her personal life to the full, written just after her death by her grief-stricken husband, William Godwin, left her impact and feminist position contested for many years.[6] Yet, the memoir, other accounts, plus her numerous letters and notes give important insight into her thinking. This mixture of personal and political is inherent to my understanding of Wollstonecraft, as is her strong physical aura. Her contemporaries described her as a vivacious, even strident, thinker and orator; upon entering a room she held a commanding and beautiful presence.[7] Her suicide attempts – psychic imbalance manifested as physical destruction – and early death aged 38, emphasise her corporeality, especially when imagining her unconscious body pulled from the Thames, or her last days.[8] Wollstonecraft's intellectual writing seems to confirm a physical presence. Conversation-like in tone and hinged around her subjective experience, it is almost as though she stands at my shoulder as I read. I am situated between her body and ideas, her death and continuing importance.

'Landscape' and 'Confinement' are interspersed with short creative texts composed whilst walking through Somers Town in search of the signs of the long-vanished Polygon. Written to Mary as 'love letters' on the back of postcards (Figures 5.1–5.4), these provide an alternative literary thread through the text, to draw out imagined, personal detail.[9] Written now into the past, and both intimate and public, the postcards recall Jacques Derrida's *The Post Card: From Socrates to Freud and Beyond* (1980) where the post card operates as a 'lever', a switch-point or gear, to reconnect time, place, and people.[10] The lever is physical object as metaphor. Where Derrida's text is an epistolary response to an image, mine is written on physical postcards in response to Wollstonecraft's archive. The object of the postcard, the forms of writing (creative, historical, handwritten), different images (painting, map, drawing, text), and the shifting temporalities are levers across a sequence of events, complicating the division of 'Landscape' and 'Confinement'. Mindful of Christine Delphy's assertion that the separation of disciplinary methods is a form of oppression, this is an interdisciplinary, 'materialist' method, that uses historical documentary with creative writing, and intersects philosophy, architectural history, and visual culture.[11] As I advance through the writing here, and on foot through Somers Town, I present the texts, objects, Mary and myself, as levers between history and the present, the personal and the intellectual. Inevitably I move towards Mary's death, increasingly composing around the absent physicality of her body.

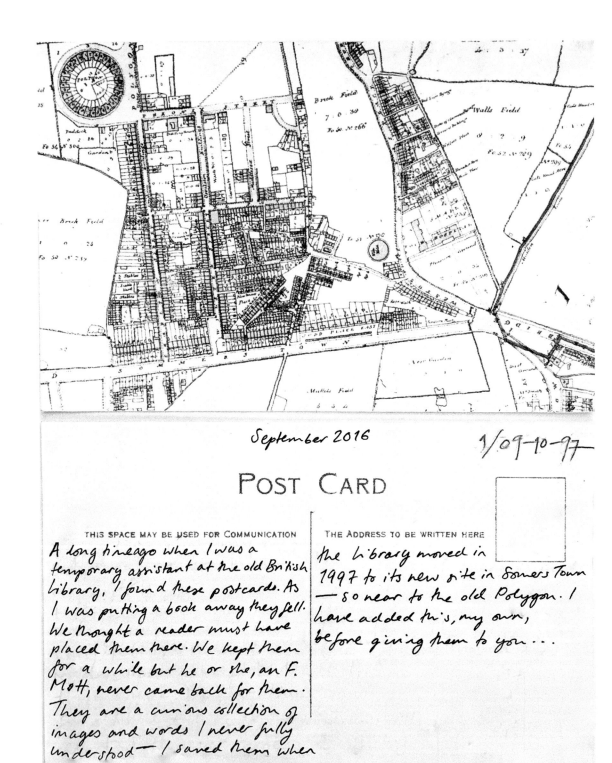

September 2016

1/09-10-97

POST CARD

THIS SPACE MAY BE USED FOR COMMUNICATION

A long timeago when I was a
temporary assistant at the old British
library, I found these postcards. As
I was putting a book away they fell.
We thought a reader must have
placed them there. We kept them
for a while but he or she, an F.
Mott, never came back for them.
They are a curious collection of
images and words I never fully
understood — I saved them when

THE ADDRESS TO BE WRITTEN HERE

the Library moved in
1997 to its new site in Somers Town
— so near to the old Polygon. I
have added this, my own,
before giving them to you ...

Figure 5.1 Postcard 1. Section of map, showing north of Euston Road and Somers Town of St. Pancras by John Thompson, c. 1803. (King's Cross and north of Euston Road). Public Domain. Postcard and text by Emma Cheatle, 2016.

Landscape

Shortly after the first stage of the French Revolution, Wollstonecraft wrote her first pamphlet *A Vindication of the Rights of Men* (1790) in swift response to Burke's *Reflections on the Revolution in France* (1790). Burke had supported the American Revolution but condemned the overturn of monarchy, stating that the French had 'shown themselves the ablest architects of ruin'.[12] Wollstonecraft was well-versed in Burke's earlier *A Philosophical Enquiry into the Origin of Our Ideas of the Sublime and Beautiful* (1756) where he proposed that aesthetics was a dichotomy of the sublime (massive or masculine/ landscape) and beautiful (feminine or soft/detail). Her 'vindication' instead invoked an everyday pastoral, the landscape of the *sans-culotte*: 'I shall not,' she stated, 'attempt to follow you through "horse-way and footpath"'.[13] Despite not *following* Burke, she identified with, and borrowed, his use of architectural terms: 'Attacking the *foundation* of your opinions, I shall leave the *superstructure* to find a centre of gravity on which it might lean till some strong blast puffs it into the air'.[14] Wollstonecraft called her pamphlet 'effusions of the moment', and incorporated ideas of air throughout, to blow apart arguments, or to re-balance them.[15] Conceptualisations of gas and air were newly understood in the eighteenth century and by 1789 their different constituents signified political states.[16] Burke likened 'wild gas' (oxygen) to the explosive nature of the French Revolution and 'fixed air' (carbon dioxide) to the rational reason of the 1688 Glorious Revolution in England.[17] For Wollstonecraft a revolutionary *blast* enabled a mere *puff* to easily, and wittily, knock over a shoddily built argument. Further, the references appear to be influenced by the destruction of buildings in Paris, as well as the structure of the guillotine. Using abundant exclamatory punctuation, Wollstonecraft's breathless style reinforced her explosive intent.

Wollstonecraft published anonymously to gain a hearing.[18] Only when the pamphlet rapidly sold out did Wollstonecraft reveal herself. She soon became known as a radical female voice and followed her success with the polemic *A Vindication of the Rights of Woman* (1792).[19] Although criticised for lacking a clear structure, *Rights of Woman* offers a clear challenge to the roles women were confined to, calling particularly for educational equality.[20] References to landscape continue: women are 'flowers planted in too rich a soil' (31) and therefore, quoting Rousseau: '"how can they leave the nursery for the camp!"' (218). Air also remains important. Thomas Beddoes, radical physician and Wollstonecraft's friend, had already linked the idea of feminist equality to the balanced constituents of air.[21] Wollstonecraft's text, decrying the lazy, 'voluptuousness' of wealth, stirs up this 'still sultry air' (212). Where *Rights of Men* calls for the destruction of the edifice that stifles its occupants, *Rights of Woman* demands 'the sharp invigorating air of freedom', seeking to ventilate it; open a window to let in fresh air.[22] Wollstonecraft's voice here seemed less revolutionary: rather than complete demolition she proposed a new equilibrium within the same structure.

Rights of Woman was written in just six weeks before Wollstonecraft was swept onwards into the continuing events in France. In 1795 Wollstonecraft had returned to London from France after nearly two years packed with change and productivity. While witnessing and documenting the ongoing bloody turmoil of the French Revolution, in

Scene of the Great Dust-heap, Kings Cross Battle Bridge 1837, from the Maiden Lane, the present York Road; it was removed in 1849 to assist in rebuilding Moscow Russia. The great heap there terminates the east. View from New Road to house in the grounds of the Small Pox Hospital in the background.

September 10th, 2017

2/09-10-97

POST CARD

WITH GREETINGS

Dear Mary —
Summer is on the cusp of autumn. It's 200 years since you died... but I'll come back to that. Right now, I am looking for the house in which you lived for the last part of your life. Well, not the house, demolished in the 1890s, but some trace of its once presence. As I walk — like you — through London towards Polygon Road, I

imagine it as it was then. The city,

FOR ADDRESS ONLY

expanding rapidly, was a dirty, noisome place. Somers Town, just to the north, is painted as a rural idyll. But really it was rough, 'a piece of common or barren brickfield' someone said. There were gravel pits and dust heaps and you could see the plague pit of St Pancras, the workhouse and the Smallpox Hospital nearby.

Figure 5.2 Postcard 2. The Great Dust-Heap, next to Battle Bridge and the Smallpox Hospital King's Cross, London. Watercolour painting by E. H. Dixon, 1837, courtesy of Wellcome Library, London. Postcard and text by Emma Cheatle, 2016.

which many of her friends were killed, she had fallen in love with American businessman Gilbert Imlay, become pregnant and borne a baby girl, Fanny.[23] After the birth, Imlay's interest in Wollstonecraft had waned and she was alone for increasingly long periods. On her return to London she found him living with another woman. Within days, she made her first suicide attempt. Imlay, perhaps to provide her with a sense of purpose (and out of guilt), persuaded her to travel to Scandinavia. She set off the following week, in what must have been a very fragile state, alone except for her maid and one-year old Fanny. The trip, purportedly to negotiate one of Imlay's ongoing business problems, became a search for strength and recalibration in the Scandinavian landscape. The ensuing *Letters Written in Sweden, Norway and Denmark* (1796), based on letters written to Imlay during the trip, is extremely beguiling. As Godwin later wrote: 'If ever there was a book calculated to make a man in love with its author, this appears to me to be the book'.[24]

In *Rights of Men* Wollstonecraft argued that Burke's notion of 'beauty' had been used to cripple women into feminine sensibilities. She instead asserted that, as exhibited in the natural world, the sublime and beautiful were interdependent: and the same should hold for men and women, in public and private life.[25] *Letters Written in Sweden* . . . offers a lyrical writing utterly immersed in the landscape and its people. Every page is a response to the places on Wollstonecraft's journey – the result is intense, critical, meditative, and creative. Enthralled by the vast sublime, Wollstonecraft traces the beauty of detail, repeatedly outlining their concomitance: 'the rocks which tossed their fantastic heads so high were often covered with pines and firs . . . The eye stole into many a covert where tranquillity seemed to have taken up her abode'.[26] We follow her from the 'wild grandeur' of 'terrific oceans', 'menacing rocks', and 'closing chasms' to trees and foliage of 'dazzling verdure' which 'relieved and charmed my eyes' (28, 29, 32), to rest where the 'prattling of the sea amongst the pebbles has lulled me to sleep' (49).

Against this backdrop of the natural landscape, she scrutinised and compared the buildings, everyday objects and social practices to those of Britain and France. The 'clean airy' towns with canals and 'rows of trees' provided a welcoming, if staid, contrast to Paris' bloody, collapsing streets. She was as vexed by the bad teeth of the women as she was reassured by the simple domesticity of plain meals in small houses and farms.[27] Most of all though, the voyage around Scandinavia instigated a deepened understanding of the relationships between landscape, politics, place, and the personal, with which she began to associate her own identity and sanity.

Confinement

Wollstonecraft was well known for her personal rejection of the Georgian aesthetics of appearance, fashion, and domesticity. She dressed plainly, and disapproved of vanity, wearing her hair 'uncombed and unpowdered'.[28] In *Rights of Woman* she stated that she had no 'sacred respect for cleanliness and decency in domestic life'.[29] She thought that the politicisation of the home was inevitable: 'women cannot, by force, be confined to domestic concerns; for they will however ignorant, intermeddle with more *weighty*

May 10th, 2005

3/09-10-97

POST CARD.

THIS SPACE MAY BE USED
FOR COMMUNICATION.
(In British Isles only.)
(Post Office Regulation.)

THE ADDRESS ONLY TO BE
WRITTEN HERE.

INLAND,
½d.
STAMP.

FOREIGN,
1d.

There is not much left of the eighteenth century here. Certainly nothing of Leroux's strange sixteen-sided polygonal building, your + Godwin's home at no. 29. The building, with its unusual form, would have attracted them both. The development was unfinished but 'poor unfortunate' Fanny, your illegitimate daughter by Imlay, could play in the dusty fields. Despite the circular form, the interiors were standard: bedchambers on the upper floor, a large dining-room on the first and a parlour on the ground. Cast iron balconies graced the first floor.

Like me, you were once again pregnant.

Figure 5.3 Postcard 3. The Polygon, Somers Town, 1850. Public Domain. Postcard and text by Emma Cheatle, 2016.

affairs, neglecting private duties'.[30] Women were naturally interested in public matters, and had something to contribute: if society did not allow them to in an organised way then, through distraction, the home would suffer. Yet to her, the very idea of home was unimportant. Moving frequently, on return from France her belongings were left in storage until she and Godwin set up home in the Polygon. The French revolutionary leader Talleyrand-Périgord, to whom *Rights of Woman* was dedicated, remembered visiting Wollstonecraft to be served wine from teacups.[31] From an early age, she had sought freedom from a troubled family life. Yet, until her sojourns in France and Scandinavia – where she was often in the thick of public life – Wollstonecraft had frequently found herself bound by domesticity: as a governess (a role she despised); a nurse to both her sister during postnatal depression, and to her mother on her deathbed. By stating that public life was 'weighty', Wollstonecraft stressed its importance. Domesticity, in contrast, was confining due to the pressing impositions of social propriety. It was also squeezed to having little importance by the same weight.

And yet, domesticity became increasingly important to Wollstonecraft. Motherhood was a role she embraced, and she believed that domestic space was a setting for a moral and equal family life. The little-known *Lessons* (1798), probably written for Fanny in 1795, gently introduces the immediate environment. Like a poem on the page, 'Lesson I' is composed of single object-words mapping the simple appreciation of a child's immediate objects: 'House. Wall. Field. Street . . . Stone. / Bed. Chair. Door . . . Cup. Box.'[32] Words then build into sentences, commands that spatialise the world. 'Lesson III' reads 'Stroke the cat. Play with the Dog. Eat the Bread. Drink the milk. Hold the cup. Lay down the knife'; 'Lesson IV': 'Let me comb your head. Ask Betty to wash your face. Go and see for some bread. Drink milk if you are dry. Play on the floor with the ball. Do not touch the ink; you will black your hands . . . Will you walk in the fields?'[33] Finally, 'Lesson XIII' extends these simple commands to suggest that the home environment builds morals and empathy. Noting that Fanny has learned that opening the door might disturb her father's sleep, Wollstonecraft states: 'thinking again, you came back to me on tiptoes. Whisper—whisper. Pray mama, call me, when papa wakes; for I shall be afraid to open the door to see, lest I should disturb him.'[34] *Lessons* maps family life and its social frameworks from the intimacy of objects in the home to the external spatial environment.

Domesticity was, nevertheless, to be approached with extreme caution, and in her gothic novel *Maria, or The Wrongs of Woman* (1798) Wollstonecraft revealed her continuing ambivalence.[35] The gothic tradition brought the sublime into the domestic, and was hence a critical agent to Burke's simple dichotomy. In *Wrongs* the eponymous heroine finds herself in a private lunatic asylum, a gothic motif indicating the *wrongs* of society. Maria is not unwell, but incarcerated as the property of her brutal husband. In *Rights of Woman* a fundamental criticism recurs around the social injustice of property. Signifying buildings, material goods, and legal conditions, just as 'aristocracy [is] founded on property', so 'one class presses on another; for all are aiming to procure respect on account of their property: and property, once gained, will procure the respect due only to talents and virtue'. Further, women are legally the property of men, and marriage is 'legal prostitution'.[36] Even the newly built asylums and hospitals, though providing charity, cannot deliver the justice of equality.[37]

Wrongs is a sustained critique of the male possession of women. With only a short 'interregnum between the reign of the father and husband' for women to decide who and what their freedoms and pleasures may be, Wollstonecraft identified the way women were kept docile and pliable.[38] With marriage for many women already a mental imprisonment, Maria's incarceration is a physical manifestation of her married state. She states: 'Marriage had bastilled me for life' (87). The allusion to the Bastille, destroyed by the revolutionaries in 1789, again references the French Revolution. Wollstonecraft hence made a powerful political statement about the private, domestic institution of marriage.

If marriage 'bastilled' women, the walls of home becoming fortress-like, they were further confined by biology. Unsurprisingly maternity, known as 'lying-in', was increasingly thought of through the term 'confinement'.[39] Earlier in the century diarist Hester Thrale had compared birth 'to being in prison' and 'confinement with hard labour'.[40] Convention stipulated remaining in the home for a month after birth, confined to the bed or bedroom, in the dark, and with little fresh air.[41] Maternity was also literally dangerous. Although delivery had better survival rates than many feared, the death rate from postpartum infection, or 'puerperal fever' was high. Concepts of air were equally influential here: in the seventeenth and eighteenth centuries, medical doctrine suggested that fever was transmitted by fresh air; in the nineteenth century, foetid air.[42] With women weakened by the exertions of labour a further danger was 'puerperal insanity'.[43]

When Maria's husband claims that she has puerperal insanity, she is locked in a 'mansion of despair' (7), in a dark room with only a 'small grated window' (9). In time she befriends the maid, Jemima, yet the gothic is ever present: 'horror still reigned in the darkened cells, suspicion lurked in the passages and whispered along the walls' (35). Jemima's own story relates even more appalling confinements: impoverished, she is bullied, raped, and enslaved in damp 'cellar-like apartments' (37), ending up as 'a common property', that is, a prostitute (43). Jemima and Maria's narratives expose and politicise, prevalent, though usually private, oppressions.

Wrongs, published unfinished after her death, is Wollstonecraft's most radical work. Where the *Vindications* experiment with metaphors of air, place, and architectural structure, and *Letters Written in Sweden* ... establish confidence through detailed descriptions of landscape, *Wrongs* uses narrative as a powerful, critical catalogue of the oppressions caused by women's status as male property. The novel foregrounds the way that women, whether defined by wifehood or servitude, are further entrapped by female biology. 'Madness' was often linked to childbirth, and accepted as particularly female.[44] One of Wollstonecraft's potential (and autobiographical) endings to *Wrongs* was Maria's suicide, her false incarceration driving her to the madness her husband has perjured. For Wollstonecraft, motherhood equated with both joy and loss. Her first labour had been easy, overseen by a local midwife in Le Havre. She was proudly up and about the next day, and against the fashion, breastfeeding her lusty baby. Yet within the year, Imlay had become estranged, leading her to depression and two suicide attempts.

In 1797, pregnant for a second time with Godwin's child, Mary prepared at home for the delivery. There is some evidence that she felt restricted by the pregnancy, which had led her to marry Godwin.[45] Her plans for the lying-in also revealed ambivalence.

On the one hand, she rejected the 'dark and airless' room: Godwin recalled she was 'frequently to ridicule the fashion of ladies in England, who kept to their chamber for one full month after delivery'.[46] Yet she chose the care of a traditional midwife over that of the newly fashionable man-midwife, stating: 'women might certainly study the art of healing, and be physicians as well as nurses. And midwifery, decency seems to allot to them, though I am afraid the word midwife, in our dictionaries, will soon give place to *accoucheur,* and one proof of the former delicacy of the sex be effaced from the language.'[47] The man-midwife, or *accoucheur* as he increasingly liked to be known, was steadily invading the space of the midwife.[48] Further, he was associated with the dreaded hospital:

> I cannot give you an adequate idea of the wretchedness of an hospital; everything is left to the care of people intent on gain. The attendants seem to have lost all feeling of compassion in the bustling discharge of their offices; death is so familiar to them . . . Everything appeared to be conducted for the accommodation of the medical men and their pupils, who came to make experiments on the poor, for the benefit of the rich.[49]

In the event Mary's labour was long and difficult but eventually she delivered. Following complications, a man-midwife was indeed summoned – from the General Lying-in Hospital – and performed a botched operation. Mary died eleven days later from puerperal fever. She did not leave the bed in which she gave birth, and, aside from several brief notes to Godwin on the morning of the labour, she was almost silent until her death. In contrast, the house was alive with movement and noise. With friends, relatives and various physicians visiting daily there were as many as eight extra people in the house at once.[50]

At this point, all the material references seem to come back together – crowded into this final domestic space of the Polygon. It was the height of summer. As the city around advanced into the pastoral fields, in the upstairs bedchamber infection made its steady creep through Mary's body. Perhaps dust from the nearby brick fields filtered through the open window as the noise of visitors seeped up the stairs. There is a hush as I enter the room, careful not to bang the door. I see a bed, its bloody linen unchanged. I smell the chamber pot, Mary's clothing, hair, and horribly, her decaying flesh. The space and her body have become wretched – dark and airless after all.

Post-card, post-script

Words were everything to Wollstonecraft. Some works she wrote quickly and passionately, others she laboured over. Effusive and candid, letters went daily to Imlay, her sisters, and friends. Her relationship with Godwin, their differences and good-humoured support of each other, is documented by a literary and often witty exchange. In contrast, his diary records her death wordlessly – three stark lines cross the page.

I claim to have written the postcards whilst walking around Somers Town seeking Mary Wollstonecraft. I also suggest that they were found objects, written by another voice. Between fact and fiction, walking and writing, the postcards change the

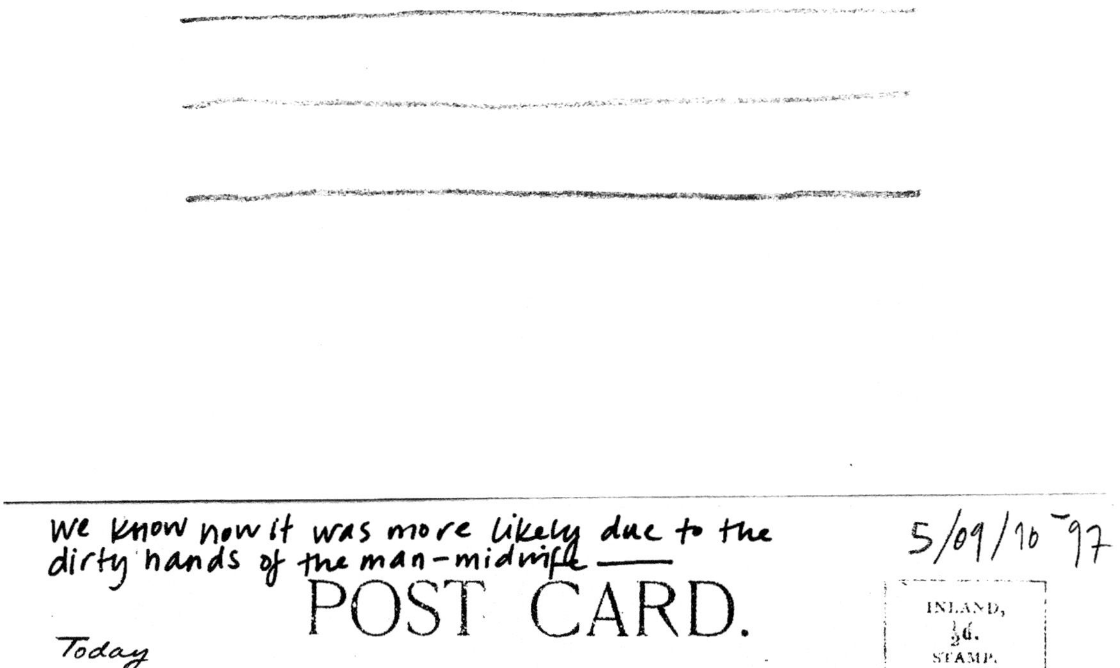

We know now it was more likely due to the dirty hands of the man-midwife ——

5/09/10 '97

POST CARD.

Today

THIS SPACE MAY BE USED
FOR COMMUNICATION.
(In British Isles only.)
(Post Office Regulation.)

THE ADDRESS ONLY TO BE
WRITTEN HERE.

INLAND,
½d.
STAMP.

FOREIGN,
1d.

It is autumn now, and I listen again to Michelle Obama's powerful speech lambasting Trump's attitudes to women. As first lady, she visited a school very near here. I wonder if she has read your work —

I, for one, see you on the streets of London and Paris. Look — there you go — striding down the path cut through Burke's field of

words. I feel for your hand on Fanny's cup. I lie on the rocks of Norway feeling the wrath of the mountainous landscape around, taste the dust in the air, cry at your pointless death. I am Fanny — when I commit suicide 19 years late, I will be found wearing your stays. M.W. Now, I reinhabit your struggle, ours, as we continue to be caught between the space and objects of public, intellectual life and the confining interiority, inferiority of domesticity and motherhood.
                                              Love.

Figure 5.4 Postcard 4. Postcard drawing and text by Emma Cheatle, 2016.

pace, temporality, place, and script of the essay. In the lines drawn between the narrow streets of eighteenth-century Paris, the little inns and craggy mountains of Norway and at a desk in a half-lit room in North London, they attempt to materialise Mary.

Notes

1   Jacques Derrida, *The Post Card: from Socrates to Freud and Beyond*, trans. Alan Bass (Chicago, IL: University of Chicago Press, 1987), 78.
2   Emma Cheatle, *Spaces of (Modern) Maternity: Architecture, Literature and Birth, 1660–1880* (forthcoming).
3   Edmund Burke, *Reflections on the Revolution in France: A Critical Edition* [1790], ed. J. C. D. Clark (Stanford, CA: Stanford University Press, 2003); Mary Wollstonecraft, *A Vindication of the Rights of Men* (London: Joseph Johnson, 1790); Mary Wollstonecraft, *A Vindication of the Rights of Woman* [1792] (London: Fisher Unwin, 1891).
4   Mary Wollstonecraft, *Letters Written in Sweden, Norway and Denmark* [1796] (Oxford: Oxford World Classics, 2009).
5   See Christine Delphy, 'For a Materialist Feminism' [1975], in eds. Rosemary Hennessy and Chrys Ingraham, *Materialist Feminism: A Reader in Class, Difference and Women's Lives* (London: Routledge, 1997), 62. See also Catriona Mortimer-Sandilands, 'Landscape, Memory and Forgetting: Thinking through (My Mother's) Body and Place' in *Material Feminisms*, eds. Stacy Alaimo and Sussan Hekman (Bloomington: Indiana University Press, 2008), 265–287.
6   William Godwin, *Godwin on Wollstonecraft* [1798], ed. Richard Holmes (London: Harper, 2005).
7   Godwin, *Godwin on Wollstonecraft*, 53.
8   Janet Todd, *Mary Wollstonecraft: A Revolutionary Life*. (London: Weidenfeld and Nicolson, 2000), 356; 450–457; Claire Tomalin, *The Life and Death of Mary Wollstonecraft* (London: Penguin, 1992), 235–236.
9   For my method see Emma Cheatle, *Part-Architecture: The Maison de Verre, Duchamp, Domesticity and Desire in 1930s Paris* (London: Routledge, 2017). Also, Hélène Frichot, 'Following Hélène Cixous' Steps Towards a Writing Architecture', in *Architectural Theory Review*, 15/3 (2010), 312–323; Jane Rendell, 'Site-Writing: She is Walking About in a Town Which She Does Not Know', *Home Cultures* 4/2, eds. Lesley McFadden and Matthew Barrac (July 2007), 177–199.
10 Derrida, *The Post Card*, xiii; 78.
11 Delphy, 'For a Materialist Feminism', 60. For my interdisciplinary method see also Emma Cheatle, 'Part-Architecture: The Manifest and the Hidden in the Maison de Verre and the Large Glass (or Towards an Architectural Unconscious)' in *Architecture and the Unconscious*, eds. John Hendrix and Lorens Holm (Farnham: Ashgate, 2016), 253–272.
12 Statement made in a Parliamentary debate, 9 February 1790. See Edmund Burke. *Reflections on the Revolution in France: A Critical Edition*, ed. J. C. D. Clark. (Stanford, CA: Stanford University Press, 2002), 66–67.
13 Wollstonecraft, *Rights of Men*, 145.
14 Ibid., 145, my italics.
15 Ibid., iii.
16 Steven Connor, *The Matter of Air: Science and the Art of the Ethereal* (London: Reaktion, 2010), 65–66.
17 Burke, *Reflections on the Revolution*, 7.
18 Many women writers, from Aphra Behn to George Eliot, published anonymously or under male pseudonyms from the seventeenth to nineteenth centuries. This was not always due to prejudice – men also published anonymously – although for women that was probably the key reason. See John Mullan, *Anonymity: A Secret History of English Literature* (London: Faber and Faber, 2007).
19 Wollstonecraft, *Rights of Woman*, page numbers hereon in brackets.
20 Godwin, *Godwin on Wollstonecraft*, 40; Tomalin, *Life and Death of Mary Wollstonecraft*, 136.
21 Connor, *Matter of Air*, 60–65.
22 Wollstonecraft, *Rights of Woman*, 72–73.
23 Mary Wollstonecraft, *An Historical and Moral View of the Origin and Progress of the French Revolution* (London: Joseph Johnson, 1794).
24 Godwin, *Godwin on Wollstonecraft*, 60–61. The original letters plead, at times angrily and plaintively, with Imlay. In the publication Mary Wollstonecraft, *Letters Written in Sweden, Norway and Denmark* [1796] (Oxford: Oxford World Classics, 2009), Wollstonecraft crafts these into a moving, mesmerising text.
25 Wollstonecraft, *Rights of Men*, 105–108.
26 Wollstonecraft, *Letters Written in Sweden*, 29. Pages hereon in brackets.
27 Ibid., 13, 57, 100.

28   Todd, *Mary Wollstonecraft*, 155; Tomalin, *Life and Death of Mary Wollstonecraft*, 150; Richard Holmes, *Footsteps: Adventures of a Romantic Biographer* (London: Harper, 1996), 92.

29   Wollstonecraft, *Rights of Woman*, x.

30   Ibid., xii.

31   Todd, *Mary Wollstonecraft*, 155.

32   Mary Wollstonecraft, *Lessons* [1795], in *Posthumous Works of Mary Wollstonecraft*, ed. William Godwin (London: Joseph Johnson, 1798), 176.

33   Ibid., 178.

34   Ibid., 196. It seems probable *Lessons* was rewritten in 1797 when Wollstonecraft was pregnant. Before the birth (of baby Mary) she and Godwin had referred to the foetus as 'William'.

35   Mary Wollstonecraft, *Maria, or, The Wrongs of Woman* [1797], in *Posthumous Works of Mary Wollstonecraft*, ed. William Godwin (London: Joseph Johnson, 1798).

36   Wollstonecraft, *Rights of Woman*, 116, 213, 212, 222.

37   Ibid., 219.

38   Wollstonecraft, *Letters Written in Sweden*, 106, 108.

39   See Adrian Wilson, *The Making of Man-Midwifery: Childbirth in England, 1660–1770* (Cambridge, MA.: Harvard University Press, 1995); Irvine Loudon, *Death in Childbirth. An International Study of Maternal Care and Maternal Mortality 1800–1950* (Oxford: Clarendon Press, 1992). The exact date is uncertain but 'confinement' became a common term across the nineteenth century.

40   Roy Porter and Dorothy Porter, *In Sickness and in Health: The British Experience, 1650–1850* (Oxford: Blackwell, 1989) , 86; see also Deborah D. Rogers, *The Matrophobic Gothic and Its Legacy: Sacrificing Mothers in the Novel and in Popular Culture* (New York: Peter Lang, 2007).

41   Wilson, *Making of Man-Midwifery*; *Midwives, Society and Childbirth: Debates and Controversies in the Modern Period*, eds. Hilary Marland and Anne Marie Rafferty (London: Routledge, 1997). See also my forthcoming book: Cheatle, *Spaces of (Modern) Maternity*.

42   Loudon, *Death in Childbirth*, 160, 13–17.

43   Irvine Loudon, 'Puerperal Insanity in the 19th Century', *Journal of the Royal Society of Medicine* 81 (February 1988), 76–9; Hilary Marland, *Dangerous Motherhood: Insanity and Childbirth in Victorian Britain* (Basingstoke: Palgrave, 2004), 57.

44   Jonathan Andrews and Andrew Scull, *Customers and Patrons of the Mad-Trade: The Management of Lunacy in Eighteenth-Century London* (Berkeley: University of California Press, 2003), 71.

45   Virginia Sapiro, 'Wollstonecraft, Feminism and Democracy: "Being Bastilled" ' in *Feminist Interpretations of Mary Wollstonecraft* ed. Maria J. Falco (University Park, PA: Pennsylvania State University Press, 2010), 43.

46   Godwin, *Godwin on Wollstonecraft*, 80.

47   Wollstonecraft, *Rights of Woman*, 26.

48   Wilson, *Making of Man-Midwifery*, 175.

49   Wollstonecraft, *Wrongs*, 51.

50   I evaluated this using Mary Wollstonecraft, *The Collected Letters of Mary Wollstonecraft*, ed. Janet Todd (London: Allen Lane, 2003), 436 n.936; William Godwin, *Letters, Vol. 1: 1778–1797*, ed. Pamela Clemit (Oxford: Oxford University Press, 2011), 230, 237 n.3, 245 n.3, 5.

Control

Chapter 6

Remodelling the Führer

Hitler's domestic spaces as propaganda

Despina Stratigakos

In 2003, *Guardian* journalist Simon Waldman came across a November 1938 edition of the British magazine *Homes and Gardens*, which included an illustrated feature on Adolf Hitler's mountain home, described as 'a handsome Bavarian chalet, 2000 feet up on the Obersalzberg amid pinewoods and cherry orchards . . . barely ten miles from Mozart's own medieval Salzburg'. The article's author, writing under the pseudonym Ignatius Phayre, had previously boasted in the journal *Current History* of being a personal friend of the Führer.[1] In *Homes and Gardens*, Phayre credited Hitler as the architect of the building and the life that took place therein, including visits from brilliant foreigner artists, droll conversations, and superb meals. With an eye to his audience's interests, Phayre described the home's furnishings, art (including Hitler's watercolours), and gardens, as well as the Führer's 'passion for cut flowers in his home'.[2] The reader was left with the impression of Hitler as a man of taste and warm hospitality – a country squire, as Phayre called him, who pampered his guests, delighted in the company of children, and spoiled his pet dogs. One could almost forget that this issue of *Homes and Gardens* appeared amid growing international fears about the aggression of Hitler's regime and just days before the events of *Kristallnacht.*[3]

Fascinated by this forgotten episode in publishing history, Waldman posted the article on his personal website and, curious to learn more about it, contacted the editor of *Homes and Gardens*, Isobel McKenzie-Price, who replied with a warning letter that Waldman had violated the magazine's copyright and must remove the scanned article. Waldman then posted McKenzie-Price's reply, and although he complied by removing the scans, they already had been widely disseminated. *Homes and Gardens'* perceived

HITLER'S
MOUNTAIN
HOME

A Visit to "Haus Wachenfeld,"
in the Bavarian Alps, written and
illustrated by Ignatius Phayre

A closer view of the house, showing the
umbrella-shaded terrace.

I T is over twelve years since Herr Hitler fixed on the site of his one and only home. It *had* to be close to the Austrian border, barely ten miles from Mozart's own mediæval Salzburg. At first no more than a hunter's shack, "Haus Wachenfeld" has grown, until it is to-day quite a handsome Bavarian chalet, 2,000 feet up on the Ober-salzburg amid pinewoods and cherry orchards. Here, in the early days, Hitler's widowed sister, Frau Angela Raubal, kept house for him on a "peasant" scale. Then, as his famous book, *Mein Kampf* ("My Struggle") became a best-seller of astonishing power (4,500,000 copies of it have been sold), Hitler began to think of replacing that humble shack by a house and garden of suitable scope. In this matter he has throughout been his own architect.

There is nothing pretentious about the Führer's little estate. It is one that any merchant of Munich or Nuremburg might possess in these lovely hills.

The entrance hall is filled with a curious display of cactus plants in majolica pots. Herr Hitler's study is fitted as a modern office, and leading out of this is a telephone exchange. From here it is possible for the Führer to invite his friends or Ministers to fly over to Berchtesgaden, landing on his own aerodrome just below the chalet lawns.

This view shows the chalet's lovely setting. In the foreground are Hitler (back to camera) with Field-Marshals Göring (left) and von Blomberg (centre).

193

Figure 6.1 Title page of Ignatius Phayre's November 1938 article in *Homes and Gardens*.

censorship quickly became an international controversy. Critics questioned the validity of the magazine's copyright claim and accused it of attempting to bury its past complicity in the whitewashing of a violent and hateful regime. The David S. Wyman Institute for Holocaust Studies, based in Washington, D.C., sent a petition to the publisher signed by seventy Holocaust scholars and educators demanding that the publisher, the conglomerate IPC Media, face up to its past and make the article publicly available. In a statement of apology negotiated with the Wyman Institute, IPC Media confessed to being 'appalled' that *Homes and Gardens* had been 'taken in by the Nazi propaganda of the 1930s'. They also admitted the lack of a clear copyright to the material and withdrew previous objections to the reproduction of the article. But they also pointed an accusatory finger at other newspapers and magazines of this era, which they claimed had been similarly duped by the Nazi regime.[4]

If the controversy stirred by Waldman's actions focused on journalism's accountability for past offenses, the deflective response of IPC Media pointed to a broader history in need of exploration. What was the nature of the Nazi propaganda that had 'taken in' *Homes and Gardens*? Ideologically speaking, where did the personal and political intersect in Hitler's garden? The first major post-war biography of Hitler, published by Alan Bullock in 1952, dismissed the meaningfulness of the Führer's private life as 'meager and uninteresting at the best of times'.[5] A wholly different attitude characterized the tell-all books that emerged in subsequent decades, which scoured Hitler's body, family past, and relationships to men and women for anomalies on a personal scale that could somehow explain a cosmic catastrophe.

Nazi mythologies about Hitler's origins emphasized his poverty and homelessness as a young man as well as his disdain for creature comforts. Nonetheless, once Hitler became chancellor, and particularly after royalties from *Mein Kampf* made him a wealthy man, he focused considerable energies on the redesign and furnishing of his residences. Hitler occupied three homes during the Third Reich: the Old Reich Chancellery on Wilhelmstrasse in Berlin; a luxury apartment at Prinzregentenplatz 16 in Munich; and the Berghof, his mountain retreat on the Obersalzberg, on the border with Austria. All three residences were fully remodelled in the mid-1930s under the direction of Gerdy Troost, a Munich-based designer and wife of architect Paul Ludwig Troost, to whom Hitler had entrusted his first monumental building projects. When the architect died unexpectedly in 1934, his young widow assumed responsibility for completing his National Socialist commissions, which set the standard for the regime's new architecture. Together with the architect Leonhard Gall, her husband's former employee, she established and ran the Atelier Troost.[6]

Hitler's domestic turn began in the late 1920s, when the Nazi Party needed to broaden its appeal, particularly to the middle classes, by appearing to be more mainstream in both its message and leadership. The death of his niece Geli Raubal on September 18, 1931 also forced Hitler to confront his domestic image. The sensationalistic press stories that erupted with her suicide – including speculation as to what, exactly, the relationship had been between uncle and niece – put Hitler and his image makers on alert. In 1932, in the midst of a presidential election battle, Nazi publicists brought Hitler's private life into the limelight in order to emphasize his moral and human character and thereby win over bourgeois voters and women. The success of this public relations campaign in reassuring Germans that Hitler was, at heart, a 'good man' ensured its continuity even after he came to power.

Indeed, by the mid-1930s, it was all but impossible to avoid images and stories about the domestic Hitler. Not only the German media covered the topic with great – indeed, almost obsessive – zeal, but it was also avidly carried by an English-language press serving a global audience, from London to Sydney, Toronto to Phoenix, and Bombay to Shanghai. In Germany, a market quickly emerged for popular consumer goods bearing images of the Führer's home or its owner at leisure on the Obersalzberg. One could decorate with a Hitler-house-themed porcelain plate or embroidered throw pillow, save pennies in a replica coin bank, play with a toy model, send a postcard showing Hitler feeding deer on his terrace, or buy one of the many photography albums that documented his life at home, from the dictator entertaining children to hiking with his dog. For a time, Hitler's mountain retreat was arguably the most famous house in the world.

This vast production of images of Hitler at home proved to be enormously seductive and continues to exert its power even today. Its appeal has largely gone unchecked by historians, who have insufficiently exposed and deconstructed the propaganda surrounding Hitler's domesticity. Apart from a small body of articles, books, and catalogues, literature about Hitler's homes tends to be uncritical and, in some cases, reproduces the ideological 'charm' of Third Reich publications. Remarkably, given how much has been written about Hitler, the significance of his domestic spaces in the visual imagination of National Socialism has remained underexplored terrain.[7]

Compared to their high visibility during the Third Reich, Hitler's domestic spaces rarely appear in political or architectural histories of the period. Those who have written about the many diplomatic meetings that occurred in these homes have had little to say about the settings, despite Hitler's desire to use them as stage sets to perform his identity as a statesman and man of culture. Studies of the Obersalzberg as an ideological and political center of National Socialism have been more attentive to its structures, but architectural historians themselves have contributed little to this literature. In general, scholars of architecture and fascist aesthetics have focused on monumental building projects and mass spectacle, overlooking the domestic and minute. And yet one could argue that the aesthetics of the mass spectacle at the Nuremberg Rally Grounds or of the Gigantic in the New Chancellery, both designed by Albert Speer and associated with the public Führer, correlate with the singular and detailed assemblage of Hitler's private domestic spaces, a choreography of objects and space that enacts the private man. The Hitler who commanded thousands and moved mountains of stone induced awe; the Hitler at home with his dogs and tea inspired empathy. Both images were integral to the Führer's seductive power and each had its architectural manifestation. Reading the official and monumental together with the domestic and minute allows us to grasp their intended and productive interplay in the representation of the Führer as both beyond and yet of the people.

Hitler himself cared deeply about the production of his domestic spaces, discussing them at length with Troost. After the war, she recalled the enthusiastic interest he had showed in even the smallest detail. The transformation of Hitler's mountain home in 1935–36 from a simple chalet (known as Haus Wachenfeld) into a residence (renamed the Berghof) befitting an emperor particularly captured his imagination. Bavarian architect Alois Degano undertook the structural expansion according to Hitler's proposals; the Atelier Troost, also working closely with the client, completed the interiors. In his memoirs, Speer, who had not been invited to help, admitted that Hitler had devoted a level of personal attention to the design of the Berghof that was unequalled by any of his other building projects.[8] It was Hitler's favourite place to be – about a third of his time in office was spent on the Obersalzberg. On July 14, 1944, Joseph Goebbels confided to his diary that he was relieved that the Führer had decided to transfer his military headquarters from his mountain home to the Wolf's Lair on the eastern front.[9] While Hitler had spent months planning battle strategies from his living room, the Allied armies had pushed ever closer to Germany's borders.

Perhaps if Speer had been involved, historians might have paid more attention to Hitler's domestic spaces. Women architects and designers have only recently begun to receive their due in architectural history books, and little is known about their involvement in the Third Reich. Troost has likewise slipped beneath the historian's radar, despite the fact that she was once the tastemaker of choice for Hitler and other prominent National Socialists. The impact of her work moreover, indicates that we need to consider more fully the role of interior design in the self-representation of the Nazi regime, to which many of its architects, including Speer, eagerly contributed.

Ultimately, the reasons for the neglect of the dictator's homes and their creators may have more to do with scholars having all too readily accepted the propaganda of the Third Reich; namely, that Hitler's domestic spaces existed outside the world of politics and ideology. I believe, to the contrary, that they were profoundly ideological spaces, which demonstrably lay at the heart of some of the most successful propaganda about Hitler produced by his regime. Representations of Hitler's home life played a critical role in the early 1930s, when his public image as a screaming reactionary needed to be softened. The attention and care lavished on Hitler's domesticity by his propagandists also transformed a potential liability – the perceived oddity of a stateless man living without deep connections to family, place, or lovers – into an asset by creating a domestic milieu that grounded and normalized him. Hitler's domestic spaces struck just the right balance with the public of heterosexual masculinity, refined but not ostentatious taste, and German roots. Thus, his publicists and designers killed two birds with one stone, making Hitler seem both warmer and less queer. And all of this was carefully crafted and communicated to German and foreign audiences through a media eager to sell the story and images of the domestic bachelor.

With views of Germany on one side of the mountain and Austria on the other, the Berghof was the most public of Hitler's private homes, and it exerted a powerful hold on the Nazi imagination of empire. Hitler and his publicists drew on mountain imagery from Germany's literary and artistic movements (particularly Romanticism) to mythologize the Führer as a mystic leader who immersed himself in – and embodied – the terrible and magnificent forces of nature.[10] At the same time, the mountain served as a means to humanize Germany's leader through his contact with animals as well as with children. In officially produced postcards, magazines and books, Germans consumed fantasies about an ideal domestic life rooted in the natural landscape. In the expansive *Lebensraum* and pure mountain air, where the sun shone and blond children frolicked, the Nazis encouraged Germans to envision a blissful future in exchange for sacrifices to their pocketbooks and freedoms.[11]

The rise of celebrity culture in the 1920s and 1930s created a voracious appetite for information about the daily lives of the rich and famous. The advent of new technologies in broadcasting, recording, and film brought entertainers and politicians into the everyday lives of people. Celebrities were both larger-than-life and a part of the family, creating a seemingly unquenchable market for information on the lives of these intimate strangers.[12] In the mid-1930s, Hitler may have been a dictator who, in the words of British Prime Minister Stanley Baldwin, cast a 'black shadow of fear' over Europe, but he was also a celebrity.

Curiosity about celebrities' homes dominated the public's desire to see beyond the mask of fame to the 'real' person within. Since the nineteenth century, American and European middle-class cultures had come to focus on the domestic milieu as the site of the authentic self. Hollywood fan magazines and newspaper gossip columns gushed about what the famous did at home – 'what they ate, what their beauty secrets were, what pets they pampered, what cars they drove, what they wore'.[13] Articles on movie stars' houses typically blended details about the architecture and interior decoration with details about the occupant's personality, thrilling readers who believed they were getting to know the actor on more intimate terms.[14] Beyond fan magazines and gossip columns, the mainstream media also embraced the popularity of celebrity homes. In the 1930s, for example, *Architectural Digest* began to run a regular feature on the homes of Hollywood movie stars and directors.

The publication of photographs of celebrities' homes responded to and stimulated the desire to visualize their private lives. In Germany, such images had become an integral part of the political effort to broaden Hitler's appeal as early as 1932, when he ran for president.[15] By 1935, the English-language press had also begun to offer 'candid' and sympathetic images of Hitler's home life to their audiences. In March 1935, *Newsweek* claimed to have 'secured first publication rights in America for these exclusive candid camera shots of Adolf Hitler. They constitute the only informal record of the Reich Leader in private life'. In the two-page feature, Hitler was shown at Haus Wachenfeld, hiking in the snow, playing with his dog, reading in the solarium, and sharing 'a bowl of stew with neighbors', among other 'candid' shots.[16] Most of the images, created by Heinrich Hoffmann, Hitler's court photographer, also appeared in *Hitler in seinen Bergen* (Hitler in his mountains), the photographic album for German audiences published that same year. By 1936, a broad spectrum of English-language publications had familiarized their readers with Hitler's home life through such ostensibly informal, behind-the-scenes images.

The growing interest in visualizing the domestic spaces of the rich and famous also had a physical dimension. Specifically, the 1920s and 30s witnessed a dramatic rise in the popularity of house museums, where one could experience first-hand the homes of history's 'great men'.[17] In a 1932 essay, Virginia Woolf noted that 'London, happily, is becoming full of great men's houses, bought for the nation and preserved entire with the chairs they sat on and the cups they drank from, their umbrellas and their chests of drawers'. The owners of these houses, she continued, may have had little artistic taste when it came to decorating, 'but they seem always to possess a much rarer and more interesting gift – a faculty for housing themselves appropriately, for making the table, the chair, the curtain, the carpet into their own image'. Here, amid their possessions, Woolf contended, one could get to know the great men of history far better than from any biography.[18]

In August 1936, *Vogue* magazine took its readers, attuned to the worlds of fashion and style, on a virtual tour of the houses of three 'makers of foreign policies': Hitler, Benito Mussolini, and British Foreign Secretary Anthony Eden. 'All of these rooms are obviously characteristic of man and country – Anthony Eden's London house, British and reticent, impersonal as British diplomacy; Hitler's chalet, German, jumbled, and *gemütlich*; and Mussolini's villa, decoratively violent, magnificently proportioned, the home for a nation's impressive pride'.[19] Going beyond Woolf's belief that individuals mirrored themselves in their home environment, *Vogue* suggested that one could also read the psychology of nations in the domestic décor of its 'great men'.

The article illustrated the interiors of the three men's houses with photographs and simple captions tying the occupant to a function appropriate to the room: 'Where Hitler dines', 'Where Mussolini plays his violin', 'Where Eden sleeps', and so forth. Hitler's domestic space was represented by the dining nook in the ground-floor *Stube,* or living room, at Haus Wachenfeld, pictured as it existed before the 1935–36 renovation. 'On the side of a mountain, the chalet has a suburban neatness, with a sun porch and canaries, and its rooms, like this one, a cozy podge of clocks, dwarfs, and swastika cushions'. True to the description, the accompanying photograph reveals dwarf figures lurking in the corner, a grandfather clock, and a prominently placed swastika cushion. One wonders what Jewish readers might have thought of *Vogue*'s insistence that this interior, with its swastika-accented décor, 'is obviously characteristic of man and country', thus rendering as alien and 'uncharacteristic' Germans who stood outside this racially coded definition of home.[20]

Compared to Phayre's *Homes and Gardens* article, which romanticized Hitler as a country squire, *Vogue*'s treatment of politicians' domestic spaces seems relatively innocuous. But even here, the magazine trod a dangerous line. In August 1936, when *Vogue* published the article, the Olympic Games took place in Berlin despite the threat of an international boycott. The Nazi regime, sensitive to its international image and eager to secure the foreign currency of tourists, countered allegations of racial discrimination by allowing one Jewish athlete to participate on the German team and by temporarily removing anti-Semitic materials from the capital's streets and public spaces.[21] *Vogue*'s article, with its comparative approach, aided in this normalizing effort by placing two fascist dictators and an elected member of Parliament on the same footing, blurring the political differences among them and transferring the reader's attention instead to issues of interior design.

This deflection of critical focus continued to characterize press stories about the domestic Hitler into the late 1930s. On August 20, 1939, the *New York Times Magazine* published 'Herr Hitler at Home in the Clouds', an illustrated article by Hedwig Mauer Simpson, a British journalist living in Munich. She began with a brief history of

Hitler's mountain house, acknowledging that its transformation from Haus Wachenfeld to the Berghof reflected the Führer's 'consolidated' powers and an accommodation of governmental and diplomatic functions, making the residence 'less private' in nature. 'Yet this does not mean that Hitler has given up the privilege of retiring when he likes', Simpson contended.[22] And as if following the Führer's lead, Simpson then shifted her attention away from the outside world to the spaces and routine of 'ordinary life' at the Berghof.

The author admired the interiors of the house, which had been 'furnished harmoniously, according to the best of German traditions' and boasted 'beautiful common rooms', including 'a sitting room facing west and overlooking the deep bowl amid Alpine heights in which the quaint old market town of Berchtesgaden is situated'. In this setting, the Führer's daily routine played itself out: a late breakfast, walks in the mountain, and vegetarian meals. Although this narrative was by now well known to readers, Simpson's account provided tantalizing details, such as the quality of the tomatoes on Hitler's table or his love of gooseberry pie. Similarly, she offered a glimpse into some of his official work duties – attending to private petitions from the 'widows and orphans of party martyrs'. Such business took 'about two or three hours' in the morning, after which Hitler received callers. Then host and guests gathered for a 'leisurely' lunch, and after taking a nap, Hitler might invite guests to go for a walk to his nearby teahouse. In the afternoon, the gates of the house might be opened up to the pilgrims who came to see their leader. Simpson described a typical scene at these encounters between Führer and *Volk*: 'a particularly pretty child with a mop of fair curls attracts his attention, and then Heinrich Hoffmann takes those photographs of the Fuehrer bending over a little child which touch Nazi hearts'.[23] (In fact, the 'walk by' had been discontinued years before.)

An elegant dinner, with the ladies in evening dress and Hitler in a 'dark lounge suit', was followed by coffee 'in front of a blazing log fire'. Hitler's guests came 'from all kinds of German circles, as well as from foreign countries'. As coffee was passed around, Hitler used this time to collect impressions. 'Hitler can be a good listener and seems to gather a good deal by letting American solo dancers or German film stars talk to him. Non-political-minded persons will often tell him inadvertently, or by implication, things which his trained staff usually keep from him'. And on this image of Hitler by the fireside, conversing with dancers and movie stars, Simpson concluded her article.[24]

This idyll about life at the Berghof was far removed, to put it mildly, from the world captured on the front page of *The New York Times* on August 20, 1939, the day that Simpson's article appeared in the Sunday magazine. A third of the stories described the growing unrest in Europe. 100,000 German troops had massed on the Polish border as the Slovak army, which had pledged its cooperation to Hitler, began its own mobilization. 'Squads of police' had been sent to Bratislava's Jewish ghetto to protect the inhabitants from repeated beatings and vandalism by the German minority. A front-page editorial in the Bratislava German-language newspaper *Grenzbote* called for 'the Jews [to] be quickly and thoroughly punished this time for their evil provocations'. Pope Pius, speaking to pilgrims, made a 'fervent plea for peace' and expressed hope that Europe's statesmen would succeed in avoiding war. Lord Halifax, then the British Foreign Secretary, cut short his vacation and returned to work at the Foreign Office in London, increasing apprehension among the British people. Switzerland began to strengthen the garrisons along her German and Italian borders.[25]

It is difficult to imagine what readers thought as they paged through the newspaper and arrived at Simpson's article in the magazine. Nothing in her happy and harmonious fable reflected the realities of the front page. The article was accompanied by recycled photographs of the Berghof and Hitler hiking as well as by an editorial cartoon drawn by the London-based artist David Low. The latter depicted Hitler, looking pensive, seated at a table at the Berghof between the lovely female figure of Peace and an ominous, shroud-covered figure of war. While the cartoon, probably added by an editor, made sense in relation to the front page, it bore no relationship to Simpson's story.

Without knowing more about Simpson's identity we can only guess at her intentions in writing a highly misleading account of Hitler and 'ordinary life' on the Obersalzberg. But it is not only the writer's intentions that raise questions. One also has to wonder about *The New York Times'* decision to publish at this highly fraught moment what amounted to an ode to life at the Berghof. Portraying Hitler as a lover of orphans and gooseberry pie made it perhaps just a little easier to hope that the stories on the front page were exaggerated. Twelve days later, when German forces invaded Poland, *The New York Times* readers, along with the rest of the world, discovered that they were not.

If consumers of English-language media stories about the off-duty Führer were soon disabused of any notion of the dictator as a champion (rather than creator) of widows and orphans, the question nonetheless remains as to whether audiences must also be held accountable in the creation of that myth. The abundance of prewar features on the domestic Hitler published outside Germany reflects not only the foreign media's willingness to disseminate flattering stories about the dictator, but also the existence of an eager audience. That Ignatius Phayre, who essentially published Nazi propaganda, was able to sell his work to so many outlets testifies to the strength and breadth of this market. While the role of the foreign press in laundering Hitler's image thus must be examined, it is important not to overlook the magazine and newspaper readers around the world who wanted to believe the sanitized version. Indeed, the tens of thousands of readers who visited Simon Waldman's Hitler pages and their subsequent reposting on websites around the globe reveal that there is still tremendous interest in such accounts, and not all of it is critical. Since being rediscovered, the *Homes and Gardens* article routinely is cited on websites as a reliable, first-hand account of Hitler's mountain retreat. Some eighty years later, the distorting mirror of Hitler at home continues to deceive.

Notes

1 Ignatius Phayre, 'Holiday with Hitler', *Current History* (July 1936): 50.
2 Ignatius Phayre, 'Hitler's Mountain Home', *Homes and Garden* (November 1938): 193–94.
3 For an in-depth discussion of Ignatius Phayre (William George Fitz-Gerald), see Despina Stratigakos, *Hitler at Home* (New Haven, Yale University Press, 2015), 194ff.
4 Ibid., 316–17.
5 Alan Bullock, *Hitler: A Study in Tyranny* (London: Odhams, 1952), 7. On the history of Hitler biographies, see Ron Rosenbaum, *Explaining Hitler* (New York: Random House, 1998), and John Lukacs, *The Hitler of History* (New York: Knopf, 1997).
6 Stratigakos, *Hitler at Home*, 107–46.

7   Notable exceptions include *Die tödliche Utopie: Bilder, Texte, Dokumente, Daten zum Dritten Reich*, eds. Volker Dahm, Albert A. Feiber, Harmut Mehring, and Horst Möller, 5th ed. (Munich: Institut für Zeitgeschichte, 2008), 52–187; Rudolf Herz, *Hoffmann & Hitler: Fotografie als Medium des Führer-Mythos* (Munich: Fotomuseum im Münchner Stadtmuseum, 1994), 242–259; and Sonja Günther, *Design der Macht: Möbel für Repräsentanten des 'Dritten Reiches'* (Stuttgart: Deutsche, 1992).

8   Albert Speer, *Inside the Third Reich*, trans. Richard and Clara Winston (New York: Touchstone, 1997), 85.

9   Joseph Goebbels, *Die Tagebücher von Joseph Goebbels*, Part II, 13, ed. Elke Fröhlich (Saur: Munich, 1995), 116.

10 Stratigakos, *Hitler at Home*, 181.

11 Ibid., 160.

12 Amy Henderson, 'Media and the Rise of Celebrity Culture', *OAH Magazine of History* 6, no. 4 (1992): 52.

13 Amy Henderson, 'From Barnum to 'Bling Bling:' The Changing Face of Celebrity Culture'. *Hedgehog Review* 7, no. 1 (2005): 44.

14 Brett L. Abrams, *Hollywood Bohemians: Transgressive Sexuality and the Selling of the Movieland Dream* (Jefferson, NC: McFarland, 2008), 119–20.

15 Stratigakos, *Hitler at Home*, 149–60.

16 *Newsweek*, 'Hitler at Bavarian Retreat', March 2, 1935, 12–13.

17 Laurence Vail Coleman, *Historic House Museums* (Washington, D.C.: American Association of Museums, 1933), 18.

18 Virginia Woolf, 'Great Men's Houses' [1932], reprinted in Virginia Woolf, *The London Scene: Five Essays* (New York: Hallman, 1975), 23.

19 *Vogue* (U.S.), 'Mussolini, Hitler, and Eden – in Retreat', August 15, 1936, 70.

20 Ibid., 70–71.

21 David Clay Large, *Nazi Games: The Olympics of 1936* (New York: Norton, 2007).

22 Hedwig Mauer Simpson, 'Herr Hitler at Home in the Clouds', *New York Times Magazine*, August 20, 1939, 5.

23 Ibid., 5, 22.

24 Ibid., 22.

25 'War Moves Go On', *The New York Times*, August 20, 1939; 'Pontiff Still Sees a Chance for Peace', *New York Times*, August 20, 1939; 'Coup Fear Takes Halifax to London', *The New York Times*, August 20, 1939; 'The Developments in Europe', *The New York Times*, August 20, 1939.

Chapter 7

Architectural preservation as taxidermy

Patriarchy and boredom

Christian Parreno

In contemporary culture, with deliberate pejorative connotations, architectural preservation is often referred to as 'the taxidermy of architecture'.[1] For instance, in April 2014 *The New York Times* wrote that although there is no harm in dismantling, storing and potentially reassembling somewhere else the façade of the American Folk Art Museum – as part of the extension plans of the Museum of Modern Art, on West 53rd Street – the act should not be mistaken as a 'gesture for actual preservation' since 'it's more like taxidermy'.[2] To the contributor of the newspaper, after the valued structure had been pulled apart, the institutional executioner pretended to safeguard the victim by keeping the outer membrane, extending the offence rather than respecting its integrity. Similarly, in April 2007 the *Chicago Tribune* assessed the redevelopment of the Farwell Building as an exemplary case of 'architectural taxidermy', explaining that its exterior was removed, cleaned and restored before being grafted onto a new structure, as though it were 'a stuffed animal'.[3] For the reporter, this kind of machination can be pleasing – preferable to the erection of massive garages or bland condominiums – but also irritating as it flattens the life of buildings, desperately holding onto the past by creating wallpapers that parody the three-dimensionality of architecture. In both accounts, following the dictionary definition, 'the art of preparing and preserving the skins of animals, and of . . . mounting them so as to present the appearance, attitude, etc., of the living animal'[4] is transposed to architecture in its most literal form. With a disapproving tone, the media describes preservation as the simple maintenance of façades with the intention to recuperate their primary condition, regardless of their historical context.[5]

The irony of preservation as taxidermy derives from its anachronism as well as from the impossibility of reviving a lost moment in the life of an object. In the first case, the current efforts of architectural preservation are likened to the investigative and re-presentational aims of a practice considered equally objective and artistic, particularly in the nineteenth and early twentieth centuries. In the second, the assumption that architectural structures pass their prime, can become extinct but are capable of recuperating their lost temporality, questions the selection criteria that determine why some parts of the built environment are enlivened and not others. Furthermore, the preoccupation with the façade as the skin of architecture reveals the essence of preservation as public and civic, as a rhetorical device in favour of memory and heritage based on stylistic realism. This ambiguous façadism – or façadomy – implies that interventions that prolong the existence of buildings not only require the acknowledgement of those who encounter them but also incorporate the political ideals and cultural preferences of the system that enabled their emergence. However, the insistence of preservation on the past problematises the construction of the future, propounding an analytical and critical threshold that facilitates the reconsideration of the present.

Teddy bear patriarchy

In 'Teddy Bear Patriarchy: Taxidermy in the Garden of Eden, New York City, 1908–1936' (1984), Donna Haraway delineates preservation as a non-neutral endeavour, underpinned by gender, race and class ideologies. The philosopher reconstructs the history behind the animals of the African Hall in the American Museum of Natural History, behind the memorial to Theodore Roosevelt, across from the heart of Central Park – an urban garden planned to counterbalance the intense modernity of Manhattan, on land formerly occupied by free blacks and Irish immigrants. According to the Museum, the exhibition, which opened in 1936 with the aim to 'provide a unique glimpse of the diverse topography of Africa and its wildlife', features a central composition of 'a freestanding group of eight elephants, poised as if to charge, surrounded by 28 habitat dioramas . . . set in a specific location, cast in the light of a particular time of day'.[6] The design of the scenes is credited to 'scientists in the field in the early 20th century and the on-site sketches and photographs of the artists who accompanied them', identifying Carl Akeley as 'the naturalist, explorer, photographer, sculptor, and taxidermist'.[7] In addition, the record states that he not only conceived the design for the hall in 1909 and collected many of the specimens for it, but also successfully petitioned the King of Belgium to create the first national park in Africa.[8] Undoing this unified and justified narrative to disclose its underlying violence and reclaim the polyphonic agency of countless workers and collaborators, 'Teddy Bear Patriarchy' denounces the official version as a construction of 'the commerce of power and knowledge in white and male supremacist monopoly capitalism',[9] actually perpetrated by women – Akeley's two wives, Delia J. Denning and Mary L. Jobe – and anonymous Africans who were recruited as labour.

The recomposed history exposes preservation as a mechanism of power, concerned with the validation, extension and fortification of the hegemony of the past and its auxiliary structures. Through the assembly of evidence, some of it jealously guarded by the archive officers of the Museum, Haraway traces the origins of biased speculations that position Akeley as a superior mind. For example, his autobiography *In Brightest Africa* (1920) is a compilation of transcriptions of conversations at dinner parties and other secondary sources – according to his first wife, 'he hated to wield a pen'.[10] The publication was researched and ghost-written by his secretary Dorothy S. Greene and edited by the publishers Doubleday and Page, without the corresponding attribution. This multiple and diffuse authorship is also evident in a photograph in which Akeley rests and smokes a pipe on top of a freshly felled elephant. Yet when the seemingly victorious image is compared to others taken the same day, the courageous and dexterous killer appears to be Delia J., who also acted as the photographer of the excursion. In her memoirs – *Jungle Portraits* (1930), penned after her divorce and omitted in *The Wilderness Lives Again* (1940) by Mary L. – the explorer and hunter is depicted as frequently sick and isolated in his tent, feeling threatened by the environment he was determined to conquer, with an endangered morale due to a mauling in British East Africa in 1910 – 'an invalid dangerously close to death whose courageous wife hunts not only for food for the camp, but also for scientific specimens so that he may hasten out of this dangerous continent before it claims him'.[11]

Inadvertently complicit with power

To Haraway, Akeley did not conspire to produce 'a history of race, sex, and class in New York City that reached to Nairobi'.[12] Nevertheless, with the purpose of constructing 'a monumental reproduction of the Garden of Eden' to tell the 'truth of natural history' through the interior architecture of the African Hall[13] – now called the Akeley Hall of African Mammals – his manoeuvres and method of work portray preservation as a subservient device, responsive and passive, in complicit cooperation with capitalism and the personal interest of influential figures. As an economic venture, Akeley's expeditions, hunting and taxidermic experimentations – financed by the trustees of the Museum, including Childs Frick, Madison Grant, H. F. Osborn, Daniel Pomeroy, Kermit Roosevelt, Henry W. Sage, J. P. Morgan, William K. Vanderbilt and John D. Rockefeller III[14] – surface analogously to the selection of which buildings are chosen to be protected and decisions as to the period of the past to which they have to return. Rather than being expressions of innocent nostalgia, laudable altruism or genuine appreciation for the past, these decisions are informed by canons that entail the politicised and polarising rummage through prime specimens of architecture. The preferred buildings are those with aesthetic qualities capable of pleasing potential consumers, usually ones in strategic locations of high economic value. Comparable to a positive eugenics implemented in the built environment, conservation becomes a priority when the state of decay and of imminent death of a celebrated structure has been verified by the governing apparatus as a commercial opportunity. As a personal project, the taxidermy of animals and the representation of nature in the African Hall are related to the territorial policies of Theodore Roosevelt, who established national parks, protected forests and erected monuments dedicated to country life.[15] The early diagnosis of *neurasthenia*, an American term for boredom resulting from the overexposure to urban civilization and the processes of industrialisation, encouraged the president – a friend and hunting companion of Akeley, the patron of the Museum and the 'Teddy Bear' that titles Haraway's investigation[16] – to explore the outdoors and be physically active. In contrast to the prescription to female sufferers of enforced immobilisation, interior confinement and overfeeding,[17] male patients were advised to exercise and embark on lengthy journeys of hunting and riding, in exclusive communion with other men, following the motto 'the true man is the sportsman'.[18]

Epitomised by the aim to protect nature and procure a genetically hygienic future, preservation, the restoration of the most pristine origin, suggests that the present – polluted, mechanised and deteriorated, predominantly urban – requires the maintenance of particular residues of the past in order to progress.[19] For Haraway, the attempt to control the effects of the passing of time through habits that procure death and sustain the act of execution is not only in confrontation with the female capacity to give birth but constitutes also a teleological anxiety. On the one hand, reinforcing the supremacy of what is considered culturally masculine, 'it is in the craft of killing that life is constructed, not in the accident of personal, material birth'.[20] On the other, responding to the romantic belief that existential meaning can be conquered in a lifetime, 'in immediate vision of the origin, perhaps the future can be fixed. By saving the beginnings, the end can be achieved and the present can be transcended'.[21] Although the mission is to extend the previous status, paradoxically the fundamental properties of what came before are erased. In the case of architecture, a building that has undergone a process of preservation, either by being renovated or altered through cuts or additions, has a new beginning that marks a new temporality. To arrest decadence and secure permanence, these interventions re-synchronise the object, forcing it to reach the level of rationalisation and development imposed by the political and economic system. The altering processes are anachronistic in relation to the origins of the treated structure, since they use the most advanced technologies. Such treatments risk fetishising a particular moment of a structure's existence and producing simulacra – a deceptive type of design that expunges time by adopting ageing as a motif, ignoring the cycles of nature and civilization.

Similar to Akeley's conviction that by immortalising the best samples of African fauna further destruction could be avoided, the survival offered by preservation appears heroic and glittering, rescuing buildings from early and unjust demises – as if they have been victims of misfortune or mistreatment by their occupants – with educational purposes and optimising resources in the name of environmentalism.[22] Yet these intentions are oblivious to interrogations such as 'how much of the past needs to be protected?'; 'how long will the new intervention last?'; and 'how many times can an edifice endure renovation before it becomes another entity?' The concern with the role of the past in the creation of the future problematises the ideation of the new, as a category that organises the design and building of the modern environment in dialogue with the fatigue with the old. For taxidermic preservation, the present is no longer a moment of difference – ideal for innovation – but the extension of what has been produced, dependent on existing material that has been scrutinised and proved effective and popular. The improvement of machineries of mapping, cleaning and ecological control provide accuracy in the recovery of history and facilitate its scientific research. Nonetheless, these modes of production not only defer to the reigning forces that allow their materialisation, but also entail a positivist approach that contributes to the perpetuation of a state of constant adjustment and change in urban centres.[23] The procedures of preservation are part of a system concerned with capital gain, industrial expansion and political power. As unveiled in 'Teddy Bear Patriarchy', Akeley's advances in photographic and filmic techniques – as prosthesis of the eye, to be sold and expended – were 'infinitely more potent than the gun' for 'the possession, preservation, consumption, surveillance, appreciation, and control of nature . . . and control of time'.[24] These appliances were adopted by Hollywood studios and the US Department of War.[25]

Considering boredom

The boredom of Roosevelt ostensibly drove his participation in the war against Spain for Cuba and the Philippines in 1898 during his vice-presidency – according to Fernand Braudel, since 'the United States needed a war' to have 'something to think about other than material gain'[26] – and the creation of the Great White Fleet in 1907 to tour the world as a testament of American supremacy while he was president. If compared to the ambition of preservation to fuel the continuation of the past, these actions arise as the contradictory will to elude the ephemeral without falling into stagnation, recovering the invested energy, securing profit and thereby perpetuating the ruling authority. As agents of power, the developers of projects that conserve existing elements of the built environment favour the monumental and what is considered the outcome of artistic virtuosity. They disregard the repetitious and mundane – the boring – without realising that what is left to deteriorate and perish is as significant in the understanding of history as what is permitted to recover and survive.

To enlighten the postmodern fixation on the past and its criteria for preservation, Fredric Jameson commends boredom as 'a very useful instrument with which to explore the past, and to stage a meeting between it and the present'.[27] Clarifying that the condition is not a stable or aesthetic property of any object but rather a revealing reaction to situations of crisis and confusion, he asserts that it acts as 'a precious symptom of our own existential, ideological, and cultural limits, an index of what has to be refused in the way of other people's cultural practices and their threat to our own rationalisations about the nature and value of art'.[28] In his view, the outcome of the production of the intentionally interesting can be boring and the experience of the accidentally boring can be interesting – as in 'the complacent eclecticism of postmodern architecture, which randomly and without principle but with gusto cannibalises all the architectural styles of the past and combines them in overstimulating ensembles'.[29] This paradox is thus productive as long as it is grasped as relational and dynamic, facilitating the identification of the need for change and reinstalling the desire for desire. By exhausting the celebrated – becoming bored with the classics – attention can then be given to what has been forgotten, the non-survivors that did not qualify for posterity because they were perceived as irrelevant at the historical moment of their reception and evaluation.

Like the omission of Akeley's wives and the Africans of his convoys in the official version of the Museum, the indifference of boredom with the past and its obstinate lingering in the present resonates with preservation in a twofold way. Firstly, following Jameson and exemplified by the aspiration of the African Hall to exhibit nature as the sacred beginning, the interest in historicity, consumed images and former fashions fuels a pervasive sense of ahistoricity.[30] The craving for the resurrection of previous eras responds to the need to fill the emptiness of the present, as if doubtful of progressivist convictions. Former configurations supply an endless source of positive material, with marginal risk of failure or inefficiency, exploiting and materialising nostalgia as the style – vintage or retro – that represents bygone periods of prosperity. Secondly, according to Emil Cioran and demonstrated by the endeavours of the Museum, the interest in history, its recording and salvation is the result of the fear of boredom brought on by the endless repetition of what has been done and achieved.[31] By implication, boredom ought to be the starting point from which the past is investigated, not only revising already told stories and divulging untold ones, but also turning history into the textbook that indicates what should be avoided – in an inverted but circular genealogy, 'no matter what you do, the starting point is boredom, and the end'.[32]

Under the structure of boredom – when the present stops providing difference, in between 'that which happens' and 'that which fails to occur'[33] – the efforts to protect and renovate the built environment can surpass the direct dragging of yesterday into today and instead become an active operation in the origination of tomorrow. Offering more than a historical account, preservation can organise a critical threshold, in between spaces and temporalities, where what has not yet been imagined can transpire.[34] This formation allows the speculative crossing from 'what exists' to 'what can potentially exist', operating in the uncertainty of waiting, not to calculate the future but to try its options at the front edge of the present. Unlike the polysemous dioramas of the African Hall, the ambiguous dismantling of the façade of the American Folk Art Museum or the irksome skinning of the Farwell Building, the activities promoted by boredom can turn into moments of experimentation, barring fixed or utopian representations. The ensuing forming, evolving and becoming are infused with the political, since – similar to boredom – they negotiate the winning of the future, principally when the future cannot be planned or accurately predicted.[35] In this manner, latency becomes manifest, as a moment after stimulation but before the determination of action, charged with the possibilities of design. This inclusiveness expands creative abilities, forcing the acknowledgement of an undesired environment only to motivate the ideation of an improved one, restoring the sense that the conservation and projection of spaces for inhabitation is a meaningful and empowering task.[36] In architectural preservation, boredom can act as a reservoir of positive energy, usable to transcend the pugnacious destruction and the determinist façadism shared with hunting and taxidermy. To overcome the exhaustion derived from the nostalgia favoured by capitalism, this vigour ought to borrow from the euphoria of what is about to come, nurturing the making of architecture.[37]

Notes

1   A shorter version of this essay was published as 'Boredom' in *Tabula Plena: Forms of Urban Preservation*. Edited by Bryony Roberts. (Zurich: Lars Müller Publishers, 2016).
2   John Freeman Gill, 'The Folly of Saving What You Kill', *The New York Times*, 23 April 2014.
3   Blair Kamin, 'The Danger of Becoming Skin Deep', *Chicago Tribune*, 8 April 2007.
4   *The Shorter Oxford English Dictionary*, 3rd ed., s. v. 'taxidermy'.
5   Academic elaborations have also used the metaphor of taxidermy to critique certain approaches to preservation in urban planning. See, for example, Steven W. Semes, *The Future of the Past: A Conservation Ethic for Architecture, Urbanism, and Historic Preservation* (New York: W. W. Norton, 2009); and Anika S. Lemar, 'Zoning as Taxidermy: Neighborhood Conservation Districts and the Regulation of Aesthetics', *Indiana Law Journal* 90, no. 4 (2015).
6   American Museum of National History. 'Akeley Hall of African Mammals', www.amnh.org/exhibitions/permanent-exhibitions/mammal-halls/akeley-hall-of-african-mammals (accessed 24 February 2017). The elephants rest on an elongated octagonal podium with incorporated seats, reminiscent of a coffin.
7   Ibid.
8   Ibid.
9   Donna Haraway, 'Teddy Bear Patriarchy: Taxidermy in the Garden of Eden, New York City, 1908–1936', *Social Text* 11 (1984): 21.
10   Ibid., 43. Quoted from Mary L. Jobe Akeley, *The Wilderness Lives Again: Carl Akeley and the Great Adventure* (New York: Dodd and Mead, 1940), 222.
11   Haraway, 'Teddy Bear Patriarchy', 48.
12   Ibid., 21.
13   Ibid., 20, 21.
14   Ibid., 54. The renovation of the dioramas carried out in 1972 was financed by Philip Morris Inc.
15   In the memorial outside the American Museum of National History, the statue of Roosevelt is surrounded by a low wall describing him as a 'ranchman', 'scholar', 'explorer', 'scientist', 'conservationist', 'naturalist', 'statesman', 'author', 'historian', 'humanitarian', 'soldier' and 'patriot'.
16   Haraway explains in a footnote, 'The Deavereaux or Hotel Colorado in Glenwood Springs, CO, contains a plaque with one version of the origin of the Teddy Bear, emblem of Theodor Roosevelt: T.R. returned empty handed from a hunting trip to the hotel, and so a hotel maid created a little stuffed bear and gave it to him. [. . .] Another version has T.R. sparing the life of a bear cub, with the stuffed version commemorating his kindness'. Ibid., 58.
17   Anne Stiles, 'Go Rest, Young Man', *Monitor on Psychology* 43, no. 1 (2012), www.apa.org/monitor/2012/01/go-rest.aspx. (accessed 24 February 2017). Allison Pease writes, 'In the 1910 *Autobiography of a Neurasthene*, written by a female doctor, the narrator notes that the passivity of women's lives makes them particularly susceptible to neurasthenia: "This anxious watching and waiting did me no good. But after all what is a woman's life, – whether wife, mother, or that of a doctor, but watching and waiting. . . . I have watched and waited every blessed minute of my life and I suppose I shall end it all by watching and waiting for death. It is a woman's life"'. Pease, *Modernism, Feminism*, 25, quoting Margaret Cleaves, *Autobiography of a Neurasthene: As Told by One of Them and Recorded by Dr. Margaret A. Cleaves* (Boston: R.G. Badger, 1910), 40–41.
18   Haraway, 'Teddy Bear Patriarchy', 38.
19   In the entrance hall of the American Museum of National History, a wall features the following quote by Roosevelt, 'conservation means development as much as it does protection'.
20   Haraway, 'Teddy Bear Patriarchy', 23.
21   Ibid., 20
22   Haraway points out that Akeley was aware of the destruction caused by his presence in Africa – 'After his first visit in 1921, he was motivated to convince the Belgian government to make of this area the first African national park to ensure an absolute sanctuary for the gorilla in the future.' Ibid., 25.
23   The state of constant construction and reconstruction is reminiscent of the description of Thekla, one of the settlements imagined by Italo Calvino in *Invisible Cities* – 'Those who arrive at Thekla can see little of the city, beyond the plank fences, the sackcloth screens, the scaffoldings, the metal armatures, the wooden catwalks hanging from ropes or supported by sawhorses, the ladders, the trestles. If you ask, "Why is Thekla's construction taking such a long time?" the inhabitants continue hoisting sacks, lowering leaded strings, moving long brushes up and down, as they answer, "So that its destruction cannot begin". And if asked whether they fear that, once the scaffoldings are removed, the city may begin to crumble and fall to pieces, they add hastily, in a whisper, "Not only the city"'. Italo Calvino, *Invisible Cities* (London: Vintage, 1997), 127.
24   Haraway, 'Teddy Bear Patriarchy', 39, 42.
25   Mark Alvey, 'The Cinema as Taxidermy: Carl Akeley and the Preservative Obsession', *Framework* 48, no. 1 (2007).
26   Fernand Braudel, *A History of Civilizations* (London: Allen Lane/Penguin, 1994), 384–85.
27   Fredric Jameson, *Postmodernism, or, the Cultural Logic of Late Capitalism* (London: Verso, 1991), 303.

28 Ibid., 72. For Jameson, in the case of art, 'it is not a great secret that in some of the most significant works of high modernism, what is boring can often be very interesting indeed, and vice versa: a combination which the reading of any hundred sentences by Raymond Roussel, say, will at once dramatize'.

29 Ibid., 229. In addition, Jameson confesses, 'I like [postmodern] architecture and a lot of the newer visual work, in particular the newer photography. The music is not bad to listen to, or the poetry to read; the novel is the weakest of the newer cultural areas and is considerably excelled by its narrative counterparts in film and video . . . Food and fashion have also greatly improved, as has the life world generally. My sense is that this is essentially a visual culture, wired for sound – but one where the linguistic element . . . is slack and flabby, and not to be made interesting without ingenuity, daring, and keen motivation'.

30 Ibid., 71–72.

31 Emil Cioran, *History and Utopia*, trans. Richard Howard (New York: Seaver, 1987), 109.

32 Emil Cioran, *Tears and Saints*, trans. Ilinca Zarifopol-Johnston (Chicago: The University of Chicago Press, 1995), 86.

33 Patrice Petro, *Aftershocks of the New: Feminism and Film History* (New Brunswick: Rutgers University Press, 2002), 57.

34 Andrew Benjamin, 'Boredom and Distraction: The Moods of Modernity', in *Walter Benjamin and History*, ed. Andrew Benjamin (London: Continuum, 2005), 162, 170.

35 Ibid., 164–65.

36 For Andreas Elpidorou, 'boredom helps to restore the perception that one's activities are meaningful or significant. . . . Boredom is both a warning that we are not doing what we want to be doing and a "push" that motivates us to switch goals and projects. Neither apathy, nor dislike, nor frustration can fulfill boredom's function'. Andreas Elpidorou, 'The Bright Side of Boredom', *Frontiers in Psychology* 5 (2014).

37 This resonates with the ethics of affirmation posed by Rosi Braidotti. She asserts that the cultivation of 'social, human, post-human, non-human relations', including those with the built environment, expands creativity and can result in joy – opposed to the 'shutting down of sadness'. The task is 'to learn to think differently about ourselves' to consciously construct a different history. If 'the energy is not immediately available due to the mourning of melancholia of trans-capitalism, . . . [then] we borrow from the future. . . . We insert it in our action here and now, and we try to work together toward schemes, discourses, study areas that will allow us to come to terms with our complexity – without giving into depression, without becoming demented hippies, without dropping out of university, without becoming data fetishists'. Rosi Braidotti, 'Affect and the Affective Turn' (keynote lecture delivered at The Fourth International and Interdisciplinary Conference on Emotional Geographies, Groningen, 1–3 July 2013).

Project 3

A cortege of ghostly bodies

Abstraction, *prothesis*, and the logic of the mannequin

Daniel Koch

Bodies are both present and thoroughly gendered in commercial environments – and, by extension, in public space. Such gendered presence is addressed in studies of both the historical evolution and current conditions of consumption and public space alike, which show that it takes many, varied forms.[1] Where much discourse on bodies in such spaces tends to focus on photographic and video material – in magazines, on billboards, and on shopfronts – somewhat less attention has been given to the role of mannequins (here, specifically wax and plastic mannequin 'dolls' used to display fashion in shopfronts and inside stores). Mannequins clearly perform something other than the photographic material used to display fashion: they are less detailed, less formulated, and less expressive.[2] This is not due to an inability to make mannequins more 'real'. Considering their prevalence and gendered presence and distribution, it is worth considering how they specifically contribute to processes of subjectification, embodiment, identity, and fashion negotiation.[3] This project builds on four primary sources: empirical research into commercial space, specifically two department stores;[4] Vanessa Osborne's 'The Logic of the Mannequin';[5] Gilles Châtelet's discussions on diagrams, space, and abstraction-*prothesis* processes;[6] and an experimental, explorative study undertaken at Dansmuseet (the Museum of Dance and Movement) in Stockholm in 2012.[7] The project aims to develop our understanding of how mannequins operate in commercial space and society – specifically, how in their abstraction these inanimate objects not only *allow for* but in fact *demand* completion from observers.

      Vanessa Osborne's 'The Logic of the Mannequin' suggests that the state of partial abstraction is central to the way mannequin dolls – and also live mannequins, or models – operate. The possibility of identifying with the mannequin, for Osborne, depends on the mannequin not having too much concreteness, or too much personality. At the same time, mannequins must provide enough upon which to build a persona, that they are effectively able to integrate parts of a self into their own construction. This 'self' that undergoes such integration is made up in turn not only of who one is, but also who one would like to be, and could like to be. There needs to be room for experimentation both with the mannequin, and with oneself, to try out whether the projected result is something that one would like to turn into. While fashion models in magazines and ads, as well as live and in video commercials, tend to have this character – which, according to Osborne, is one reason that models are generally not replaced by people much more known to the general public (with a few notable idol exceptions) – this becomes more evident in mannequin dolls because they more deliberately play with a degree of abstraction in their concreteness.[8] (When it is present in live mannequins, arguably such abstraction can start to border on the uncanny.)[9]

Drawing on Gilles Châtelet's definition of diagrams as *concrete abstractions*, a parallel can be constructed between mannequins and diagrams. In science, diagrams are concrete representations of abstracted (concrete) phenomena (as distinct from abstract abstractions or abstract concretions). It is this particularity of diagrams, that they are *meaningless*, which, he argues, engenders them with a creative capacity. Châtelet's argument can be linked to Osborne's, in that more precisely, diagrams contain too little information to be meaningful 'as they are', but contain enough information to suggest that they hold meaning, imposing on the observer the task of completing the information required to make the diagram meaningful.[10] To understand diagrams, we therefore need to *add in* information that has been *removed* in the abstraction of phenomena into diagrams. This adding of information is described by Châtelet as an act of *prothesis*, which he defines in the following terms:

> The Aristotelian theory of abstraction-addition, which relates however not only to the relationship between mathematics and physics, establishes a *reversible* action that makes it possible to add or subtract determinations at leisure. Stripping a physical being of its matter and mobility, I can also produce by abstraction a mathematical being – to which the geometer's wit will lend an existence – and then simply reintegrate this being into the order of physical natures, by restoring the determinations of which I had deprived it. This is the action of '*prothesis*' or addition of determinations.[11]

Châtelet adds that *prothesis* is only partially predictable, and remains independent of what was originally removed through abstraction.[12] This makes diagrams doubly transformative, as both the abstraction and the consecutive *prothesis* by necessity transform that which the diagram represents. A fair portion of such *prothesis* is performed on a pre-conscious (which is not to say untrained) level, and in initial contact with the diagram. Seen in this light, mannequins are diagrammatic devices that compel us to complete them, by transforming them into personas or even persons – a completion that is pre-conscious and which tends to take the form of, more often than not, ourselves or someone we know.[13]

Because of their degree of abstraction, mannequins arguably allow for an experimental inhabitation of the other – they allow us to 'try-on', so to speak, another body.[14] Such inhabitation is not only about observing how we could look, but also entails a more involved experience of how it would be to be that (other) person, wearing that clothing, in that, or a similar, context.[15] By staging a wide range of mannequins and allowing visitors to interact with them the situated material context of Dansmuseet, a museum in Stockholm dedicated to dance, offered a unique opportunity to play out some of the implications of these processes, and to examine the logic of the mannequin I sketch above, including the degrees of abstraction, interrelations, and contexts being produced. Concretely, this was done by the deployment of masks and personas,[16] and by making living bodies take on degrees of abstraction by dressing them in costumes. This experiment challenged the notion of who is a person and who is not, and equally what is an object and what is not, thereby destabilising the subject-object binary on two fronts.

In interacting with the mannequins at Dansmuseet, and in responding to photographs of the experiment afterwards, viewers tended at first to describe a stronger identification with the mannequin doll than with the masked persons, even though the latter are more clearly living beings and the former inanimate material. Secondly, they tended to agree that the masked persons and their actions more easily became 'uncanny' – staging mannequin dolls to resemble living people seems, in light of this reception, less prone to produce unease than the other way around. Even more so if the masked persons are staged to 'act on' the mannequin dolls, compared to if mannequin dolls were staged to 'act on' masked persons. The mannequins seemed to be interpreted by viewers as being situated on a path *towards subjectivity* – their identity was, in this sense, able to be 'added on' by the viewer, via an act of *prothesis*. Conversely, living subjects (albeit masked and posed) seemed to be interpreted occupying a path leading *away from subjectivity* – their identity was understood as having to undergo a process of *abstraction* before *prothesis* might become possible.[17] In the case of the mannequin, the viewer needs only to extend the direction of subjectification (in relation to what is ostensibly an object), whereas in the second, the viewer needs to first complete the act of abstraction (in relation to a specific, living person) before engaging in the *prothesis* that enables what I earlier termed 'an experimental inhabitation of the other'. This latter operation can, perhaps unsurprisingly, be experienced as something uncanny when performed in relation to living subjects. A limit to the mannequin-object is thus suggested here – to how much 'subject-ness' it can portray before it loses its suggestive power, and, perhaps more disturbingly, to how far removed from a 'subject' any mannequin – living model or shop dummy – must be for this particular consumption process of projected bodily inhabitation to take place.

In an environment like a department store, where the importance of the body is highly differentiated – that is, where how important your body is for the fit of the clothing varies – mannequins are used to push consumers to consistently try bodies out, by trying clothing on. The question becomes 'do I fit this body, and does my body thereby fit the clothing?' rather than 'does the clothing fit me?' This shift is built into the abstraction-*prothesis* reading of mannequins, which stresses the possibility of inhabiting other bodies. If this interpretation is correct, then it is noticeable how different stagings of mannequins

– concretely explored in the Dansmuseet project – communicate differences in *who you can be*, *for whom*, and *in what way*. In department stores, these same mechanics can be seen in the number of mannequins placed to be seen from behind, the side, or frontally, which differs radically according to the intended gender of the future (living) wearer of the clothing on display.[18] Such stagings, at their limit, might also affect the importance, relevance, and validity of considering one's own body as malleable, or even faulty.

The efficacy of the logic of the mannequin, as it is theorized here, depends on particular social and cultural contexts, which form an integral part of the architecture of fashion consumption: in order for mannequins to stimulate the acts of *prosthesis* described here, their context needs to be one wherein completing the mannequin's proto-identity with 'you' – the human subject – is a reasonable impulse, which is not a constant given but culturally and contextually conditioned. This implies relations to self and body that are perceived as malleable and changing – as projects of becoming rather than entities to express. The impulses of *prothesis*, which are often pre-cognitive or at least pre-conscious, need to draw on the self rather than on the other, and insofar as the impulse of completing-with-self is there, *prothesis* is likely to be a process that is self-reinforcing, and continuously reinforced, trained, and expanded until broken. Despite tending towards completion, this process however also has the capacity to move towards transgression: it contains within it the possibility of transgressing personality, gender, and sex via experimental, projected inhabitation of other genders, identities, and even bodies. Fashion here, by necessity, can be understood not in terms of specific items of clothing or general trends of clothing, but as situated bodily practices of wearing.

Notes

1   See Nicole Kalms, 'Provocations of the Hypersexualized City', *Architecture and Culture* 2, no. 3 (2014); Nicole Kalms, 'Digital Technology and the Safety of Women and Girls in Urban Space: Personal safety Apps or crowd-sourced activism tools?' in *Architecture and Feminisms: Ecologies, Economies, Technologies* eds. Hélène Frichot, Catharina Gabrielsson, Helen Runting (London: Routledge, 2017); Chuihua Judy Chung, 'Ms. Consumer', in *Harvard Design School Guide to Shopping*, ed. Chuihua Judy Chung, et al. (Köln: Taschen, 2001); Mica Nava, 'Modernity's Disavowal: Women, the City and the Department Store' in *Modern Times: Reflections on a Century of English Modernity*, eds. Mica Nava and Alan O'Shea (London: Routledge, 1996); Lauren Rosewarne, *Sex in Public: Women, Outdoor Advertising and Public Policy* (Newcastle: Cambridge Scholars Publishing, 2007); Tom Reichert, *The Erotic History of Advertising* (Amherst, N.Y.: Prometheus Books, 2003).

2   Mark B. Sandberg, *Living Pictures, Missing Persons: Mannequins, Museums and Modernity* (Princeton, N.J.: Princeton University Press, 2003).

3   Subjectification e.g. Judith Butler, *Precarious Life: The Powers of Mourning and Violence* (London: Verso, 2004); Fashion and identity negotiation e.g. Elisabeth Wilson, *Adorned in Dreams: Fashion and Modernity*, 2nd ed. (New York: I.B. Tauris, 2003); specifically fashion as situated bodily practice of wearing e.g. Joanne Entwistle, *The Fashioned Body: Fashion, Dress and Modern Social Theory* (Cambridge, UK: Polity Press, 2000).

4   Åhlens City and Debenhams in Stockholm, studied in 2005 and 2006, e.g. Daniel Koch, *Structuring Fashion: Department Stores as Situating Spatial Practice* (Stockholm: Axl Books, 2007).

5   Vanessa Osborne, 'The Logic of the Mannequin: Shop Windows and the Realist Novel,' in *The Places and Spaces of Fashion, 1800–2007*, ed. John Potvin (New York: Routledge, 2009).

6   Gilles Châtelet, *Figuring Space: Philosophy, Mathematics and Physics* [Les enjeux du mobile: Mathématique, physique, philosophie], trans. Robert Shore and Muriel Zagha (Dordrecht: Kluwer Academic Publishers, 2000).

7   Charles Koroly, *Korolys Kostymdrama*, 2012. Dansmuseet. I would like to express my gratitude to Dansmuseet for allowing the experiment to take place, and also the participants in various roles: Malin Blank, Magnus Helgesson, Thomas Koch Blank, and Jenny Wiklund.

8 In research on mannequins, dolls tended to be treated as individuals, as phenomena, or as a historical emergence, whereas their emplaced, spatial, situational interdependency with architecture is less often discussed beyond the notion of the shop window. For a discussion on shifting degrees of abstraction in mannequin dolls, see Emily R. King, 'Allure of the Silent Beauties: Mannequins and Display in America, 1935–70' in *The Places and Spaces of Fashion, 1800–2007*, ed. John Potvin (New York: Routledge, 2009). Additionally concerning living mannequins and de-personalisation/abstraction, see Lauren Rosewarne, 'Pin-Ups in Public Space: Sexist Outdoor Advertising as Sexual Harassment', *Women's Studies International Forum* 30, no. 4 (2007); Osborne, 'The Logic of the Mannequin'; or Caroline Evans, 'The Ontology of the Fashion Model,' *AA Files* 63 (2011).

9 For the relation between mannequin, model, automata, body, femininity, and subjectivity see further 'The Ontology of the Fashion Model'.

10 Compare to Daniel Libeskind, *Chamber Works: Architectural Mediations on Themes from Heraclitus* (Architectural Association, 1983).

11 Châtelet, *Figuring Space*, 17–18.

12 'We have just touched on the weak point of the theory of abstraction: a certain casualness with regard to what makes it possible to attach or detach determinations. For to abstract is always to mutilate . . . It seems that the theory of abstraction-prothesis exacerbates the opposition of the terms it was supposed to bind back together.' Ibid., 18.

13 See for instance Osborne, 'The Logic of the Mannequin'; Nicholas Blomley, '"I'd Like to Dress Her All Over": Masculinity, Power and Retail Space' in *Retailing, Consumption and Capital: Towards the New Retail Geography*, eds. Neil Wrigley and Michelle Lowe (Essex: Longman Group Limited, 1996).

14 e.g., as dependent on what Sandberg calls 'mobilized bodies', not only of mobility in the geographical sense, but in a cognitive and subjective sense. For Sandberg, mannequins here form a part of a culture effigy that 'body forth' a newly mobile body, with 'both the presence effects that made them convincing and the absences that made them portable.' Sandberg, *Living Pictures, Missing Persons*, 5.

15 'And, in fact, this monadic body, which we call 'our own', is always attended by the mobile horizon of its virtual sites. Everything happens for this body as if a cortege of ghostly bodies, all equally its own, always followed it and always preceded it, marking out its possible places of occupation, according to a form of spacing out which is unfolded within it and by it.' Jean-Toussaint Desanti, 'The Liberation of the Gesture and the Bias of the Visible' in *Figuring Space: Philosophy, Mathematics and Physics*, ed. Gilles Châtelet (Dordrecht: Kluwer, 2000), xxx.

16 Katarina Bonnevier, 'The 1893 Faire of Masks: The Spectacle of the World's Columbian Exposition,' *Nordic Journal of Architectural Research* 16, no. 1 (2003).

17 It is tempting here to draw parallel between Lacan's and Châtelet's discussions on gestures, but this should be done only with care. However, in the context, it may be interesting to consider this 'directionality' as the way in which mannequins embody 'gestures' that condition the consecutive understanding of the mannequin, and furthermore whether these gestures are 'there' or contextually actualized. See Jacques Lacan, *The Seminar of Jacques Lacan. Book 20, On Feminine Sexuality: The Limits of Love and Knowledge: 1972–1973* (Encore), [Le Seminaire, Livre XX, Encore] (London: W. W. Norton & Company, 1998). See also Slavoj Žižek, 'Class Struggle or Postmodernism?: Yes Please!' in *Contingency, Hegemony, Universality: Contemporary Dialogues on the Left*, eds. Judith Butler, Ernesto Laclau, and Slavoj Žižek (London: Verso, 2000).

18 See Lacan, *Book 20*; also Laura Mulvey's 'to-be-looked-at-ness', Lara Mulvey, 'Visual Pleasure and Narrative Cinema', *Screen* 16, no. 3 (1975).

Project 3 The exhibition *'Korolys kostymdrama'* (Koroly's Costume Drama) at the Museum
of Dance and Movement in Stockholm employed mannequins in different
combinations of dress and wear, including decay, and allowed physical interaction
with the exhibited objects. Photograph by Daniel Koch. Copyright Patchwork
Architecture Laboratory.

Chapter 8

Subaltern bodies in the digital urban imaginary

Alison Brunn

The twenty-first century has so far seen responsive sensing technology, digitally networked infrastructure and ubiquitous computing increasingly presented as the solution to the myriad problems facing both the contemporary and the future city. The networked environment is posited as a means of averting environmental crisis and coping with projected population swells and their attendant fallout – notions of urban crisis that are invoked to convey the urgency with which the city must be reimagined and optimized through emerging digital technologies. In such scenarios, residents of the 'digital city' become generators of data to be used by both state actors and other residents in complex feedback loops. Citizens not only sense, but *are sensed*. People's presence, behaviour and even biorhythms register in and on the digital city – a prospect that has elicited criticism around notions of privacy, surveillance, transparency and power imbalances between average citizens and larger entities, be they private corporations or government actors. In the wake of 2013's Edward Snowden leaks, disclosures of surveillance programmes have revealed a collapse of the distinctness separating surveilling entities, as data collected by private companies is conscripted by the state.

What such technological critiques typically fail to address are differentiated notions of what it means to be seen, heard and, in turn, sensed. Questions around data and sensing in the built environment are necessarily complicated by the fact that those outside of dominant social classes often struggle to be visible at all, or are at times made hyper-visible. This chapter begins by discussing differentiated notions of visibility in regards to paid sexual labour, elaborating on two approaches to the monitoring and regulation of sex work – the 'Prostitution Free Zones' of Washington, D.C. and Portland,

Oregon, and the micro-surveillance of sex workers in Bengal. These case studies illustrate how notions of sex workers' visibility are complex and, at times, contradictory.

Shifting momentarily away from sex work, I will then discuss transformations in subjectification and governmentality that are made possible through 'smart' cybernetic environments. Building on an existing body of scholarship that exposes the smart city's potential for new modalities of governance, I will argue that the smart city's unprecedented capacity for the self-regulation and monitoring of behaviour extends to sexual behaviour. My intent is to highlight how complex and differentiated notions of visibility might play out within cybernetic environments and how the smart city, as an exemplar of such environments, could function as the ultimate zone of either exclusion, surveillance, or both for the figure of the sex worker as a feminized Other.

The prostitution free zone

Throughout the twentieth century, the zoning of sexual commerce into specified locales contributed to the sex worker's appearance as a figure existing outside of the social interior. The imagery associated with such places has become part of a visual lexicon of vice, which turns red light districts and 'seedy' urban areas into places of iconography, notoriety and tourism. Popular culture has produced images of the sex worker that are also absorbed into the public imagination, in depictions that range from celebratory to depraved. In terms of the governance and management of urban space, the figure of the sex worker was seen as a hallmark of 'urban blight', whose existence in public space served as a stand-in for the existence of other stigmatized or illegal activities, such as drug use and violent crime.

In the 1990s and 2000s, some American cities instituted policies known as Prostitution Free Zones, or PFZs as I will refer to them from now on. These essentially amounted to reverse zoning ordinances that, rather than relegate sexual commerce or 'adult entertainment' inside the boundaries of a specified locale, such as a red-light district, took an inverted approach. The implementation of the PFZ established areas of 'zero-tolerance' in which the enforcement of anti-prostitution laws was especially stringent. These measures were undertaken with the explicit objective of expelling sex workers from those areas.

Filmmaker PJ Starr's short documentary, *Prostitution Free Zone*, opens with images of a posted sign on a Washington, D.C. street. The sign notifies passers-by that the area has been declared a PFZ, and that any person in a group of two or more who fails to disperse at the order of police is subject to arrest. Sharmus Outlaw, a trans activist and advocate for sex worker rights who is interviewed in the film, describes an incident where she was stopped during the day for assisting a man who had asked her for spare change. Officers claimed she was offering him drugs and ordered her to disperse.[1] The obvious unconstitutionality of the ordinance – its propensity for racial profiling and the sweeping power granted to individual police officers – finally led to its repeal there in 2014.

Though no longer in effect, the policy remains relevant to a discussion of the management of sexual behaviour by the state. Not only could those who refused to disperse be arrested under the PFZ ordinance, but even those who did disperse were subject to a literal banishment – once ordered to leave the zone, an individual could not return to that area for the duration of the zone. In Washington, D.C., this was up to ten days. In the city of Portland, Oregon, the period of exclusion could last from 90 days to one year.

Portland's PFZs, along with drug-free zones, were instituted as a crackdown in reputed 'high-vice areas' during the 1990s and were finally repealed in 2007. As mentioned, exclusion from a Portland PFZ could last up to 90 days on suspicion alone. If convicted of prostitution-related activities, the individual would be excluded from the zone for a full year. If caught anywhere within the zone during that time, they would be subject to an additional arrest on the grounds of trespassing.[2] These ordinances delineated areas of the city from where those merely suspected of prostitution were effectively banished. Once excluded, it became illegal for these people merely to exist in public space, even when not taking part in sex work or any otherwise illegal activity.

The rhetoric of those who tout such policies is couched in terms of 'quality of life' and zero-tolerance for criminality.[3] A 2008 editorial in *The Oregonian* urged the city to consider reintroducing the exclusionary practice, asserting '[t]he approach gave police a quick and invaluable way to disperse hot spots of criminal activity, and make life bearable for the people who have to live next door to it'.[4] The underlying implication is that those who at any time – even temporarily – engage in sex work exist *permanently* outside the threshold of the Social. The very existence of the sex worker in spatial proximity to 'everyday people' is a threat to those whose citizenship is legitimized through property ownership, legality and also through sexual normativity. These bans amounted to more than just the temporary removal of an individual from an area of the city. Lisa E. Sanchez, in a 2004 study of the policies, describes them as amounting to 'a denial of the prostitute's legal subjectivity and cultural existence'.[5] Their desired effect was to render sex work, and thus the sex worker, invisible via a complete expulsion from the social interior. While the PFZ is a useful case study in the legislated invisibility of the sex worker, it is equally important to examine scenarios in which sex workers are rendered hyper-visible, and represented as sources of risk needing supervision and control.

Micro-surveillance and peer education

To discuss the emergence of the sex worker's body as a hyper-visible site of management and regulation, I turn to a 2005 case study by Swati Ghosh which details the micro-surveillance of sex workers in Bengal in response to the global AIDS epidemic. According to Ghosh, the status of prostitution during the post-Independence period in India was 'relatively settled'.[6] The global crisis of HIV-AIDS in the 1990s, however, brought new forms of attention and scrutiny to the subaltern body and the bodies of sex workers in particular. The image of the sex worker as a site of disease propelled collaboration among the Indian government, local organizations in Bengal, international NGOs and donors to develop public health intervention programmes. The platform they developed was conceived specifically to stop the spread of HIV and AIDS by targeting the bodies of sex workers as sites of infection. Between 1992 and 1997, their approach transformed from mere medical intervention into a system of surveillance and peer education.

Former sex workers were deployed into communities to identify infected workers and gather data on patterns of sexual behaviour. The data furnished to NGOs – and, by extension, to the state – included workers' names, income, social status, number of clients per day, 'nature of sexual act performed',[7] infection with other STDs, use of contraception, visits to clinics, as well as their assets and economic standing.

Beyond collecting information, the former sex workers engaged in counselling active workers to adopt safe-sex practices and seek medical check-ups. Ghosh describes this as the institution of a 'watch-care system, whereby the prostitute is subordinated at once to supervision, careful concern, regulation, and control'.[8] No authority figure or legal impetus were required to either gather the information or modify sex worker behaviour, since in this atmosphere sex was medicalized and the sex workers themselves were reframed as recipients of care.[9] The modification of sexual behaviour was initially seen by those involved as a question of public health, rather than any question of morality. Furthermore, the employment of former sex workers to undertake such activities made the institutional backing of the programmes less visible. Because the collected data would become an important factor in predicting the course of the AIDS pandemic, the act of surveillance was seen as a 'public good'.[10] In this way, the notion of global crisis heightened the perceived need for control over the bodies and behaviour of individuals. This dynamic persists today, though the contemporary crisis is not HIV/AIDS, but climate change.

Subjectification and the smart city

While definitions of the smart city are multiple and often quite vague, they tend toward common themes. One is efficiency, both financial and environmental. Such definitions often allude to non-specific notions of 'quality of life' as a central objective. At the heart of all smart city proposals are information and communication technologies (ICT) with an immense response capacity.[11] While 'smart city' might once have only connoted the integration of computing with urban life and infrastructure, in the last decade it has converged with the idea of the sustainable city.[12] The spectre of global environmental crisis has heightened the perceived urgency with which urban environments must be remade to save humanity from itself; giving designers, planners and corporations alike a license to propagate a highly computed, highly responsive vision of a 'sustainable' or 'green' city.

The prospect of ICT embedded in daily life is not new. In 1994, David Lyon described surveillance as concerning such mundane activities as 'taking money from a bank machine . . . using a credit card . . . picking up books from the library or crossing a border on trips abroad. In each case mentioned, computers record our transactions, check against other known details, ensure that we and not another are billed or paid, store bits of our biographies, or assess our financial, legal or national standing.'[13] The list of surveilled mundane activities has only expanded with the proliferation of smartphones, social media, facial recognition software, browser cookies and so on. Until recently, smart city technologies have largely been promoted by vendors rather than demanded by governments and citizens. Some of the most high-profile smart city proposals have been collaborations among universities, governments and private companies, notably IBM and Cisco. In 2011, it was estimated that annual spending on smart city technology would reach $108 billion by the year 2020.[14]

MIT and Cisco's 2008 Connected Sustainable Cities project similarly envisions the home as a site of data generation and response. In 'Programming Environments', Jennifer Gabrys describes dwellings in which '[the] organization of activities unfolds through programmed and activated environments so as to realize the most productive and efficient use of time and resources . . . Monitoring residents' behaviors in detail through sensors and data is essential for achieving efficiency.'[15]

The above scenarios speak to the surveillance potential of the smart city, but to understand the broader shifts in urban life and governmentality that smart cities entail, it's necessary to move beyond a dialectic of surveillance versus privacy. Unlike Bentham's Panopticon, where surveillance is identifiable as originating from the figure of the guard tower, smart cities integrate data collection and sensing technologies to the point that they are nearly imperceptible. Yet, since citizens participate in their own surveillance – by generating data, responding to data and observing the city's responses to data all around them – the individual is constantly exposed.

Surveillance is no longer bound to vision in a literal sense. Instead, it operates through the circulation of information and thus transcends any fixed locale. In the smart city, the sovereign figure is diffuse, embodied by no person in particular, but dispersed throughout the environment itself. The very interfaces and technologies that are, for urban citizens, a 'means of life'[16] become the ideal site for their management and administration. As the networks of feedback mechanisms deployed in urban contexts grow ever more dense and ubiquitous, surveillance is increasingly dispersed throughout the environment. The smart city endows the built environment with an unprecedented capacity for the self-regulation of behaviour. It's an environment of subtle and invisible coercion where inhabitants respond, often subconsciously, to a series of signals and stimuli.

The Prostitution Free Zone and the micro-surveillance of sex workers in Bengal illustrate two different strategies of managing othered groups through a biopolitical framework of regulation and behaviour modification, and suggest varying potential outcomes for paid sexual labour within the context of the data-rich, cybernetic environment. In the Prostitution Free Zones of Portland and Washington, D.C., sex workers (or those merely *perceived* to be sex workers) were identified by either citizens or police and given a literal 'exclusion notice', with the intent of erasing their existence in public space and rendering them invisible. The crux of the smart city's potential for governmentality is that it seeks not only to produce itself – the 'smart environment' – but to produce a certain kind of person, the 'smart citizen'. Who the smart citizen *is* is a question necessarily bound up with normativity.

Smart citizens perform their citizenship not because they are threatened by an authority figure but because their environment prescribes that they monitor and adjust their behaviour – this is made possible through the collection of data, which produces a sense of constant visibility and exposure. Behaviour is modified to coincide with valorized norms which centre not only around energy consumption or carbon reduction but other forms of 'smart' behaviour as well – this is inclusive of social and sexual behaviour. Norms are perpetually reinforced through acts of observation and self-regulation, to exclude and expel non-conformers. This suggests that the smart city could function as the ultimate zone of exclusion for the sex worker as a feminized Other whose sexual labour is non-normative, even if it is not criminalized outright.

In Bengal, after the onslaught of HIV made sex workers hyper-visible as critical sites of public health intervention, sex worker communities were not erased or expelled but rather infiltrated so that management and behaviour modification could occur in the form of peer education. Under the watch-care system, sex was medicalized and the sex workers themselves were reframed as recipients of care. Intimate details of the women's lives were recorded and furnished as data to NGOs. In the smart city, where monitoring individuals is essential to achieving 'intelligence', the body of the sex worker would inevitably emerge as a target of surveillance.

Both case studies that I've discussed exist in a period of time that somewhat pre-dates our current discourse of smart cities. Accordingly, they highlight the ways in which the forces that regulate sexual normativity and manage the visibility of Others in urban environments have existed apart from highly networked infrastructure and ubiquitous computing. The smart city – as an imaginary – would enable a hyper-coordination of data and thus a degree of enforcement in urban environments that is perhaps unprecedented. When notions of an 'intelligent' city converge with normative notions of a 'successful' city, then 'intelligence' becomes linked with the ability to manage, expel or modify that which is not normal.

Notes

1   PJ Starr, *Prostitution Free Zone*. Web, directed by PJ Starr (Washington, D.C.: Moral High Ground Productions, 2009).
2   Lisa E. Sanchez, 'The Global E-rotic Subject, the Ban, and the Prostitute-free Zone: Sex Work and the Theory of Differential Exclusion', *Environment and Planning D: Society and Space* 22, no. 6 (2004): 868–69, doi: 10.1068/d413.
3   Sanchez, 'The Global E-rotic Subject', 863.
4   Mary Kitch, 'Look Again at Prostitution Free Zones', *The Oregonian/OregonLive* (Portland, Oregon), 21 August 2008.
5   Sanchez, 'The Global E-rotic Subject', 865.
6   Swati Ghosh, 'Surveillance in Decolonized Social Space: The Case of Sex Workers in Bengal', *Social Text* 23, no. 2 (2005): 58, doi: 10.1215/01642472-23-2_83-55.
7   Ibid., 60.
8   Ibid., 55.
9   Ibid., 60.
10 Ibid., 59.
11 Gemma Galdon-Clavell, '(Not So) Smart Cities? The Drivers, Impact and Risks of Surveillance-Enabled Smart Environments', *Science & Public Policy (SPP)* 40, no. 6 (2013): 718, doi: 10.1093/scipol/sct070.
12 Jennifer Gabrys, 'Programming Environments: Environmentality and Citizen Sensing in the Smart City', *Environment and Planning D: Society and Space* 32 (2014): 33, doi: 10.1068/d16812.
13 David Lyon, *Electronic Eye: The Rise of Surveillance Society* (Minneapolis: University of Minnesota Press, 1994), 4.
14 Galdon-Clavell, '(Not So) Smart Cities', 717.
15 Gabrys, 'Programming Environments', 38.
16 Bruce Braun, 'A new urban dispositif? Governing life in an age of climate change', *Environment and Planning D: Society and Space* 32 (2014): 55, doi: 10.1068/d4313.

Chapter 9

Digital technology and the safety of women and girls in urban space

Personal safety Apps or crowd-sourced activism tools?

Nicole Kalms

The ubiquity of smartphone technology has shaped contemporary culture over the past decade with mobile devices connecting users to new forms of data and an endless array of communities. Voice calls and text messaging have been extended by mobile internet access, live camera and video feeds, navigation tools and Apps – all of which amplify communication – and also introduce new and novel ways to consider and critique urban experience. With nearly two-thirds of people connected to the world wide web via a smart phone device,[1] mobile technology provides the opportunity to connect and collaborate as well as a ways to monitor and moderate participation and practices in cities.

In this chapter, I examine two forms of mobile geolocative technology aimed at mitigating the sexual violence faced by women and girls in urban spaces. Firstly, I explore the emergence of personal safety Apps that allow family members and friends to monitor the movements of users and to alert 'guardians' of possible risk or calamity. Secondly, I examine crowd-sourced activism tools used by women to auto-ethnographically document their experience of sexual assault and in doing so, to collectively map unsafe territories and untold perspectives of their cities. My aim is to question whether these digital tools offer heterosexual women and girls agency and protection or if, in contrast, they reinforce the message that violence against women and girls is their own responsibility to manage?

I will also draw on my own research undertaken as the Director of the Monash University XYX Lab. The XYX research laboratory examines the nexus of space, gender and communication in cities and has recently partnered with Plan International Australia to examine the *Free to Be* geolocative mapping project. The tool, piloted in 2016, crowd sourced over 1300 comments from women and girls living in Melbourne in a two-month period. The project exposed women's and girls' perceptions of safe and unsafe spaces in Melbourne and revealed 'hotspots' of sexual harassment as well as areas of the city where women and girls 'self-excluded' as a result of perceived risk. *Free to Be* was co-designed with young women for young women and the XYX Lab synthesized the outcomes. My research into the geolocative spots and comments given by women and girls will provide an example of a gender-sensitive approach to sex crimes perpetrated against women and girls.

By examining the individualist safety App, the crowd sourced activists' map, and my own research with the *Free to Be* project, I will reveal the complexity of women's relationship to sexual violence in urban space. I will suggest that crowd-sourced activism allows for a nuanced understanding of women's experience in the city, and that, by revealing the potential for collaborative power with stakeholders and communities, new dynamics emerge for feminist scholarship and feminist activism.

Here/Her

Women's contemporary fear of crime is a significant social problem that has been well documented in the field of geography.[2] Yet the progress of women's capacity to engage fully in cities remains unchanged despite the multiple waves and multifarious methods of feminism. Mobile Apps and social media technology have responded to the risks faced by women in cities, where sex crimes are presently estimated to affect over 80 per cent of women worldwide.[3] Sex crimes include: stalking; unwanted touching; obscene gestures; voyeurism; unwanted sexual comments or jokes; sex-related insults; pressuring for dates or demand for sex; indecent exposure; and unwanted offensive and invasive interpersonal communication through technologies such as mobile phones and social media.[4] These crimes are acknowledged internationally as a large, growing and underreported threat to women's safety.[5]

It is well established that sexual harassment is not about the desire for sexual favors or even sexual contact, but 'the enforcement of gender expectations.'[6, 7] In societies where sexual harassment is a significant part of constructing women's fear of more serious violent attack, the fear of sexual violence is a powerful means of maintaining gender inequity.[8] Nearly one-third say that 'girls should not be out in public places after dark' where the prevalence of sexual harassment reinforces existing power inequalities.

Digital bodyguards

When negotiating city spaces, some women take action to preserve their personal safety. They may avoid strangers, pretend to have a conversation on their phone, grasp their keys as a weapon and limit their movement through particular urban areas where sex crimes are perceived to be rife.[9] The personal safety App is a smart phone tool that responds to women's fear of sexual violence in everyday life by enabling the woman's or girl's friends and family to remotely monitor her location and to track her movements. The user herself may record events of sexual violence as evidence for later prosecution and – in cities where the saturation of media and consumer culture dominates – safety Apps seem to offer women and girls new 'empowered' forms of navigating and negotiating cities.

While the 'relationship between the environment and opportunity for offending and victimization is well established in criminology,'[10] crime prevention strategies are still developing, and gender-sensitive approaches are lacking. In most cities, the importance of women's safety is inadequately acknowledged, and CCTV cameras, 'safety zones' and alarm buttons are generalized measures for all users, and only become useful after the sexual harassment or assault has occurred.

While the effectiveness of personal safety Apps is still being researched, the preliminary evidence suggests that the use of the smartphone Apps provides an opportunity for women to reflect on their sense of safety.[11] By introducing and undertaking a brief overview of a sample of safety Apps available to women, I will highlight the distinct aspects of product marketing and product functions as a way to reveal the socio-cultural regulation of women's behaviour that accompanies safety Apps.

Companion is a safety App that lets users 'reach out to family, friends, or your public safety department to have them keep an eye on you as you travel late at night.'[12] Developed by students as a response to sexual violence on university campuses,[13] the App reinforces that women are not safe in and around university spaces, and need to manage their behaviour to mitigate the risk of sexual assault.[14] Users shown in the App's online media are only female – confirming that this is a tool for managing violence against women. Playing out a scenario, the video shows a young woman inputting her destination and mode of transport into the App; family and friends are then shown connecting to their own smart phone technology as 'companions' to ensure remotely that she arrives safely. If required, the user can trigger the App to sound an alarm, alert the police and will send an automatic message to the guardian if the user's destination is not reached. Once the user arrives safely at her destination, the 'companion' is notified.

bSafe supports empowered and individual users to be undeterred by the risks of occupying urban space and markets itself as 'the end of worry.'[15] With features such as 'I'm Here', 'Follow Me' and 'Fake Call', women using bSafe communicate their agency to family members or partners while paradoxically being continually monitored.[16] While the App is ungendered in the marketing, the online reviews and promotion of the App reflect the complexity of contemporary agency for women:

> My husband doesn´t have to worry about me anymore and neither do I!
>
> This App is my personal hero. I have no problem walking by myself in heels to meet up with friends in the city now cuz they are always with me on bSafe.
>
> I hated that my girlfriend got out of work late in the city and walked home. With 'Follow Me' feature I can walk with her and know she´s home safe.[17]

The marketing of many of the Apps focus on stories about sexual assaults and attacks, with particular emphasis on women expressing concern about their own safety.[18] bSafe markets the App as a 'new world of safety tools' that allows users to set up a 'personal safety network.'[19]

Watch Over Me views women as passive, potential victims. If users fail to check-in on time, the App will then send out alerts to emergency contacts with information to help them locate the user. The App also offers a 'shake to alarm' feature that activates emergency alerts and turns on the camera to record what is happening. It also allows women to report any crime witnessed, and to warn others about a possible threatening situation. The co-developer of the App states: 'Safety starts with taking precautions and being more aware of what's going on around you,'[20] reinforcing that safety is women's concern and responsibility to bear.

Musketeer is a personal safety App that connects people in distress with others who can be of support. Using geolocative technology that includes video, audio, pictures and text, emergency response is marketed as a 'social safety network' where users can 'be a hero' by responding to 'someone's call for help' and 'change two lives – yours and theirs.' Users of the App can also receive help from other users. The App profile states:

> One example of a use for the App is if someone needs to walk home late at night through dark streets. While it isn't exactly an emergency, sometimes it is comforting to have someone accompany you so you feel safe.[21]

A potentially valuable aspect of this technology may be the ability to connect socio-spatial places with communities in cities. Yet the dominant ways that the technology is marketed is to promote the ever-present risks of being in space, and it works with women's *perceptions* of the risk of violence as opposed to the *actual* risk of violence.

Furthermore, the geolocative technology that is used in the App to keep women safe is also used in more concerning software that has precipitated incidents of online stalking, where geolocation tracking allows another person to monitor someone's movements without consent.[22] Online surveillance software can be downloaded to watch behaviour remotely, and this has led to an increase in the use of online forms of control by partners or former partners of women. This is part of a concerning shift in forms of sexual violence perpetrated against women.

Digital chaperones

Making safety women's 'thing' to manage and negotiate does little to address the crisis of sexual assault in cities. Problematically, women's perceived fear of violence in urban space may be amplified by the Apps' use of geospatial technologies. By using 'an App that turns your friends into digital chaperones'[23] the tool mimics ways that women have historically been monitored and may mirror the controlling behaviour of perpetrators, which is part of the disempowerment of women.

While feminism has many multiplicities and a singular surviving 'feminism' is an impossibility, the personal safety Apps' alignment does not reflect a territorial transformation that echoes women's expanding sexual empowerment and liberation.[24] In contrast, I suggest that the personal safety App reinforces self-surveillance and discipline – now a normative requirement for women to ensure that the problems of women's bodies are controlled and monitored.[25] Laura Garcia-Favaro states that: 'women are constituted as adaptive factors fully responsible for their self-care and enhancing their own well-being through strategic cost-benefit calculation.'[26] Women's behaviour and relationships continue to be changed or modified as a result of using the Apps – indeed, with some of the Apps this is the intent. While the safety App is marketed as a way to keep women safe from violence, many have mechanisms that in effect serve to control and prohibit women's full participation in city life, or to imbue a sense of protection when no real protection from risk exists. To reinforce that safety is women's responsibility limits women's independence in public life and is a 'gendered driver of violence against women.'[27]

Crowd feminism: The new fabric of women's security?

In contrast to personal and individualistic safety Apps, geolocative crowd mapping is a tool that provides women and girls with the opportunity to pool their experiences in cities for action and activism. Maps like Harassmap, Safecity, Free to Be and Not Asking For It make visible not just the individual incidents of sexual violence but the cumulative crisis across cities, cultures and demographics by productively registering gendered 'security and insecurity.'[28] The developers of Safecity state:

> Through the Safecity platform, women and girls can anonymously share and read each other's experiences of sexual violence, serving to break the myth that we are alone as victims. Furthermore, data generated pinpoints trends which can be used to find effective neighborhood solutions.[29]

As a tool for women to share their diverse female and feminist voices, the maps enable women and girls who participate or observe, to be informed about the various experiences of safety and risk in the city. This form of data combats the under reporting of sex crimes by allowing women to report 'in their own words, without the restrictions on narrative form associated with the traditional justice system.'[30] Given the lengthy history of women's exclusion and invisibility in cities and the difficulties of accurately collecting information about and collating sex crimes in cities, crowd-sourcing projects such as *Free to Be* offer a new methodology. The fine-grained analysis of the map entries and their locales reveal not only the locations of safe spaces as well as the unsafe areas in the city, but also the perception of these spaces as described by women themselves. This, and other, gender-sensitive participatory tools record women's and girl's experience in cities, and the 'data' collated becomes a significant asset. Crowd sourcing provides evidence that can prompt and potentially shape government policy, gendered behaviour and cities themselves.

By providing an alternative position for women moving around the city, crowd sourced feminist activism opens 'new technological and geopolitical contexts,' and follows Doina Petrescu's approach to feminist praxis where interdisciplinary practitioners are engaged to juxtapose various emergent positions.[31] As Petrescu suggests, these reconstructions alter identities and re-territorialise domains through 'subverting the critical division between "thinking" and "doing"'.[32] For example, the online Not Asking For It project in India focuses the crowd-sourced map on what women were wearing and their individual story of when and where the sex crime occurred, and collates personalised experiences beyond a number and a post or zip code. Not Asking For It reveals women's stories, the qualities of the city space in which the assault occurred and the artifacts of sexual violence. By including an important critique of the clothes worn by women (and with women uploading images of the ordinary and unsexualised clothes that they were wearing at the time of assault) the activist project draws into question and indeed, totally opposes, the notion that women 'ask for it.'[33] Outfits become artifacts of women's inequity and pose questions about who assumes responsibility for sexual violence.

Aspects of crowd-sourced gender activism intersect the discourses of urbanism, gender studies, policy and planning, psychology, politics and sociology. This activism reflects Petrescu's position that 'translations and trans-disciplinary moves' are a familiar and necessary feminist approach, as gender relations are difficult to contain within a single discipline.[34] Other earlier interdisciplinary approaches to urban space are valuable reminders of the longevity of the activist project via technology. In *Design and Feminism* by Joan Rothschild[35] and *The Sex of Architecture* by Diana Agrest, Patricia Conway, and Leslie Kanes Weisman,[36] examples are provided of the challenges of re-situating feminism and examining architecture in relation to media. The aim of these works, published twenty-five years ago, was to prompt new approaches to the ways that gender stereotypes manipulate and regulate the construction of gendered identity, encouraging 'critical contributions women can and must make as designers and users of created environments.'[37]

The acceptance and value given to crowd-sourced material reflect how cities are increasingly indistinguishable from technology, and that there is a need to reconceptualise both as a result. Scott McQuire suggests cities are undergoing a radical shift, and are intertwined with media to the point where the formation and structure of urban events are determined equally and reciprocally by urban spaces, networks and community.[38] Crowd sourcing reflects changes to how women occupy urban space, but also offers insight into feminist resistance in urban spaces, with the potential to shape cities that are 'more sensitive to the needs of a diverse population' and alert to aspects of space and culture that might be left out of design process and normative ideologies.[39]

Sara Rabie uses the word 'Crowd-Feminism' to describe the way that women are using crowd mapping as a tool for activism.[40] The results, for example from the *Everyday Sexism Project* in the UK in 2012, attest to the impact. *Everyday Sexism* has been collecting stories of women's experiences of sexual harassment and assault, and has helped to increase reporting of sexual assault. In London, this has led to a 40 per cent increase in summons and charges.[41] It is however, argued that the tool is not without bias and its application needs testing and refining. Political scientist Nicole Grove points out:

> Aerial targeting via crowd mapping and online mapping applications attempts
> to subject whole populations to scrutiny and intervention, and treats them as

targets that can, without careful scrutiny, be abstracted from political, cultural, and geographical contexts, thereby reducing difference that might otherwise highlight the moral and political ambiguity of the map.[42]

Yet the Free to Be map makes visible the violence in areas of Melbourne with precision. The analysis of the data undertaken by myself and the XYX Lab indicates how different sides of the same street – less then 20 metres apart – can have entirely different risks and tendencies for sex crimes against women and girls. The map also tracks women's and girls' paths of exclusion and avoidance in the city and identifies areas in need of intervention. The analysis then calls for preventative strategies to break through the cycles of cause and effect.

Through reflecting on Petrescu's 'thinking and doing,' and synthesizing the Free to Be data, the XYX Lab collaborated with Plan International Australia to convene a Design Thinking workshop. The event welcomed participants from all sectors of the community,

Figure 9.1 Workshop image of the Free to Be/Design Thinking co-design workshop undertaken by the Monash University XYX Lab and Plan International Australia. Image: XYX Lab, 2016. Copyright Nicole Kalms.

from different jobs, ages, ethnicities, and most importantly, with diverse experiences and different (even conflicting) perceptions of the same city – Melbourne. Harnessing the differences between people was a key objective of the workshop, and designing together helped individuals articulate and discuss their experiences and perceptions with empathy.

Municipal and state powers were held accountable and – as shown in our research – city councils, public transport service providers and designers were eager to participate in co-design workshops with women and girls, with the commitment to make Melbourne's urban spaces safer.[43] By the end of the workshop, more than fifty participants had proposed policy recommendations, physical and tangible interventions, digital or virtual ideas, and experiences and events aimed to support women's and girls' experiences in cities in response to the Free to Be project. Most importantly, the ideas developed throughout the workshop were co-created, and challenged the traditional ways that architects and designers propose and build cities. The XYX Lab instead relied upon the experts in room: each and every participant's own lived experiences of Melbourne, both personal and professional.

Conclusion

Mapping is a tool for governance, surveillance and knowledge.[44] Contemporary maps bring together social media technologies to create a tool that is able to adaptively perform a 'more discursive practice' rather than a singularly directed and passive one.[45] Crowd-sourced mapping connects the value of publicly driven data collection to spatial locations and women's experience of sexual violence. Crowd sourcing per se allows for large numbers of people to work on collective projects from diverse and distributed positions in cities and, indeed, across the globe.[46] Spatial mapping of violence clearly articulates areas of the city that can be publicly avoided, but more importantly, identifies locations that must be addressed by municipal, state or federal powers that have influence over urban planning. The identification of areas in need of safety interventions is not simply based on the socio-economic reputations of place, but on actual real time events. The growing potential of crowd mapping as a means to prompt early intervention has been identified; crowd sourcing is another form of a surveillance that utilises recent technological infrastructure to deploy resistance power in specific frameworks. Resistance in this regard is not a complete dismissal of the role of sovereign powers, but an undeniable shift in the global power hierarchy.[47]

The immediacy of updatable information leaves traditional media floundering for relevance when it comes to data relating to key societal problems such as gendered violence. With direct access to information pertaining to gendered violence, and the ability to contribute to the dialogue surrounding it, crowd sourcing provides both agency and power to women. In contrast, the individual safety Apps suggest agency yet lack connection to the larger systemic issues of sex crimes which violate women's physical integrity or autonomy.[48] Geolocative mapping should be considered as an approach that can support actions towards more gender-sensitive cities in which the risk of violence perpetrated against women no longer threatens their access to city life.

Notes

1 Janna Anderson and Lee Rainie, *The Future of Apps and Web*. www.pewinternet.org/2012/03/23/the-future-of-apps-and-web/ (accessed October 20, 2016).

2 Rachel Pain, 'Whither Women's Fear? Perceptions of Sexual Violence in Public and Private Space', *International Review of Victimology* 4, no. 4 (1997): cites the work of Conklin, 1975; Hough and Mayhew, 1983; Lewis and Salem, 1986; Smith, 1983 in 'Space, Sexual Violence and Social Control', *Progress in Human Geography*, 1991: 415.

3 Cindy Tarczon and Antonia Quadara, 'The nature and extent of sexual assault and abuse in Australia', ACSSA Resource Sheet No. 5 — December 2012, *Australian Institute of Family Studies*, 2012. Molly Johnson and Ebony Bennett, 'Everyday Sexism: Australian women's experiences of street harassment', (accessed December 2, 2016). www.tai.org.au/content/everyday-sexism2015.

4 Centre Against Sexual Assault. 'Fact Sheet and Statistics 2016', http://bit.ly/1NoBN1b (accessed February 2, 2017).

5 WHO, Australian Human Rights Commission, http://bit.ly/2neNX60 (accessed February 18, 2017).

6 Gita Neupane and Meda Chesny-Lind, 'Violence against women on public transport in Nepal: sexual harassment and the spatial expression of male privilege', *International Journal of Comparative and Applied Criminal Justine* 38:1 (2014): 23–28.

7 Plan International Australia 'A Right to the Night: Australian girls on their safety in public places', http://bit.ly/2n4IYE6 (accessed December 12, 2016).

8 Pain, 'Whither Women's Fear?', 300.

9 Johnson, Molly, and Ebony Bennett, 'Everyday Sexism: Australian women's experiences of street harassment', www.tai.org.au/content/everyday-sexism2015 (accessed December 2, 2016).

10 Manish Mada and Mahesh K. Nall. 'Sexual Harassment in Public Spaces: Examining Gender Differences in Perceived Seriousness and Victimization', *International Criminal Justice Review*, 26(2), 2016: 82.

11 Nancy Glass, Amber Clough, James Case, Ginger Hanson, Jamie Barnes-Hoyt, Amy Waterbury, Jeanne Alhusen, Miriam Ehrensaft, Karen Trister Grace and Nancy Perri, 'A safety app to respond to dating violence for college women and their friends: the MyPlan study randomized controlled trial protocol', *BMC Public Health* (2015) 15: 871.

12 Lisa Heffernan, 'Not Just Pepper Spray: Apps and Devices to Keep College Students Safe'. www.nbcnews.com/feature/college-game-plan/not-just-pepper-spray-Apps-devices-keep-college-students-safe-n563356 (accessed February 10, 2012).

13 Companion website. www.companionapp.io/ (accessed February 12, 2017).

14 The prevalence and normalisation of sexual assault has been termed 'rape culture'.

15 bSafe website, http://getbsafe.com/ (accessed February 21, 2017).

16 One under researched area is the way that safety Apps simultaneously (and problematically) mimic characteristics of relationships of intimate abuse, where perpetrators track women's movement and activities as a way to control and dominate with threatening behaviour.

17 bSafe website, http://getbsafe.com/ (accessed February 21, 2017).

18 In this study I have analysed bSafe, Companion App, Watch Over Me and Musketeer.

19 bSafe website, http://getbsafe.com/ (accessed February 21, 2017).

20 Cassandra Khaw, 'How one woman's abduction led to the Watch Over Me App', PC World, www.pcworld.com/article/2038644/how-one-womans-abduction-led-to-the-watch-over-me-App.html (accessed October 20, 2016).

21 Musketeer website, www.getmusketeer.com/ (accessed January 12, 2017).

22 Jessica Sier 'The frightening reality of how modern tech helps stalkers terrorise and harass', *The Financial Review*, www.afr.com/technology/web/the-frightening-reality-of-how-modern-tech-helps-stalkers-terrorise-and-harass-20170326-gv72pq#ixzz4eSFs75TZ (accessed April 3, 2017).

23 Hannah Verdier, 'Companion: the app that walks you home at night', *The Guardian*, November 2, 2015, www.theguardian.com/technology/shortcuts/2015/nov/01/companion-app-keep-you-safe-walk-home (accessed June 12, 2016).

24 Angela McRobbie describes post-feminism as playing directly into the hands of corporate consumer culture, *The Aftermath of Post-Feminism: Gender, Culture and Social Change* (Los Angeles: Sage, 2009), 158.

25 This is discussed by Rosalind Gill in 'Empowerment/Sexism', *Feminism and Psychology* 18, no. 42 (2008).

26 Laura Garcia-Favaro, 'Porn Trouble', *Australian Feminist Studies* 30, no. 86 (2016): 373.

27 'Change the story: A shared framework for the primary prevention of violence against women and their children', in *Australia. Our Watch*, Australia's National Research Organisation for Women's Safety (ANROWS) and VicHealth, 2015.

28 Nicole Sunday Grove, 'The cartographic ambiguities of HarassMap: Crowdmapping security and sexual violence in Egypt', *Security Dialogue*, Volume 46, 4: 2015, 346.

29 ElsaMarie D'silva, 'Safer cities with ICT? How crowd mapping can help stop sexual violence', *Vital Voices Global Partnerships*, www.vitalvoices.org/blog/2015/06/safer-cities-ict-how-crowd-mApping-can-help-stop-sexual-violence (accessed October 20, 2016).

30   Bianca Fileborn, 'Special Report', *Griffith Report Law and Violence*, Volume 2 (1): 2014.
31   Doina Petrescu, *Altering Practices: Feminist politics and Poetics of Space* (London: Routledge, 2007), xvii.
32   Doina Petrescu, *Altering Practices: Feminist politics and Poetics of Space* (London: Routledge, 2007), 5.
33   Diane Richardson and Hazel May 'Deserving Victims?: Sexual Status and the Social Construction of Violence', *The Sociological Review* 47, no. 2 (1999).
34   Doina Petrescu, *Altering Practices: Feminist politics and Poetics of Space* (London: Routledge, 2007), xvii.
35   Joan Rothschild, *Design and Feminism: Re-Visioning Spaces, Places, and Everyday Things* (New Brunswick, N.J: Rutgers University Press 1999).
36   Diana Agrest, Patricia Conway, Leslie Kanes Weisman, *The Sex of Architecture* (New York: Harry N. Abrams 1996).
37   Rothschild, *Design and Feminism*, 1.
38   Scott McQuire, *The Media City: Media, Architecture and Urban Space* (Melbourne: Sage, 2008).
39   Rothschild, *Design and Feminism*, 2.
40   Sara Rabie, *Crowd-Feminism: Crowdmapping as a Tool for Activism*, (Masters Thesis, Goldsmiths University, 2013).
41   Transport for London, '"Report it to Stop it" increases public confidence to report unwanted sexual behaviour', February 24, 2016, https://tfl.gov.uk/info-for/media/press-releases/2016/february/-report-it-to-stop-it-increases-public-confidence-to-report-unwanted-sexual-behaviour (accessed January 5, 2017).
42   Groves, 'The cartographic ambiguities of HarassMap', 360.
43   The XYX Lab conducted stakeholder workshops with Plan International Australia in March 2017. This work is the subject of a larger series of research projects.
44   Michel Foucault, *The History of Sexuality Volume 1: An Introduction*, translated by Robert Hurley (London: Allen Lane, 1979).
45   Beth Baron, *Egypt as a woman* (Berkeley: University of California Press, 2007), 2.
46   Jeremy W. Crampton, *Mapping: A critical introduction to cartography and GIS*, (Wiley-Blackwell: London, 2010).
47   Rabie, *Crowd-Feminism*, 2013.
48   Marianne Junger, 'Women's experiences of sexual harassment: Some implications for their fear of crime', *The British Journal of Criminology* 27, (1987): 364.

Chapter 10

Machinic architectural ecologies

An uncertain ground

Janet McGaw

Jennifer Bloomer's writing in the 1990s was largely concerned with what was 'othered' in architecture. 'The other' she defined as the secondary term in a range of binary pairs. In 'The Matter of the Cutting Edge', Bloomer considered the binaries of masculine/feminine, mind/body, form/matter, structure/ornament, objective/subjective, interpreting/making, avant-garde/nostalgic, clean/dirty . . . and the list went on.[1] At the heart of her essay was a concern that with the advent of computer aided design software, architecture had moved into infinite, rational, electronic space at the expense of the sensual, the material, and the corporeal. She argued that the endless search for the 'cutting-edge' by avant-garde architects was, ironically, an unrecognised and nostalgic desire for something never attainable, as unattainable as the primordial home, one's mother's womb. Her challenge to the field was to either invert the value systems so that what was 'othered' became the new territory for architects to play in or (and this was the final 'other') move to the garden where the binaries do not exist. It is in the garden, she proposed, that culture and nature intersect.

Over the past two decades architectural practice has challenged many of these distinctions: creative works are recognised in the academe as research practices and we write and think about making; surfaces have folded, curved, wrinkled, and perforated to become simultaneously structure and ornament; landscape and buildings have merged into constructed grounds. Borderlands of all varieties are increasingly liminal spaces for negotiation. Feminist theorists were instrumental in shifting the terrain in architectural discourse. But so too, (ironically, perhaps), was the binary code of computational design. Digital codes written in 1s and 0s are now enabling design to become more sensual, decorated, and corporeal. The last five years have been particularly fruitful. This chapter considers the growing body of experimental designs that slip between digital space and the material world: architecture where human designers enlist non-human biological and technological 'actants'[2] as co-creators. 'Hylozoic grounds',[3] 'material ecologies',[4] and 'protocellular architecture',[5] will be the focus.

I want to think about the slipperiness that exists in these borderlands, enlisting Donna Haraway's concepts of the 'cyborg'[6] and 'oddkin'[7] and Félix Guattari's concept of 'animal-, vegetable-, Cosmic-, and machinic-becomings'[8] as theoretical tropes. Guattari writes about the hope that emergent natural-technological ecologies offer to address the degradation of natural systems wrought by 'integrated world capitalism'. The 'cyborg' is a concept Haraway used to dismantle totalising theories but it is also a 'thick' description of our particular historical moment in which technologies are interior to humankind.[9] I am interested in Haraway's caution that 'cyborgs do not remember the Cosmos. They are the illegitimate offspring of militarism and patriarchal capitalism'[10] and as such, it would seem, they intrinsically present an ethical risk to natural ecosystems. In Haraway's most recent work she creatively imagines a future in which the cyborg is transformed through intimate relations with non-human living systems – she calls them 'oddkins' – so they not only remember the cosmos, but become creative actants in its restoration. Scientists like Tim Flannery have argued that it is too late for natural systems to re-calibrate without radical intervention by super-scale machinic ecologies.[11] But others have raised ethical concerns about the extent to which humans are meddling with natural processes. Protocells have been dubbed 'frankencells'[12] alluding to Frankenstein's monster who turns against its maker. Rachel Armstrong, co-director of the Advanced Virtual and Technological Architectural Research (AVATAR) group states that we are approaching an 'information singularity' where materials and technologies will emerge, evolve, and behave in unpredictable ways.[13] These are ethical dilemmas that need thinking through.

Architecture and the Anthropocene

There is broad acceptance in the scientific community that we are now living in a new geological age produced by anthropogenic interference in earth systems. It began with the Industrial Revolution in the late 18th century and entered what is known as 'The Great Acceleration' circa 1950. Since then graphs on a multiplicity of variables – soil degradation, species loss, carbon dioxide in the atmosphere, and growth in human population – follow exponential curves that continue despite recognition and global commitments to address them.[14] Peg Rawes has charted the architectural profession's response to the environmental crisis noting that the focus has been on improving environmental building performance and reducing operational energy consumption in buildings with little effect.[15] She argues that environmental discourse and practice in architecture needs to broaden to consider the complex and reflexive 'relational architectural ecologies' that exist between the material, cultural, social, and political.[16] That is, that environmental milieus are not only shaped by non-human living ecologies – soils, flora, fauna, and atmospheres – but by the broader socio-political and economic relationships that frame how these environments are valued and cared for. Our environmental crisis is human-made, and cannot be solved through technologies alone. Transformations to these other relational ecologies are also necessary.

It is a concept that recalls Guattari's 'three ecologies'. Guattari observed a 'nagging paradox': despite the continuous development of techno-scientific solutions to address environmental problems, political and economic forces seem to undermine them at every turn.[17] To respond to the ecological crisis, he argued, we need to cultivate an 'ecosophy' that takes in three ecological registers: social ecologies, mental ecologies, and environmental ecologies. He asserted that contemporary global capitalism produces social forces that consolidate power hierarchies, maximise profit to an empowered elite, and exclude minority groups at the expense of environmental conservation. Haraway concurs, preferring the term 'Capitalocence' to the 'Anthropocene',[18] for its foregrounding of the economies of greed that underpin the transformation to the earth. The consequent internalisation of these values by ordinary people, Guattari argues, has led to passivity, mental entrapment and a lack of belief that they have the power to make a difference.[19] What is necessary are new 'social ecologies' that radically decentre politics by rebuilding human relations; new 'mental ecologies' that emerge in contexts that support local, cultural, and interpersonal difference; and 'machinic ecologies', a variety of restorative technological interventions into dynamic environmental systems, from super-scale planetary and geo-engineering innovations to tackle climate change to small bio- and nano- engineering interventions in plant, animal, and human biological systems to address toxicity, food security, and failing health. In the future, Guattari argues, it will not be enough to defend nature; we will need to recreate it:

> The creation of new living species – animal and vegetable – looms inevitably on the horizon, and the adoption of an ecosophical ethics adapted to this terrifying and fascinating situation is equally as urgent as the invention of a politics focussed on the destiny of humanity.[20]

The work of architects and installation artists such as Philip Beesley, Neri Oxman, and Rachel Armstrong arguably do just this. Straddling the boundaries of computational design, material engineering, and biological systems, their designs fundamentally rethink human-environment relations. Neri Oxman is scripting with 'maxels'. Maxels are 'material voxels,'[21] a computer coding practice that dissolves the distinction between formal and material concerns. She is also using additive fabrication technologies to construct architecture from biological polymers. Philip Beesley is fabricating responsive, 'near living' environments which foster new socialities. Rachel Armstrong is working with protocells, which she anticipates can create materials that actively transform in response to environmental pressures. Protocells are chemical cells that exhibit life-like characteristics. All three conjure up religious and mythological references of the feminine when they discuss their work; Oxman refers to the Jewish scriptures, and Arabic and Greek mythology; Beesley draws on medieval Christian art and mysticism; Armstrong, Greek mythology. They beseech us to have faith and believe that their machinic ecologies will save us. Let's look a little closer at the new ecologies they propose and question the extent to which the transgression of boundaries between technological, human, and biological are liberationist practices, and the extent to which they pose new risks of anthropogenic transformations of the earth's biomes.

Hylozoic series

Architect and installation artist Philip Beesley's series of hylozoic works from 2007–2015 are an exploration of hylozoism, a philosophical construct that considers all matter to be alive. Using 'geotextile mesh', an intricate acrylic network supporting fronds and whiskers covered with proximity sensors, microcontrollers, and actuators, Beesley creates magical landscapes that react to human presence. Waves of light, soft murmuring sounds, and the movement of artificial feathers that respond as people move under their protective, forest-like canopies conjure up a sense of being alive. As Beesley explains: 'Hylozoic has Greek origins; it suggests that life comes out of material things, and it suggests that there are no strict boundaries between the inert matter of rock, gases and liquids, and living things. All things are potentially animate'.[22]

The series has had many iterations: 'Grounds', 'Groves', 'Soil', and 'Veils' at scales that range from garments, through interior installations, and environmental landscapes to urban interventions. Each has an immersive, diffuse, convoluted spatiality, and fragile, responsive, changeable materiality. The underlying armature of each installation is made from small interconnecting chevrons that comprise a net that can curve in three dimensions to form arches, vaults, and columns. Onto this are hitched a number of other responsive elements connected electronically using the open source software Arduino: feathers made from shape-memory alloys that contract, curling the feathers upward when a small current is passed through them; gland-like bladders containing chemical solutions that produce power; traps that impart humidity or contain salts that absorb moisture; lights, sounds, and kinaesthetic devices that are switched on by thousands of human motion sensors. It has, he claims, the intelligence of a 'swarm' and feels like it is a complex organism; a 'cloud' that appears to breathe, pulse, and sigh.

Aesthetically seductive, the sensory experience produces emotional responses in participants. With names like 'Vesica' that allude to spiritual auras and the transitional space between heaven and earth, and 'Sibyl', the female Greek oracle, Beesley seeks to invoke a sense of otherness. He acknowledges the precariousness of working at the boundaries of living systems but is quick to counteract the otherwise scary associations with the predatory triffids of science fiction, preferring to consider his works benign. The gentle motions that caress human participants, the soft murmurs of comfort, the warm lights that flicker in an otherwise darkened space seem to reinforce his contention. But is this sense of reassurance a deception? Let's hold this thought while we consider the work of Neri Oxman.

Material ecologies

While Beesley's hylozoic series are machinic-ecological assemblages, complex wholes made from an array of varied component parts, Neri Oxman describes her work with the

Mediated Matter Group at MITs Media Lab on a trajectory away from synthetic assemblage towards technologies modelled on organic growth. Just as each living cell carries the genetic code of a whole organism, her complex forms begin with a simple digital code. And just as organisms grow, so too do her material designs. The algorithm directs the nozzle of a 3D printer to squirt a single, tangled line of matter that grows into a complex, holey solid. Most digital printers use petroleum-based plastics. Oxman experiments with organic materials: chitin, a biopolymer found in the exoskeletons of crustaceans, calcium and other minerals, bacteria, and silk.

Imaginary Beings: Mythologies of the Not Yet, (2012) developed in collaboration with W. Craig Carter and inspired by Jorge Luis Borges' *Book of Imaginary Beings* is a collection of part-animal and part-mythological designs that augment the human body. *Medusa*, a protective helmet, its naming recalling the mythical female Gorgon, is an ultra lightweight construction with increased mechanical strength due to its perforated, wrinkled, and folded surface. Brain-augmented electrodes are imagined to be incorporated into its material fabric to interact with the electrical impulses in neurological circuits to increase the cognitive performance of the wearer. *Remora*, a corset or hip splint, attaches itself to the pelvic region with barnacle-like cellular 'suction cups' to promote circulation within bodily arteries, veins and capillaries. It is modelled on and named after the symbiotic sucker-fish that travels with sharks. *Arachné*, named after the weaver who was transformed into a spider by the goddess Athena, is a web-like corset of soft flexible material filled with stiff cells that protects the muscles between the ribs and enhances and augment movement within the chest wall. These architectural forms are closer to prostheses than shelter, technologically augmenting the (female) human body, in the spirit of Haraway's cyborg, to enable it to better adapt to new and changing environmental conditions. They equally celebrate the curvaceous sensuousness and particularity of the female form, challenging the dominance of male figures – from Vitruvian to Modulor man – in architectural discourse and practice.

The *Wanderers: Astrobiological Explorations* (aka 'wonderers') series (2014), developed in collaboration with Christoph Bader and Dominik Kolb, are musings on a mythical future of astronomical roaming on planets with hostile atmospheres, temperatures, and gravitational forces. This series of 'wearables' are conceived for different planetary contexts and recall, through their namings, the ancient Arabic art-science of astronomy. *Mushtari: Jupiter's Wonderer* are modelled on the human gastrointestinal tract, hosting colonies of photosynthetic cyanobacteria (which converts light into sugar) and E. coli microorganisms. Not only will they protect the (again, female) body from environmental variation, they produce colonies of bacteria that can sustain bodies and repair damaged tissue.[23] *Otaared: Mercury's Wonderer*, is a 3D printed exoskeleton designed to contain calcifying bacteria. The formal design is parametrically developed from the shape of a woman's scapulae and sternum and is a prototype for a bony exoskeleton. These later design explorations move beyond technological augmentation to imagine new techno-biological couplings.

Oxman has also extended the collaboration beyond bacterial life. Perhaps inspired by research for the earlier *Arachné* project, in which she observed that 'spider spinnerets are the antecedents of multi-material printers',[24] Oxman enlists silk-worms as co-creators of a 'Silk Pavilion'.[25] Attaching sensors to silkworms, she was able to program robotic arms to mimic their weaving pattern and manipulate a silk thread into a woven, domed structure. She then co-opted the labour of 6,500 silk worms, raised in her laboratory, to thicken the web. The worms constructed their cocoons, metamorphosed into moths and left leaving eggs for a next generation of weavers behind. Unlike sericulture, the industry that creates silk fabric, which boils silkworms so that they do not perforate their cocoons damaging thread on the way out, not a single silkworm was deliberately killed for her pavilion.

Neri and her collaborators' ambiguous, polemical pieces challenge architecture to think beyond traditional forms of shelter. Enlisting non-human biological actants as co-creators – organic and machinic – they design interventions that grow out of and interact intimately with the varied specificities of the human body. The vision of these prostheses is to respond rapidly and instinctively to the intensities and unpredictability of environmental changes predicted for our planet.

Protocellular architecture

Aspects of Oxman and Beesley's current experiments with metabolic processes are built on research into protocells led by Rachel Armstrong and Neil Spiller. A protocell is an artificial cell-like system that is able to self-maintain, self-reproduce, and potentially evolve. Although not actually alive, it is a chemical ensemble that behaves in ways that resemble living things. While there is disagreement over whether protocells even exist yet, Spiller and Armstrong assert the protocell model is the first technology that can challenge the top-down imperatives of DNA, modeling a new evolutionary process.[26]

Armstrong's current project is Project Persephone, a collaboration with the Icarus Interstellar Foundation. It is a design in evolution for a living starship 'grown from the ground up' with artificial soils made from protocells that are responsive and evolutionary.[27] Unlike Oxman's speculative and fantastical Wanderer garments, the collaborators imagine Persephone will become a reality by 2100, its machinic 'living' environment able to support humans in space for hundreds of years.

Protocells are unlike any previous technology and as a consequence their development has unknown consequences. Just like splitting the atom yielded both cheap, abundant energy and weapons of mass destruction, so too do protocells present equally contrasting prospects. Their benefits to the building industry include self-repairing materials, films that deploy to protect against corrosion, and chemical sensors that can drive autonomous, adaptive systems. With the prospect of unpredictable environmental futures, smart, responsive building materials architecture that can sense changes to their surroundings and transform themselves are appealing.[28] Armstrong imagines protocells deploying in the watery foundations of Venice, for example, to grow an artificial reef that props up the sinking city. Oxman, on the other hand, imagines personal microbiomes that will repair damaged skin.

But as Mark Bedau and Emily Parke caution, there are equally reasons to believe that protocells pose risks to human health and earth systems for two reasons:

protocells self-replicate and therefore any danger would be magnified; and protocells evolve, changing in ways their creators could never predict, including competing with existing life forms, and resisting eradication. Bill Joy imagines that exponential advances in protocells along with nano-technology and genetic engineering have the potential to infiltrate and damage living cells:

> Tough omnivorous 'bacteria' could outcompete real bacteria: They could spread like blowing pollen, replicate swiftly, and reduce the biosphere to dust in a matter of days. Dangerous replicators could easily be too tough, small, and rapidly spreading to stop . . . We have trouble enough controlling viruses and fruit flies.[29]

Bedau and Parke believe Joy's speculations to be naive and uninformed, but they do acknowledge that there are ethical risks that we have not even begun to explore.[30]

Despite these concerns, development marches on. Multi-million dollar grants are funding research and development of protocellular, artificial life forms, according to Miller and Gulbis, and commercially viable production looks like it is only a decade away. That protocellular research is now being controlled by commercial interests should raise concerns.[31] Guattari has warned that history has shown contemporary global capitalism to be driven by profit rather than ethics, usually at the expense of environmental conservation.

Ecosophies of hope? Or new practices of environmental subjugation?

At the outset of this chapter I said I wanted to occupy the slippery, liminal space between the digital and the material. I will hold the discomfort and the anxiety that these speculations raise, and resist taking an easy route out via a path of technophobia too quickly, which has often been the approach of feminist theorists,[32] I am prepared to accept Haraway and Guattari's argument that we are to some extent already cyborgs; machinic ecologies in which human-animal-vegetable and technological coincide. However I do want us to consider the ethical implications of transgressing boundaries between human and other non-human living systems. It is not an either-or argument, rather one of thinking through degrees.

Two decades ago theorists like Bloomer and Haraway could not foresee the extent to which digital technologies could be transformed in a generation. Computer aided design, from Bloomer's perspective, was all about lightness, immateriality, and an unrecognised homesickness for *mater*.[33] The virtual needed to be resisted by way of the garden, a place of mess and uncontrollability. 'A Cyborg Manifesto' was the first paper Haraway ever wrote using a personal computer while the internet was in its infancy.[34] Although Haraway was interested in 'thick' description of real-life relationships between humans and technology, the concept of the cyborg in the 1990s was primarily a rhetorical device for critiquing binary ways of thinking. Bloomer is sadly no longer in a position to continue to contribute to the discourse, but Haraway's theoretical and creative journey has meandered and charged in new and original directions knitting together her varied interests in zoology, biology, linguistics, and philosophy to imagine the material world ever-differently. Two key concerns compel her forward: the exponential projections of human population growth to 11 billion by the century's end, unsustainable by most scientists' measures, and the projected loss of 'refugias' – places of complex and diverse species from which biological life can re-emerge after catastrophes through anthropogenic destruction. How to imagine a future with these dire predictions? Like Bloomer, she reconsiders the material world of the garden:

> Matter is never 'mere' medium to the 'informing' seed; rather in terra's carrier bag, kin and get have a much richer congress for worlding . . . Matter mater, mutter, make me – make us, that collective gathered in the narrative bag of the Chthulucene – stay with the naturalcultural multispecies trouble on earth.[35]

Haraway's garden is reimagined through creative, collaborative writing – a 'muttering' - with filmmaker Fabrizio Terranova and psychologist, philosopher and ethologist, Vinciane Despret, in a Narration Spéculative workshop at an Isabelle Stengers colloquium.[36] Haraway describes the approach as an SF writing practice, an acronym that conjures multiple pairings: science fiction, speculative fabulations, speculative feminisms and string figures, a Navajo story telling method coupled with images woven, unwoven and re-woven in string by the two hands of the story teller. Together they fabricate a tale of five generations in which new relational ecologies between humans, non-human and technological critters evolve to produce a depopulation of human species and recreation of refugias. Camille 1 emerges in 2025 as an act of radical hope amidst the environmental and social crises that are unfolding in our present. What distinguishes the Camilles 1 through 5 is a decision by the community within which she is born to 'choose kin' rather than 'make babies'. Kin include at least three parents for every child and a chosen migratory animal symbiont, whose genetic code is selectively implanted into the child.

The Camille stories chart a future that uncannily circles back on ancient pasts, remaking Indigenous ways of knowing, living and being: kinship networks that include animal totems and practices of environmental care and nurture. The significant point of divergence is the connection with the non-human living world in Indigenous cultures practiced through observation, ceremony, reciprocity and respect. In Camille's world, the relationship is also genetic: an 'oddkin' coupling.[37] While Haraway and her collaborators coin the term 'animal symbiont', suggesting a mutually beneficial relationship between co-evolving critters, I can't help but wonder if it as a new form of colonisation: not of land, but of bodies and genomes.

While Haraway explores the garden through the creative and imaginative practice of speculative fictions, Beesley, Oxman and Armstrong explore similar concepts through an expanded architectural practice. In each of these practices, design authorship is no longer singular but enacted through a collaboration between social, technological and biological actants. Materials are no longer inert but are responsive and changeable. There is a reflexive relationship between virtual and real to produce dynamic, complex machinic ecologies. Bodies are augmented by machines and other living ecological systems – messy, unpredictable, micro-biological gardens. These architectures are material, sensual, organic and corporeal – I'm thinking here of Oxman's chitin wings, bodily prostheses, woven silken shells, and Beesley's warm, embracing 'near-living' architectures. But there are also concerning moments where they seem to slip beyond the earth's gravitational pull and depart from the cellular building blocks of organic life. Oxman's extra-terrestrial garments and Armstrong's starships grown from artificial, protocellular soils seem to give up on their ambitions for a sustainable environmental future, preferring to escape the 'gravity/*gravida*' of '*mater*' earth to start all over again.[38]

Bloomer, I think, had it right all along: the way out of our current dilemmas is still by way of the garden. As designers, now more than ever, we must choose to exercise an ethic and aesthetic of respect for earth's many and diverse eco-systems, protecting the few remaining refugias we still have. But nostalgia for a lost Garden of Eden will not bring it back. As Haraway says, we have no option but to stay with the trouble we have made for ourselves. A designer's task now is to invent new machinic ecologies for intervening, whilst being ever wary of just how far she should go in messing with the building blocks of life.

Notes

1 Jennifer Bloomer, 'The Matter of the Cutting Edge', *Assemblage*, No. 27, Tulane Papers: The Politics of Contemporary Architectural Discourse, August 1995: 106–111.
2 The term 'actant' is used in Actor-Network Theory to describe both human and non-human actors in a network of relationships.
3 Philip Beesley, 'Being Responsive,' *Architecture Australia*, Vol 101, No. 5. (2012): 84–85.
4 Neri Oxman, 'Material Ecology' in *Theories of the Digital in Architecture*, eds. Rivka Oxman and Robert Oxman (London: Routledge, 2014), 319–326.
5 Neil Spiller and Rachel Armstrong, *Protocell Architecture, Architectural Design*, Vol. 81, Iss. 2. (London: John Wiley & Sons Ltd, 2011).
6 Donna Haraway, 'A Cyborg Manifesto: Science, Technology and Socialist-Feminism in the Late Twentieth Century' in *Simians, Cyborgs, and Women: The Reinvention of Nature* (New York: Routledge, 1996), 181.
7 Donna Haraway, *Staying with the Trouble: Making Kin in the Chthulucene* (Durham and London: Duke University Press, 2016), 145,
8 Félix Guattari, *Three Ecologies* trans. I. Pindar and P. Sutton (London and New Brunswick: Athlone Press, 2000). Original work published 1989.
9 Hari Kunzru, 'Donna Haraway Interview Transcript, 1996', 2009. Available at www.harikunzru.com/archive/donna-haraway-interview-transcript-1996 (accessed 20 October 2016).
10 Haraway, 'A Cyborg Manifesto', 151.
11 Tim Flannery, *Atmospheres of Hope: Searching for Solutions to the Climate Crisis* (Melbourne: The Text Publishing Company, 2015).
12 Mark Bedau and Emily Parke, 'Social and Ethical Issues Concerning Protocells' in *Protocells: Bridging Nonliving and Living Matter*, eds. Rasmussen *et al* (Cambridge, Mass. And London: MIT Press, 2009), 644.
13 Rachel Armstrong, 'The Post-epistemological Details of Oceanic Ontologies' *Architectural Design* Vol. 84. Iss. 4. (2014): 113.
14 The United Nations Brundtland Report 1987, The Kyoto Protocol 1992, The Climate Change Conference in Copenhagen 2009, The Doha Amendment 2012 and the Paris Agreement 2015.
15 Peg Rawes, *Relational Architectural Ecologies: Architecture, Nature and Subjectivity* (London: Routledge, 2013).
16 Rawes, *Relational Architectural Ecologies*, 10.
17 Guattari, *Three Ecologies*, 31.
18 Haraway, *Staying with the Trouble*, 47–51.
19 Guattari, *Three Ecologies*.
20 Guattari, *Three Ecologies*, 66–67.
21 Oxman, 'Material Ecology', 322.

22 Beesley, 'Being Responsive', 84–85.

23 Hari Mendoza, 'Neri Oxman Creates Wearable Skin Embedded with Organisms Using 3D Printing Tech from Stratasys', May 13, 2013. Available at www.3dprint.com/65025/neri-oxman-skin/ (accessed 30 March 2016).

24 Neri Oxman, 'Arachne (Autoportrait / Self Portrait) 2012' *Neri Oxman: Projects*. Available at www.neri. media.mit.edu/ (accessed 20 October 2016).

25 Neri Oxman, J. Laucks, M. Kayser, J. Duro-Royo, C. Gonzales-Uribe, 'Silk Pavilion: A Case Study in Fiber-based Digital Fabrication', *FABRICATE: Negotiating Design and Making* Conference Proceedings, eds. Fabio Gramazio, Matthias Kohler, Silke Lan enber ta Verla, 2014, 248–255.

26 Neil Spiller and Rachel Armstrong, *Protocell Architecture*.

27 Rachel Armstrong, 'Black Sky Thinking', Available at www.blackskythinking.org/ (accessed 20 October 2016).

28 Philip Beesley, N. Yen-Wen Cheng, R.S. Williamson, 'Introduction' in *Fabrication: Examining the Digital Practice of Architecture* (Toronto: Coach House Press), Proceedings of the 2004 AIA/ACADIA Fabrication Conference 8–13 November, 2004. Cambridge and Toronto, Ontario, Canada.

29 Bill Joy, 'Why the future does not need us', *Wired, 8* (April 2000) www.wired.com/2000/04/joy-2/

30 Mark Bedau and Emily Parke, 'Social and Ethical Issues Concerning Protocells', *Protocells: Bridging Nonliving and Living Matter*, ed. Rasmussen et al. (Cambridge, Mass. and London: MIT Press, 2008), 641–655.

31 David Miller and Jacqueline Gulbis, 'Engineering Protocells: Prospects for Self-Assembly and Nanoscale Production-Lines', *Life (2075–1729)* Vol. 5 Iss. 2, (2015) 1019–1053, DOI: 10.3390/life5021019.

32 Sadie Plant, 'Learning and Building in the Feminine' in *Altering Practices,* ed. Doina Petrescu (London: Routledge, 2007), 297–306.

33 Bloomer, 'The Matter of the Cutting Edge'; Bloomer, 'The Unbearable Being of Lightness' in D. Petrescu, ed., *Altering Practices: Feminist Politics and Poetics of Space* (London and New York: Routledge: 2007), 288.

34 Kunzru, 'Donna Haraway Interview Transcript, 1996'.

35 Haraway, *Staying with the Trouble*, 120–121.

36 Haraway, *Staying with the Trouble*, 134.

37 Haraway, *Staying with the Trouble*, 3.

38 Bloomer, 'The Unbearable Being of Lightness', 288.

Project 4

Gender and anonymous peer review

Sandra Kaji-O'Grady

Academia is sometimes perceived as a kind of sanctuary for women and minorities, at least relative to architectural practice. It is not just that most universities have equal opportunity policies and practices, but that the western intellectual foundation of academe privileges intellectual work as a disembodied activity. In academia what one thinks and writes is supposed to count for more than one's identity or physical appearance. One of the perceived advantages for academic women has been that the pressure to conform to societal expectations of femininity can seem less than in many other professions. The historian Mary Beard's looks, for example, had little bearing on her impressive academic career but became the subject of misogynist ridicule when she appeared as a television presenter for the BBC2 program 'Meet the Romans'. Of course, the idea that only one's intellect counts in academia has never actually been true – the fact that Beard is white, English, public-schooled and respectably married to an art historian educated at the Courtauld most likely helped her a great deal. Being a woman, however, probably didn't make her path easy. Indeed, Beard recalls that she discovered active discrimination against women when she arrived at Cambridge as a student.[1] Few women survived as well as she did. At the University of Cambridge, where Beard is Professor of Classics, women account for less than sixteen per cent of the professoriate.[2] So much for the mythology of the university as a place for bright women to escape gender inequity.

According to a report by Universities UK titled *Patterns and Trends in UK Higher Education 2015*, white women make up almost twenty-one per cent of professors in the UK and black and minority ethnic women less than two per cent. There are just seventeen black female professors in the UK, but the nation is not an outlier. Women similarly hold just eighteen per cent of full professorships in Europe.[3] The figures are comparable for the US and Australia but even more dire in less socially-progressive industrialized societies such as Japan, where women represent less than thirteen per cent of academics at all levels at the nation's top-rated universities.[4] And everywhere, as a 2016 American Council on Education report found, 'men make more than women at every rank, in every discipline.'[5] At Harvard University, for example, in the 2013–2014 academic year, male full-time professors on average were paid about US $15,000 more than female full professors.[6]

Some argue that there isn't the pipeline of women holding doctoral degrees who are qualified to enter academia, yet women receive slightly more than fifty per cent of the doctorates awarded by American universities and have done so for the past decade.[7] Recently more women have been graduating from universities than men in Europe, North America and Australia. According to a 2016 report by the Higher Education Policy Institute, men are currently less likely than women to go to British universities, those who do are more likely to drop out and those who complete their course are less likely to get a good degree. On the other hand, there are fewer women than men at the top of the academic hierarchy, those women are paid less and are less likely to hold a tenure track position, and, what's more, they are much less likely than men to have had children. It becomes clear that participation in universities, be it as a student or an academic, is not a measure of one's intellect or scholarly aptitude, but a complex reflection of cultural practices and policy as they intersect with identity. The picture is even more complex when we take into account the variations between disciplines. The proportion of women academics in mathematics and engineering, for example, is outrageously low. And in the arts, where women are often found in higher numbers, it varies between institutions. At the Royal College of Art, for example, women make up forty-seven per cent of its academic staff, but only twenty-five per cent of its professoriate.[8]

There has been one academic domain, however, in which identity is – ostensibly – irrelevant. The double-blind peer review process. Peer review was introduced to scholarly publication in 1731 by the Royal Society of Edinburgh to ensure the maintenance of intellectual standards and objectivity. Double-blind peer review is when neither the authors nor the reviewers are aware of the others' identities. Authors tend to believe – for obvious reasons – double-blind reviews are less biased than single-blind. Advocates of double-blind peer review argue that it eliminates biases based on gender, ethnicity, seniority, standing in a research community and affiliation. It enables the disadvantage that accrues to some individuals in society to remain outside the question of the quality of the academic contribution. Despite instances of corruption and bias, anonymous peer review has enabled minority and emerging voices to be heard. But many journals, especially in science, medicine and economics, practice single-blind review where the reviewers are aware of the authors' identities, but the authors are not aware of the reviewers' identities. *Nature*, the peak international journal of science, only introduced double-blind peer review in 2015, and then as an option for contributing authors. It did so in the face of evidence of the impact of involuntary bias at work in science communication. When the journal *Behavioral Ecology* introduced double-blind peer review, they experienced an increase of thirty-three per cent in the representation of female authors.[9] It may be that women now felt more comfortable about submitting work, but research suggests that it is more likely that their work was now more fairly reviewed. One recent experiment had participants rate conference abstracts ostensibly authored by females or males, with author associations rotated. Publications from male authors were associated with greater scientific quality, and especially so if they worked on topics perceived to be masculine.[10]

Academic publishing is under pressure, however, and with it double-blind peer review. Journals and small publishers are being gathered up by large commercial publishing conglomerates, with the result that academic books are becoming increasingly costly and rare. Many journals are charging authors for the privilege of publishing, and then charging readers, too. Online publishing offers quicker and shorter routes to larger audiences. In theory, online open publishing leads to a greater diversity of texts, challenges the commercialization of knowledge and provides open access to both readers and authors. It can give readers and authors the opportunity to engage in a dialogue that approximates the 'chat-room'. These new modes are increasingly important in promotion and in justification of one's research in terms of impact and engagement.

In the context of formulating new approaches to academic publication, anonymized peer review has come under attack. The review process is thought to slow the dissemination of knowledge. It is also seen by some to stifle risky ideas, with reviewers producing a kind of normalizing or gatekeeper effect on ideas and experimental modes of research and writing. Authors are at the liberty of reviewers whose comments they cannot refute and this, too, is seen to suppress difference and debate. Building on this critique, MIT Media Lab's new *Journal of Design Science*, declares itself an experiment in 'radical transparency', with almost every part of the journal open and editable. Readers can annotate each paper, adding comments and context to what the author wrote. The editing history is visible to everyone, so authorship is no longer an opaque attribution. Reviewers are known and accountable. It sounds liberating but is such a model actually politically radical or will it replicate social inequity?

Many of the newer forms of disseminating research, for example, the TED talk, advantage individuals with English as a first language and with the social skills and the confidence that social privilege and a quality education bring. Of the speakers named in 2014 by blog site ArchDaily as the '20 most inspiring TED talks for Architects', it is telling that just three are women and nineteen are white. Indeed, it is arguable that novel modes of publishing academic research will see intellectual discourse narrowed precisely *because* identities are known. One way to test this argument in our field is to examine the impacts of different modes of review as they currently play out in print journals. It is possible to do because we already have scholarly publications in architecture that operate with models of review where the author's identity is known, and others where anonymity is maintained during review. To understand the impact of these different modes, recent issues of eight leading English-language journals in the field of the architectural humanities were examined for the gender of their contributors and the results graphically represented.

The grey area of the pie charts represents male authors, and the white female authors. It's a quick and dirty analysis that counts every contributor, sole or co-author, as equal since it would take considerable resources to determine the proportionate contribution of co-authored papers. A subtler analysis would unlikely change the results significantly, though, as co-authorship is as prevalent for men as women and the same counting method was used for all journals and both genders. Curiously, co-authorship in architectural discourse as pairs tends to be between authors of the same sex, but that is a puzzle for another time.

Contributions to three of the journals – *AA Files*, *Log* and *Volume* – are reviewed by an editor, guest editor or editorial board without anonymity. *Architecture and Culture*, *Architecture Research Quarterly*, *The Journal of Architecture, the Journal of Architectural Education* and *Footprint* use double-blind peer review process. All journals are open to submissions, but each of them rely heavily on solicitation, actively courting authors for special issues. Some of this encouragement is direct, some is through networks and venues where prospective authors might be found. A marked gendered difference of authorship in the discipline's journals is evident and seems to relate to how contributors are engaged and their work reviewed. This is most clearly apparent when one compares the *AA Files* to *The Journal of Architectural Education*. The *AA Files* averages twenty-three per cent women authors over eight recent issues, dating from May 2013 to December 2016. As you can see, 2015 was a particularly grim year for women in the *AA Files*, with its three issues averaging less than fourteen per cent female authors. This, however, is a solid effort compared with the bad old days of 2011 when issue 62 arrived with just one woman out of twenty contributors (and that author, Baroness Vivien Stern, while impressive in her research field of penal reform, is not an architectural scholar). The proportion of women publishing in *The Journal of Architectural Education* over its past seven issues, from March 2014 to March 2016, stands at forty-three per cent, almost double that of the *AA Files*.

The representation of women in the Architectural Association's flagship journal and its other scholarly publications suggests a social conservatism quite at odds with its status as a center of avant-garde thinking and design experimentation. The AA lists on its website all those in employed in its academic mission, from casual tutors and consultants, to studio leaders and continuing faculty – an impressive 251 people drawn from all over the world. Just thirty-five per cent of these are women. Yet, the proportion of women contributors in the *AA Files* does not even reflect women's participation in its home institution. It is unlikely that this is because women's writing, thinking or designing is of inferior quality, or that women are not interested in publishing in that venue. Either women do not submit to the *AA Files* at the rates they do to *JAE*, or they have higher rejection rates than men. Or both. My suspicion is that editors solicit work from individuals in their personal and professional networks and that unconscious bias creeps into this process. The social visibility afforded to men sees them more likely to be noticed by and, perhaps more importantly, recommended to the editor. The involuntary bias that saw scientific papers ranked differently according to the perceived gender of their author (by both men and women) is likely also at work in architecture as papers are procured, and then, again, as they are reviewed by the editor. Thus, we see that there is little difference between *Log* and the *AA Files*, despite one having a female editor, the other a male editor. One can only speculate on the loss of content. The *Journal of Architectural Education*, by comparison, has a large board of sixteen members. The current Executive Editor, Marc Neveu, has actively pursued candidates for the board with a diversity of geography, expertise, gender and race. This means that the editorial board's reach goes beyond a small circle of academics attached to elite institutions. Anonymity of peer review subsequently guarantees quality and prevents bias entering at this stage. Neveu argues that the board's breadth is simply because 'we are the journal of the ACSA.'[11] The ACSA is a nonprofit association of over 200 member schools in the US and Canada, representing over 5,000 faculty. The ACSA cites equity, diversity and inclusiveness as its core values, alongside creative scholarship, research and practice.

My quick analysis suggests that in architecture, as in other fields, anonymity decouples scholarly work from the identity of the scholar and in doing so, goes some way to mitigating against gender bias. It is the academic equivalent of the famous switch to blind auditions at the New York Philharmonic Orchestra that saw increased representation of women from ten per cent to forty-five per cent.[12] On the other hand, an editorial board or editor motivated to include authors outside a narrow group of established male scholars and practitioners could make a positive difference for both author diversity and the richness of intellectual contribution. Aggregate Architectural History Collaborative, for example, have opted for a dual system of transparent and double-blind peer review at the discretion of the author, and denote which process a paper has undergone on its publication. Their very active model of solicitation and inclusion has seen women's participation in its publications reach forty-four per cent.

How review processes suppress or elicit content is something we need to keep in mind when we take on editorial board roles, when we edit anthologies or journals, when we act as referees and when we submit our work for academic publication. Incrementally, the impact of even a small bias in journals translates into large impacts on women's career progress over time. It is one of the things at play in the diminishing proportion of women in academia as we move from junior, untenured roles to the professoriate. These biases are repeated in the context of grant proposals, promotion and tenure reviews and hiring decisions. Anyone committed to intellectual quality should advocate for the removal of bias against minority voices in this critical area of academic life. One way to actively make a difference would be for male colleagues to apply Jeremy Till's '30 percent pledge' to their own participation in academic journals and other multi-authored publications.[13]

Notes

1   Robert Crum, 'Up Pompei with the Roguish Don', *The Observer*, August 24, 2008, accessed February 1, 2016, www.theguardian.com/books/2008/aug/24/classics

2   See Jack Grove, 'Gender Survey of UK Professoriate, 2013', *Times Higher Education*, June 13, 2013, accessed March 20, 2017, www.timeshighereducation.com/news/gender-survey-of-uk-professoriate-2013/2004766.article

3   Isabelle Vernos, 'Research Management: Quota are Questionable', *Nature* 495, no. 7439 (2013): 39.

4   Jack Grove, 'Global Gender Index, 2013', *Times Higher Education*, May 2, 2013.

5   Heather L. Johnson, *Pipelines, Pathways, and Institutional Leadership: An Update on the Status of Women in Higher Education* (Washington, DC: American Council on Education, 2016), 9, www.acenet.edu/news-room/Documents/Higher-Ed-Spotlight-Pipelines-Pathways-and-Institutional-Leadership-Status-of-Women.pdf

6   Based on a database of faculty salaries compiled by The Chronicle of Higher Education and reported in Samantha Allen, 'Ivy League Stiffs Its Female Profs', *The Daily Beast*, April 9, 2015, www.thedailybeast.com/articles/2015/04/09/ivy-league-stiffs-its-female-profs.html

7 Johnson, *Pipelines, Pathways, and Institutional Leadership.*

8 Jack Grove, 'Gender Survey of UK Professoriate, 2013', June 13, 2013, Appendix 1, *Times Higher Education*, 'Academic Staff Full Time Equivalent by Institution, Professorial Status and Gender 2011/2012,', www.timeshighereducation.com/news/gender-survey-of-uk-professoriate-2013/2004766. article

9 Amber Budden et al., 'Double-blind Review Favours Increased Representation of Female Authors', *Trends in Ecology and Evolution* 23, no. 1 (2008): 4–6.

10 Silvia Knobloch-Westerwick et al., 'The Matilda Effect in Science Communication: An Experiment in Gender Bias in Publication Quality Perceptions and Collaboration Interest,', *Science Communication* 35, no. 5 (2013): 603–625.

11 Email to author, February 16, 2017.

12 Claudia Goldin and Cecilia Rouse, 'Orchestrating Impartiality: The Impact of "Blind" Auditions on Female Musicians,' *The American Economic Review* 90, no. 4 (2000): 715–741.

13 Jeremy Till, '30 percent Pledge', www.jeremytill.net/read/86/30-pledge

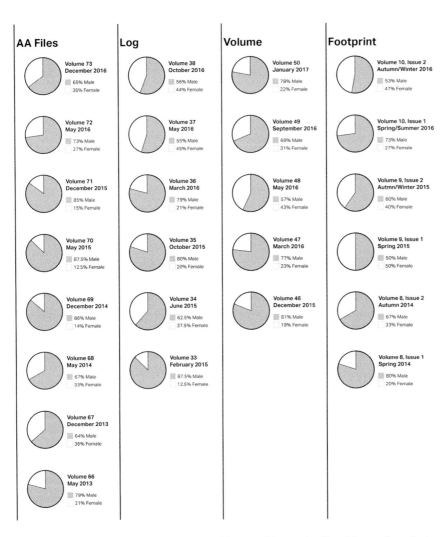

AA Files

Volume 73
December 2016
65% Male
35% Female

Volume 72
May 2016
73% Male
27% Female

Volume 71
December 2015
85% Male
15% Female

Volume 70
May 2015
87.5% Male
12.5% Female

Volume 69
December 2014
86% Male
14% Female

Volume 68
May 2014
67% Male
33% Female

Volume 67
December 2013
64% Male
36% Female

Volume 66
May 2013
79% Male
21% Female

Log

Volume 38
October 2016
56% Male
44% Female

Volume 37
May 2016
55% Male
45% Female

Volume 36
March 2016
79% Male
21% Female

Volume 35
October 2015
80% Male
20% Female

Volume 34
June 2015
62.5% Male
37.5% Female

Volume 33
February 2015
87.5% Male
12.5% Female

Volume

Volume 50
January 2017
78% Male
22% Female

Volume 49
September 2016
69% Male
31% Female

Volume 48
May 2016
57% Male
43% Female

Volume 47
March 2016
77% Male
23% Female

Volume 46
December 2015
81% Male
19% Female

Footprint

Volume 10, Issue 2
Autumn/Winter 2016
53% Male
47% Female

Volume 10, Issue 1
Spring/Summer 2016
73% Male
27% Female

Volume 9, Issue 2
Autmn/Winter 2015
60% Male
40% Female

Volume 9, Issue 1
Spring 2015
50% Male
50% Female

Volume 8, Issue 2
Autumn 2014
67% Male
33% Female

Volume 8, Issue 1
Spring 2014
80% Male
20% Female

Project 4 Gender of authors in eight architectural journals. Graphics and analysis by Malakai Smith, 2017.

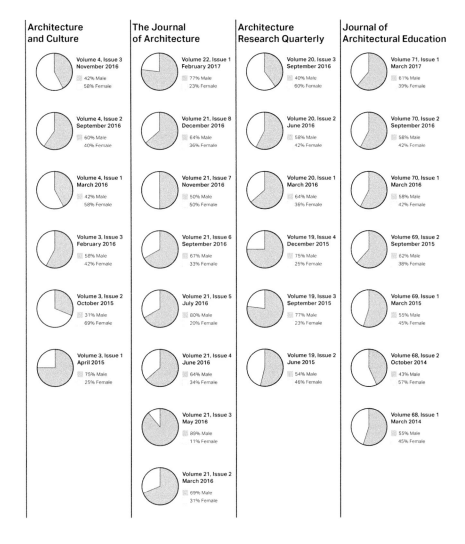

Architecture and Culture

Volume 4, Issue 3
November 2016
42% Male
58% Female

Volume 4, Issue 2
September 2016
60% Male
40% Female

Volume 4, Issue 1
March 2016
42% Male
58% Female

Volume 3, Issue 3
February 2016
58% Male
42% Female

Volume 3, Issue 2
October 2015
31% Male
69% Female

Volume 3, Issue 1
April 2015
75% Male
25% Female

The Journal of Architecture

Volume 22, Issue 1
February 2017
77% Male
23% Female

Volume 21, Issue 8
December 2016
64% Male
36% Female

Volume 21, Issue 7
November 2016
50% Male
50% Female

Volume 21, Issue 6
September 2016
67% Male
33% Female

Volume 21, Issue 5
July 2016
80% Male
20% Female

Volume 21, Issue 4
June 2016
64% Male
34% Female

Volume 21, Issue 3
May 2016
89% Male
11% Female

Volume 21, Issue 2
March 2016
69% Male
31% Female

Architecture Research Quarterly

Volume 20, Issue 3
September 2016
40% Male
60% Female

Volume 20, Issue 2
June 2016
58% Male
42% Female

Volume 20, Issue 1
March 2016
64% Male
36% Female

Volume 19, Issue 4
December 2015
75% Male
25% Female

Volume 19, Issue 3
September 2015
77% Male
23% Female

Volume 19, Issue 2
June 2015
54% Male
46% Female

Journal of Architectural Education

Volume 71, Issue 1
March 2017
61% Male
39% Female

Volume 70, Issue 2
September 2016
58% Male
42% Female

Volume 70, Issue 1
March 2016
58% Male
42% Female

Volume 69, Issue 2
September 2015
62% Male
38% Female

Volume 69, Issue 1
March 2015
55% Male
45% Female

Volume 68, Issue 2
October 2014
43% Male
57% Female

Volume 68, Issue 1
March 2014
55% Male
45% Female

Chapter 11

In captivity

The real estate of co-living

Hélène Frichot and Helen Runting

This is a chapter about disruptive real estate strategies, bloody capsularisations, and unsupportive environments that captivate and mould the subjectivities of their inhabitants. We deploy feminist architectural theory to critique the innovative and community conscious approaches to real estate that are currently being designed and marketed under the banner of 'co-living'. In order to understand what might be at stake in the co-living model, we here consider two projects that are close to home for us, in Stockholm, Sweden, and one that is further afield. Drawing on the statements of their architects, and the popular reception of either the concept (if unbuilt) or the building (if built), we address: 1. The development Old Oak in Willesden Junction, London, which is owned and managed by London-based real estate developer and property manager The Collective; 2. The KomBo initiative, led by Stockholm-based architects Utopia Arkitekter with Swedish property owner Järntorget; and 3. The Conscious Co living initiative led by the Stockholm-based real estate venture TechFarm and the Stockholm-based architecture office CoDesign (specifically, we look at the proposed Flagship building).

If we accept that we have a fundamental right to shelter, to an 'inhabitable ground', whoever we are, the environment (both constructed and 'natural') must be viewed less as a resource to be used than as a facilitative milieu that supports and shapes us. Taking this position seriously in relation to an emerging housing model, we here argue that despite what may be the best of intentions on the part of interested parties, upon closer inspection, co-living in fact relies on a disavowal of dependencies, vulnerabilities, and intimacies, of bodies, and of politics. It is this disavowal which we believe places these real estate infrastructures in direct conflict with the feminist project of, to parse Judith Butler, 'a life liveable for everyone.'[1]

Real estate infrastructures

By now, the devastating story of the American sub-prime mortgage crash of 2007–2010, which led to a global economic meltdown, is well known. Further compounding this crisis, shifts in the global political landscape demonstrate the ease with which nation states wildly swing toward right-wing conservative politics. The dark promise of violence and terrorism amidst a state of permanent exception, the expression of fundamentalisms of all kinds, and the exclusion of minorities, refugees, and migrants begin to threaten precarious environment-worlds, including what it means to be at home. Amidst social and environmental inequalities how do we grapple with what Isabelle Stengers has called, after the political activist Rosa Luxemburg, 'the coming barbarism'?[2] Because this, it would appear, is our contemporary situation.

Against this barbaric backdrop of world affairs in the early 21st century, with a desire to offer a critical account of the present and its vicissitudes, it is no wonder that architecture as a discipline, a profession, and a practice has expressed a distinct interest in real estate.[3] Architecture is a spatial and material art, well-practiced in raising signature edifices and dressing interiors according to 'organisartorial' logics.[4] The discipline thus holds a longstanding relationship with real estate interests, participating in the economic transaction of spatial goods, and beyond this in the production, circulation and exchange of seductive effects and stimulating atmospheres required to produce 'propertied' subjects and their associated debts.

Architecture not only frames the point of view of a subject tied up with real estate, architecture and its curated interiors mould the subject. In a celebrated essay from the early 1990s Beatriz Colomina suggests that 'Architecture is not simply a platform that accommodates the viewing subject. It is a viewing mechanism that produces the subject. It precedes and frames its occupants.'[5] The logic of subjectification extends far beyond the disciplining panopticism of architecture's visuality – in fact, we align ourselves with an ontological position that holds that *the subject never comes first*, but is always something more larval, formed in process through disciplining routines and controlling atmospheres mounted by means both architectural and environmental. To rework a phrase from feminist thinker Zoë Sofia [Sofoulis]: aside from their local environment-world, the subject is not.[6] Or, to cite Donna Haraway, a source close to Sofia, 'nothing comes without its world'.[7] A similar position is present in Judith Butler's recent argument that: 'We cannot talk about a body without knowing what supports that body and what its relationship is to that support, or lack of support.'[8] Butler positions such a formulation as fundamental to feminism's resistance to a phallocentric understanding that posits the subject as sovereign and independent, and as capable of acting without being acted upon. Rejecting this ontology, she theorises the human body as 'a certain kind of dependency on infrastructure, understood complexly as environment, social relations, networks of support and sustenance.'[9] The infrastructures that form an intimate and co-constitutive part of the subject are also fragile: not only can they recede or fall apart, but they can become 'emphatically unsupportive,' leaving us, ultimately, to fall.[10] Butler's position, like a long line of feminist thinkers, emphasises a dependent and interdependent, embodied subjectivity: to be left to fall, like being left out in the cold, ultimately puts the life of the body (and those who in turn depend on that body) at risk. Infrastructure is thus something that we *can* in fact take a 'normative' stand on, to the extent that 'the norm that life should be liveable for everyone, that norm is not one we should refuse as normalising and policing – that norm is one . . . that we embrace and seek to realise in more and more concrete ways.'[11]

Writing from the midst of a moment of economic exuberance in the late Welfare State of Sweden, we have, in a series of previous essays gathered under the auspices of a fledgling feminist theory of real estate, addressed a number of emerging real estate infrastructures – from the 'gentrifictions' of the 'world's third hippest neighbourhood'[12] to the performance of a 'housing career'[13] to the 'wide, white, and scattered' interiors of the real estate website hemnet.se[14] and the 'pastel cells' of architecture and interiors as displayed in gallery settings.[15] The subjects of these infrastructures – who we have variously named indebted women, entrepreneurs of the self, and involuntary architects – are, despite being exposed to cripplingly high levels of risk and debt, always discouraged from seeing themselves as 'vulnerable.' In each case, it is the agentic and entrepreneurial capacities of the subject of real estate that are valorised (rather than their vulnerabilities), because making the best of the opportunities that present themselves is what counts in a contemporary world of real estate transactions. We have critiqued this entrepreneurial spirit on the grounds that it excludes the possibility of structural change and of solidarity: this is because lack, in the context of neoliberalism's facilitative environments, is presented as a promise and an opportunity for the exercise of agency through tasteful and bold acts of purchase, sale, and interior decoration. Failure in such a set-up, as the work of Michel Foucault has demonstrated, and as Wendy Brown explains, is presumed to be a failure of management: 'the rationally calculating individual bears full responsibility for the consequences of his or her action no matter how severe the constraints on this action.'[16]

Mechanisms of debt will remain in the background of this essay, as we now foreground the quasi-utopian gestures of a real estate project that exists under the nomenclature of 'co-living', seeking to show that even these fail us when it comes to the feminist project of producing a radically emancipatory 'designed living environment.'[17]

The co-living formula

'Greater Stockholm's housing crisis', we are told by Stockholm-based architects Utopia Arkitekter, 'has become acute. If we are to manage to produce the number of attractive and economical dwellings required in coming years, we must embrace new ways of thinking and working.'[18] The result of Utopia Arkitekter's attempts to do just this is KomBo, a real estate scheme for co-living that is first and foremost to be sold to 'municipalities, developers, architects, and property managers,' and then once built, rented to a target group that includes, beyond the core demographic of 18–35 year olds, 'friends, the divorced, the aging, temporary residents, long-distance commuters, or people with a shared interest like sports clubs.'[19] The scheme is concretised in a complex of buildings that are proposed for a site in Sundyberg, in the city's north, to be funded by the private real estate firm Järntorget. These buildings, and the model they are based upon, comprise apartments that accommodate between three and five sound-insulated bedrooms that are arranged in a linear sequence (in the Sundyberg example, these bedrooms are each approximately nine square metres); an entertaining space (dining table and couches); several toilets and showers (in the Sundyberg example, which is a four-bedroom apartment, at least two toilets and a bathroom are shown in plan); a kitchen with individual food storage cupboards; a personal closet of one square metre in the shared space; and a balcony. The entire apartment is 105 square metres, and each resident is to sign an individual rental agreement with their landlord, according to the website, intimating that residents do not necessarily choose their flatmates. The interior visualisation that accompanies the architect's description of the scheme shows a dinner party taking place, with 11 people occupying different parts of the space. They appear to be in their late twenties or early thirties. The set-up resembles a 'student corridor' – a common form of budget student accommodation offered by student housing associations across the country – a sense reinforced by the bright colours and untreated wood of the interior. Far from subsidised student accommodation, however, these apartments can be expected to command only very marginally less ('between GBP £4 and GBP £11 per week less in rent') than a small (non-student, non-shared) apartment 'with a similar floor area.'[20]

Across the North Sea, 'disruptive'[21] property developer The Collective offer a very different vision of co-living. The Collective's Old Oak development on the western fringe of London comprises some 546 hundred 'suites', of which the vast majority (452 to be exact) are classed as 'twodios', which comprise of two 10-square-metre rooms each of which accommodate a double bed, a desk, and an ensuite, and which share access to a kitchenette and two-person 'breakfast bar' (we estimate the size of the whole 'package' to be approximately 25 square meters).[22] Each room is rented separately (one presumably shares with an unknown 'roomie') for GBP £230 per week.[23] The other components of a home – kitchen, laundry, living room – are 'shared' between the residents of a floor (with an apparent height of 10 residential floors, that's 54 'members' per floor).[24] Three dining rooms, an unknown number of 'communal entertainment spaces', 'curated retail outlets', 'events spaces', 'roof terraces', and a gym, spa, cinema room, library, restaurant, and bar are also available to 'members'.[25]

Returning to Stockholm, in addition to their two existing properties (the 33-room K9 in wealthy Östermalm and the 13-person Hus 24 in the medieval town centre), the real estate venture TechFarm are currently in the planning phase of their first new-build project, the aptly named Flagship, the location of which is yet to be disclosed but is somewhere 'in urban Stockholm, not too far away from the city centre conveniently located close to nature.'[26] The Stockholm-based architecture office Codesign have developed both the concept and the design for the Flagship building and the 'Conscious Living' initiative to which it is a part.[27] In both KomBo and TechFarm, we see a model of architectural practice that exceeds the traditional client-architect relation, wherein the architects take part-ownership over the concept, its framing, its execution, and its marketing (they are entrepreneur and architect). In the Flagship, residents will, we are told, live in 'micro-apartments', which are categorised as accommodating either 'long-term' or 'short-term' stays. In the case of the former, micro-apartments are to range from

10 square metres (specified as being 'for single persons') to 30 square metres (specified as being 'for couples or small families'); in the case of the latter, they are to range from an astonishing 4 square metres to 26 square metres. The smaller micro-apartments are to have shared bathrooms, while the larger micro-apartments have been provisioned with private bathrooms. In addition to bathrooms, and like The Collective, residents, we are told, have access to a shared sauna and showers, a laundry room, a yoga room, a gym, a juice bar, an open kitchen, a bookable kitchen, a living room, a small bookable hobby room with a roof terrace, and three greenhouses. Like the location of the building, the price of rooms is not yet listed, but we note that the starting price for a traditional bedroom in an existing TechFarm property (which in some cases are fitted out with bunk beds) is GBP £450 per month at the time of writing.[28] Presumably, a new-build will fetch considerably more. Whilst legal minimum requirements for a habitable room are no longer specified under the regulations of the Swedish National Board of Housing, Building and Planning, the Swedish Mapping, Cadastral and Land Registration Authority continue to define a 'room' as having at least seven square metres and access to daylight.[29] The smallest of the mini-apartments are, therefore neither clearly 'apartments', nor even 'rooms'. They are perhaps best described as 'cells'.

Under confinement

The 'bloody mystifications of the new world order', as Lieven de Cauter has called it (citing Agamben), includes the increasing capsularisation of the human subject into cells both stationary and locomotive.[30] This is what Peter Sloterdijk further theorises as cell-building, the self-container, and egospheres, suggesting that the co-isolated unit of the apartment dwelling is ideally composed for the singular New Human Being who, 'flexibilised in the capital stream, devotes itself to the cultivation of its self-relationships.'[31] The cell is what initiatives like Conscious Co-Living or KomBo undertaken by 'real estate ventures' like TechFarm, developers like Järntorget or The Collective, and architects like Codesign and Utopia Arkitekter are seeking to exploit by way of a critical reversal of terms, promising in the minimal cell alternative ways of achieving community and being together. One well-appointed and comfortably designed cell nestled alongside the other, just the right distribution of private and shared resources, and a wall strong enough to keep the local urban wilderness at bay. This vision might allow a spatial dispensation for a community, but, as Sloterdijk argues, the minimum is merely a misnomer for the concept of habitat cell as 'life-world' atom.[32] For Sloterdijk, while clusters of cells appear to form a habitat that performs like 'foam', each cell remains isolated and self-contained. Likewise, Cauter discusses an increasing propensity toward the capsularisation of life. He explains that the word 'capsule' not only designates a container or box, it describes a grasping, a capturing, forms of spell-bound captivation that subsequently risk becoming captivity.

Kept to a minimum area that is potentially smaller than has previously been considered a 'habitable room', we can wonder what kind of subject and what kind of 'living' this foam-like infrastructure of captivated cells and shared spaces, owned by private companies and rented at a premium, supports? In particular, we remain curious about the cells themselves, as these are the only rooms that are visually accessible to others.

What can one do in a co-living cell? What kind of production and reproduction do these spaces make possible? What acts are possible in a nine-square-metre bedroom, with a single bed, in a KomBo apartment, or in a four-square-metre Flagship micro-apartment, or in a 10-square-metre bedroom in an Old Oak 'twodio', with your randomly allocated 'roomie' not metres, but centimetres away? These are the contemporary conditions of confinement that we face, when a human body cannot move or stretch or flex. What about sex or private discussion, relations that one wishes to limit to a given circle, relations one cannot, or simply does not wish to, extend to all members of the co-living community? The cell provides privacy for a prone body glued to a laptop or asleep, but if it cannot physically accommodate more than one body, the infrastructure as a whole cannot support intimacy. Anywhere.

Fear of joining in (FOJI)

Under neoliberal governmentalities, as Wendy Brown reminds us in her reading of Foucault's biopolitics lectures, 'moral autonomy' is measured by 'the capacity for self-care.'[33] It is not by accident that the shared spaces in the co-living model tend to be equated with 'wellness'. This can be seen in the careful placement of the 'wellness floor' in TechFarm's Flagship, which – much like the swimming pool in J.G. Ballard's *High Rise*[34] – divides the two different classes of 'long-term and short-term' micro-apartments. This space for self-care is the point at which the long-term and short-term residents meet, and the point at which the short-term residents can rise no further in the vertical circulation system. The wellness floor constitutes a 'border zone' in which subjects with radically different access to resources (four square metres and a shared shower; 30 square metres and the possibility of a family) meet. Here, in this shared space where political agonism might be possible, energies are concertedly directed inwards, through a program comprising of 'a recreation area with sauna and showers, a laundry room, a yoga room, a gym and a juice bar.'[35]

What can one do in a shared space? The shared spaces that are so vital to the co-living models – that are used to justify the confines of the cell – emerge in this account (which builds primarily upon the marketing material of the architects and developers pushing these schemes) as spaces within which one works, under the purview of others, on oneself or with others. These are spaces subject to a familiar, panoptical visual regime: in the sight of others, we discipline our bodies and internalise and perform routines that shape our conduct. This 'bottom-up policing' extends previously state-controlled apparatuses of education, of hygiene, and of health, as well as the logics of the market (compulsory productivity described in terms of entrepreneurship), deep into the machine for subjectivation that is 'the home'. In this, we are reminded of Douglas Spencer's quip, that '[i]n neoliberalism, everything is productive, but nothing is labour.'[36] Beyond the heavy-handed optimisation of private and shared space described in the previous section, we also encounter an equally pervasive optimisation of lived time. As one tenant of an existing TechFarm property describes her home life:

> What makes Tech Farm unique is the attention to detail and passion for personal growth and lifestyle design. I'm surrounded by highly driven and entrepreneurial people, yet I don't feel any anxiety or pressure. I'm relaxed. I'm productive. I'm energised. I'm at home.[37]

The atmosphere of mindfulness that pervades the co-living concept seems to be something one arrives at through the act of co-living. It is not, perhaps, there from the beginning. Having been given an apartment in Old Oak for a couple of weeks, *Glamour* magazine journalist Leanne Bayley repeatedly describes an experience she terms FOJI (Fear of joining in):

> . . . as I walked into reception at The Collective tonight, a gig was happening in the bar. Cool! Definitely. Did I go in? No. I am going to have to overcome this fear because right now I'm fighting against what The Collective is striving for. Here's that word again: community.[38]

Leanne may have the official job title 'resident basic bitch' on the magazine's website, but her fight against the kind of community being offered by The Collective is understandable. She realises she has few choices in this situation: she can literally 'get back in her box' or she can 'join in' with a 'community' built upon principles of compulsory conviviality. In both instances, the possibility of any form of politics seems evacuated: we are either in agreement or we are alone. Resident Vijay Kannan, 20, who's on a placement at healthcare company General Electric in Amersham, describes the paradox to journalist Samuel Fishwick: 'You can be who you want to be here, do exactly what you want and there are 500 people who feel the same way as you do.'[39]

At this point, it would be useful to differentiate between the compromises to space and privacy, and the injunctions to socialise that occur in 'share house' living, and those that we here situate as integral to the 'co-living' model. It is crucial that our audience understand that 'a rented bedroom in a share house' (or even 'a very small, rented, studio apartment,' which is more common in the Swedish context) and 'a rented cell in a co-living environment' are entirely different forms of 'real estate' and support entirely different forms of 'living'. TechFarm might be 'co-created' but it is (importantly) *not* 'co-owned'; KomBo might make reference to Sweden's private and public history of collective living, but its nine-square-metre bedrooms and optimised shared spaces are less accommodating of different bodies (the bodies of children, for instance) than the models that mark Sweden's experimental history regarding collective housing.[40] While The Collective might talk of 'roomies' and 'community', access privileges are contained in a smart card, and are not revoked via a discussion 'around the kitchen table' (as in bourgeois civil society) or via a set of regulations enforced by a State and applied to an entire population (the Welfare State model), but rather by a corporate landlord who owns the property. Unlike the vast majority of share houses, the co-living apartments discussed here are designed by architects with *the production of a specific subject in sight*: a subject who takes their life into their own hands. The entrepreneur of the self.[41]

We will all be homeless

At the Tech Open Air Festival in Berlin on July 14, 2016, Chief Operating Officer of The Collective James Scott made the astonishing statement that: 'In the future we will all be homeless.'[42] The co-living concept is one that values transience highly, and in ways that are mystifying to those not initiated into the Silicon Valley's unique language of failure. Jessica Guzik writes of her co-living experience:

> When I was in my 20s I thought nothing of living with a roommate or several to save money . . . But as I got older, I bought into the narrative that I was supposed to graduate into a one-bedroom apartment of my own. That is until last July, when – at 32 years old and with a six-figure income – I moved into WeLive. I missed the sense of community that came with roommates but didn't want to sacrifice too much of my personal space. I also wasn't particularly price-sensitive. Fast-forward to the present. I've been sleeping in eight-bed dorms for the past seven weeks and haven't had a full-time job in four months. I care less about personal space, more about saving money. Basically I'm 22 years old again.[43]

In case the tenor of this female subject's testimonial is missed, what she is celebrating is the liberty she has claimed in her conditions of precarious labour and provisional accommodation. For some, the thought of sleeping in an eight-bed dorm, of being unemployed for four months, and of being 22 years old again are hardly attractive conditions. Their celebration by Jessica above seems coherent with 'the promise of lack' that we have situated as the psychic motor of neoliberal governmentalities of the self.[44] At the same time, such a disavowal seems almost theatrically staged in the co-living scenario. 'Privilege,' write Wade Cotton and Isabelle Kirkham-Lewitt, 'is a blindness to one's own needs or blindness to the fact that one's needs are being met on their behalf.'[45] It is only by prioritising our 'broader condition of dependency and interdependency' that we can understand 'what a body can do'. It might be then, and only then, that we can get our bodies (homeless, disposed, and de-sexed) and our bodies politic (relaxed, energised, and compulsively productive) to do things.

The co-living arrangements we discuss briefly here seem to sweep vulnerability and the question of a precarious life under the carpet by seemingly liberating inhabitants from anything other than their creative labour (when they can get it) and capacity for crowd-thinking. We should be wary of too quickly romanticising the neatness of the bare cell and the hush of adolescent sex it requires, the celebration of transience and creative labour 24/7, and the permanent exceptions of dispossession and being ready to leave at less than a moment's notice. We should be alert, because: 'The dependency on infrastructure for a liveable life seems clear, but when infrastructure fails, and fails consistently, how do we understand that condition of life?'[46] As Butler, Gambetti, and Sabsay argue, rather than pitching critical resistance against vulnerability, the two can be seen to operate conjunctively, which offers one way out of the paternalistic logic of 'protection'.[47] As human bodies, not just as women, children, and the wretched of the earth, we are all vulnerable, and rely on our facilitative environments for support. Isabelle Stengers suggests that to counter the coming barbarism we need 'new powers of acting, feeling, imagining, and thinking' and the means to shake up old habits and produce new connections instead.[48] But is independent, sovereign entrepreneurial action the only mode available to us? Beyond the sales pitch of co-living, which is by no means an answer to how we might share our resources, we must secure the means of co-governance, and for a politics able to extend beyond the cell and the perimeter wall.

There is an uncanny similarity between the co-living model and Cauter's account of capsules thrown upon a sea of chaos. We have become an archipelago of insular entities, a seething, multiplying human foam exhausting global territories. For some this is a good thing, for others a questionable state of affairs that has contributed to what is now called the Anthropocene.[49]

Notes

1   Judith Butler, 'Rethinking Vulnerability and Resistance' in *Vulnerability in Resistance*, eds. Judith Butler, Zeynep Gambetti, and Leticia Sabsay (Durham, NC: Duke University Press, 2016), 13.

2   Isabelle Stengers, *In Catastrophic Times: Resisting the Coming Barbarism* (Open Humanities Press, 2015), accessed April 12, 2017, http://openhumanitiespress.org/books/download/Stengers_2015_ In-Catastrophic-Times.pdf.

3   See: Jack Self and Shumi Bose, eds., *Real Estates: Life without Debt* (London: Bedford Press, 2014); Martin, Reinhold, Moore, Jacob, Schindler, Susanne, eds., *The Art of Inequality: Architecture, Housing and Real Estate* (New York: The Temple Hoyne Buell Center for the Study of American Architecture, 2015).

4   'The organisartorial regime' is a term that we have introduced in order to describe 'a retreat into place', into the building of worlds via the dressing of interiors (a nesting impulse). See: Helen Runting and Hélène Frichot, 'Wide, White, and Scattered: Picturing her housing career' in *This Thing Called Theory*, eds. Teresa Stoppani, Giorgio Ponzo, and George Themistokleous (London: Bloomsbury, 2016), 231–241.

5   Beatriz Colomina, 'The Split Wall: Domestic Voyeurism' in *Sexuality & Space*, eds. Beatriz Colomina and Jennifer Bloomer (New York: Princeton Architectural Press, 1992), 84.

6   Zoë Sofia, 'Container Technologies', *Hypatia* 15, no. 2 (Spring, 2000): 183.

7   The Australian feminist Zoe Sofia, who also publishes as Zoe Sofoulis, was a PhD student of Donna Haraway in the 1980s. Donna Haraway, *Modest_Witness@Second_Millennium. FemaleMan©_Meets_ OncoMouse™: Feminism and Technoscience* (New York: Routledge, 1997), 137. See also Maria de la Bellacasa, 'Nothing comes without its world: thinking with care', *The Sociological Review* 60 (2012).

8   Judith Butler, 'Rethinking Vulnerability and Resistance,' accessed February 17, 2017, http://bibacc.org/ wp-content/uploads/2016/07/Rethinking-Vulnerability-and-Resistance-Judith-Butler.pdf

9   Ibid.

10 Butler, 'Rethinking Vulnerability and Resistance' in *Vulnerability in Resistance*, 15.

11 Ibid.

12 Helen Runting and Hélène Frichot, 'Welcome to the Promenade City.''

13 Hélène Frichot and Helen Runting, 'The Promise of a Lack: Responding to (Her) Real-Estate Career,' *The Avery Review* 13 (2015).

14 Runting and Frichot, 'Wide, White, and Scattered.'

15 Runting and Frichot, 'Welcome to the Promenade City.'

16 Wendy Brown, 'Neoliberalism and the End of Liberal Democracy' in *Edgework: Critical Essays on Knowledge and Politics*, ed. Wendy Brown, (Princeton, N.J.: Princeton University Press, 2005), 42.

17 Here, we refer to the title of a recent Swedish government inquiry on the built environment. See: The Swedish Government, *Gestaltad livsmiljö – en ny politik för arkitektur, form och design* (Designed Living environment – a new policy for architecture, form and design) (Stockholm: Statens offentliga utredningar, 2015).

18 Utopia Arkitekter, KomBo, accessed April 13, 2017, www.utopia.se/se/projekt/kombo. Translated from Swedish by the authors.

19 Ibid.

20 The architects describe KomBo as a product that 'delivers lower rent than having one's own small apartment with a similar floor area,' however they estimate the difference in rent to be 'between 200 and 500 Swedish crowns per month less,' which is between GBP £4 and GBP £11 less per week. Prices converted from SEK to GBP on April 13, 2017. Ibid.

21 'The Collective has also formed a partnership with property technology accelerator Property Innovation Labs (Pi Labs) in a bid to support other start-up companies seeking to disrupt the current property market.' Jessica Mairs, '"In the future we will all be homeless" says co-living entrepreneur,' *Dezeen* (July 15, 2016), accessed April 12, 2017, www.dezeen.com/2016/07/15/in-the-future-we-will-all-be-homeless-says-co-living-entrepreneur-the-collective-james-scott-housing/.

22 The Collective, 'Welcome to Old Oak', accessed April 12, 2017, www.thecollective.co.uk/coliving/old-oak.

23 The Collective, 'Ensuite Room (Standard)', accessed April 12, 2017, www.thecollective.co.uk/coliving/old-oak/ensuite-standard.

24 Height calculated from image of the exterior, accessed April 12, 2017, at www.standard.co.uk/.lifestyle/esmagazine/the-collective-inside-london-s-most-luxurious-commune-a3333526.html#gallery.

25 See www.thecollective.co.uk/coliving/old-oak#coliving-overview, accessed April 12, 2017.

26 TechFarm, 'Flagship', accessed April 12, 2017, www.techfarm.life/flagship.

27 Codesign, 'Tech Farm', accessed April 12, 2017, www.codesign.se/tech-farm/.

28 TechFarm, 'How Much Does It Cost?' accessed April 12, 2017, www.techfarm.life/faqs.

29 Mäklarsamfundet, 'Vad är ett rum?' accessed April 12, 2017, www.maklarsamfundet.se/vad-ar-ett-rum.

30 Lieven De Cauter, *The Capsular Civilization: On the City in the Age of Fear* (Rotterdam: NAi Publishers, 2004), 154–155.

31 Peter Sloterdijk, *Foams: Spheres III*, trans. Wieland Hoban (New York: Semiotext(e), 2016), 530.

32 Ibid.

33 Wendy Brown, 'Neoliberalism and the End of Liberal Democracy', 42.

34 J.G. Ballard, *High-Rise* (New York: Holt, Rinehart and Winston, 1975).

35 TechFarm, 'Floorplan', accessed April 13, 2017, www.techfarm.life/flagship.

36 Douglas Spencer, *The Architecture of Neoliberalism: How Contemporary Architecture Became an Instrument of Control and Compliance* (London: Bloomsbury, 2016), 76.

37 TechFarm, 'Community', accessed April 12, 2017, www.techfarm.life/community.

38 Leanne Bayley, 'I swapped one flatmate for 500 in London's first co-living community,' *Glamour* (October 10, 2016), accessed December 1, 2016, www.glamourmagazine.co.uk/article/the-collective-old-oak-review.

39 Samuel Fishwick, 'The Collective: inside London's most luxurious commune', *The Evening Standard*, accessed April 12, 2017, www.standard.co.uk/lifestyle/esmagazine/the-collective-inside-london-s-most-luxurious-commune-a3333526.html.

40 Sweden has a rich history of experiments in collective housing, including Kolletivhuset, which was designed by Sven Markelius, in collaboration with Alva Myrdal, in 1935. Kollektivhuset was built upon principles which included the socialisation of domestic tasks, including those relating to child rearing.

41 The architects of the Flagship building specifically state that their concept 'is based on an analysis of the target audience and their lifestyle. Co-living is aimed at the people involved in start-ups.' CoDesign, 'TechFarm.'

42 Mairs, 'In the future we will all be homeless'.

43 Jessica Guzik, 'Co-Living: Group Homes for the Self-Conscious and Gainfully Employed?' accessed April 12, 2017, https://medium.com/@jessicaguzik/co-living-group-homes-for-the-self-conscious-and-gainfully-employed-1f7c4922802b.

44 Frichot and Runting, 'The Promise of a Lack.'

45 Wade Cotton and Isabelle Kirkham-Lewitt, 'Model Wombs', *Avery Review* 22 (March 2017).

46 Butler, 'Rethinking Vulnerability and Resistance', 12–13.

47 Butler, et al. 2016, 1–11.

48 Stengers, *In Catastrophic Times*, 24.

49 While there has been a proliferation of uses and definitions of this term, a term the coinage of which is most often associated with Nobel Laureate atmospheric chemist Paul Crutzen, we offer Haraway's concise account, which can be found in Donna Haraway, *Staying with the Trouble: Making Kin in the Chthulucence* (Durham and London: Duke University Press, 2016), 44–46.

Milieu

Chapter 12

Material and rational feminisms

A contribution to humane architectures

Peg Rawes and Douglas Spencer

Opening Remarks

The following dialogue was stimulated by the 13th International AHRA (Architectural Humanities Research Association) conference invitation to explore the relationship between feminist architectural practices, economics and technologies. In response, we chose to question the roles and current usage of two key terms associated with the formation of positive and negative subjectivities under economic and technological modes of production. These two terms, 'affect' and 'rationalism', are often seen as necessarily conceptually and politically antithetical to each other. On the one hand, while feminism tends to see affect as an agent of leftist and radical critique of normative society, the 'affective turn' in architectural design and authorship has become an uncritical and essentialist form within neoliberal markets. On the other hand, rationalist modes of critique are aligned with normative techno-scientific thinking and consequently seen as necessarily opposed to materialist feminist politics. In order to examine these positions, we have attempted to draw attention to the way in which 'affect' and 'rationalism' are structured in contemporary political philosophy and critical theory. Drawing from our work on philosophical and feminist critiques of subjectivity, architecture and power, we question the continuing opposition between affect and rationalism as principal means for resisting neoliberal practices and cultures. Instead, with reference to the 'radical' rationalism of Baruch Spinoza and Theodore Adorno's philosophies we have attempted to rethink this opposition as a meaningful contribution to developing humane feminist architectural practices in the 21st century. For example, we consider how architectural affect produces and also conceals neoliberal interests, and argue that when affect is located in essentialist forms of matter, it divorces us from *other* histories of rationalism that may helpfully mobilise critical feminist practices.

Peg Rawes: The current political situation in the UK and the US highlights that feminisms, including feminist forms of rationality, are even more societally necessary. Might reasoning or rational thinking be tactics, modes or strategies that feminism can take up in its practices? I ask this as someone trained in feminist philosophy, where reason and rational thinking have been considered the 'opposition' or 'the problem': normally associated with universal, transcendental and male forms of Enlightenment philosophy, and therefore very actively critiqued by significant feminist continental philosophers.[1] However, given the strong denigration of reasoning in the public sphere by 'charismatic' politicians who claim power through an abandonment of rational thinking, perhaps we need to rethink this. Also, in the UK, expertise and experts are being discredited in ideological attacks on the Higher Education sector by populist, anti-institutional ideologies from both sides of the political spectrum. There is a very *real* sense that knowledges derived from engaged, rational or technical practices – which I take to also include specific feminist histories, knowledges and practices – are not being promoted or defended in the public political sphere.[2]

Douglas Spencer: Our discussions have also been prompted by my recent critique of the discourse of affect in architecture.[3] I've been arguing that the so-called 'affective turn' is complicit with processes of subjectification within and for neoliberalism, especially with respect to how we are fashioned as essentially emotive and affective beings, and in terms of the denigration of our reasoning capacities accompanying this process. I would want to note that these same affirmations of affect can also be found within certain currents of feminist thinking, such as its 'new materialist' forms.

My argument is not that we should recover reason at the *expense* of affect, but that we need to find ways of thinking the two things together, especially if we are to overcome conceiving of them as essentially opposed terms. To this end I find especially pertinent the thought of Theodor Adorno, particularly as expressed within his and Max Horkheimer's *Dialectic of Enlightenment*.[4]

Materialisms and ecologies

PR: Feminist thinking and materiality are intimately linked. Very important and creative work has been done on this, which has produced pre-histories – e.g., Judith Butler's matrixial etymologies[5] and significant feminist architectural histories, theories and design practices, including many colleagues who are participating in this conference.[6] Two modes of feminist materialist thinking are, in particular, important for architecture. Both are related to Marxist critiques of capital, and an affirmation of affect. First, Luce Irigaray and Silvia Frederici's work on reproductive labour and difference is in sympathy with colleagues who have discussed women, work and architecture.[7] These have a renewed value in relation to the detrimental impact of unpaid labour that affects significant numbers of female and male academics and practitioners. Over the past few years, unpaid labour and poor reproductive rights and caring provision (and, by extension, 'care of the self') in the academic and architectural professional environments, have come to be defined as 'affective' forms of labour; for example, the precarious job security of young lecturers is reflected in *The Guardian's* recent report on an academic who earns a salary of £6,000 from three different institutions.[8] These critiques are also relevant in relation to tendencies amongst leading UK universities to now use zero-hour contracts for part-time lecturing positions: this is a situation very familiar to part-time architectural lecturers, especially those who teach in the architectural humanities.

The second reason to advocate materialist feminism is because of the techno-scientific formation of architecture and the built environment.[9] Very good examples of feminist thinkers who have shown the ethical and societal significance of this kind of critique includes Donna Haraway's work on 'companion species', Isabelle Stengers' 'ethics of practice' and Karen Barad's 'agential realism'.[10] These writers present critical and creative analyses of science and technology within humanities and aesthetic research, revising rationalism so that it can then be used to tackle pressing issues about the techno-scientific formation of society. As a consequence, feminisms may critically engage with techno-science, rather than oppose narratives of reasoning, in order to question biological and political definitions of 'society', 'self' and 'care', which the sciences produce and reproduce. For example, very powerful forms of normative representation used in neuro-cognitive science are often taken as dominant material and social 'truths', but without any reconstruction of subjectivity or of politics. Such 'proof' lies in some of the most universal (and, for feminists, obsolete) concepts of subjectivity that reconfirm normativity. Despite all the 'brilliance' of these sciences, their positivist origins are also used to undermine understandings of reciprocity or responsibility with the societal and political forces within which we live and work. Beyond the rise of the neuro-sciences, commercial architecture and our cities are also being substantially transformed by other large-scale techno-scientific systems – especially the drive towards automated and industrialised forms of computational design, including BIM. Architectural feminists (men, women and 'other') need to directly engage in these discussions. If feminist architectural critique fails to debate science, technology and rationalism, is it in danger of being permanently consigned to an irrelevant 'anti-rationalist' margin that is deemed viable only at the small scale rather than at the public and private infrastructural large scale? Of course, I also say this as someone who shares in the responsibility to develop new ways to engage, to learn and to challenge pedagogies which reproduce the 'same' instrumental forms of practice and standard models of power and control (and which exclude feminine forms of reasoning).

DS: Thinking of the relationship between materialism and feminism, it strikes me that we have, on the one hand, an older 'materialism', a 'dialectical' or historical 'materialism' with which Simone de Beauvoir was, of course, very much engaged.[11] This was critical to her understanding of how 'woman' was produced as a historical category, and of how 'woman' was produced as the 'other' to man through a range of material, political, cultural and technological means. On the other hand, we have a so-called 'new materialism' which has in some sense presented itself as an advance over all those older and critical practices that have been invested in the study of the linguistic, the semiotic, the textual.[12] The progressive promise of this new materialism is that in bypassing such forms of mediation we will somehow bypass systems of power; that we will achieve some more immediate engagement with the material world. But this is a false immediacy. Within our field, it implies that we can study and understand architecture simply in terms of its apparently obvious presence, in terms of its immediate materiality. Any properly critical theorisation of architecture, though, would want to stress that architecture is not immediate but *mediated* and *mediating*. Think, for, instance, of Fredric Jameson's statement that architecture is 'that constitutive seam between the economic organization of society and the aesthetic production of its (spatial) art'.[13] Architecture is also mediated by, and mediating of, the environmental, the political, the cultural the technological and, perhaps most of all, conditions and practices of labour. An exclusive focus on matter will tend to obscure the nature and work of those mediations.

The promises and problematics of affect

PR: My interest in affect concerns its efficacy for biopolitical thinking and practices. Feminist philosophies of affect, particularly through Rosi Braidotti's writing,[14] take affect to be a necessary counter-argument to the negative forms of oppositional debate in contemporary politics: for example, the kind of debate found in the UK's parliamentary chamber, which spatially reflects the negatively-defined form of political difference in policy and party position, and is therefore also, politically, a repetition of the same. As is so currently evident in the UK, there is very little opportunity for political transformation in this order; this shows the need for and potential of *political* affect, rather than just *sensory* affect.

I find Baruch Spinoza's discussion of affect valuable here, particularly because he is a rational philosopher of the late 17th century writing in the Dutch Republic at a time of intensive urbanisation and in an early-modern neoliberal society: a very sympathetic setting with respect to northern Europe today. Also, as a Jewish thinker, his subjectivity and position of thinking is with, and of, difference. His notion of affect in *The Ethics* [1677][15] is a political philosophy, which materialises the 'passions' – i.e. the *powers* of the emotions – through a forensic analysis of their differences, yet presented in a 'geometric method' which repurposes Euclid's geometry. Placing science and emotion together, this is an early form of psychoanalysis. It advocates for our passionate powers of reasoning but, importantly, a reasoning that is not divorced from our capacity to produce rational forms of agency. This is the rationalism that Gilles Deleuze and Félix Guattari remove from Spinoza, because of their anti-Enlightenment project, but perhaps we could benefit from returning to it? Particularly if we understand Spinoza to be a practitioner of affective powers and alterity, he is linked to Michel Foucault's biopolitical philosophy. Nevertheless, unlike Foucault's negative definition of biopolitics and biopower,[16] Spinoza releases affect so that it becomes a production of care of the self, where ratio is not only inhumane (as Foucault suggests), but can be the humane care of self, and hence society. This seems very valuable to me, because it produces a kind of rational power, which is lost in many other narratives of sensory or bodily affect. Instead, for Spinoza, affect is produced as a form of ratio or reasoning, which produces difference rather than same-ness.[17] Also, historically, Spinoza's thinking is located in an early phase of the Enlightenment, when there is a dynamic and mobile understanding of individuation, before 18th-century Enlightenment philosophy and law codify subjectivity into universal, moral, autonomous forms of individuation.

After Spinoza, then, feminist *ratio is located in human difference*, not sameness; in an affirmative dissimilarity that is constituted between our bodily, mental, ecological and political realities, and through which differentiated societies can be built, rather than normative, technocratic monocultures. Unlike Giorgio Agamben's influential but negative theory of the human as lack or exception,[18] Spinoza's relational theory is a 'biopower' which has 'a care with' poststructuralist ethical imaginaries that do not exclusively return to oppositional forms of individuation. His proto-materialist essay about *humane ratio* has a 'critical sympathy'[19] that accords with feminist practitioners, for instance with the work of economists Julie Graham and Katherine Gibson[20] (also underpinning Katherine Gibson's dialogue with Doina Petrescu in this volume), or architectural professionals who promote ethical, affirmative and diverse modes of practice.

DS: Deleuze and Guattari's treatment of Spinoza occurs in the context of their own particular project. The pronounced anti-Hegelian aspect of this project means that they seek to circumvent theories and practices of mediation and the dialectic, rather pursuing an affirmative philosophy of immediacy and immanence. This is the context in which we ought to understand the quote that Deleuze famously takes from Spinoza, that 'we do not even know what a body is capable of'.[21] Prior to the intellect, and to any linguistic mediation of experience in the form of ideas, we can locate the immediacy of the body as a site of experience and affirm its potentials. This quotation, in turn, becomes endlessly repeated and recycled by others, in other contexts and to other ends, to the point where it *seems* like a body can do anything and everything, and that therefore *all* we need is a body. So this notion of what a body can do is supposed to be grounded in immediacy but is in fact itself the product of the multiple mediations on which its affirmation depends.

As for my own concerns around the so-called 'affective turn' in architecture, I'll start by referring to Sylvia Lavin's *Kissing Architecture* (2011). Lavin's statement that 'no one can speak when kissing'[22] captures her absolute affirmation of affect and the body, her belief that these can and will do everything for us, and that we do not need language, speech or interpretation because meaning is of little concern. Similar arguments can also be located in Farshid Moussavi's affirmations of affect in architecture and her claims regarding the end of the efficacy of language.[23]

These affirmations of affect are typically conceived as being opposed to the apparently intellectualised, distanced and essentially negative practices of critical theory, practices for which Adorno has come to stand as a figurehead in this context.[24] If we step away from the common caricatures of Adorno's thought, though, we find something within it that is both important and pertinent to an analysis of the relations between reason and affect. For Adorno, the subject can never be *identified* with its body. Nor can it be *identified* with its thought. In fact, at the heart of patriarchy – and this is precisely the term used by Adorno and Horkheimer in their *Dialectic of Enlightenment* – there is a constitutive split between reason and feeling, and it is on this split that a whole raft of further dualisms and hierarchical relations are founded. So, from this perspective, I find the splitting off and valorising of the body and affect from the negatively defined reasoning and intellectual capacities of the subject troubling.

A further concern around the affirmation of affect is that when isolated in itself it can easily and readily be deployed as an instrument of subjectifying power, especially when we are invited to respond to our experience of the world *only* in terms of our immediate perceptions. Much recent architecture has been only to happy to assume this role, especially in its use of ornament, in absorbing the attention of the subject in a sensually charged individual experience of the city, as opposed to a collectively reasoned critique of its existing conditions.

Architecture and reason

PR: My interest in architectural aspects of ratio is developed in a project that deploys Spinoza's ratio to critique the chronic dysfunctions in housing equity in the UK:[25] issues which are of course also very evident in the EU and globally. I am also interested in re-evaluating reasoning in the architectural discipline, against the tendencies of an anti-rationalist debate that is naturalised in some feminist thinking (cf. Irigaray), yet at odds with the positive ways in which women architects are trained and work. Women (and men) in architecture clearly do experience significant issues of alienation as a result of techno-scientific and economic pressures, but these feminist architects also possess affective powers of reasoning – humane ratios – that constitute critical and ethical practices. For me, ratio therefore partly concerns its utility in the valorisation of the work of feminist practitioners in the built environment – for example, in the work of Parlour and ArchiteXX, who redirect professional, legal, political and rational languages to expose inequalities, enable equity and feminist strategies. These techniques also resonate with the work of researchers outside the education sector, including housing and welfare charities' research into the histories and formation of housing inequality.[26] Such researchers create powerful empirical and rational critiques that have political affect and demonstrate material history. Of course, we all know that data is not neutral, but such research exposes the effects of its negative values, something which Spinoza also recognised in his philosophy of powerful and weak affects. Again, here ratio operates as a valuable power of critique for rational feminist practices.

DS: Adorno and Horkheimer's *Dialectic of Enlightenment* presents a strong critique of enlightenment rationality. This is not a call to abandon reason altogether, but to understand it dialectically. The core of this critique is located in Adorno and Horkheimer's retelling of the Sirens episode from Homer's *The Odyssey*. In this episode, the Sirens lure unwitting sailors onto the rocks with their irresistible song. Prototypically entrepreneurial forms of reasoning, identified with masculinity, are threatened by expressions of sensuality personified as feminine and characterised as archaic. Sailors heeding the call of the Sirens are rewarded with absolute knowledge of past and future, but the cost of this knowledge is death. In this mythic episode the relationship between knowledge and the passions is figured as troubled and troubling. For Adorno and Horkheimer, Odysseus' solution to this quandary is itself equally fraught, and their own retelling of the Sirens episode is presented as an allegory of how the dualisms on which patriarchy depends are founded.

The cunning Odysseus identifies an escape clause that will enable him to encounter the Sirens without succumbing to their enchantments. He will have himself tightly bound to the mast of the ship he commands, so that when he hears the Sirens' call he will be physically unable to respond to it. When Odysseus – the master – calls upon his oarsmen – the labour force – to steer the ship toward the rocks they cannot respond because he has commanded them, in advance, to block their ears with wax. This is, for Adorno and Horkheimer, a foundational moment in the establishment of patriarchal dualism and of a whole unresolved problematic of the Enlightenment, precisely because of the separation of reason from affect that it implies. This moment marks a turn after which the sensuous can only be experienced under the categorical conditions of art. Odysseus, the prototypically entrepreneurial figure, can only experience the sensuous at some remove. He is, say Adorno and Horkheimer, like the concertgoer bound to his seat for the duration of the performance. On the other hand, the workers, here represented by the oarsman at Odysseus' command, are rendered insensible. The division of labour also divides conditions of experience.

So Odysseus' victory over the Sirens is Pyrrhic. *The Odyssey* is recast in Adorno and Horkheimer's retelling as a tragedy because when thought and feeling are separated from one another, both are impoverished, damaged. Thought and feeling need to be reunited in order to remedy the suffering that follows from their separation, in order to escape the 'infinite regression' of enlightenment.

Critique

PR: Reason and ratio are consistent with the work of demystifying ideological structures of thought, and, as I mentioned earlier, very necessary practices at the moment. I also see this affective ratio as a kind of biopower which is cognisant of Foucault's biopolitics, but also differentiated from the inhumane form of ratio that he critiques (i.e., not of a humane humanism). It is only at the very end of his writings, in the mid 1980s, that Foucault acknowledges humane ratio when he examines 'technologies of the self'.[27] In contrast, in Spinoza and also in feminist architecture, I would suggest that there are very good forms of humane ratio, as well as work being done on the demystification of inhumane powers.

DS: Wherever we read that dualisms must be challenged, and that this involves rejecting critical theory, this is in fact a reinforcing of dualisms but with a reversal of the polarity between the affirmed and the negated, rather than any real overcoming of the binary oppositions through which they are conceived. This happens when the material and the immediate are affirmed over the critical and the mediated. I also think that Deleuze and Guattari are deeply implicated in this shortcoming, not only in their own writings, but also in the ways that these have been appropriated. Their thought often works with and through binaries – the striated and the smooth, the tree and the rhizome, for instance – and they are, however they might qualify this, always affirming one of the terms in the binary over the other.[28] In terms of maintaining the dualism between feeling and reason, I find Deleuze's remarks in his book on Francis Bacon especially egregious.[29] Here he praises Bacon's painting because, he claims, it works on the basis of affect, operating directly upon the nervous system and entirely bypassing the brain and its cognitive labours. This makes little sense physiologically and experientially. More importantly, it is symptomatic of Deleuze's outright rejection of the dialectic and of the philosophy of Hegel that leaves his thought unable to countenance mediation and ill-equipped to overcome the binaries which it encounters. Instead, he resorts to affirming bodily affect over mental reasoning.

Adorno's encounter with Hegel's dialectic is itself dialectical and consequently far better able to work through the binary of feeling and reason so as to suggest how their dualistic conception can be overcome. Adorno's complaint with Hegel's dialectic is that its teleology is charted on a course toward the realisation of pure spirit, of spirit knowing itself. For Adorno this is a forgetting of the body, specifically the 'belly',[30] and he seeks to bring this back into the dialectic, without it being at the cost of the absolute rejection of spirit.

Labour

PR: Moving on from this theme of critique, I want to come back to the importance of labour, and end with a few comments about the inhumane ratios that currently undermine sustainable inhabitation in the Higher Education sector and architectural spheres, and to consider whose responsibility this is. These remarks come from conversations with my students and contribution to The Architecture Lobby's *Asymmetric Labor* volume, edited by Peggy Deamer and an international 'union' of students.[31] First, as a member of the pedagogic elite, I am partly responsible for educational practices that create productive young 'architectural bodies'. With my colleagues, I help to develop affirmative discursive environments which produce students with professional and political aspirations, and critical powers about their employability. But this is also a precarious set of skills for many graduates, because when work is available, it is often poorly paid, and has little security. Secondly, many graduates undertaking doctorates have to balance the labour of their academic qualification alongside the labour of parenting (rather than previous generations who were advised to produce a PhD before a family): again challenging expectations, given the competitiveness of the PhD/young career researcher markets combined with parenting responsibilities and child-care costs. The final element in this nexus is housing, which includes the unaffordability of rents, and unsustainable travel between home and work. Again, these are discussions that were present 20–30 years ago, but are back as the norm for researchers who may well be into their 40s (rather than in their late 20s, as was the case in earlier generations). These are real life ratios in architectural work that feminist practices can directly address, and often do.

DS: The types of labour that Peg refers to are largely invisible, and this is a critical issue, especially where we are concerned with affective and so-called immaterial labour. There is work, in itself, to be done on making such forms of labour visible that bears, in particular, upon the upper strata of architectural production, which seems unable to acknowledge any type of labour whatsoever. It can't acknowledge the conceptual labour of design, preferring to attribute this to algorithimic operations or to putatively natural processes of computation, nor the forms of labour involved in the construction of its phantasmagoric and architectural productions. As a critical response, we need to practice the forms of cognitive, and not just affective, labour that will allow us to critically comprehend and interpret these productions and the various forms of labour they involve.

Notes

1   See, for example: Luce Irigaray, *This Sex Which Is Not One*, translated by Catherine Porter with Carolyn Burke (Ithaca NY: Cornell University Press, 1985); Judith Butler, *Bodies that Matter: On the Discursive Limits of Sex* (New York, London: Routledge, 1993; Elizabeth Grosz, *Architecture from the Outside: Essays on Virtual and Real Space* (Cambridge Mass.: MIT Press, 2001).

2   This opening remark has been tempered to some extent by the international Women's Marches on 21 January 2017, against Trump and in support of women in the US, marking a brief public and affecting occupation of major city spaces for women's rights.

3   Doug Spencer, *The Architecture of Neoliberalism* (London: Bloomsbury Academic, 2016).

4   Max Horkheimer and Theodore Adorno, *Dialectic of Enlightenment* (NY: Seabury Press, 1972).

5   Butler, *Bodies that Matter*.

6   See Jane Rendell, *Site Writing: The Architecture of Art Criticism* (London: IB Tauris, 2010) and the work of colleagues who are in this anthology and the accompanying *Architecture and Culture* journal issue.

7   Luce Irigaray, *This Sex Which Is Not One*, 1985; Silvia Frederici, *Revolution at Point Zero: Housework, Reproduction and Feminist Struggle* (New York: PM Press & Common Notions, 2012); Jane Rendell, *The Pursuit of Pleasure: Gender, Space and Architecture in Regency London* (London: Continuum, 2002); Lori Brown, *Contested Spaces: Abortion Clinics, Women's Shelters and Hospitals* (London: Ashgate, 2013); and Parlour, *AA Dossier: The State of Gender Equity* (Melbourne: Parlour Press, 2014), www.archiparlour.org (accessed 30 November 2016).

8   Sally Weale, 'Part-time lecturers on precarious work: "I don't make enough for rent"', *The Guardian*, 16 November 2016, www.theguardian.com/uk-news/2016/nov/16/part-time-lecturers-on-precarious-work-i-dont-make-enough-for-rent (accessed 19 November 2016).

9   Peg Rawes 'Biopolitical Ecological Poetics' in *Poetic Biopolitics: Relational Practices in Architecture and the Arts*, edited by P. Rawes, T. Mathews and S. Loo (London: IB Tauris, 2016).

10 Donna Haraway, *When Species Meet* (Minneapolis, London: University of Minnesota Press, 2008); Isabelle Stengers, *Power and Invention: Situating Science, Theory Out of Bounds*. Vol. 10 (Minneapolis: University of Minnesota Press, 1997); Karen Barad, *Meeting the Universe Halfway: Quantum Physics and the Entanglement of Matter and Meaning* (Durham CA: Duke University Press, 2007).

11 Simone de Beauvoir, *The Second Sex* (New York: A.A. Knopf, 1978).

12 Jane Bennett, *Vibrant Matter* (Durham: Duke University Press, 2010); Diana Coole and Samantha Frost, *New Materialisms* (Durham NC: Duke University Press, 2010); Rick Dolphijn and Iris Tuin, *New Materialism: Interviews and Cartographies* (Ann Arbor, Mich.: Open Humanities Press, 2012).

13 Frederic Jameson, *Postmodernism or the Cultural Logic of Late Capitalism* (London: Verso 1991), 121.

14 Rosi Braidotti, *The Posthuman* (Cambridge: Polity Press, 2013).

15 Baruch Spinoza, *Ethics, Treatise on the Emendation of the Intellect and Selected Letters*, translated by E. Shirley, edited by S. Feldman (Indianapolis: Hackett Publishing Company, 1993).

16 Michel Foucault, *The Birth of Biopolitics: Lectures at the Collège de France, 1978–1979*, translated by G. Burchell (Basingstoke: Palgrave Macmillan, 2008).

17 Peg Rawes, 'Dissimilarity: Spinoza's Geometric Ratios and Housing Crisis', in *Spinoza's Philosophy of Proportion and Ratio*, edited by B. Lord (Edinburgh: Edinburgh University Press, 2017 in press).

18 Giorgio Agamben, *Homo Sacer: Sovereign Power and Bare Life* (Stanford: Stanford University Press, 1998).

19 Donna Haraway, *When Species Meet,* 2008.

20 J. K. Gibson Graham, *The End of Capitalism (As We Knew It): A Feminist Critique of Political Economy* (Minneapolis: University of Minnesota Press, 2006).

21 Gilles Deleuze, *Expressionism in Philosophy* (New York: Zone Books, 1992), 226.

22 Sylvia Lavin, *Kissing Architecture* (Princeton: Princeton University Press, 2011), 14.

23 Farshid Moussavi, *The Function of Form* (Barcelona: Actar, 2009).

24 Simon O'Sullivan, 'The Aesthetics of Affect: Thinking Art Beyond Representation', *Angelaki*, Vol. 6, No. 3 (2001):125–135.

25 See Peg Rawes and Beth Lord, *Equal By Design*, with Lone Star Productions, www.equalbydesign.
    co.uk (accessed 1 December 2016), and Peg Rawes, 'Housing Biopolitics and Care' in *Critical and
    Clinical Cartographies: Embodiment, Technology, Care, Design*, edited by A. Radman and H. Sohn
    (Edinburgh University Press: Edinburgh, 2017). Also see Danny Dorling, *All That is Solid: How the Great
    Housing Disaster Defines Our Times, and What We Can Do about It* (London: Allen Lane, 2014); Rowan
    Moore, 'Britain's Housing Crisis is a Human Disaster. Here are 10 Ways to Solve It', *The Observer*,
    14 March 2015, www.theguardian.com/society/2015/mar/14/britain-housing-crisis-10-ways-solve-rowan-
    mooregeneral-election (accessed 1 November 2016); Oliver Wainwright, 'Revealed: How Developers
    Exploit Flawed Planning System to Minimize Affordable Housing', *The Guardian*, 25 June 2015, www.
    theguardian.com/cities/2015/jun/25/london-developers-viability-planning-affordable-social-housing-
    regeneration-oliver-wainwright (accessed 1 November 2016).
26 See Alice Martin, 'Why the UK Leads the Way on Inequality', New Economics Foundation, 9 January
    2015,   www.neweconomics.org/blog/entry/why-the-uk-leads-the-way-on-inequality   (accessed   1
    November 2016); Deborah Garvie and Shelter, 'Little Boxes, Fewer Homes – Why Housing Space
    Standards Will Get More Homes Built', in *Equalities of Wellbeing*, April 2015, www.equalitiesofwellbeing.
    co.uk/publications-from-equalities-ofwellbeing-housing-workshop   (accessed   1   November   2016);
    Joseph Rowntree, *Housing and Poverty Blog*, www.jrf.org.uk/topic/housing-and-poverty (accessed 1
    November 2016).
27 Luther Martin et al., *Technologies of the Self: A Seminar with Michel Foucault* (Amhurst MA: University
    of Massachusetts Press, 1988).
28 Gilles Deleuze and Guattari, *Anti-Oedipus: Capitalism and Schizophrenia* (Minneapolis: University of
    Minnesota Press, 1983); Gilles Deleuze and Félix Guattari, *A Thousand Plateaus* (London: Continuum,
    1987).
29 Gilles Deleuze, *Francis Bacon* (London: Continuum, 2008).
30 Theodore Adorno, *Negative Dialectics* (London: Routledge, 1973), 23.
31 Peg Rawes, 'Humane and inhumane ratios', *Aysmmetric Labors: The Economy of Architecture in Theory
    and Practice*, edited by A. Cayer, P. Deamer, S. Korsh, E. Peterson and M. Shvartzberg (New York: The
    Architecture Lobby, 2016).

Project 5

Slow watch: A sci-fi novel about the ecology of time in the society of fear

Malin Zimm

It is the third time this week that the ergonomist adjusts her work station. Suri walks down the hall to get some coffee, a walk and a task that always reminds her how different her world is to others. People around her walk in slow motion, their clothes flapping and their cheeks bouncing unflatteringly around stout lips, an effect of gravity that most people perceive only on flat screens in sport playbacks – boxers taking a blow, every drop of spit leaving their mouths backlit, or footballers being tackled, knees awkwardly twisted or elbows poked into softer parts – yet this is a frame-by-frame-perception that Suri is incapable of turning off. Pressing the button for 'double espresso' and then 'steamed milk' puts her in what feels like a lunch break of waiting, before the brew begins to pour into the cup, in a beam that looks sculpted in tar.

Suri Moucha is a genetically designed surveillance footage analyst, specialized in face reading and global digital tracking. The security industry is growing in multiple fields in the public, military, and private sectors. The speed and accuracy of analysis is crucial since everyone is exposed to an abundance of information. Suri is a key figure in this industry of fear, and much hope is projected on her, as she is often the last instance in a chain of failed digital readings. Security and safety are terminological derivatives of fear, and stress is a physical and psychological reaction in its spectrum.

What makes Suri Moucha exceptional is that she has the heart rate and metabolic ratio of a mouse. As a function of their fast metabolism, time passes more slowly for small animals and insects.[1]

Perception of time is measured by establishing at what frequency a species can distinguish light flashing, showing that humans perceive 60 Hz, while flies perceive 250 Hz. Suri is capable of perceiving nearly two and a half times more visual information per second than the average human, a processing power that renders everything in slow motion from her point of view. Perception of time is strangely uniform to humans, with few exceptions beyond the fact that children, who are smaller and have faster metabolisms, perceive time as passing at a slower rate than adults do. An incoming swat appears to a fly like a slowly closing gate. To the smaller animals, the pace of the surrounding world is slow, like the bullet dodge in the film *The Matrix*. Humans, in turn, perceive the animals to be impossibly fast. Suri perceives her surroundings like a mouse would – not as slow as a fly (the rate of an insect's metabolism would kill her), but rather the speed of a small mammal's perception, which can be accommodated by her body's rate of energy conservation, as long as she follows her dietary advice and checks her body temperature regularly. Time is both external (objective, universal, and absolute) and internal (subjective, individual, and relative) and as a result Suri's external surroundings are perpetually lagging in relation to her high-resolution senses. [2] People's voices are distorted, their motions are performed as if their bodies are submerged in water. As a child, her genome was carefully mapped and studied. Her sensory development was followed by a team of researchers and physicians. At some point in all of this, a linguistic researcher wanted to show her how human voices sounded like, undistorted. They had wanted to equip her with devices they promised would restore 'normality'. She never felt more alone than when they tried to adapt her body to meet the reality of others.

Suri Moucha sits back in her chair, comfortable enough following the slight alterations recently made to her lower backrest. As she places her fingers on the sensor-fitted armrests, a stream of images floods the minute screens, like billions of multi-coloured shooting stars. A perfect storm of visuals, to anyone who could stomach to watch more than a few seconds. A bystander would not be able to make any sense of the flow, but Suri spends an adequate amount of time with each picture, discerning the patterns and identifying people as they move from one camera to the next, sometimes across continents, disappearing from one screen and appearing in another. She sprinkles target markers by means of brain wave control: simply thinking 'mark' leaves a perfectly traceable digital line of footsteps behind each of her targets. Her keyboard, integrated in the right armrest, allows her to add new targets, save complex tracks for closer inspection, save stills for reports, and report hidden angles, glitches, or poor coverage. She puts time markers on targets using, or dropping off or picking up, communication devices.

The armrest to the left holds the keys with which she adds mood markers, categorizing facial expressions into either one of the universal emotions: happiness, neutrality, surprise, sadness, contempt, wrath, or fear. Yes; the (four) negative emotions outnumber the (one) positive and (two) neutral ones. It makes her think that happiness is banal, both taken for granted but also idealized beyond reach. A paraphrase of Tolstoy comes into her mind: all happy faces are alike; each unhappy face is unhappy in its own way. The left-hand keyboard corresponds to the right side of her brain, which is more specialized in reading empathy. The whole set-up was carefully tested of course: Suri's brain is, after all, one of the most well-studied lumps of grey matter in the world. Her flow allows her to sift through the most important security footage in the world, to literally track hundreds of people around the earth. When computers and feds have tried everything, they apply for Suri's time, and she rarely fails.

For some time, it looked as though facial recognition technology, whereby a computer identifies a face in a photograph or video, was fool-proof and that the digital readers were winning: Nec's Neoface, 3VR, Microsoft, Google's Facenet, the Ukrainian company Viewdle, the Swedish company Polar Rose (eventually bought by Apple), Visage Technologies… All these companies were founded between 2010 and 2020, and whilst they were still growing, they found themselves increasingly in trouble as entire communities were formed around the reverse-engineering of facial recognition, as a kind of liberation movement.[3] People had learned to outsmart the digital systems that had been built to interpret human behaviour and detect risks, such as the American system FAST (Future Attribution Systems Technology), developed around 2015.[4] The future is a race between machine intelligence mapping human irrationality and biological entities responding with precision-acting and body control. The increasingly ingenious ways of confusing the digital readers included impeding the reading of biometrics by visually dislocating some of the eighty key nodes used in face identification. There were also strategies aimed at the AI development programmes. Hacker attacks on the 'training systems' for facial recognition were increasingly successful in disrupting the code that teaches a computer what a face look like. The 2018 attack on Eigenfaces gradually displaced its vectors until the computers trained by this PT failed even to tell human subjects from showroom dummies.[5] The anti-face movement grew strong in the late 2010s, as the number of arrests sky-rocketed in the aftermath of the new loitering laws introduced at the initiative of President Trump. Wearers of anti-faces were rarely criminals, in Suri's experience, and simple enough to track as unsuspicious entities, but there were of course always the hard cases. In a cat and mouse game of vision dazzle, Suri would find these individuals again and again and they in turn would again disappear from her screens, summoning a whole new set of war paint and ingenious camouflage techniques each time. Like World War I razzle-dazzle ships, skilled anti-faces had developed some amazing choreographies in combination with optical clothing and reflecting hoods, which made it difficult to tell which direction they were even moving in.

War is about getting the informational upper hand: watching the other, tracing them, and revealing a map of intentions that is almost always the result of a body in motion. You cannot switch off your body, but you can reconstruct the image of it. People would learn how to act different ages, adopting the way of walking and motion pattern of an elderly person, for instance. The menu of tricks had also expanded from simple physical costumes to digital masquerading, from trying to hide by means of invisibility cloaks, to multiplying, using kaleidoscopic projective software running on display surface clothing. These technologies were known as 'digital masks' or force fields, able to turn one person into four or fourteen people. A covering face was beginning to be more common, which contained liquid crystals that did virtually the same thing as the invisibility cloak. This also gave wearers a severe skin condition, since it was developed off the legal market. Body doubling has even spiralled to become a gadget on the market: first for security purposes and then for a whole range of services, from party tricks to kinkier stuff. To back-hack these rogue technologies and bring quality back to the surveillance data was the job of a squadron of 'reverse-reverse-engineers'. Suri's job, in contrast, was to stay ahead of the game, applying her unique perception and analysis to penetrate the strategies that fooled the digital face readers. Her skills were not merely physical – although she handled vast amounts of data at a speed impossible to follow for a normall consciousness – in fact, this physical ability has paved the way for a highly developed capacity for reading social dimensions. Although she hid it well, her 'condition' gave her enormous amounts of time to study the facial expressions, the pitch of voice (which was of course, always distorted, but also stretched, allowing her to notice the very composition of the frequencies that the voice is a compound of), and the minute twitches, glances, and hints that the human body gives off inadvertently.

Suri knows fear. She knows it from the wired heart of surveillance industry. She knows it from twenty years of sitting in front of ever more upgraded interfaces, ever more advanced systems, and ever more multiplied processors. Whatever they throw in front of her, her speed reading never falters, her skills are always able to be further perfected. In the beginning, Suri felt like she was the figurehead on the prow of the ship of fear. Of course, the company had always provided the highest class of healthcare, and her physician psychiatrist, dietician, and neurologist formed a perfect team to make sure that her mind was in order for the titanic tasks. The biology of fear is a field of study that includes all animal species. Some scientists have claimed that fear has a particular location in the brain (in rodents), while others argue that fear cannot be a psychological construct since in humans, neuroimaging does not show any uniform circuitry for fear. Despite being a feeling shared across phylogeny, scientific researchers have yet to establish a uniform ecological theory of fear that is functional.[6] In general, science is far behind in the study of feelings across species, a field that would emphasize empathy and understanding across biological systems. We have, as a society, quite willingly adopted fear as a central state. It creates communities, based on the infectious assumption of a common enemy or threat. Talking about anxiety, passing it on, becoming a group that shares fear: these are the mechanisms of the transfer of fear. Fear is rarely addressed directly, but there are rhetorical markers of its hold on society, the most common being 'safety' and 'security'. Fear triggers both a biological and a psychological response. The output of fear is both feelings and behaviour. Anxiety, however, cannot be treated in the mind only, it also needs body work.[7] Surveillance footage has become one of the most demanding storage forms in the world. The incessant CCTV footage and the documentation of the banalities of everyday life – people passing in and out of subway ticket lines, elevators, and lobbies – occupies more server space today than all the literature, film, and photographs recorded in history. Fear is the triumph of the banal.

The fears of society are manifested in Suri's body: her resting heart rate is equivalent to a normal person's pulse in the event of a car crash or childbirth. People are not designed to endure stress levels like these, but Suri has adapted to her augmented body functions and fully alert biochemistry. Her body temperature alone would be a fatal fever to most people. Having a heart rate like Suri's is like being a rabbit running in the headlights without stopping for years. Fear prepares an organism to react to danger, by triggering the release of hormones and slowing or shutting down functions not needed for survival (such as the digestive system), while sharpening senses and functions that help us survive, like vision. The heart rate increases in order to deliver blood to all muscles to prepare for flight, and a hormone flush reaches the amygdala to help us focus on the danger and store it in our memory.[8]

Suri closes her eyes and meditates, as she is advised to do between sessions, her eyes rolling in to the point between the nose, where the 'third eye' sits. She likes the idea of a third eye, but she does not think of it as a part of her own body; rather she sees it as the body part of another being, whose eye is placed inside of her. The first thing she sees when she opens her eyes is the bobble-head Jeremy Bentham doll she got from a witty and grateful FBI executive.

Today, she is scheduled for a meeting with the city-planning group that she reports to on a regular basis. They are all waiting for her when she enters. The meeting revolves around plans for an extension to the city airport. The architects explain: 'We have created a large, open space without support columns, which will easily accommodate any future reconfiguration needs in relation to the next generation of screening machines.' Suri looks at the drawing and routinely scans it for dead angles and broken sightlines. She says, half to herself, 'I can't help but think about the irony: in order to find specific bodies, the environment becomes all the more generic.' The plans are assessed in line with Suri's troubleshooting of placement of cameras, of sight-impeding spatial features like niches and recesses, and of the impact of revolving doors that almost function as photo booths. She suggests the space might be equipped with even more close-up equipment, since people are forced to slow down for a generous amount of time to ensure their faces are caught on camera. The more sophisticated the surveillance systems become, the more elaborate the reconstruction and camouflage of bodies. The design team is increasingly responsible for reducing congestion in non-secure areas, creating more off-site checkpoints, and optimizing crowd-control infrastructure.[9] Before Suri leaves the meeting, one of the architects turns to her and comments: 'I guess we're learning from Las Vegas – all over again.'

```
        .;*rt1(!rtj!r1}j]+jfxrjv)c.,
     Tī+sc(!!*"<!~!\r\!||""""*!\^jr6;
     Q9stj~\^r~*!i~!!***~r1tc5%SDQW-
     AWOKOQNWNBOWRBQOXOBWWWWWBBOBNs
      uWODS%6BPbU6AkbkdXVkkaUOBWM
       TOKBWBQXS9$a23AA555DWWQOR\
       QWkzS$QWOQBWWBWWDOX6!NWA
       WWe)U4?j~!tj!\jj+j1PjVM9
       QN54zj!,  ,  ,  ,:*\[k4dMa
       RWWr(!_,  ,  ``_r;;\!4]VW*
       XNT;svⅼr\!t!1ī<r<34b35W?
       4U<rS34~;~ir+)tt25S!4W2
       kNr_5Ek^*~(1j1[T2DO<  VWc
       6M\ \VdT"*5O9KE9SAv   4W1
       UMr  l3X5"!b3sCU5z*   CW'
       $W-    "TU35VkkUOT"   dQ!
       dW'     !u6SAQDXT;    zW
       VW'       !z5RW6(:    2W'
       5Wr        |fNN[;     3W
       VW)        ,]5kl      3Wr
       VW!        *]]Ts      VW!
       6W-        ]<?!a1     dW)
       VW!       r[\"ttkl    5Qr
       kB|     ,fj+`:~ts4(     %Br
       aW`    :?~*`|~`*i4s_   UW!
       jW!    `V*;  ,*:`  ,;!3X`  $Rj
       2W*   4r!*;_!!   _!tSD 3Qj
       UW'rd';_,`*:  ̄"\zWk[R3
       QWb?_~;,kr ,_!!tkDEW3
       NQ"Cj ̄`r%Vkz!`,<szR4Bk
       WW'3k;  ,<k!!\c$5!lr?A3B5
       RW"23~;rl~<Jx[4GP[V4kW5
       WWrf%k!;<ssj?e3k$BA*3Mk
       WWT4e7kKa?kT3TdKS3Af_%M
       2QWkrxd2AOXdKKOO5a%S\*SW6_
      _rkWWA<v9QKSSGK5VAEKWKnkDSk:!!
     j̄?VkORNVUNNWWWWWWNQWRQQ%SkTcSb*
     5Qk5X52DQAb3Vsjv]]kV5s5U4k5SWO
     !BGDN%kCSPk3kAnJ[jVsTTV$OWWWWU
      j%GBWNWANRWUPEDOXURKNBWBWWW.
       <kBWWOQWWNSQRDOWNNWWWEVT~
        kUUNSUNSXDBk2x<:;
```

Later that afternoon, Suri is standing in a body scanning box that looks like a shower cubicle, that Tammie, her physcian, invites her to enter with her standard joke, 'Right, time to beam you up.' Her daily scan is performed, and her body temperature is measured. While being scanned, she asks if it's ok to join the badminton team later in the week. 'Sure, I mean, that's totally up to you, in fact we had an evaluation of your long-term stats and I must say, they've never been better. Your body temp is way more stable than even two years ago, and cardio-wise, you know, you've nothing to worry about.'

Suri knows why she feels better than ever, but has decided to keep this a secret, as an experiment in reverse psychology, and not for any particular reason, just spite. Since everything about her is monitored, she thinks it fair to exercise some integrity and leave the team out of the loop regarding the game she has invented, letting them think they will have the analysis before she does. Her employers are still captives of fear, while she has liberated herself. Gradually, then suddenly, she let go of fear. She felt her body reach a platform, like the state you might achieve by years and years of meditation, she reached that point where the storm got quiet, and the waves stopped rolling. It was impossible to see it coming, and impossible to turn back once she had experienced this total bliss. In the beginning, her work was satisfying; it became the outflow of a sense of acuteness. But over the years she'd become more and more detached from that acuteness, from the fear-driven industry around her, and increasingly fascinated by the meditative qualities of her work, as she perfected the art of finding, following, tracking, and marking the people she was asked to find in the wired world of people watching over people. A feeling of fondness had come over her, a tender but firm hold of her fast-beating heart, as the incessant flows of people flushed through her screens. The predictability of the behaviour of these masses had become as interesting to her as the ingenuity of the dissidents. She had learned to love all of them, these people passing by. And nobody had seen more people passing by than Suri.

Postscript

I have constructed the name Suri Moucha from the French words for mouse, *souris*, and fly, *mouche*. Suri Moucha is genetically equipped with very sharp vision, not in the depth of space but in the depths of time. Suri is offering her body functions and unique services to a society driven by fear and the need for control. Society rebuilds itself to accommodate fear,[10] while people adjust to resist the architecture of fear by reconstructing their bodies, in an act of defiance.

Notes

1   Emilie Reas, "Small Animals Live in a Slow-Motion World," *Scientific American* (July 1, 2014), www.scientificamerican.com/article/small-animals-live-in-a-slow-motion-world/#
2   H. E. Lehmann, "Time and Psychopathology," *Annals of the New York Academy of Sciences* 138 (1967): 798–821.
3   Linus Larsson, "Ansiktet kan avslöja vem som helst," *Dagens Nyheter* (October 15, 2016), www.dn.se/nyheter/vetenskap/ansiktet-kan-avsloja-vem-som-helst/
4   DHS Science and Technology Directorate, Department of Homeland Security, "Future Attribute Screening Technology (FAST) Fact Sheet" (November 18, 2014), www.dhs.gov/sites/default/files/publications/Future%20Attribute%20Screening%20Technology-FAST-508_0.pdf
5   "Eigenface," *Wikipedia*, last modified January 9, 2017, https://en.wikipedia.org/wiki/Eigenface
6   Ralph Adolphs "The Biology of Fear," *Current Biology* 23, no. 2 (January 21, 2013): 79–93.
7   New York University, "Researchers outline barriers to treating fear, anxiety," *ScienceDaily*, September 9, 2016, www.sciencedaily.com/releases/2016/09/160909094831.htm
8   University of Minnesota, "Impact of Fear and Anxiety," *Taking Charge of your Health and Wellbeing*, accessed on July 14, 2016, www.takingcharge.csh.umn.edu/enhance-your-wellbeing/security/facing-fear/impact-fear
9   Alwyn Scott and Daniel Trotta, "Architects Fight Airport Security Threats with Flexible Design," *Reuters* (July 2, 2016), www.reuters.com/article/us-turkey-blast-airportsecurity-idUSKCN0ZI0ET
10 Nan Ellin, *The Architecture of Fear* (New York: Princeton Architectural Press, 1997).

Chapter 13

Academic capitalism in architecture schools

A feminist critique of employability, 24/7 work and entrepreneurship

Igea Troiani

Figure 13.1 Charlie Chaplin, Stanley Sanford, from *Modern Times,* 1936
Copyright Photographer Chaplin/United Artists/REX/Shutterstock

Figure 13.2 Charlie Chaplin, from *Modern Times*, 1936
Copyright Photographer Max Munn Autrey/Chaplin/United Artists/REX/Shutterstock

In the 1936 comedy film, *Modern Times*,[1] Chaplin is employed on an assembly line where he screws nuts onto pieces of machinery in a steel factory at an ever-increasing rate. As the machine is sped up on the instruction of the President of the Electro Steel Corporation, Chaplin is forced to work faster. In an ingenious move by upper management to maximise production, a piece of new technology, the "feeding machine" is brought onto the shop floor and the workers are force fed in a way that ensures their hands are free to work for greater productivity. Unable to keep up Chaplin goes mad and runs into the machine that continues regardless.

> If this [the university] is a firm, . . . and if President Kerr in fact is the manager; then I'll tell you something. The faculty are a bunch of employees; and we're the raw material! But we're a bunch of raw materials that don't mean to be . . . Don't mean to be made into any product . . . Don't mean to end up being bought by some clients of the University, be they the government, be they industry, . . . be they anyone! We're human beings!

There's a time when the operation of the machine becomes so odious, makes you so sick at heart, that you can't take part! . . . And you've got to put your bodies upon the gears and upon the wheels . . . upon the levers, upon all the apparatus, and you've got to make it stop! And you've got to indicate to the people who run it, . . . that unless you're free, the machine will be prevented from working at all![2]

Academic capitalism

Universities have long been free institutions. In the United Kingdom, they are becoming less so, in both their demand for (ever-increasing) student fees and their positioning in relation to the marketplace outside the university. Marketisation (or increased market and market-like behaviour) has allowed many public universities worldwide to transition from Foucault's 'premodern or medieval university'[3] to entrepreneurial businesses. During the Industrial Revolution, academics were able to 'position themselves between capital and labor, protecting themselves from the harsh discipline of the market'.[4] But the nature of academic labour changed dramatically during the late 20th century due to the 'globalization of the political economy'[5] resulting in academic capitalism.[6] Since then, 'changes in funding [have] work[ed] to bring the university and its faculty in line with economic production and the managerial revolution'.[7] The implementation of a New Public Management (NPM) approach means that governments require public universities to fund and manage their own budgets, transacting according to a neoliberal system of consuming and producing students, staff, knowledge and research for the purpose of improving national economies through continuous growth from the engine of entrepreneurial innovation.

While this is a universal phenomenon experienced across all disciplines, here I focus in detail on the negative impact academic capitalism has had on schools of architecture in the UK. While many academics will identify with what is discussed, it can be uncomfortable and depressing for some to acknowledge because it sheds doubts about the future of architectural education. My argument is that architectural academics are too acquiescent and polite to react against the neoliberal demands imparted on us. Denialism will do little to improve an unhealthy model of architectural education because it debilitates academics from targeting precise areas of change. I propose that 'a feminist politics of resistance'[8] that can be practiced by sceptical, politically active women and men architecture academics, is a vital way to resist the diminishing of quality in architectural education.

This chapter is indebted to work of the political scientist, Wendy Brown, on the impact of neoliberalism in academia, and (in general) on democracy, freedom of speech, power and gender equality. In higher education, an established patriarchal model of academic labour constructs and obstructs the formation of alternate values and identities of diverse educators and students opposed to the prioritisation of economically driven architectural education. Following the post-1970s era of Thatcher, architectural education in the UK altered, veering away from a qualitative model to a quantitative self-centred model of higher education. At the core of this shift is the imperative for universities to create highly employable architectural graduate technicians faster and as many as the architecture schools are allowed to recruit. Because of this, some critics have compared universities to factories both in their design and modes of production.[9]

Employability in architectural education

James Mayo explains that, 'Operating like a factory has economically served architecture schools moderately well in the past'.[10] Prospective students (and their parents) often choose architecture as a career because, as a profession, it is seen to offer greater job security and income generation post-university. Because of their already healthy intakes, architecture schools are seen as departments that can expand. In order to create new 'markets', the number of undergraduates has increased disproportionately to teaching staff. Some schools have developed the digital learning experience with little or no direct teaching contact or established architecture courses in other countries that capture new markets, such as China, attracting post-graduates into their UK programmes. Summer courses are run during non-teaching time and the shift to two shorter semesters rather than three terms means there is less teaching delivered.

In order to increase their revenue, NPM university administrators (often with no connection with the disciplines they are managing) 'work with the mentality of the managerial class'[11] by increasing student intake in national and international markets and changing the demographic of their academic workforce. Architecture academics who teach are morphing from a workforce of predominantly full time or tenured experts into a part-time, casual, temporary or contingent staff[12] teaching design studios or delivering lectures and seminars with fewer workplace benefits for job security and progression. Academic staff work many more hours than they are remunerated. Casual staff often accept these contracts because they offer them, in the short term, a rate of pay (comparable or higher to the income they are making in practice) and intellectual stimulation (which they might be denied in practice) that can in the long term increase their reputational capital. To quote Brown, 'Younger faculty, raised on neoliberal careerism, are generally unaware that there could be alternative academic purposes and practices to those organized by a neoliberal table of values'.[13] Their labour exploitation is a key way in which schools of architecture justify their 'bang for buck' or cost-to-benefit ratio. When professors or other full time staff leave or retire they are often replaced with staff without equivalent qualifications for cost saving reasons. While the university gains from its economically rational business model, there are detrimental effects on the quality of teaching delivered to students but this is camouflaged through the reason for an architectural education.

Neoliberalism in schools of architecture focuses on the short-term vocational goal of making students instantly employable, efficient "factory workers" (who can maximise the money they can make for their employers). Free student labour, undertaken as 'live projects' for outside clients in architecture schools, is practice exploitative. On the teaching shop floor, areas of the architecture curriculum – its liberal arts aspects, namely history and theory – that are deemed to be speculative or less obviously economically generative can be devalued under academic capitalism. Technical skills enhancing revenue-generating productivity in students are given equal if not greater value because they increase the chances of employability. This has a detrimental effect on architectural practice and architecture because it disables a graduate's long-term goal to be an independent and critical architectural thinker and designer. Nowadays students are encouraged to gain employment in a firm or to start their own practice as soon as possible without having developed their own architectural position, steadily over years of practice mentoring. There is also the more insidious suggestion that one trains as an architect to become a consultant whose rate of pay is higher than that of a salaried architect. Alternatively because of the low rate of pay in the profession, some students are veering towards starting their own entrepreneurial multidisciplinary visualisation company (a new market for the profession) or model-making company rather than architectural practice, creating a division of labour in the architectural production process prioritising the image of architecture for advertising, selling or winning jobs.[14]

The university's administratively heavy methods of assessment have also followed neoliberal quantitative, checking systems used in manufacturing. Laurence argues that, 'the university, like the hospital or the prison, can be understood as an apparatus of perpetual examination'.[15] He contends that a process of standardisation or normalisation occurs in order to acculturate students into disciplinary norms: 'The student is constantly evaluated, graded, measured, created. The abnormal is marginalized, rejected, and excluded. The human sciences develop and the university introduces the student to a world where everything can be measured, including their imaginations'.[16]

The consequence of this 'examinatorial power is the invention of a new type of . . . calculable individual'.[17] NPM driven universities present students as consumers or "clients" of measurable academic services and academics as "service providers". Many educators accept this unquestionably. The shift in relationship from educator/mentor-student/mentee to educator/manufacturer-student/client has dire consequences in terms of pedagogical practice. National Student Surveys (NSS) in the UK and university rankings are the indicators of an undergraduate programme's strength, and with that the strength and quality of a school of architecture. Happy "clients" in high revenue generating universities lead to a good NSS ranking. Students often have more power, than staff, to complain and to get response from senior managers. "Client satisfaction" means that staff complaints are devalued or ignored and staff, particularly younger staff, are fearful to voice their opinions. For staff with full time and fractional posts teaching and research are both under constant quantitative surveillance.

More permanent staff are required to teach and offer pastoral care to increasingly large student numbers while actively researching to produce internationally recognised research and obtain funding (to buy out their research and teaching time). Operating like a factory worker, producing and satisfying clients and producing and disseminating world-renowned research, requires that architecture academics work such long hours that they have limited time or opportunity to slowly evolve and construct new research or knowledge. The academic is given minimum time to think and to produce 'deliverables', from which the university can make revenue. As work hours grow, the time to rest decreases. This imbalance has detrimental affects on staff mental and physical health.

A 24/7 work life

According to Jonathan Crary, 'in relation to labor, [a 24/7 work life] renders plausible, even normal, the idea of working without pause, without limits. It is aligned with what is inanimate, inert, or unageing'.[18] Crary notes the 'features that distinguish living beings from machines'[19] include the need for pause or for rest. But '24/7 markets and a global infrastructure for continuous work and consumption'[20] undermine this. Globalised architectural practice (where a firm creates architecture across multiple time zones and countries so that a job never stops being worked on) is not questioned under neoliberalism. In fact, many profit-driven practitioners see this as the sign of a successful, 'healthy' practice.[21]

Some universities have shifted to 24/7 architectural studio and library opening hours to support, enable and encourage high productivity. Building in part upon the model of the Beaux-Arts architect working tirelessly and happily in their arts studio, architectural programmes encourage students to work continuously 'without breaks' and to demand email responses from their educators 24/7. New technology allows 24/7 labour and penetrates the domestic domain of architectural students and academics. Crary contends that time to regenerate 'is now simply too expensive to be structurally possible within contemporary capitalism'.[22]

In *The Time Bind: When Work Becomes Home and Home Becomes Work* Arlie Russell Hochschild refers to the 1936 comedy film, *Modern Times*, starring Charlie Chaplin (Figures 1 and 2).[23] Hochschild notes that the speedup of labour in modern life is no longer confined to work and now 'extends to the home'.[24] The architecture student or academic is hurried and stretched in their university workplace and, if they have family or carer commitments, hurries others.[25] Like Chaplin's character in the film, more and more architecture students and academics are suffering mental and physical illness, burnout or exhaustion. In a work-oriented paradox, rather than reduce excessive workloads, most architecture schools create more work within the university through elaborate bureaucratic systems for medical and psychological support for staff and students or externally run wellbeing classes and courses for employees, often outside set work hours. Those able to survive and thrive in high-pressure work environments are rewarded for their ability to be tirelessly productive for the university's success. In *The Second Shift: Working Parents and the Revolution of Home*, Hochschild and Machung contend that universities favour 'family-free people' because they are able to be optimally productive.[26]

Economic man, creativity and entrepreneurship

From 1978 to 1979, Michel Foucault examined neoliberalism through a series of lectures that considered the link between governmentality (or 'the art of government') and the exertion of power. In the book of the collated lectures entitled *The Birth of Biopolitics* Foucault notes the changing relationship between biology and politics (biopolitics) and the powerful role that *homo oeconomicus* or economic man plays in neoliberalism.[27] Economic man is highly employable and productive. They are family-free (this does not mean they are without a family but that they do not have primary care responsibilities, thereby giving them more time to work). They are entrepreneurial, using creativity to gain a market edge in the global economy. Economic man is consumed with self-interest, and adopts rationality for maximum economic gain. In her reflection on Foucault's lectures, Brown notes that under neoliberalism's free market advocacy economic man 'takes its shape as human capital seeking to strengthen its competitive positioning and appreciate its value'.[28] Economic man today acts out the 'ever-growing intimacy of corporate and finance capital with the state'[29] and ensures that everything is for sale. Economic rationalism demands that education, healthcare, falling pregnant and even dating are commoditised to maximise return on investment.[30]

Homo oeconomicus in a university setting is family-free, productive and entrepreneurial. Slaughter and Leslie argue that 'globalization [has created] new structures, incentives, and rewards for some aspects of academic careers and is simultaneously instituting constraints and disincentives for other aspects of careers'.[31] Pressure has risen in universities for academics to bring in external money from industry or research funding bodies, taking them out of what some have called the 'ivory tower' into corporate life. In public UK institutions 'state funding of universities is "tied" to a set of academic productivity metrics that measure knowledge according to "impact"'.[32] The rationality of *homo oeconomicus* working in the university quantifies and measures outputs and the numbers of people on social media networks reading that research through tweets, LinkedIn followers etc. Those who elect not to participate at this level of being quantified for their 'academic credit rating' become uncompetitive and unattractive for university promotion. Because as Brown notes, neoliberalism accentuates inequality rather than fosters it, as it falsely claims, all of those who are not 'socially male and masculinist within a persistently gendered economic ontology and division of labor' are disadvantaged.[33] To quote Brown further, 'this is so regardless of whether men are "stay-at-home fathers," women are single or childfree, or families are queer. . . . With only competing and value-enhancing human capital in the frame, complex and persistent gender inequality is attributed to sexual difference, an effect that neoliberalism takes for the cause'.[34]

While the *homo oeconomicus* is a phrase that is not gender specific, entrepreneur meaning 'to do something', comes from the 13th century French masculine verb *entreprendre*. Because of its use in John Stuart Mill's *Principles of Political Economy*, it became popular and was used to describe an entrepreneur as both a risk taker and business manager.[35]

There are parallels between the entrepreneurial business outside the university and the entrepreneurial university surrounding global market capture. The entrepreneurial university aims to spread 'throughout the world (encouraging excellence and innovation in an environment of mutual competitive rivalry)' in order to 'enhance . . . their own institution' in the 'global university space'.[36] According to Biernacki, 'Economics instrumentalizes creativity as a factor of production'.[37] Creativity in an academic arena is co-opted by neoliberalism for revenue making. As Schvartzberg explains: 'The popular notion of "creativity" is particularly interesting because it has become a generalized imperative of neoliberalized societies: creativity (and its proxies, "innovation" and "disruption") are seen today as an essential component of any "competitive" worker'.[38] It is because of the ability of 'creativity [to] ma[k]e new worlds out of nothing' and to 'measure . . . productivity as a kind of surplus value relative to other inputs' that economists such as Richard Florida have defined the value of the 'creative class' in which architects and architectural researchers sit comfortably.[39]

Before graduation, universities offer incentive programmes to enhance student entrepreneurship. Career academics (who never leave working in the university) typically construct one path of research through which to consolidate their, and their university's, reputation for innovation. Creating a unique field of research requires long-time research (better done in large teams) on a topic that has been chosen early.

Students and academic researchers who are not 'family free' in universities are disadvantaged by the entrepreneurial turn. The persistent gender attainment gap, pay gap and promotion gap in universities attests to inequalities premised on long working hours.[40] Morley contends that women (and I would add men) academics with family care responsibilities are 'caught between two greedy institutions – the extended family and the university . . . A dominant view is that time expended on role performance in one domain depletes time available for the demands of the other domain'.[41]

Pillay writes that academic mothers find it difficult to balance 'two lives' because the juggle can lead to 'going nowhere slowly'.[42] She suggests that the transitional space in-between motherhood and the intellectual self is not always 'smooth'.[43] Academics with family care responsibilities are pressured because 'each role absorbs enormous psychological, intellectual, and emotional energy'.[44] Academic mothers, fathers and carers have to rationalise the tasks required of them in both their domestic and professional spheres so as to 'become highly efficient, serious and single minded by compartmentalising work life and family life'.[45]

Resisting academic capitalism

Unlike private corporations, universities have had a shorter period of running their own 'businesses' and are not currently supporting gender equity of their academic staff within their organisations. Koppes Bryan and Wilson note that 'It is a somewhat perplexing reality that higher education lags behind other sectors . . . Major corporations long ago recognized the need to adjust personnel policies to attract and retain men and women seeking to better "balance" career and family . . . While colleges and universities are perceived as being highly progressive, the fact of the matter is that higher education is an extremely conservative enterprise when it comes to change'.[46] In this period of transition to entrepreneurial university, many schools of architecture are currently exploiting both their 'human (academic) capital' and 'cultural capital'. Architecture academics, supported by upper management, need to actively acknowledge and resist many of the economically instigated changes presented to them by their universities for reasons I will explain below.[47]

The absorption of neoliberalism does not sit comfortably within the academic community because it disempowers the fundamental role that universities have as agents for social correction. As Simon Sadler notes: 'The model of the university as a locus for criticism within the dense relations of capitalism depends on the possibility of immanent critique – on locating the contradictions in the rules and systems necessary to production'.[48] Academics need to have a critical distance from production, but the co-option of neoliberalism by universities contradicts this. Olssen claims that neoliberalism's departure from the welfare state tradition has attacked the notion of public interest, which had formerly underpinned western models of bureaucracy and government.[49]

The nurturing of competitive marketplace tactics that pit design studios or research clusters against one another are gender biased because they advocate macho aggression.[50] According to Olssen, 'although it is essential in economic contexts to ensure norms of fair cooperation in order to avoid monopolies and the centralization of economic power, in many community contexts, including families, and frequently in work places, reciprocal social relations depend upon cooperative behaviour, and facilitation, rather than competition. One of the crucial failings of unbridled neoliberalism from the perspective of educators, . . . is that it seeks to institute competition as the central structuring norm of a society on the grounds that this best promotes efficient institutional and behavioural forms'.[51]

Academic selflessness, rather than selfishness, will allow the employment of tactics of resistance. Some tactics invite academics to look after the wellbeing of themselves and their family and their colleagues by resisting the demands put on them by their managers. Others encourage academics to look after the wellbeing of their students and public welfare as their professional responsibility.

The eleven female authors and members of the Great Lakes Feminist Geography Collective argue that a slow scholarship movement is one way of resisting the university pressures put on academics for high productivity.[52] The authors set out a range of 'strategies to resist the compressed temporal regimes of the neoliberal university [so as] to stop, reflect, reject, resist, subvert, and collaborate to cultivate different, more reflexive academic cultures'.[53] They are to: 1. Talk about and support slow strategies; 2. Count what others don't; 3. Organize; 4. Take care; 5. Write fewer emails; 6. Turn off email; 7. Make time to think; 8. Make time to write (differently); 9. Say no. Say yes; and 10. Reach for the minimum (number of outputs and amount of grant funding). These are some practical proactive steps to surviving short-term pressures and go some way to challenging the efficiency and quantitative valuing demanded of *homo oeconomicus* academics.

Still, for disciplinary specificity, I would add that it might simply be enough to question, at every moment of our working life, the labour we are asked to perform. It might be enough that we do not simply acquiesce to top-down governance that prioritises only the economic value of humanity and self-promotion. We must critically examine the relationship between our biology and politics and between the city and the soul. Over the twenty years I have been in architectural education, women, men, gays and lesbians who have been disadvantaged or discriminated against have offered, from their marginalised spaces, voices of reason in what is otherwise a peculiarly 'macho' masculinist world that propels us uncritically towards a future few of us are brave enough to challenge. Resistance will be most effective, as Brown has exemplified, through free academic speech represented in our writing and talking with our academic peers, students and the public. We need to work actively to ground our students and us through retaining pity, empathy and generosity within an academic community. I encourage us to work specifically to re-value citizenship over economic growth and self-interest in our individual careers. Architecture academics need to acknowledge and question at every opportunity the neoliberalisation of schools of architecture premised on marketisation, economisation and optimisation. The mistrust of the 'ivory tower' intellectual realm instigated by industry, and implemented by governments, undermines the importance of the academic voice and we must resist this to retain quality in architectural education and in architectural production outside the university.

Acknowledgements: Thank you to Tonia Carless and Philip Baker for their generous feedback to this chapter.

Notes

1   Charlie Chaplin, dir., *Modern Times* (USA, 1936).
2   Mario Savio, quoted in Frederick Turner, *From Counterculture to Cyberculture* (Chicago: University of Chicago Press, 2006), 11. Quoted in Franco Berardi, 'Dynamic of the general intellect,' in *The Architect as Worker: Immaterial Labor, the Creative Class and the Politics of Design*, ed. Peggy Deamer (London: Bloomsbury Academic, 2015), 3.
3   Michel Foucault, *The Order of Things* (London: Routledge, 2002/1966). In the premodern university, Foucault contends people's limits were defined in relation to God or outside the living world. After modernity, people's limits became defined within the living world and the role of scholars was to direct society. It was the state's role to support this cultural trajectory, not demand direct economic returns.
4   Sheila Slaughter and Larry L. Leslie, *Academic Capitalism: Politics, Policies and the Entrepreneurial University* (Baltimore and London: John Hopkins University Press, 1997), 4.
5   Slaughter and Leslie, *Academic Capitalism*, 1.
6   'Academic capital' was defined by Pierre Bourdieu, 'The forms of capital,' in *Handbook of Theory and Research for the Sociology of Education*, ed. J. Richardson (New York: Greenwood, 1986) 241–258.
7   Michael Gibbons et al., *The New Production of Knowledge: The Dynamics of Science and Research in Contemporary Societies* (London, California, New Delhi and Singapore: Sage, 1994), quoted in Slaughter and Leslie, *Academic Capitalism*, 2.
8   Alison Mountz et al., 'For Slow Scholarship: A Feminist Politics of Resistance through Collective Action in the Neoliberal University,' *ACME: An International E-Journal for Critical Geographies* 14, no. 4 (2015): 1235–1259.
9   Pier Vittorio Aureli, 'Form and Labor: Toward a History of Abstraction in Architecture,' in *The Architect as Worker: Immaterial Labor, the Creative Class and the Politics of Design*, ed. Peggy Deamer (London: Bloomsbury Academic, 2015), 111.
10 James M. Mayo, 'Dilemmas of Architectural Education in the Academic Political Economy,' *Journal of Architectural Education* 44, no. 2 (1991): 80–89, 81.
11 Ibid., 81.
12 Contingent labour describes on-demand labour in a neutral way so that businesses can camouflage their motives. Casual and temporary have different connotations.
13 Wendy Brown, *Undoing the Demos: Neoliberalism's Stealth Revolution* (New York: Zone Books, 2015), 198.
14 Factory Fifteen www.factoryfifteen.com/home), Squint/Opera www.squintopera.com/) or DBOX www.dbox.com/).
15 Mike Laurence, 'Reconstituting the Political: Foucault and the Modern University' (paper presented at the annual meeting of the American Political Science Association, Ontario, Canada, September, 2009). Laurence refers to Gilles Deleuze writings on Foucault but not to Deleuze's control societies specifically.
16 Ibid.
17 Ibid.
18 Jonathan Crary, *24/7: Late Capitalism and the Ends of Sleep* (London and New York: Verso, 2014), 9–10.
19 Ibid., 14.
20 Ibid., 3.

21 Graham Owen ed., *Architecture, Ethics and Globalization: Ethics, Efficacy and Architecture in the Globalized Economy* (London: Routledge, 2009).

22 Crary, *24/7*, 14–15.

23 Arlie Russell Hochschild, *The Time Bind: When Work Becomes Home and Home Becomes Work* (New York: Metropolitan Books, 1997).

24 Ibid., 225.

25 Laura Koppes Bryan with Cheryl A. Wilson, *Shaping Work-Life Culture in Higher Education: A Guide for Academic Leaders* (New York and London: Routledge, 2015), 12. 'High demands and expectations for job performance that result in more time at work increase negative stress in family life.'

26 Arlie Hochschild with Anne Machung, *The Second Shift: Working Parents and the Revolution of Home* (London: Piatkus, 1989).

27 Michel Foucault, *The Birth of Biopolitics: Lectures at the Collège de France, 1978–1979*, ed. Arnold I. Davidson, trans. Graham Burchell (Basingstoke: Palgrave Macmillan, 2010).

28 Brown, *Undoing the Demos*, 33.

29 Ibid., 29.

30 Ibid., 31.

31 Slaughter and Leslie, *Academic Capitalism*, 1.

32 Brown, *Undoing the Demos*, 23.

33 Ibid., 107.

34 Ibid., 107.

35 John Stuart Mill, *Principles of Political Economy* [1884], abridged and edited by J. Laurence Laughlin (New York: 2009), Project Gutenberg e-book.

36 Ansgar Allen, 'The Idea of a World University: Can Foucauldian Research Offer a Vision of Educational Futures?' *Pedagogy, Culture & Society* 19, no. 3 (2011): 370.

37 Richard Biernacki, 'The Capitalist Origin of the Concept of Creative Work,' in *The Architect as Worker*, ed. Deamer, 40.

38 Manuel Shvartzberg, 'Foucault's "Environmental" Power: Architecture and Neoliberal Subjectivization,' in *The Architect as Worker*, ed. Deamer, 181.

39 Biernacki, 'Capitalist Origin,' 40; Richard Florida, *The Rise of the Creative Class: And How it's Transforming Work, Leisure, Community and Everyday Life* (New York: Basic Books, 2002).

40 Joyce P. Jacobsen, 'The Human Capital Explanation for the Gender Gap in Earnings,' in *Women, Family and Work: Writings on the Economics of Gender*, ed. Karine S. Moe (Malden, MA, Oxford, Melbourne and Berlin: Blackwell, 2003), 161–176.

41 Louise Morley, 'Women and Higher Education Leadership: Absences and Aspirations,' Leadership Foundation for Higher Education Stimulus Paper (London: Leadership Foundation for Higher Education, 2013), 7.

42 Venitha Pillay, *Academic Mothers* (Stoke on Trent, UK and Sterling, USA: Trentham Books, 2007), 30.

43 Ibid., viii.

44 One mother, quoted in ibid., 30.

45 Chester 1990: 7, quoted in Pillay, *Academic Mothers*, 31.

46 Koppes Bryan with Wilson, *Shaping Work-Life Culture*, ix.

47 Koppes Bryan and Wilson argue that academic leaders should take the lead in changing the work culture in colleges and universities through 'facilitating a work-life culture that is supportive of faculty, staff, and students.' Ibid., 2.

48 Simon Sadler, 'The Varieties of Capitalist Experience,' in *Architecture and Capitalism: 1845 to the Present*, ed. Peggy Deamer (London: Routledge, 2014), 125.

49 Mark Olssen, *Liberalism, Neoliberalism, Social Democracy: Thin Communitarian Perspectives on Political Philosophy and Education* (New York and London: Routledge, 2010), 14.

50 Ibid.

51 Ibid.

52 Mountz et al., 'For Slow Scholarship,' 1249–1253.

53 Ibid., 1249.

Chapter 14

Environmentalising humanitarian governance in Za'atri Refugee Camp through 'interactive spaces'

A posthuman approach

Aya Musmar

Humanitarian deafness

In Za'atri, a refugee camp with a population of almost 80,000, more than twenty Western humanitarian NGOs have been working to respond to the Syrian refugees' everyday needs.[1] A review conducted by MSF (Médecins Sans Frontières) in October 2013 to evaluate the quality of the camp management contrasted the weighty administration and coordination of Za'atri with the critical view taken by refugees of their circumstances there.[2] The report of that review referred to refugees' attitudes to different probabilities of 'failure' by agencies in Za'atri to effectively facilitate refugees' participation in decision-making and to take into account refugees' desired changes in the camp.[3]

Today, five years after the camp was established, Western NGOs in Za'atri still seem to struggle to bridge the gap between what they think they should offer and what actual life in the camp might require. It is apparent to visitors to the camp that refugees there are not satisfied with how their lives are run by the NGOs; discussing camp governance with refugees tends to elicit responses tinged with irritation. For example, one Syrian refugee complained to me: 'we know how to do things if they ask us what we think! It is ironic for us how they come up with some decisions while abandoning others without any logical reason; we just watch from a distance and smile, waiting to see what happens next!' Another refugee who was more involved in the decision-making process said, 'Even if they do ask us what we want, they end up doing what they think is right anyway!' These objections address two main opinions among refugees about camp governance: one sees the NGOs as strongly implicated in the currently despised governance of the camp; the other opinion is that the refugees themselves need to be included in the camp's governance structure. The perception that NGO frameworks resist offers of practical input and ideas from their clients widens the gap between the Western NGOs as the camp's governors and the refugees as the governed population. This gap gestures towards an accountability that humanitarian NGOs have failed to achieve in the camp.

While Western humanitarian NGOs aim to respond to people in crisis, their legitimacy and accountability should be questioned in light of their ideological and pragmatic paradigms.[4] The legitimacy, which they seek with their governmental counterparts, is established in Za'atri by their pledges to abide by the humanitarian principles of the UNHCR with which they are partnered.[5] While these principles are assumed to be universal, their accountability is still measured against 'their ability to argue persuasively that they contribute to the welfare of the governed'.[6] To establish their accountability, many Western NGOs lean on their pragmatic agendas to show how their frameworks work towards engaging with or representing those who are governed. However, as suggested above, the governed are often dissatisfied with the quality of the services or programmes delivered by the humanitarian NGOs.

Mindful that NGO activities tend to reflect their respective ideological frameworks, I argue that Western NGOs are hampered by their ideological commitment to humanistic approaches with their presumed universal applicability. Since Western humanitarian NGOs are structured upon a universal description of the human, they usually bring the Western construct of basic definitions to other contexts without accounting for the culture, language, or belief systems of those contexts. Derived from Eurocentric subjectivity, with reference to the Vitruvian white, perfectly proportioned male human, such definitions have not only excluded others, they have also failed to fulfil subsequent promises to incorporate 'otherness'.[7] The Eurocentric mind-set has glorified the Europeans' vision of themselves as imperial powers, and it has also led them to 'objectify' the other.[8] When Western NGOs address the agency of the 'victimised' refugees out of 'pity', they become blinded by their certainty of knowing the answer to how best to offer aid, and by their superior, egotistic attitude when responding to criticism, especially criticism coming from those they seek to help.[9] As a result, this disposition, which assumes the embedded privilege of the white as a saviour,[10] causes what Geoffrey Pfeifer and Chioke I'Anson describe as 'dialectical deafness'.[11] As their 'humanistic' mode of thought is built into their frameworks, they are not only blind but also deaf to refugees' authentic needs, desires, and aspirations, as well as unable to identify new effective technologies that can be learned from the refugees themselves.[12]

Politics of location

The posthumanist critical stance has emerged not only to refute a long-lasting humanistic attitude that is exclusive, but also to provide a methodology to construct posthuman subjectivities.[13] When introducing her account of the posthuman, Rosi Braidotti proposes 'the politics of location or situated and accountable knowledge practices' as a methodology to facilitate the process of becoming a posthuman.[14] Questions that address located complexities and multiplicities of place and time are an important point of departure in her thought. For example, how we can constitute ourselves without an emphasis on 'self-centred individualism',[15] and instead acknowledge our relations with others? [16] Interrelations with 'others' are not limited to other humans, but also include 'all non-anthropomorphic elements', allowing other elements to be species, ecologies, or even machines.[17] A situated approach that is based upon a 'heterogeneous politics' imposes an ethical responsibility on the researcher to look for channels of communication with all forms of 'otherness'. In the following section, I will address the complexity of Za'atri refugee camp where I position myself as a visitor to the camp.

Za'atri as a hybrid organism

Mindful of the complexity amidst which the life of the camp materialises, Za'atri refugee camp can be described as what Michel Agier calls a 'hybrid organism.'[18] The life of Za'atri as an 'organism' does not reproduce any existent form of life but its own. Conditioned by the 'extraterritoriality'[19] and 'exceptionalism'[20] that were destined when its boundaries were decided by the UNHCR and the Jordanian government, Za'atri camp has opted out of the normative order of life to develop its own norms. It has developed as a composition of diverse bodies, materials, technologies, spaces, and languages. Due to the 'dialectical deafness' that the Western NGO frameworks suffer from, the composition of this lively organism is fractured into two structures: on the one hand, the structure of Western NGOs as suppliers of aid, and on the other hand, the new social structure of refugees who receive the aid and are governed by the NGOs.[21] Each of these structures features its own bodies, equipment, mobility, and technologies. Whenever each of these multiplicities confronts the other, hierarchies are upset.[22] In this chapter I want to ask: How can such fractures between the two structures be approached with a level of sensitivity to the refugee subject? How might an approach to the posthuman subject enable the dialogue between the Western NGOs and the refugee community to avoid the stalemate of 'dialectical deafness'?[23]

In his essay *Can the Subaltern be Heard?*, [24] [25] which is a reading of Gayatri Spivak's well-known essay *Can the Subaltern Speak?*, J. Maggio argues that the subaltern subject already speaks, it is just a matter of hearing her. To displace the limited transcendental Western subject,[26] which Spivak challenges in her essay, Maggio suggests the concept of translation as a way to approach and understand other cultures; cultures that Western discourse usually stands at a distance from.[27] The significance of translation lies in its intermediate position in enabling an open intellectual dialogue.[28] According to Walter Benjamin, translation cannot give the full meaning of the original, but can only echo it.[29] To be made accountable, translation needs to exceed the emptiness of a literal conversion to involve instead the translation of a people's culture and social practices.[30] Gayatri Spivak argues that to interpret a people's everyday practices requires the translator to 'inhabit' the host language.[31] A real understanding of language takes place through the interconnections between the translator and the environment of everyday spatial and social forms.[32]

So for the posthuman, understood as a mediated body that is interconnected with human, non-human, and 'earth' others,[33] translation as non-systematic and a non-linear approach[34] is a responsibility that the posthuman subject not only takes on, but is ethically accountable for. By translating the language of the refugee subject through its vitalist and materialist interrelations in the camp environment, posthuman experiments can break away from the Western Eurocentric framework to work with other alternatives. This experimentation in posthuman subjectivity actualises 'the virtual possibilities of an expanded, relational self that functions as a nature-culture continuum and is technologically mediated.'[35] How does the posthuman subject's inhabitation of the linguistic, social, and spatial forms of life in Za'atri Camp offer an alternative to Western NGOs accountability? While 'environment' is constructed in Western NGOs' frameworks to indicate a place that surrounds passive subjectivities, how can the posthuman subject's experience contribute to redefining the 'environment' as a more dynamic milieu that is inhabited by intentional subjectivities? What other alternatives does this posthuman approach suggest?

Linguistic deafness

'Environment' can be related to the verb, to environ, which also means to surround. 'Environment' indicates circumstantial variables that surround persons and things in a generic form. Mindful of the controversy that envelopes the inactive representation of refugees inside the temporal boundaries of a refugee camp,[36] I argue that associating 'environment' as given in its western construct to a 'refugee camp' contributes to a further reduction of the camp's subjects as passive recipients, rather than as active actors. Western NGOs are deafened by their own language and discourse. They become unable to hear other languages, such as those spoken by refugees. Nevertheless, 'environment' understood as 'Bee'ah- بيئة' in the Arabic linguistic discourse is derived from the verb 'bawa'a-بوأ', which indicates any intentional inhabitation of spaces, relations, or ideologies. This linguistic variation offers a new alternative for a consideration of the context of the camp environment by activating the subjectivity of the refugees inside the camp, and by understanding the environment less as generic than as concrete and specific.

Spatial deafness

The spatiality of the refugee camp has always been related to the way in which the camp is governed. How space presents itself in the camp is captured in two main images. The first is an image of a policed life and large-scale technologies: fortified and policed gates with guards and checkpoints; an asphalted wide ring road encircling twelve districts; long, tight queues hemmed in with wired fences and watch towers leading to large-scale nongovernmental spatial units that provide food items and non-food items; fenced-in hospitals, fenced-in schools, toilet units, and so forth. The other is an image of a social life and small-scale technologies: people chatting while sitting together at the side of a street; planted backyards and small front gardens; shaded courtyards where coffee and tea is served; laundry lines suspended between vertical surfaces; busy markets and mobile street merchants, and shops to hire and sell wedding dresses.[37]

The refugee camp as a built environment has been structured in accordance with specific guidelines that follow humanitarian frameworks. Regardless of the prevailing circumstances of its location, geography, environment, or inhabitants, 'the physical design of refugee camps . . . originates from a single UN design manual applied and adapted in different contexts.'[38] Humanitarian government initiatives that 'construct, manage, and control camps' by corresponding to priorities that are concerned with controlling 'undesirable' populations have long used the same UN design manual to sketch out the main principles for the layout of refugee camps.[39] These principles are then associated with the agenda of local or international NGOs.[40] Referring to the work of the architect Manuel Herz, Eyal Weizman describes a development of refugee camp spaces following medical and military logics:

> Hygiene, sanitation, the management and containment of plague, the circulation of services, infrastructure and the provision of water, electricity, medicine and nutrition, along with the disposal of sewage and waste, all become the organisational principles of a new spatial regime of multiple separations and regimentation of time and space, intersecting quasi-military with quasi-medical principles.[41]

The problem with the UN design manual, and with the technologies of the hastily produced spatial regimes of humanitarian management, is their practice of total governmental control, whether the goal of this government-through-the-construction-of-refugee-camps is perceived as the production of what Rony Brauman, a former president of MSF, calls 'humanitarian spaces' or is closer to what Agier calls 'waiting rooms.'[42] Whether the apparatuses deployed towards achieving these respective ends are administrative programs or sets of necessary operations, humanitarian government action homogenises a whole population into the figure of a refugee, a victim, or a beneficiary figure. This 'macro-scale' approach de-socialises refugee subjects. Through the following section and by discussing field explorations I have undertaken, I aim to counter the assumed narrative about the camp as a place of mass representation. I will argue that in spite of 'the managerial representation' that humanitarian governments inflict on the refugee camp, understood as a large space that confines a large number of people,[43] refugees can develop their own micro-scaled 'environmental subjectivities.'[44] To reveal these micro-scaled 'environmental subjectivities', I will dwell on linguistic and physically embodied approaches as new lenses through which I search for alternatives.[45]

Linguistically and physically embodied situated knowledges

I am attentive to the criticism that linguistic approaches might receive where they risk being uninformed in relation to the practical demands of the built environment. As Amos

Rapoport has argued, 'in linguistics itself, there has been increasing criticism of the neglect of pragmatics.'[46] The sociolinguistic approach that I follow is accompanied by a situated position whereby I physically inhabit the context, both as Braidotti's posthuman subject, and as Spivak's translator. Inhabiting the context is part of being inside Za'atri Camp, of positioning my own subject position there. This subject position I inhabit and perform is not only conditioned by attending to the daily life in the camp, but also by speaking the Arabic language, living in the culture, and practicing a similar religion.

I present this section by reflecting on my field experience, enabled after I volunteered with one of the NGOs working inside Za'atri Camp, within a component called Community Mobilisation. Community Mobilisers work as mediators to facilitate platforms of dialogue between refugees and NGO management. Mediators are responsible for both disseminating NGO operational decisions to refugees, and transmitting refugees' needs to NGO management. Community Mobilisers apply walking as a methodical approach to observing and engaging with the everyday life of people inside of Za'atri. By following in the steps of Community Mobilisers for two months, my aim was to observe the role of different spaces in steering the dialogue between refugees and NGOs, specifically through an acknowledgement of everyday embodied practices in these spaces. By highlighting what I call 'moments of interactivity', I critically analyse how a space relevant to a specific moment becomes interactive, and thus socially productive in developing relations between NGO representatives and refugees.[47] To achieve the aim of the walks I undertook, I commenced my study by mapping out the possible scenarios that might support such moments. For example, the occurrences of those moments varied in tactic (social, organisational), frequency (on a daily basis, occasionally), activity (verbal, physical), scale (between two persons, three to ten persons, more than fifteen persons), actors (Community Mobilisers, men, women, or children), and spatial settings (a refugee's place, street, NGO centre). At the same time as encountering spaces in which moments of interactivity occur, my concern is also with any representation of agency.[48] Below, illustrations of two such moments of interactivity, *Moment 1* and *Moment 2*, capture glimpses of spaces where acts of interest manifested.

As Anthony Giddens explains, the agency of actions is linked to the ability of an action to influence 'a specific process or state of affairs.'[49] To act with agency is to transform a flow of procedures by exercising 'some sort of power' whether this happens by intervening or refraining from intervention.[50] In the context of the camp, where I look at existing NGO frameworks as the representation of what Giddens describes as a *state of affairs*, an act of agency is that which has the capacity to affect a state of affairs. These affects may be produced by deterritorialising a situation's structured hierarchies, by abstaining from attending to its order, or by forming a new state of affairs that counters the current one.[51] The significance of the two moments lies in the overlapped processes that bring into that space other moments and actors. By coming together they form the force of a multiplicity that can challenge the regulated structure inside the camp.

By presenting these moments of interactivity, the attempt is to describe each within its setting. To unknot how a space's configuration rendered these moments as important, I will describe the occurrence of these moments. Despite the stagnancy attributed to the image as a static form of representation, moments of interactivity will

Figure 14.1 Moment 1: Al- Madafah. Photograph and image copyright Aya Musmar.

be recalled with spontaneity, or as they were encountered in the field. I will arouse each of the moments by attending to both movement and sound.

Moment 1: This moment is captured in the 'Madafah' of Abu Al Waleed, one of the respected leaders in Za'atri. 'Madafah' [مضافة] is a noun in Arabic that designates a place that is derived from the verb 'Daf' [ضاف]; 'Daf' [ضاف] means visited as a guest. Madafah is the 'place of guests', with specific spatial arrangements in which a powerful man in a community hosts guests from the same community to discuss their issues and use his connections to resolve them. Sitting there in his own Madafah, Abu Al Waleed spends most of his time in expectation of visitors. He has never been an official leader and never aspired to be one. However, people in his community trust him and look up to him. During the time I spent in the camp, many of the formal and the informal meetings between refugees and NGO representatives took place there. While I was sitting there with NGO representatives, many of his neighbours came in to discuss their daily issues. Abu Al Waleed listens to people carefully and when he speaks it is always with confidence. With his euphonic and assertive voice, when he speaks everyone listens. It is only when he mentions NGOs that his tone become tense. When I ask him about how happy he is with the NGO services inside the camp, he says: 'I have never needed an NGO to provide me with aid and I will not ask for it. They owe me, I do not owe them. I know how to sustain myself and keep my extended family sustained too.'

Reflection: While it is assumed that NGOs dominate a place at the top of the power structure in the camp, I suggest that the encounter in *Moment 1* destabilises this hypothesis. The space of Madafah opens up a new position that NGOs find they must adapt to. Madafah has not been limited to the visits of people from the refugee community, but has also served as a stage for other actors to politically perform their

Figure 14.2 Moment 2: The Wagon. Photograph and image copyright Aya Musmar.

agencies. While refugees and NGO representatives sat there together, Abu Al Waleed succeeded in mediating the discussion between them.

Moment 2: This moment was captured as we stopped by a mobile street merchant to look at his vegetables. At the same time and in the same place where he had stopped at the edge of a main street, a few women came along to check the wares in his wagon. One woman walked towards the wagon and was joined by other women, 'this is the time my daughter returns from school; I am here to pick her up' she said. One of the NGO representatives asked the seller about his vegetable prices. 'Vegetables here are much cheaper than vegetables in Amman. I usually shop for groceries from the camp', she whispered into my ear. When I asked the seller about the source of his vegetables, he simply said 'from outside.' I used to see wagons in the camp before, but not with such frequency. Some wagons are pushed by mobile street merchants, other wagons are pulled by donkeys.

Reflection: Emerging from previous social constructs that are based upon gender distinctions, women's movement is bounded to specific spaces and restricted to a few specific practices. However, the arrival of the street merchant's wagon and the situation it creates interrupts this construct. For example, while women find it hard to visit the market to get their groceries without a male companion, the wagon, as a mobile spatial element, deconstructs the boundaries constraining women's movements by providing them with a temporal space that performs like a market place.

Human vs posthuman

Both the Madafah and the Wagon and the moments of interactivity they manifest represent spaces that were initiated by refugees. Although each has its own specificity, both were configured, created, made, remade, or collected in response to an embryonic need for such spaces. In both moments acts of agency can be witnessed at a micro-scale. Agency according to Giddens' notion of Structuration Theory is fundamentally linked to the power of an action and how it holds a transformative capacity; a capacity that involves a logic and intention that precedes the emergence of a given subjectivity.[52]

Structuration Theory, according to Giddens, situates the body of the human as a medium interconnected with its surroundings, where human acts take place.[53] This deliberation gestures towards the mediation of the body that Braidotti has described in many places through her work on the posthuman, and yet it is substantially different.[54] Where agency in Giddens' terms is restricted to human beings, limiting intermediation to human bodies, Braidotti's approach to the posthuman also acknowledges actors that are other than human. Braidotti aims to destabilise the limited focus on the human subject, questioning the assumption that the human subject is the only actor that exerts influence in a situation.[55] How can the agency manifested in *Moment 1* and *Moment 2* be reread through the lens of the posthuman? What alternatives does this new approach avail us with? Will this rereading of space and situation illustrate a new layer of agents that have otherwise remained invisible?

To destabilise the limits that the human subject occupies, the posthuman subject position aims to break down the boundaries surrounding the human by flattening structures and opening up spaces for alternative points of view.[56] What follows is a possible subversion of power structures revealing how subject-positions come to be located. By allowing a consideration of the posthuman into the scene, a cartography of epistemic and ethical accountabilities emerges, which not only offers a critique of such locations, but an alternative representation of the subject as 'a dynamic non-unitary entity.'[57]

Now, looking back at *Moment 1* and *Moment 2*, which I highlight as moments of interactivity, the emerging acts of agency witnessed in each extends beyond the human actor, to include the non-human, which in turn requires recomposing and reconceptualising each moment's assembled parts.[58] Each of the moments should instead be witnessed as a dynamic collective, that is, an assemblage of human and non-human actors.

Environmental subjectivities

By being immersed in the camp, whether by walking, socialising, or formally interviewing refugees or Community Mobilisers, I have been exposed to different complexities that are associated with the camp as a hybrid environment. This was an exposition through which I had to locate myself in a position, interrelate to its actors, materials, and adapt to its surrounding circumstances, only to dislocate myself again through acts of transposition, reconfiguring my own subject position in relation to others.[59] The significance of the different accounts amidst which I have transposed myself lies in their capacity to draw attention to other possible substitutions that may allow a better understanding of the refugee subject-position as one that is not fixed or pre-determined. Understanding refugees' subjectivities in the camp is conditioned by understanding their relations to their surrounding environment. Their subjectivities are rendered vivid through these transpositions. They are not passively confined by camp boundaries, but become active subjects through their everyday life practices.[60] Refugees are dynamic environmental subjects.

Despite the 'dialectical deafness'[61] and the homogeneity that Za'atri suffers from as a UN refugee camp, Syrian refugees in Za'atri have produced spaces, however minor and fleeting, that correspond to their own specific needs in the everyday life of the camp. These are spaces, or dynamic assemblages, that feature refugee environmental subjectivities. As many of these spaces reproduce and influence other subjectivities inside the camp, a careful reading of specific spaces and situations, what I have called 'moments of interactivity', is crucial for an understanding of how alternatives are actively produced through the spatial configurations created by refugees. Following a posthuman approach is one tentative step towards a careful reading of such moments and spaces.

Notes

1   UNHCR. *Za'atri Refugee Camp*. http://data.unhcr.org/syrianrefugees/settlement.php?id=176&region=77&country=107.
2   Sean Healy and Sandrine Tiller. 'A review of the humanitarian response to the Syrian refugee crisis in Jordan, 2012–13'. *msf*. October 2013. www.msf.org.uk/sites/uk/files/jordan_case_study_final_external_0.pdf.
3   Ibid., 9.
4   Michel Feher, with Gaëlle Krikorian and Yates McKee, *Nongovernmental Politics* (New York: Zone Books, 2007).
5   Ibid.
6   Ibid., 16.
7   Rosi Braidotti, *The Posthuman* (Cambridge: Polity Press, 2013).
8   Ibid.
9   Chioke I'Anson and Geoffrey Pfeifer, 'A Critique of Humanitarian Reason: Agency, Power, and Privilege', *The Journal of Global Ethics* 9, no. 1 (2013): 49–63.
10 Teju Cole, 'The White-Savior Industrial Complex', *The Atlantic*, March 2012, www.theatlantic.com/international/archive/2012/03/the-white-savior-industrial-complex/254843/
11 I'Anson and Pfeifer, 'A Critique of Humanitarian Reason', 4.
12 Ibid.
13 Braidotti, *The Posthuman*.
14 Ibid., 51.
15 Ibid., 48.
16 Rosi Braidotti, *Transpositions: On Nomadic Ethics* (Cambridge: Polity Press, 2006).
17 Braidotti, *The Posthuman*, 60.
18 Michel Agier, *Managing the Undesirables: Refugee Camps and Humanitarian Governance* (Cambridge: Polity Press, 2011), 53.
19 Ibid.
20 Giorgio Agamben, *State of Exception*, trans. Kevin Attell (Chicago: University of Chicago Press, 2005).
21 Agier, *Managing the Undesirables*, 64.

22   Eyal Weizman, *The Least of All Possible Evils: Humanitarian Violence From Arendt to Gaza* (London, New York: Verso, 2011).

23   I'Anson and Pfeifer, 'A Critique of Humanitarian Reason'.

24   Joe Maggio, '"Can the Subaltern Be Heard?": Political Theory, Translation, Representation and Gayatri Chakravorty Spivak', *Alternatives* 32, no. 4 (2007): 419–43.

25   Gayatri Chakravorty Spivak, 'Can the Subaltern Speak?', in *Colonial Discourse and Post-Colonial Theory: A Reader*, ed. P. Williams and L. Chrisman (New York: Columbia University Press, 1992), 66–111.

26   Donna Haraway, 'Situated Knowledges: The Science Question in Feminism and The Privilege of Partial Perspective', *Feminist Studies* 14, no. 3 (1988): 575–99.

27   Maggio, 'Can the Subaltern Be Heard?', 432.

28   Ibid.

29   Walter Benjamin, *Illuminations* (New York: Schocken Books, 1968).

30   Maggio, 'Can the Subaltern Be Heard?'.

31   Ibid., 434.

32   Michel de Certeau, *The Practice of Everyday Life*, trans. Steven Rendall (Berkeley: University of California Press, 1984).

33   Braidotti, *The Posthuman*, 48.

34   Maggio, 'Can the Subaltern Be Heard?'.

35   Braidotti, *The Posthuman*, 61.

36   Giorgio Agamben, *Homo Sacer: Sovereign Power and Bare Life*, ed. Werner Hamacher and David E Wellbery, trans. Daniel Heller-Roazen (Stanford: Stanford University Press, 1998).

37   Michel Agier, *On the Margins of the World: The Refugee Experience Today* (Cambridge: Polity Press, 2008).

38   Weizman, *The Least of All Possible Evils*, 139.

39   Agier, *Managing the Undesirables*, 201.

40   Ibid.

41   Weizman, *The Least of All Possible Evils*, 139.

42   Ibid., 134, 135.

43   Agier, *Managing the Undesirables*, 182.

44   Arun Agrawal, *Environmentality: Technologies of Government and the Making of Subjects* (Durham, NC: Duke University Press, 2005).

45   Ibid.

46   Amos Rapoport, *The Meaning of The Built Environment: A Non Verbal Communication Approach*, second edition (Tucson: University of Arizona Press, 1990), 43.

47   Henri Lefebvre, *The Production of Space*, trans. Donald Nicholson-Smith (Oxford: Blackwell, 1991).

48   Anthony Giddens, *The Constitution of Society: Outline of the Theory of Structuration* (Cambridge: Polity Press, 1984).

49   Ibid., 14.

50   Ibid.

51   Ibid.

52   Ibid.

53   Ibid.

54   Braidotti, *The Posthuman*.

55   Ibid.

56   Ibid.

57   Ibid., 164.

58   Deleuze, Gilles, and Felix Guattari, *A Thousand Plateaus,* trans. Brian Massumi (London, Minneapolis: continuum, 1987).

59   Braidotti, *Transpositions*.

60   Agrawal, *Environmentality*.

61   I'Anson and Pfeifer, "A Critique of Humanitarian Reason."

Chapter 15

Feminisms in conflict

'Feminist urban planning' in Husby, Sweden

Maria Ärlemo

In autumn 2015, phones started ringing more frequently than usual at the School of Architecture, KTH (Royal Institute of Technology) in Stockholm. The first calls were received from a reporter for public radio, Sveriges Radio, in search of experts to comment on a new initiative in the suburb of Husby called 'feminist urban planning' (*'feministisk stadsplanering'*).[1] Husby is a large-scale postwar residential suburb in the northwest of Stockholm, marked by economic disadvantage and racial segregation but also noted for its level of civic engagement. Many other phone calls followed, and over a period of some months the 'feminist urban planning' initiative gained extensive coverage across both local and national media in Sweden.[2]

I was one of those who received a call. At the time, I was conducting an ethnographic exploration of local discourse on justice among grassroots organisations in Husby. Due to the thematic similarity I expanded my research to include participant observation in a workshop series hosted by Svenska Bostäder (a municipally owned housing company and the dominant property owner in Husby) as a response to the media interest aroused in the formulation of a 'feminist urban planning'. This chapter presents my account of this workshop series by drawing on my observation of the five workshops, qualitative interviews undertaken with four of the women involved in them and an exploration of related media discourse, in order to respond to the question: What feminisms were expressed, embodied and practised within the initiative of 'feminist urban planning' between spring 2015 and spring 2016?

There is a debate among feminists about how best to counteract oppression of women. Within this debate, one extreme seems to be the promotion of broad mobilisation based on shared values, a more universalistic approach often promoted by proponents from the Left. Another is the promotion of mobilisation based on shared experience of specific conditions of oppression, a more particularistic approach in line with what has been termed 'identity politics'.[3] A central thread in this debate, as can be seen in a reply by Brenna Bhandar and Denise Ferreira da Silva to an article written by Nancy Fraser,[4] is the experience by some feminists of oppression imposed upon them by other feminists through universalising accounts of feminism that render their experiences, perspectives and struggles invisible.

In this chapter, feminisms expressed within the 'feminist urban planning' initiative in Husby will be explored using an intersectional perspective. Intersectional theory presents a view of oppression as marked by several overlapping, or intersecting, social identities and their related systems of discrimination. To make negative effects of intersecting oppressions visible, intersectionality promotes multidimensional analyses of discrimination on the basis of factors including gender, race, ethnicity and class.[5] Drawing on intersectional theory, specifically the concept of 'hegemonic feminism'[6] as elaborated by Paulina de los Reyes and Diana Mulinari, which emphasises the plurality of feminist perspectives and the hierarchy among them,[7] I will argue that a specific feminist perspective came to dominate the workshop series and the events surrounding it. The feminist perspective that, according to my account, became dominant focused on the perceived oppression of women in Husby by Muslim men. The problem I want to open with concerns how this perspective was furthered by members of the white middle-class project leadership. As I will explain below, experiences of oppression by Muslim men described by the women of Husby were given time, attention and encouragement by the project leadership, while other often more demanding accounts were neglected or even silenced.

What appears to have taken place is an uneven representation by the workshop leadership group of the experiences and concerns of the women in Husby. I argue that for the initiative in Husby to be considered 'feminist', in the sense of inclusive and non-oppressive, such a power imbalance would need to be acknowledged. The chapter concludes with a reflection on what critically engaged architectural practices could learn from this case, and with the question: How can space be made for a more polyphonic discourse on 'feminist urban planning'?

Reversed planning in practice

In 2014 the political regime in the municipality of Stockholm shifted from a centre-right liberal alliance led by the Moderate Party to one led by the Social Democratic Party in alliance with the Left Party, the Green Party and the Feminist Initiative. A central aim in the latter's initial common statement of intent was to enhance what they called 'democratic sustainability', that is, to enhance the degree of local democracy and influence across the municipality of Stockholm. They argued for 'a deepened democracy where input from everyone makes Stockholm a better place. More decisions need to be taken in closer contact with citizens. An open, anti-racist, equitable Stockholm with diversity and equal rights is the Stockholm we are proud of.'[8]

In line with this political aim, the municipality's Housing and Democracy Commissioner expressed a desire to meet with women in Husby to discuss the potential for a 'reversed planning process' in relation to the upcoming renovation of the local centre. This is a planning process that aims to take as its point of departure desires expressed by local actors and residents. Two young women, residents in Husby and members of the same political party as the commissioner, posted a call for expressions of interest to participate in the reversed planning process on a female online network called StreetGäris. The network had been initiated by a young woman in Husby about two years previously. 'Gäris' is slang for 'girls' and the network is open to all in Sweden who identify themselves as female or non-binary (gender identities defined as neither female nor male). Prospective members are asked to subscribe to a set of values promoted by the network, respect for and appreciation of difference being a central component of these. As the network explains, 'we embrace and respect each other's thoughts and opinions and have no need to agree on all issues'.[9] It promotes a more equitable society to be achieved through solidarity, mentorship and empowerment.[10] As a result of the above call for expressions of interest a group of young, politically active and educated women, most of whom were 'second-generation immigrants',[11] and all current or former residents of Husby or neighbouring areas, came to a meeting with the Housing and Democracy Commissioner at the library in the Husby centre in early spring 2015. A representative from Svenska Bostäder, which owns the centre designated for renovation, also took part. As retold by members of StreetGäris, the conversation centred on issues of how women in Husby could gain greater influence over the forthcoming renovation of the centre. As one of them explained, 'I was very clear that for us not to be seen [again only] as angry citizens we needed to be informed.' She clarified that what they demanded was to be given an introduction to the planning and renovation process in order to know 'when [in the renovation process] we can influence what, so that we can discuss the right thing at the right time. So that we do not become these angry citizens on the outside, and when we complain they say no, [too late], the budget is already set.' According to her, the representative from Svenska Bostäder responded positively to their demand, and the young women interviewed believed an agreement was reached that occasions for knowledge transfer about the renovation process were to be arranged by the representative from the housing company. As concluded by the young woman quoted above, 'we came to an agreement in the group that we were going to be given that insight to make it real, that was the precondition [for our involvement in the reversed planning process]'.

But then nothing much happened, until a local reporter for Sveriges Radio in Järva, the area of Stockholm where Husby is situated, called one of the young women from StreetGäris who had been part of the meeting. This reporter was the one who later was the first to call the School of Architecture seeking clarification of the term 'feminist urban planning'. At this stage the reporter was picking up on a media debate that erupted during the summer of 2015 about radicalisation, Muslim fundamentalism and male oppression in Husby and similar suburbs across Sweden.[12] The debate was initiated by a politically active middle-aged first-generation immigrant woman who had long been a prominent figure in Husby. In her article she conveyed an experience of no longer feeling at home in Husby due to the heightened Muslim fundamentalism, patriarchal oppression and control of women in public space there. Her article was followed by many others, at times written by other Husby women, but more prominently by journalists from local or national newspapers, who further elaborated on her argument. One outcome of this was the emergence of the proposition that a specific 'suburban feminism' (*förortsfeminism*) was needed as, implicitly, the character and degree of male oppression of women in Husby and similar suburban areas was deemed to be specific and extraordinary.

There were also strong reactions against what was felt to be a stereotypical and harmful account of Husby. In one article, members of StreetGäris argued that by singling out Husby and similar suburban areas as sites of oppression of women by men, inequalities produced and reproduced elsewhere, for instance within and by the majority society, were made less visible. The authors, on behalf of the members of StreetGäris, called for a more nuanced and productive narration of Husby and the story of women's oppression. In their closing remarks the authors, in line with this reasoning, referred to the 'feminist urban planning' initiative as one positive development.

Following the redirection of the media's attention from claims about increased Muslim fundamentalism in Swedish suburbs such as Husby to the 'good example' of 'feminist urban planning', a theme that subsequently received extensive media coverage, Svenska Bostäder turned the initiative into a series of five workshops with women in Husby between autumn 2015 and early spring 2016. With the exception of one woman, it is worth noting that the women from Husby who came to take part in the first workshop were not from StreetGäris. Instead a group of older, politically active first-generation immigrant women, most if not all of them members of the local women's association Kibele, joined the workshop. Kibele is an association that aims to further integrate immigrant women into Swedish society by offering courses to enhance their ability to earn an income, and by acting as a bridge to authorities and institutions.[13] The central figure in this group was the woman who had initiated the media debate on increased fundamentalism and male oppression in Husby.

Members of StreetGäris note there is a difference in perspective between older first-generation immigrant women and younger second-generation immigrant women in Husby. As explained to me by one of them, 'younger women in Husby own Husby in a different way than the older women. It has to do with being part of society in another way; you may be part of the public debate, you may go to school, and so on.' The difference as expressed by this young woman seems to relate to degrees of marginalisation. This difference can also be seen reflected in the aims of their associations: where the older women within Kibele strive to further integrate immigrant women into Swedish society, the younger women of StreetGäris instead aim to offer support and sisterhood to all women who share their basic values of diversity and tolerance. Hence, although StreetGäris aims for a broad mobilisation, the unity is not envisioned to be based on the suppression of difference; instead, heterogeneity is celebrated and defined as a strength of the network. The embracing feminist perspective advocated by the young women contrasts with the narrower feminist perspective promoted by the older women as 'suburban feminism'. According to the older women, the experiences of women in Husby and similar neighbourhoods differ from the experiences of more privileged women to such a degree that they cannot possibly share the same feminist perspective. More importantly, the implicit argument made is that mobilisation based on broader feminist perspectives is not helping the cause of immigrant women in Husby, as their distinct views and experiences risk being made invisible by more dominant feminist perspectives and thereby losing their potential influence.

Why, then, was it the older and not the younger group of women who joined the first workshop hosted by Svenska Bostäder? As explained by one of the young women, their understanding of the situation was that the window of opportunity to influence the renovation of Husby centre had now closed. About half a year had passed, they had not been given any insight into the ongoing renovation process, and now they had instead been invited to take part in what they understood to be a series organised to discuss feminism and urban planning in general. As she explained when interviewed: 'If you have a local engagement with your community and are working for it, you want to put your energy into the right things – and now we were being told that we would not be able to influence [the renovation], there would be discussions instead.' She continued: 'I would rather use my energy where I can make a difference for my local community. I don't want to sit around with a lot of middle-class women to discuss feminism.' As viewed by most of the young women, the local-democracy aspect of the initiative had been lost and with it the incentive for them to engage.

If the young women distanced themselves from the initiative after having their demands to be afforded insight into and influence over the renovation project disregarded, the older women too distanced themselves following the first workshop, though for different reasons. As one of them stated in the first workshop, 'we want a space for women in the Husby centre'. She further asserted that 'there needs to be a space for women and there needs to be a reason for them to go there; how else will we know what they think and want?' The primary demand for them was thus not, as for the young women, influence over the renovation project per se but instead access to indoor space in the centre of Husby to establish a women's centre. Even so, their aspiration was forcefully rejected at the workshop by a representative from Svenska Bostäder, who stated that programmatic issues not pertaining to outdoor public spaces were not up for discussion.

Due to the distancing by the first two groups of local women from the workshop series, a new, third, set of women from Husby took part in discussions at the second workshop. These women were assembled by the white middle-class project leadership, brought in by the moderator and the representative from Svenska Bostäder based on their previous connections in Husby. This group of women was marked by a greater diversity than the previous groups – the women were of different ages, ethnicities and religions – but most of them were first- or second-generation immigrants. This final group was less outspoken in terms of political engagement and explicit agenda than the women who took part in the two former groups. Nevertheless, these were the women who came to form the basis of local representation in the last four workshops.

It was within the third group that the conversation centred on issues of male dominance in the public spaces of Husby. Different reasons for the perceived dominance were discussed: cramped housing conditions, unemployment, inadequate schooling resulting in grades too low for entry into higher education, responsibility for domestic chores being allocated to women. Issues of religion, culture and respect also emerged, and a tension surfaced between two immigrant women, a Muslim and a non-Muslim. The non-Muslim woman first insinuated and later stated that it was Islam itself that was the source of the problem. The Muslim woman responded in defence that there is nothing in her religion that tells young men to be disrespectful. This tension resurfaced repeatedly and in an increasingly aggressive manner during the remaining workshops. A young woman participant, the only member of StreetGäris still attending, said she was appalled that this conversation was allowed to continue by the moderator and the project leadership, contending that 'no real feminist space would ever let such oppressive statements be made'.

But there were also women from Husby, part of the third group, who objected to the dominant theme in the last four workshops of oppression of women in Husby by Muslim men. A white non-immigrant woman said that she did not recognise the image being conveyed of a suburban centre dominated by young men who spent their time harassing women. She also objected to what she found were generalising accounts of men in Husby, asking: 'Who are we talking about? Say that it's twenty young men – that's only twenty!' In an attempt to redirect the discussion, she pointed instead to something she found to be a shameful problem in the centre of Husby, namely the group of non-Muslims sitting drinking alcohol all day at the pizzeria. Yet none of her comments were picked up for further discussion. Similarly, an account given by a Muslim woman about how a man spat at her in front of her daughter on the subway travelling from Karlaplan, a high-status area in the centre of Stockholm, although met with dismay, was left unexplored. She told how the man screamed at her in a crowded subway carriage, calling her a witch and telling her to go home, and no one in the carriage other than her daughter reacted. The lack of elaboration of these accounts could be partly explained by the limitation of Svenska Bostäder's influence to those spaces where the company owns properties. The workshops were also designed to address the contexts of Husby and Järva exclusively. But the silence could also indicate a fundamental assumption built into the project that male domination and oppression in public space is especially high in Husby and similar areas – an assumption which could lead to the interpretation and treatment of male oppression reported in other urban contexts as anomalies.

The production of otherness

Husby is what is called a 'Million Home Program area', that is, a large-scale postwar residential area built between the mid-1960s and 1970s as an integral part of the Swedish welfare society. A central aim was to provide good-quality and affordable housing to all, but over the years many of these areas have become increasingly segregated along economic and ethnic lines.[14] Some argue that the segregation is racialised.[15] It has been demonstrated by Per-Markku Ristilammi, among others, that understandings of such areas have been constructed over time as counter-images against which understandings of Swedishness have been produced.[16] Following this argument, the 'feminist urban planning' initiative risks contributing to the construction of a binary opposition that links understandings of inequality to religion, more specifically to Islam, and thereby makes the surrounding, mainly secular majority of society appear as relatively non-oppressive and equitable. While such a construction is probably unconscious, undertaken by means of a selective focus on a delimited space, as well as on specific accounts of male oppression exerted by Muslim men within this space, nevertheless, I argue that this is a valid concern.

I make this point not to diminish or neglect the male oppression that is taking place in Husby, but to direct attention to male oppression that is also taking place elsewhere. Informed by intersectional theory, I also want to highlight the multiplicity of oppressions playing out within the initiative itself – such as the dominance imposed by Svenska Bostäder when they dismissed the demands of the first two groups of women who were keen to offer their ideas about the renovation of the centre. There is a critique of consensus-oriented collaborative planning practices for not adequately taking into account issues of power and dominance.[17] In this case, relative consensus among the women involved in the workshop series seems to have been reached due to the dismissive approach by representatives from Svenska Bostäder towards the first two groups of women. These more dissensual women then, due to disillusion, chose not to take part in the workshops.

The dominant role of the professional and academic white middle-class feminist perspective must also be considered. The project leadership at Svenska Bostäder and the architect employed to curate the workshops and to moderate the conversations were white middle-class women. Also, white middle-class academics, such as myself, were brought in to share our views of what 'feminist urban planning' might comprise. These accounts took up about half of each workshop. As the workshop series developed, interested officials, academics and students joined in. By the fifth and final workshop twenty people attended, less than half of whom were women from Husby.

Paulina de los Reyes and Diana Mulinari argue that there is a 'hegemonic feminism' in Sweden, within which privileged – that is to say white, well-educated, heterosexual, middle-class – women develop awareness and critique of gender inequalities based on their own frames of reference and experience. Although feminism within the dominant discourse is discussed as plural, in an attempt to signify inclusion, the hierarchy among feminisms is not acknowledged, according to de los Reyes and Mulinari: 'when we talk of hegemonic relations within feminism we simultaneously argue that there is a hierarchical relation between different feminisms, a relation which makes some feminist interventions marginal, invisible or impossible'.[18]

In the currently widespread tale of the 'feminist urban planning' initiative in Husby, which is offered as a 'good example' of citizen participation and feminist spatial practices among architects, planners, officials and politicians in Stockholm, and to some degree across Sweden, several feminist interventions along the way have been made invisible, such as the demands put forth for influence in the renovation of the local centre, and access to indoor space in the centre. Some interventions seem to have been made more or less impossible, such as for the Muslim woman and working-class mum to convey her experience of male oppression and harassment in public space, not by

Figure 15.1 The Husby centre, autumn 2016. The decorative elements on the fencing surrounding the ongoing renovation of the centre were made by women in Husby during a 'knitting graffiti project' launched by Svenska Bostäder in summer 2016. Photograph by Maria Ärlemo, 2016.

Muslim men in Husby, but when surrounded by white, presumably mainly secular, non-immigrants in one of the most privileged areas of the inner city of Stockholm.

Following the five workshops the dialogue concluded, but as explained by a representative from Svenska Bostäder the initiative is being further developed within the company. In summer 2016 a 'knitting graffiti project' was launched by the housing company, which invited women to collaboratively, and in a peaceful manner, reclaim public space in the centre of Husby. The outcome of the 'feminist urban planning' initiative in Husby does not seem to have achieved a greater local democracy or 'democratic sustainability' by means of a 'reversed planning process'. The result so far has instead been the collective exercise of knitting decorative elements to adorn the fencing that surrounds the ongoing renovation, directed by the housing company.

How could space for a more polyphonic discourse on 'feminist urban planning' be made?

In autumn 2016 all municipally owned housing companies in Stockholm were given the political directive to work with 'feminist urban planning', though it remains to be seen how they will achieve this. As the initiative is further elaborated and implemented, what can be learnt from the case of Husby? How could space for a more polyphonic discourse on 'feminist urban planning' be made? How could a more equitable society be speculated upon through critically engaged architectural practices?

Drawing on the writings of Doreen Massey and Gillian Rose, Irene Molina argues for the relevance of a relational and dialectic view of space as both constituted by and constitutive of power structures. She wants to see a further elaboration of intersectional theory that allows for explorations of intersections not only between sexism, racism and class but also through time and space. Such a theoretical perspective would offer means for critical spatial interventions into nexuses where oppressive structures intersect, thus offering a view of spatial, architectural and planning practices informed by intersectional theory as a potential means for resistance.[19]

For such a destabilisation of power structures to take place within the 'feminist urban planning' initiative in Husby, the privileged positions held by the different actors need to be acknowledged. The women in Husby need to be able to influence – not only to decorate – the ongoing renovation of the centre of Husby. Architects and planners skilled in spatial analysis and informed by intersectional theory could contribute to such a process by arguing for a loosening up of the spatial delimitation of the focus. In the case of Husby this would mean recognising that while male oppression may be a factor there, other oppressions taking place across the geography and hierarchy of Stockholm, and Sweden, also need to be addressed. This broader view would make apparent the difference in privilege among the women who were part of the initiative, but also potentially contribute to the forming of a basis for solidarity and collective action as acts of oppression take place everywhere, even if to differing degrees and according to context-specific intersections.

Notes

1   In media interviews on the 'feminist urban planning' initiative, a representative from the housing company Svenska Bostäder referred to expertise within the field at the School of Architecture, Stockholm, as well as implying that the initiative was carried out in collaboration with the School. The calls by reporters to the School of Architecture were thus seeking clarification of both what 'feminist urban planning' comprises and the role played by the School in the project. It should be noted, though, that there was no formal collaboration between Svenska Bostäder and the School of Architecture.
2   Banar Sabet and Vian Tahir, 'Förtrycket finns inte bara i Husby', *Aftonbladet*, 4 June 2015; Christy Chamy, 'Husby centrum anpassas för kvinnor', *Sveriges Radio*, 13 October 2015; Hanna Westerlund, 'Nya Husby centrum ska byggas för kvinnor', *Stockholms Fria*, 22 October 2015; Lina Lund, 'Männen får maka på sig', *Dagens Nyheter*, 26 November 2015; Lina Lund, 'Feministisk arkitektur, vad är det?', *Dagens Nyheter*, 27 November 2015. The references above are a selection of the debate in the Swedish media between spring 2015 and spring 2016 on the 'feminist urban planning' initiative in Husby.
3   'Identity politics' is a term that denotes a field of theorising around shared experiences of oppression among members of marginalised social groups, as well as political activities that aim to achieve greater justice, freedom and self-determination for such groups.
4   Nancy Fraser, 'How Feminism Became Capitalism's Handmaiden – and How to Reclaim It', *The Guardian*, 14 October 2013; Brenna Bhandar and Denise Ferreira da Silva, 'White Feminist Fatigue Syndrome: A Reply to Nancy Fraser', in *Critical Legal Thinking: Law and the Political*.
5   Paulina de los Reyes and Diana Mulinari, *Intersektionalitet: Kritiska reflektioner över (o)jämlikhetens landskap* (Malmö: Liber, 2005).
6   All quotations used in the text from written and oral sources in Swedish have been translated by the author.
7   Paulina de los Reyes and Diana Mulinari, 'Hegemonisk feminism? Ett försök att identifiera ett diskursivt fält', in *Intersektionalitet*, 78–88.
8   Karin Wanngård, Daniel Helldén, Ann-Margarethe Livh and Sissela Nordling Blanco, *Stockholm – en jämlik och hållbar stad*.
9   StreetGäris, 'Om StreetGäris'.
10 Ibid.

11 There is no consensus within Swedish popular, policy and academic discourse on how to denote persons who have themselves migrated to Sweden or have parents who have done so. In this text I will make use of the distinction between 'first-' and 'second-generation immigrants' as the empirical material indicates that there is a difference in feminist perspective between these groups of women within the 'feminist urban planning' initiative.

12 Zeliha Dagli, 'Jag kan inte längre vara mig själv här', *Aftonbladet*, 1 June 2015; Banar Sabet and Vian Tahir, 'Förtrycket finns inte bara i Husby', *Aftonbladet*, 4 June 2015; Amineh Kakabaveh, 'I förorten växer männens diktatur', *Expressen*, 22 June 2015; Manijeh Mehdiyar and Maimuna Abdullahi, 'Hatkampanjen mot förorten är rasistisk', *Expressen*, 25 June 2015; Christina Höj Larsen, Aron Etzler and Rossana Dinamarca, 'Att peka ut förorten ökar bara splittringen', *Aftonbladet*, 6 July 2015. The references above are a selection of the debate in the Swedish media between spring 2015 and spring 2016 on radicalisation, Muslim fundamentalism and male oppression in Husby and similar suburban areas.

13 Kibele, 'Om oss'.

14 Roger Andersson and Anneli Kährik, 'Widening Gaps: Segregation Dynamics during Two Decades of Economic and Institutional Change in Stockholm' in *Socio-Economic Segregation in European Capital Cities*, edited by Tiit Tammaru, Maarten van Ham, Szymon Marci czak and Sako Musterd (New York: Routledge, 2015), 110–31.

15 Irene Molina, 'Miljonprogrammet och förortens rasifiering', in *Bor vi i samma stad?*, edited by Ola Broms Wessel, Moa Tunström and Karin Bradley (Kristianstad: Pocky, 2005), 102–114.

16 Per-Markku Ristilammi, *Rosengård och den svarta poesin: en studie i modern annorlundahet* (Stehag, Stockholm: Brutus Östlings bokförlag, 1994).

17 Metzger, Jonathan, Phil Allmendinger and Stijn Oosterlynck, 'The Contested Terrain of European Territorial Governance' in *Planning against the Political: Democratic Deficits in European Territorial Governance*, edited by Jonathan Metzger, Phil Allmendinger and Stijn Oosterlynck (New York: Routledge, 2015), 1–27.

18 de los Reyes and Mulinari, 'Hegemonisk feminism?', 81–82.

19 Irene Molina, 'When Space Intersects Feminism' in *Feminist Futures of Spatial Practice: Materialisms, Activisms, Dialogues, Pedagogies, Projections*, edited by Meike Schalk, Thérèse Kristiansson and Ramia Mazé (Baunach, AADR: Spurbuchverlag, 2017), 95–100.

Chapter 16

Abandoned architectures

Some dirty narratives

Karin Reisinger

Buildings have become monuments.

Swimming pools have been used to incarcerate prisoners of war.

Bars have been converted into nature observation points for scientists.

Nature observation points have been transformed into gun turrets for soldiers.

Nazi education centres have become youth hostels.

Abandoned guestrooms have been taken over and inhabited by snakes and lions.

The house at the centre of town has become the house at the end of the street.

Architectures of preservation reveal conflicted genealogies that draw attention to the tension between preservation and exploitation, especially during periods of drastic change. The territories I will discuss house elastic architectures of humans and non-humans. I speak of architectures in the plural, because these architectures are many and diverse, and many different actors live in interdependencies with different architectural environments. '[N]ot only are human beings embodied and shifting and multiple and complex, they are also within a multitude of environments'[1] – and non-humans add to the complexity of all of that.

Far beyond nature preservation areas, defined as '[l]arge natural or near natural areas set aside to protect large-scale ecological processes, along with the complement of species and ecosystems characteristic of the area, which also provide a foundation for environmentally and culturally compatible spiritual, scientific, educational, recreational and visitor opportunities,'[2] this chapter considers the dynamics of *naturecultural assemblages*[3] and is concerned with ecologies of assemblages, and how the architectures' ecosystems allow, or do not allow, for the specific practices of certain protagonists – human and non-human alike. 'Staying with the trouble' of each territory means moving beyond the comfort zone of research within 'the discipline of architecture', or, according to Haraway, to 'be truly present'.[4] Situated in territories that have become radically transformed from conflict zones to contact zones, and vice versa, the architectures I address are built in line with macro-practices, macro-narratives and macro-policies, but support new micro-practices and micro-narratives that traverse them. Large and small scales are deeply intertwined.

Including architectures within preservation areas in Mozambique and Germany, and vanishing architectures near mining areas in Sweden, I draw from feminist political ecologies, queer ecologies and above all from Rachel Carson, who in the 1920s shifted from the discipline of English literature to biology. Like naturalists 'who have learned to think in the presence of ongoing facts of destruction,'[5] Carson shows how destruction leads to further unexpected destruction. She assembled reports on large-scale ramifications and long-lasting effects, such as species extinction, but also directed attention to located and situated small-scale impacts on diverse individuals by assembling fragments of *becomings*. In 'A Fable for Tomorrow', the first chapter of the book *Silent Spring*, Carson assembled fragments of silence to show the ubiquitous future of pollution: no birds singing in spring, no anglers because the fish have died and various cases of illness among the inhabitants of the polluted areas – a 'strange stillness', due to an 'evil spell'.[6]

> This town does not actually exist, but it might easily have a thousand counterparts in America or elsewhere in the world. I know of no community that has experienced all the misfortunes I describe. Yet every one of these disasters has actually happened somewhere, and many real communities have already suffered a substantial number of them.[7]

Silent Spring commences by assembling situations of death and dying in order to compose an image of a future yet to come. Despite the dystopian character of the first pages of *Silent Spring*, the assemblage unfolds a conjunction of situated stories and transformations, territories, substances and applied practices and their effects: assembled voids and absences. Most of the stories highlight substances called 'elixirs of death', specifically applied against what were considered weeds or vermin, impacting on private households and gardens as well as industrial agricultures.

'The balance of nature ... is fluid, ever shifting, in a constant state of adjustment',[8] but where do architectures, women and non-humans find themselves in this ubiquitous connected-ness? What if 'architectures' were to appear as a posthumous chapter in Rachel Carson's book? In *Silent Spring* Carson assembles a wide range of domains and sites: tobacco plantations; hop farms in Washington and Idaho; a typical US American household where the 'housewife' dies of acute leukaemia after spraying spiders with DDT. To respond to Carson's modes of assembling I will compile architectural fragments to form a compound of different forms of pollution: architectures polluted with life. In the following sections I will describe the unexpected *becomings* of significant architectures of three different territories, their cultures and politics.[9]

Three territories

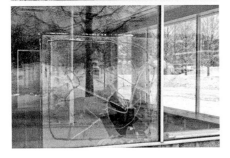

Figure 16.1 Wollseifen, Eifel National Park, Germany, 2010; Chitengo Camp, Gorongosa National Park, Mozambique, 2011; Malmberget, Sweden, 2017. Photographs by Karin Reisinger.

Territory one

Assemblage extremities and post-human adjacencies

Eifel National Park, Germany

In Germany, the former leadership education centre called Ordensburg Vogelsang, a sturdy example of National Socialist (NS) architecture using the middle ages as a stylistic precedent, was built between 1934 and 1941 as a setting of buildings and public spaces for NS education: a security area 'Malakoff', the force's cinema 'Krypte', the house of knowledge, a castle tavern, a house for female staff, hall of honour, comradeship houses, sports facilities, 'Thingstätte' (an open-air theatre), houses for groups of one hundred etc.,[10] installed in an elevated area so that nature and buildings support each other with effect and dramatic expression.[11] After World War II the assemblage was used by the military.

On a minor scale, a similar drastic shift happened to a small village nearby: Wollseifen. In 1946 its 550 inhabitants were displaced so the village could be used as a military training ground after World War II.[12] After many decades, in 2004 the territory was placed under nature preservation with the help of activists, becoming the Eifel National Park. The former village was re-occupied by nature, wilderness, but after long discussions the Ordensburg was renovated and now houses a visitors' centre that educates visitors on the 'nature' of the national park and the 'history' of the area. Nature and history are shown as distinct; whereas the aim of this chapter is to consider the continuum of the *naturecultures*. We could argue that this history is very extreme, but that does not disconnect it from nature. Put simply, precisely because of its particular history the area remained free from human settlement and was later able to become a national park, re-used in a different mode of assemblage:

> The assemblage of conservation is heterogeneous. In addition to lively human and animal bodies, it comprises nature reserves, fences, and guns; scientific instruments, maps, papers, and databases; legal designations, action plans, and market mechanisms; and films, websites, and online transfers . . . Assemblages allow certain actors to speak for, commodify, govern, and thus shape the world, often in conflict with other representations . . . Assemblages allow elites to act at a distance.[13]

As Lorimer showed, the theory of preservation too is an assemblage. At the 'conversion conference' in 2002, the territory's transformation into a national park was announced, and Ordensburg Vogelsang in Eifel, Germany, was to take its place as a visitor's centre[14] within the assemblage – to remind of the NS past instead of being left to rot. Within the centre of the nature preservation area, in two separate gallery spaces, an exhibition on 'nature' and an exhibition on the Nazi past are hosted. The choice made between renovating and leaving the architectures to nature is one that always disappoints the imaginaries and needs of some because 'people's sense of themselves and their place is often in friction with how resilience planners imagine they might foster social capital and harness networks'.[15] The practice of preservation unveils enormous conflictual potential and can lead to peculiar spatial arrangements. Today, groups meet in front of NS architectures at the centre of Eifel National Park to set out on their hiking tours.

In her writing from the late 1980s onwards, Donna Haraway makes a point of dismantling dichotomies, such as nature/culture, body/machine, feminine/masculine. Instead, in place of such dichotomies she insists upon 'situated *naturecultures*, in which all the actors become who they are *in the dance of relating*'.[16] Judith Butler teaches us: 'Who is acting is not always separable from who is acted upon.'[17] The architectures assembled here add to the blurriness of the threshold between architecture and life, following catastrophe, interruption, abandonment and (nature) preservation. Life is affected, sometimes even nurtured, by imposed structures and architectures. In my account of these architectures I embrace what Michelle Murphy describes as the *alterlife*, 'a historic moment when life on earth shares the condition of already having been altered'.[18] In the *alterlives* human-made architectures have been radically altered by non-human uses and adaptations.

The assembled buildings of Wollseifen perform a queer ecology, making use of 'the gaps in and overlaps among existing lenses',[19] no more a human habitat, but not yet a non-human one. Thus, even this area can be seen as a queer one, in which nature re-claims architecture and makes it complex and diverse: architectures for humans and at the same time for non-humans. The hikers cross a site of a hastily abandoned village, with additional buildings for military training exercises, and can experience how non-humans re-occupy the architectures. Architectures transform through lifecycles of typological resilience, often becoming reoriented to a function nobody had expected.

Territory two

Queering assemblages of preservation and knowledge

Gorongosa National Park, Mozambique

The Chitengo Camp in the Gorongosa National Park was built during colonial times when Mozambique was administered by the Portuguese. It was a meeting place for the rich and famous. The land was taken from its indigenous inhabitants, and practices of doing architecture were imported. In colonial wildlife style, luxury bungalows were built, as were restaurants, a shop, a swimming pool etc., across the plains of Mozambique. Chitengo Camp was like a small village that could house four hundred guests. It accommodated scientists and European and US American visitors who went on safari, discovered the wildlife, had great parties, relaxed by the pool and learned about the park's ecosystem. The colonial period ended in 1975, and the camp was one of the first targets of the resistance forces during Mozambique's bloody path to independence. Shots were heard and tourists were evacuated. In these years the architectures of Chitengo Camp took on different functions. Today a bullet-pocked slab of concrete reminds of the 1973 attacks during the war of independence against Portugal.[20] Many buildings were destroyed in the battles, and the neglected camp suffered from degradation following the long civil war. Despite renovation, warthogs use some of the houses because they are perfect places for their families. All that remains of some of the houses of the camp is their foundations – which the local monkeys appreciate for their meetings.

> For each of us, as for the robin in Michigan or the salmon in the Miramichi, this is a problem of ecology, of interrelationships, of interdependence. We poison the caddis flies in a stream and the salmon runs dwindle and die . . . We spray our elms and the following springs are silent of robin song . . . They reflect the web of life – or death – that scientists know as ecology.[21]

Carson compiles the argument of her book, a written 'assemblage' of multiple interrelated fragments as a close reading of interdependences across a number of single narratives. She acts by writing, accumulating small-scale changes and the ways they impact on larger scales. Her work was not initially appreciated, quite the contrary: journalists and reviewers called Rachel Carson 'an hysterical woman' using 'emotion-fanning words', author of a book 'more poisonous than the pesticides she condemns'.[22]

Political ecology, a basic tool-set to look at these narratives – concerned with 'politics of environmental degradation and conservation', 'neoliberalisation of nature', 'accumulation, enclosure and dispossession', 'access and control of resources, and environmental struggles around knowledge and power, justice and governance'[23] – looks at various perspectives enmeshed with global interrelations. It opens different possibilities for looking at worlds and livelihoods, also accommodating feminist points of view on complex ecosystems. For instance, Wendy Harcourt and Ingrid L. Nelson's *Practicing Feminist Political Ecologies* is a feminist political ecology that creates 'connections and knowledge on environment, gender and feminism at an international level.' To deal with complex interdependencies they look for ways of 'collectively sharing and understanding our common "naturecultures" ', and 'gifting and sharing diverse worldviews'.[24] They explore different ways to express how they 'live and practice feminist political ecology – through stories, narratives and analysis from many different parts of the world.'[25]

Architectures are the places where the stories happen. Sometimes exterior influences put an end to the stories and narratives prematurely, but leave the architectures behind. The architectures then serve to house new stories. In my examples these become post-human stories. Warthogs raise their babies in the neglected buildings of Chitengo Camp. Architectures accommodate different stories and serve different needs. They became livelier than they had been before. New materials move into and through the houses, new varieties of foods are stored. Nearby, in an earlier camp destroyed by a flood and abandoned by humans, windows were broken, and first the insects, then the larger non-humans, and finally the lions arrived to occupy the architectures. Unexpected forms of life flourish in unexpected places. Furniture was re-used, and an assortment of insects moved into the slits and cracks of the houses. Plants grew where once a wooden floor had been polished weekly. During colonial times proud lions were seen standing on the flat roofs of houses.

Whereas political ecologies teach us where to look, feminist political ecologies teach important *ways* of looking and doing. Harcourt and Nelson direct their practice 'against bureaucratic and modernist approaches to environmental protection pro-grammes'[26] – equally important for preservation assemblages as potential operations of power. For Carson, ' "control of nature" is a phrase conceived in arrogance, born of the Neanderthal age of biology and philosophy, when it was supposed that nature exists for the convenience of man'.[27]

Critiquing dichotomies in science, the Mozambican philosopher José P. Castiano identifies a dance in current discourses, one between a subject which knows and an object to be known about.[28] Who acts as the knowing subject in spatial transformations? Camp Chitengo was not built on empty ground, but amidst the living environments of indigenous people, and was again violently appropriated during the civil wars. After a focus on nature preservation the area might now head back towards (armed) political tensions. Encouraging the search 'for cracks and fissures in identities, dualisms, living with other species, landscapes and sense of scale', Harcourt and Nelson raise awareness of 'uncomfortable histories, realities and memories that inform our critical praxis in decolonial projects, in anti-racism, in feminism and in environmentalism'.[29]

Possible conflicts between eco-management and everyday use pivot on places and their located histories 'of interaction between living things and their surroundings.'[30]

Territory three

Doing and un-doing assemblage

Malmberget, Sweden

Another powerful assemblage that unveils destructive capacities of *becoming* altered or becoming otherwise will compose my third case study of extractive and exploitative regimes: similarly complex and powerful relations of humans, non-humans, technical devices, infrastructure, knowledge production, etc. are at work. The mines in the north of Sweden exist in a complex entanglement with their respective communities. Malmberget and parts of the town of Kiruna are about to be resettled due to recent mining developments. Former neighbourhoods will be transplanted to other sites. New houses will be provided to residents. Abandoned architectures will be carefully dismantled and taken away. The *alterlife* of architecture and society will not become possible, *the house in the centre becomes the house at the end of the street*. First, formerly lively neighbourhoods will be emptied of humans, and then of houses. These changes demonstrate economic power and its impact on spatial and migratory changes, as well as the inescapable entanglements of humans amidst their immediate environments, which cause the migratory changes. When I visited Malmberget and asked why nobody is protesting against the changes, the answer was: 'We came for the mining, and now we will go because of mining.'

Jane Bennett engages a vital materialism in the assemblages she describes in *Vibrant Matter* in order to 'highlight some of the limitations in human-centred theories of action and to investigate some of the practical implications, for social-science inquiry and for public culture, of a theory of action and responsibility that crosses the human-nonhuman divide.'[31] She describes 'things' and materials as potential actions that operate in assemblages. In the mining towns of north Sweden, it is the dominant material *malm* (ore) that has been determining the everyday lives and big decisions of pioneers and later companies. These decisions are spread throughout the town and its community, originally settled in 1888 with a deep faith in ore.[32]

Women's participation in the assemblages as workers in maintenance, social service and other organisations shows their roles as being enmeshed in the complexities and agencies of the town's history, with different impacts. Between the late 19th and early 20th centuries, various supportive roles were undertaken by women,[33] but today, the local documentation project *Dokumentera Malmberget* predominantly reveals their private lives in the mining environments.[34] An important political dimension was added through the political engagements of the women's association *Malmbergets kvinnoclubb*.[35] Paying attention to influential actors and their environments, I understand architectures as operative parts of assemblages. Both preservation and exploitation rely on them. '[D]eemed orderly, clean and therefore in need of protecting and sustaining',[36]

Tabassi explains 'dirty resilience' vis-a-vis more 'orderly' concepts, which I often see applied in forms of exploitation or preservation. Life does not care about programs or imposed structures or about the master identity that is built into and at work in territories of preservation and exploitation. It re-claims spaces left behind after humans have disappeared.

> The ability to imagine – and therefore create – alternative assemblages, alternative material embodiments – more equitable forms is, for me, the value of queer ecologies.[37]

Conclusion: Ecological politics and dirty resilience

Greta Gaard formulates the ecofeminist project of being 'concerned with the preservation and expansion of wilderness' and suggests 'replacing the master identity with an ecofeminist ecological self, an identity defined through interdependence.'[38] The architectures I have been studying have demonstrated enormous resilience when considered across expanded timescales. They have housed, one after the other, Nazis and tourists, lions and colonisers. Tough architectures, between the devil and the deep blue sea, often need to alter in order to endure. They will be obliged to accommodate unexpected inhabitants, and enter into new alliances. In interdependence with their political, social, ecological environments they are obliged to traverse vital new seas of possibility, contending with the dirty complexities of 'embodied, material subjectivities'.[39]

Shifts in the assemblage demonstrate sustainable strategies of endurance. The notion of decaying architectures assumes a human point of view on things. Rather should we see it as skilfully and collaboratively surviving in ruins and 'open-ended assemblages of entangled ways of Life'.[40] From my privileged perspective it seems easy to write about the alterlives of abandoned architectures and dirty resilience while the park rangers of Gorongosa risk their lives for their work because the park is considered a political enemy, while people have to give up their homes because of political unrest or because of the enlargement of areas of resource exploitation. However, it is not as easy as it may sound. My proposed shift of attention to the productivities and mediations of *naturecultures* is still not welcomed onto the centre stage of architectural discourse. Without these shifts in perspective, in position and scale, this reading of specific ecosystems would not be a feminist one, dismantling prevailing oppression structures and questioning traditional hegemonies. As Castiano is aware, a critique can be a type of thinking, which understands reality together with possibilities or alternatives of existing of the same reality.[41] It becomes a political project.

Rachel Carson's 'politics were ecological'.[42] Her driving concern was to show the effects of poisonous substances and to educate the public about the dangers in order to multiply the voices to instigate change – to create awareness.[43] Assembling stories, situations, materials and their effects at small and large scales, her work had an impact on politics and environmental policies. With the assembled architectures I have discussed in this chapter I want to contribute to enjoying the queer ecologies in which architectures are a welcome part of the ecological assemblage. 'Dirty, but tough architectures' ask us to get our hands dirty in theory and in practice, which means submitting them to *becomings* and mutations that allow for lines of escape, first, from the architect's design intention, and second, from human control and programming. Architectures grow, regress and vanish in relation to the environment on which architectures depend. They dissipate into the environmental milieu where material maintenance is no longer provided. Tara Tabassi calls this *dirty resilience* in her stories from her 'world-otherwise focus', the 'resilience of this mineralled, microbially rich matter'; 'what could be queerly termed *dirty resilience*'[44] – a resilience that allows architectures to endure through getting dirty and serving non-humans as immediate environments.

Architectures are embedded in ecological lifecycles, and at the same time it is important to acknowledge that the lifecycles of societies are inextricable from ecological lifecycles. To respond to these relations and interdependencies, I frame a mind-set for considering architectures. To gain insights and deal with ecologies of space, I argue that we need to take a step back from working solely with numbers, power structures, politics of territorialisation (zoning), functions, sustainability, great divides, politics of displacement, regulation, large-scale zones, guidelines and instead assemble an ethics of care, relational and queer ecologies, potentials and dispositions, response-ability and companionships, shared responsibility, politics of alterlives, small-scale environments in a careful way and to meet and learn from feminist political ecology.

Notes

1   Knox in the published conversation: Wendy Harcourt, Sacha Knox and Tara Tabassi, 'World-wise Otherwise Stories for Our Endtimes: Conversations on Queer Ecologies,' in *Practising Feminist Political Ecologies: Moving Beyond the Green Economy*, ed. Wendy Harcourt and Ingrid L. Nelson (London: Zed Books, 2015), 294.
2   See 'Category II: National Park,' IUCN, accessed 11 April 2017, www.iucn.org/theme/protected-areas/about/protected-areas-categories/category-ii-national-park.
3   Donna J. Haraway, *Staying with the Trouble: Making Kin in the Chthulucene* (Durham and London: Duke University Press, 2016).
4   Ibid., 1.
5   Isabelle Stengers, 'Introductory Note on an Ecology of Practices', *Cultural Studies Review* 11 (2005): 185–6.
6   Rachel Carson, *Silent Spring* (London: Penguin Books, 2000), 21–2.
7   Ibid., 22.
8   Ibid., 215.
9   The genealogies of the preservation areas were discussed in Karin Reisinger, *Grass Without Roots* (PhD diss. Vienna University of Technology, 2014).
10 'Vogelsang IP,' accessed 11 April 2017, www.vogelsang-ip.de/.
11 Monika Herzog, *Architekturführer Vogelsang* (Cologne: Biermann Verlag, 2007), 8.
12 A. F. Heinen, *Vogelsang. Von der NS-Ordensburg zum Truppenübungsplatz in der Eifel* (Aachen: Helios Verlags- und Buchhandelsgesellschaft, 2007), 60.
13 Jamie Lorimer, *Wildlife in the Anthropocene: Conservation after Nature* (Minneapolis: University of Minnesota Press, 2015), 10.
14 Heinen, *Vogelsang*, 197.
15 Andrea J. Nightingale, 'Challenging the Romance with Resilience: Communities, Scale and Climate Change', in *Practising Feminist Political Ecologies: Moving Beyond the Green Economy*, eds. Wendy Harcourt and Ingrid L. Nelson (London: Zed Books, 2015), 183.
16 Donna J. Haraway, *When Species Meet* (Minneapolis, London: University of Minnesota Press, 2008), 25.
17 Judith Butler, 'Interpreting Non-Violence: Why Perserve the Life of the Other?' (presented at Tanner Lectures on Human Values, Yale University, 30 March 2016).

18 Michelle Murphy, 'Work in Progress: Alterlife in the Ongoing Aftermaths of Chemical Exposure', accessed 11 April 2017, https://technopolitics.wordpress.com/technoscience-meets-biopolitics/.

19 Nicole Seymour, *Strange Natures: Futurity, Empathy, and the Queer Ecological Imagination* (Urbana: University of Illinois Press, 2013), 3.

20 Edward O. Wilson, 'War and Redemption in Gorongosa', *American Scientist*, May–June 2014, accessed 4 October 2014, www.americanscientist.org/issues/feature/2014/3/war-.and-.redemption-.in-. gorongosa/1.

21 Carson, *Silent Spring*, 169.

22 Summarised in Linda Lear, Afterword to *Silent Spring* by Rachel Carson (London: Penguin Books, 2000), 261. See also Charity Edwards' paper presented at the conference 'Architecture & Feminisms', KTH Stockholm, 21 November 2016.

23 Rebecca Elmhirst, 'Introducing New Feminist Political Ecologies', *Geoforum* 42 (2011): 129.

24 Wendy Harcourt and Ingrid L. Nelson, 'Introduction: Are we "Green" Yet? And the Violence of Asking Such a Question', in *Practising Feminist Political Ecologies: Moving Beyond the Green Economy*, eds. Wendy Harcourt and Ingrid L. Nelson (London: Zed Books, 2015), 1–7.

25 Ibid., 9.

26 Ibid., 1–2, referring to Diane Rocheleau and Padini Nirmal, 'Feminist Political Ecologies: Grounded, Networked and Rooted on Earth', in *OUP Handbook on Transnational Feminist Movements*, ed. Ravvida Baksh and Wendy Harcourt (Oxford and New York: Oxford University Press, 2015).

27 Carson, *Silent Spring*, 257.

28 José P. Castiano, *Referenciais da Filosofia Africana: Em busca da Intersujectivaçao* (Maputo: Sociedade Editorial Ndjira, 2010), 123.

29 Harcourt and Nelson, 'Introduction', 6, 9.

30 Carson, *Silent Spring*, 23.

31 Jane Bennett, *Vibrant Matter: A Political Ecology of Things* (Durham and London: Duke University Press, 2010), 24.

32 Gunilla Tagestam, *Med malmen under våra fötter – kvinnor i Malmberget berättar* (Malmberget: Grafex Malmberget, 2016), 5.

33 Lis-Marie Reinfors, *Kvinnoliv i kåkstadssamhället Malmberget 1890–1914* ['Women's Life in 'Kåkstad' Malmberget'] (Stockholm: Universitetet, Institutionen för folklivsforskning, 1989).

34 Tagestam, *Med malmen*.

35 Sveriges socialdemokratiska kvinnoförbund (Malmberget), *Malmbergets kvinnoklubb 1933–1987* ['Malmberget's Women's Club 1933–1987'] (Malmberget: Malmbergets socialdemokratiska kvinnoklubb, 1987).

36 Harcourt, Knox and Tabassi, 'World-wise Otherwise Stories,' 299.

37 Knox in Harcourt, Knox and Tabassi, 'World-wise Otherwise Stories', 306.

38 Greta Gaard, 'Living Interconnections with Animals and Nature', in *Ecofeminism: Women, Animals, Nature*, ed. Greta Gaard (Philadelphia PA: Temple University Press, 1993), 5.

39 Knox in Harcourt, Knox and Tabassi, 'World-wise Otherwise Stories', 291.

40 Ana Lowenhaupt Tsing, *The Mushroom at the End of the World: On the Possibility of Life in Capitalist Ruins* (Princeton and Oxford: Princeton University Press, 2015), viii, 4.

41 Castiano, *Referenciais*, 232.

42 Ellen Leopold, 'Seeing the Forest *and* the Trees: The Politics of Rachel Carson', *Monthly Review*, 52, no. 1 (2000). Accessed 27 April 2017, https://monthlyreview.org/2000/05/01/seeing-the-forest-and-the-trees/.

43 Carson, *Silent Spring*, 141.

44 Knox in Harcourt, Knox and Tabassi, 'World-wise Otherwise Stories,' 298–9.

Project 6

Infrastructural love

Hannes Frykholm and Olga Tengvall

We first encountered the abandoned railroad Inlandsbanan by mistake. Lost in the green sea of forest that covers much of northern Sweden, and outside the range of our navigational devices, we stumbled upon its emptiness: a three-metre wide void in the thicket. Placed on a low embankment of ballast, sand, and wood railway sleepers, a single steel track forms a tunnel through the green. Located in the geographical center of the Scandinavian Peninsula, along backlands, rural areas and provincial towns, the Inlandsbanan-railroad had the double ambition to bring ongoing industrial development to municipalities far from Stockholm, and to serve as an auxiliary service line for the military. In 1937 the 1,289-km-long railroad was completed, but already in 1964 the first part of the railroad was closed for traffic, and by 1991 the entire railroad was abandoned, due to low commercial use. Today much of the architecture of Inlandsbanan still remains: water towers, station houses with waiting rooms and staff apartments, engine car stables, repair workshops, and small restrooms. These buildings form a dilapidated monument over a geopolitical project to colonize the hinterland.

But beyond the tiring consumption of ruins, Inlandsbanan seems to hold a promise. In its most basic sense—a railroad—it is still there. A three-meter-wide exoskeleton between the soles of our feet and other places. A prosthetic limb made up of wood, ballast, and steel that extends into the horizon with promises of other landscapes, buildings, people, animals, plants, weather, and brief moments of love before the whistle signals departure again. Laid out like a string of encounters and sensations, this horizontal void holds the promise of connecting vastly different parts of the country, and of mapping new relationships between travelers and environment.

Building on a critique of Sylvia Lavin's analysis of kissing architecture, this project investigates ways in which a confounding meeting, or a kiss, between architecture, infrastructure and environment can produce affects beyond the curatorial love in museums and art institutions.[1] As Claire Colebrook suggests, affect is an intensity that in response to the existing world can map and set up new relations for a different one.[2] Unlike feelings and emotions, affect exists prior to consciousness, as intensity in the passage between two different bodily experiences and in the forces of encounter.[3] Affect is therefore not limited to an emotion produced by experiences in art museums or in shopping malls, but is rather an unstructured force, that can push us into a range of directions, some of which challenge the very institutions where kissing happens, according to Lavin.

Thinking about Inlandsbanan as a site for an architectural investigation of kissing and affect, we asked the following questions: Can a series of small additions to an infrastructural system allow a wider range of affects than the usual postcard experience of the tourist? Can travelling along the railroad make us fall in love with the surrounding environment? Can such a love affair support greater empathy and care between anthropocentric and non-anthropocentric natures along the tracks?

In response to these questions we propose eight minor additions along the tracks. These additions re-introduce the hinterland environment to the concern and attention of the traveller, all the while serving multiple users, both human and non-human. Like any infrastructural device, these interventions can be repeated and distributed along the tracks, both adapting to specific site conditions and forming a reliable system for movement. The project takes an interest in the possible encounters between passengers and the surrounding environment, be it in the form of plant and animal life, in the atmosphere with its gusts of wind, rain, and snow, or in the sensorial understanding of the past labor required for the construction of this railroad.

To fall in love implies a bodily response that is prior to the feeling of love or the expression of such feeling through emotions of love. To fall is to change position and point of view, to experience an intensity that augments the ability to act. It opens up for unstructured and unformed responses. It describes a moment of unknown possibilities, where the moment of landing is not clear. Infrastructural love does not operate around normative constructions of romance, but happens in the immediate bodily response to repeated encounters with the environment. It juxtaposes sensorial experiences that are usually kept apart and as such it could engender greater empathy for other beings, what Guattari refers to as "a new gentleness."[4]

Our proposal is not meant to be a complete remedy for the future of Inlandsbanan. Initiatives for sustainable long-term development of the region need to happen on a political level before the railroad can have an impact in revitalizing the hinterland. However, we are convinced that in the moment when such initiatives appear there is much to be won in also implementing a set of love affairs along the tracks, allowing passengers to fall in infrastructural love with this 1,200-km-long corridor in the green sea.

Infrastructural love image captions

1. Grotto

   The grotto is a place for both introspective and retrospective gazing. It is a waiting room for the next train and it introduces the passengers to fragments of the railroad's past. Inside the grotto, images of the past are projected and broken up against the craggy surface. All the past hours of labor in constructing Inlandsbanan are here condensed into a montage of images. Unlike the museum exhibition, these images are not static or descriptive, but distorted as they are projected onto the tunnel walls.

2. Neon meadow

   The meadow is a circle of soft and flexible neon sticks that sway in the wind and glow through the snow. It serves as a joint café and feeding station for humans, elks, and reindeers.

3. Cloud sauna

   As the passengers step off the train they disappear into the hot clouds of steam in the Cloud sauna. The vision is blurred and familiar faces of fellow passengers fade away. An adjacent lake provides a temporary escape into cold water before the whistle blows and the train continues.

4. Love nest

   Over the years, some of the disused structures of Inlandsbanan have been appropriated for other purposes: housing, storage, animal dwellings, and spaces for romantic encounters. In addition to an existing water tower, the love nest is an addition of eight new towers. Together these function as a combined hotel and archive of past love affairs. Each of the towers holds a history of embraces, memories of liquids, smells, and the temporary excitement of love.

5. Sidetracks into the past

   In order to deal with possible increased traffic on Inlandsbanan, there will be a need for multiple "siding tracks" where two trains going in opposite directions can meet. A wall divides the platform between the two tracks. Gates provide access to the opposite train for passengers changing direction. On each side of the wall, a projector displays video footage of an elevation view of the other side of the wall, streaming the footage to the respective projectors with a delay of 24 hours, a glimpse into the nearby past.

6. Royal theatre

   The royal theatre revisits a small town's endeavour to impress and celebrate at the occasion of an historical royal visit. The rails are used for sceneries transforming its environs into a stage. The theatre acts as a reconstruction, its plays inviting to worlds and ideas yet unknown. Although we know of its former existence, its peculiar characteristics makes us wonder, are the stories of it true? Is what we perceive real or faux and what difference does it make anyway?

7. Champagne bar

   As a combined champagne bar and amphitheater, this space flirts with the glamour of travelling. It allows the passengers to access a small bar via a marble stair leading up to an old disused water tower. A central hole in the staircase magnifies an ongoing kiss between the bricks of the ruin and the roots of birch trees. Sitting on the staircase the passengers overlook parts of the tracks, the embankment and the weeds growing along its edges.

8. Tower for tree tops

    This tower allows passengers to move inside and just above the tops of the trees. Stairs circulate around a core of restrooms, and from each of the floor plans there's a narrow footbridge aiming into the woods. Some of the bridges have bird feeding stations, others have chairs for sitting. On the upper floors, above the tree tops, the bridges give a new perspective on the forest from above. Occasional bird chirps combined with the gentle rustle of wind in the trees is all that can be heard up here.

This work was supported by the Swedish Property Board.

Notes

1   Sylvia Lavin, *Kissing Architecture* (Princeton: Princeton University Press, 2011).
2   Claire Colebrook, *Death of the Posthuman: Essays on Extinction Vol. 1* (Ann Arbor, MI: Open Humanities Press, 2015).
3   Melissa Gregg and Gregory J. Seigworth, "An Inventory of Shimmers," in *The Affect Theory Reader*, ed. Melissa Gregg and Gregory J. Seigworth (Durham, NC: Duke University Press, 2010).
4   Felix Guattari, *The Three Ecologies* (London: Bloomsbury, 2014), 34.

1. Grotto

2. Neon meadow

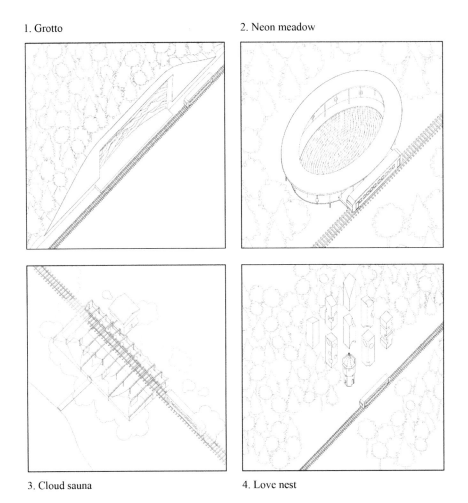

3. Cloud sauna

4. Love nest

Project 6 **Kisses and romance: On infrastructural love. Drawings by Hannes Frykholm and Olga Tengvall.**

4. Sidetracks into the past

5. Royal theatre

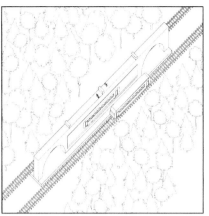

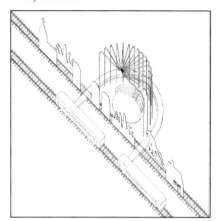

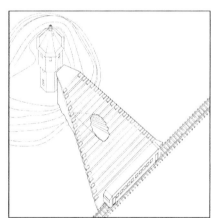

7. Champagne bar

8. Tower for treetops

Chapter 17

Diverse economies, ecologies and practices of urban commoning

Doina Petrescu and Katherine Gibson

This chapter is presented as an edited dialogue between the architect and theorist Doina Petrescu and the feminist economic geographer Katherine Gibson, whose long-time collaboration with Julie Graham is known under the joint authorial persona of J. K. Gibson-Graham.[1] The dialogic form is of particular importance for these scholars and activists, Petrescu and Gibson, especially in relation to their participatory, community-based project work, and their aspiration to imagine a post-capitalist world.[2] The dialogue offers a means of listening to stakeholders within live project settings in order to acknowledge different points of view on an identified matter of concern, and subsequently to coordinate diverse expressions of expertise. J.K. Gibson-Graham's deployment of asset mapping has proved specifically beneficial in enabling a community to recognise their shared capacities and share and coordinate their resources by means of 'commoning', likewise Doina Petrescu's approach to mapping. The dialogue form is also fitting here in that Petrescu and Gibson have previously collaborated together on atelier d'architecture autogérée's (aaa) R-URBAN project in Colombes, France. R-URBAN is a project designed as a 'bottom-up framework for urban regeneration,'[3] and will be the focus of the dialogue below.

Petrescu's work within atelier d'architecture autogérée, alongside her partner Constantin Petcou, is well-respected. Their collaborative and community-based work expands beyond a cursory participatory approach, as they invest their time exhaustively in the long-term trajectory of live projects, such as the famous ECObox community garden project.[4] Petrescu, who wrote her PhD thesis with the guidance of French feminist philosopher Hélène Cixous,[5] is renowned for the way in which she brings a poetics together with a politics, as demonstrated in her edited book *Altering Practices*, which Karen Burns has discussed in passing in this volume's opening chapter. Petrescu is also a professor in the School of Architecture, Sheffield University, a school well known for its socially engaged outreach programme, and for the live community projects in which students are encouraged to participate.

Gibson is an economic geographer, and, as she explains, a feminist political economist. Much of what she has discovered about architecture has emerged through her conversations with Petrescu.[6] What she shares with Petrescu is a desire to overcome the separation between theory and action, the conjunction of which can be animated through feminist strategies. Often this means simply starting where you are, and making the decision to address the problems of your immediate environment. One of J.K. Gibson-Graham's personal and planetary slogans is 'start where you are!'[7] Both are feminist activists and thinkers who make reference to the enduring legacy of the conceptual and practical work of Félix Guattari, and also the thinking of Gilles Deleuze.[8] In addition to her role within the pseudonym J.K. Gibson-Graham (while Julie Graham passed away in 2010, the signature J.K. Gibson-Graham continues to flourish), Gibson is a founding member of the Community Economies Collective (CEC),[9] a group of 40 scholar activists, and the Community Economies Research Network (CERN), which includes over 140 researchers, all engaged with rethinking economic diagrams of power, and reimagining and enacting post-capitalist economies. For both Gibson and Petrescu, the role of collective action and thinking together is key.

Katherine Gibson: The work that I have done with Julie Graham, as J.K Gibson-Graham, and then more recently within the Community Economies Collective, aims to represent and perform the economy as a project of becoming. From a feminist point of view, our project challenges how economies have been conventionally thought in such a way that capitalism has come to be normalised. To mount our challenge we've used the very simple image of an iceberg, which is a classic metaphor that brings things that are invisible into visibility. We propose that the economy as we know it includes a certain set of practices and relationships – the production of commodities for markets, the performance of wage labour, and the operations of businesses identified specifically as capitalist. These can all be represented at the tip of the iceberg. Underneath the visible tip we find all the other less visible, or undervalued practices that sustain life – practices taking place in households, in communities, on farms and in nature. If we look at all the people living in the world, the greater proportion are producing their livelihoods through means of subsistence, self-provisioning, and self-employment. That is to say, they are producing outside of those relationships that we associate with the normal economy; the so-called real economy.

Using the potent image of the iceberg we theorise instead a diverse economy in which a range of labour practices, different kinds of transactions, a variety of forms of enterprise, and ways of deploying surplus, different forms of property and of financial transactions co-exist. Our most recent book, *Take Back the Economy*,[10] offers simple inventory tools that help to identify the diversity of what we have to work with when transforming our communities. Our approach is to look at the heterogeneity of the economic landscape and then start from there in order to ask what kind of world do we want to build? And how might this world be composed from the multiple and heterogeneous economic relationships that are co-existing?

The feminist contribution to this mode of thinking is the critique of capital-ocentrism whereby the economy is understood as a singularity modelled on capitalist relations. This dominant understanding of economy excludes other practices and ignores the interdependence of diverse economic relations. A feminist approach aims to redress the imbalance and bring what has been seen as dependent and subordinate to view as interdependent. This includes bringing the household and the community into visibility as crucial contributors to the economy. It also means acknowledging the co-existence of multiple class processes (i.e. ways of producing, appropriating, and distributing surplus labour), not just capitalist class processes, which is to rethink an essentialist Marxist analysis.

The CEC is interested in how we might build economies through ethical negotiations that take place amidst in-between spaces, where there is no pre-determined pathway to follow. The real spaces of negotiation are where ethico-political decisions are made. We identify these key concerns around which negotiation is crucial: How do we survive well through the work that we do? What kind of ethical encounters do we have in market and non-market transactions, via monetary exchange as well as household sharing, gifting, volunteering, or fairtrade? How do we acknowledge the multiple forms of surplus that support life? Not just surplus that becomes surplus value, but surplus labour in all forms, and of course, all that we've habitually taken from nature and considered surplus. How do we think about commoning the property, knowledges, and resources upon which we depend? How do we think about finance and its role in enabling?[11]

In our book *A Postcapitalist Politics* Julie and I outlined three different, but related, kinds of politics. We draw attention to the need for a politics of language, whereby we develop a different language so that we can bring to visibility those things about which we are concerned; the 'matters of concern', as Bruno Latour would put it, that are energizing us.[12] At the same time we have to bring in a politics of subjectivity. What kind of subjects can occupy the space of post-capitalism? How would we (change ourselves) as individuals, as groups, as subjects who are convinced by certain kinds of economic discourse, and who can only see other economic discourses as romantic, futuristic, utopian, and not possible to participate in? And lastly, what kind of politics of collective actions can we engage in to reshape economies?

More recently the CEC has acknowledged how all of these politics have, to a certain extent, been human-centred. We are currently working on shifting our thinking to address the ecological nature of what is confronting us, and to work with the environments and ecologies that are supporting us. The huge challenge ahead is to find ways of extending our sense of interaction with environments and ecologies in terms of our co-productive relationships.

To help us here we can draw on feminist thinkers like Rachel Carson, Val Plumwood, Donna Haraway, and others. In order to move toward a more ecological world-view, the economy needs to be understood as embedded in ecologies, where ecologies are seen as the multiple ways that different life species create habitats that help us survive.[13] The human economy is one kind of economy, but the bee economy is yet another, then there is the economy of mitochondria, the economy of fungus – these are all other ways of organizing relationships that support lives, and we need to start seeing ourselves as interdependent with these other kinds of economies within ecologies. So, how do we start to think about not just community economies, but more-than-human economies? How do we start to see ourselves as not just human subjects, but in relation to other kinds of subjectivity, other forms of life? As such, we are searching for a different kind of language to explain the kinds of entanglements we share with non-humans. How do we start to think about a politics of collective action that is not just centred on the performativity of human actors, but the performance of more-than-human assemblages? As part of a project of rethinking our politics, we need to bring materiality and technology and other life forms and non-human entities into our sense of livelihood as an assemblage.[14]

I think what's interesting – as I move toward introducing the work that Doina Petrescu has done – is that we have an experiment going on in urban space that is beginning to do many of these things, gesturing towards the ways in which economies can be embedded in ecologies.

I want to describe an image that for me is instructive, and also architectural. It's a bamboo bridge that extends across the Mekong River in Cambodia to a Ko Pan Island. This bridge is washed away by the river every year, and is built again every year. To construct it, the builders need to go and negotiate with the bamboo clumps along the Mekong River, taking only the amount of bamboo that will allow the bamboo to regenerate itself. They need to negotiate with the landowner about how much they'll be paid to rebuild this bridge, year after year. The building process produces livelihoods for people who are fishermen at other times of the year. It signifies a relationship between human and non-human survival, and it also produces a different temporality to that which is normally manifested in buildings, in the sense that it confronts its own destruction and creation every year. To me – and I've discussed this in a paper that Doina asked me write for the journal *Building Research Information,* which was a challenge for us both – I've attempted to articulate how to think of a community economy in a human/non-human assemblage.[15] With the example of the bamboo bridge, we have a demonstration of how human and non-human habitat maintenance takes place. We have ecological and economic diversity being reproduced regularly, and we have a new relationship to what we might call durability in this built form. This is also a different way of reflecting on architecture where the focus is not on the longevity of a built form. As it turns out, just a kilometre down the river there is a counter-example in the form of a huge concrete bridge built by the Chinese, involving some coercion and corruption behind the scenes. With the effects of climate change, we'll have to see how many years the concrete bridge stands there. The bamboo bridge highlights different relationships. Its annual destruction paradoxically expresses resilience, as well as ecological and economical relationships that are embodied and performed again every time it is rebuilt.

The bamboo bridge offers a great introduction to the building and rebuilding process that the R-URBAN project by atelier d'architecture autogérée is confronting. I'd like to let Doina introduce R-URBAN, and then we'll go back and forth between us in order to discuss the economic and ecological relationships that are embodied in what R-URBAN is doing, and some of the connections between our respective projects.

Doina Petrescu: You forgot to say, Katherine, that you have also worked on R-URBAN, conducting research on the economy of the different hubs of the project. We started R-URBAN in 2008, and when I say 'we' I mean the atelier d'architecture autogérée (aaa), which is a practice I cofounded in 2001, in Paris, France, with Constantin Petcou. aaa is an architecture and design practice set up as a collective and as a professional organization in order to include non-architects as co-authors of our projects. In the past, we had completed several projects, all of them 'small' projects from the point of view of the profession of architecture: e.g. ECObox, Passage56. In 2008, the year of the global financial crisis, we realised that we had to be bolder and progress from small practical intervention to more lasting and strategic projects that could have an impact at a larger scale. We imagined a strategy model called R-URBAN as an open-source framework that enables residents to play an active role in changing the city while at the same time changing their way of living in it. The 'R' in R-URBAN stands for resilience, terms that we understood as empowering when speaking about the capacity of community not only to take risks but also to transform themselves in the face of rapid global economic and environmental changes. Within the R-URBAN framework we wanted to create a network of bottom-up resilience in order to give more agency to citizens and grassroots organisation around a series of self-managed collective hubs. These self-managed collective hubs host economic and cultural activities and everyday life practices that contribute to boosting the capacity of resilience within the neighbourhood.

The 'neighbourhood' is a key urban scale for addressing an approach like this, because this is the scale where citizens can express their agency,[16] and we wanted to involve the investment of a local community, as well as other organisations, including public organisations and local authorities, with different responsibilities in an approach to urban regeneration. We also thought that these hubs could be a new form of urban commons, and the interrelations between them would take place through processes of commoning. We understood 'commoning' as ways of ensuring the expansion and sustainability of the shared pool of resources around these collective hubs, but also as ways of practising commonality as a social practice.[17]

The first step in the implementation of this strategy is the installation of a physical infrastructure that would create assets for these new hubs. This can be achieved by using available land as an opportunity, as well as other existing assets that could be used temporarily through reversible use. In these spaces change can be initiated, tested, learned, and practised. The second stage would involve the emergence of stakeholders who could use the space provided, and share the resources and the training, provided by the hubs. Existing organisations and initiatives could also be plugged into the proposed network of civic hubs. We imagined that the strategy would enable locally closed ecological circuits at the level of the neighbourhoods, balancing the activities of production and consumption: CO_2 emissions would be reduced, water and compost carefully managed, waste would be collected and transformed locally under the control of all of the people involved in the network.

In 2009, we contacted the municipality of Colombes, a suburban city near Paris with this model and subsequently set up a partnership for an EU bid on environmental governance, with which we were successful. It is very important to mention that the power relation in this partnership was unusual: aaa was the coordinator of the European project in which the municipality was not a client, but a simple partner. In 2011, we identified assets for three possible civic hubs, one for urban agriculture, one for recycling and ecoconstruction, and the third for cooperative housing. Agrocité was the first hub, which we set up on a social housing estate, on a plot that belonged to the city and was available for about 10 years. As a response to this projected timeline, we imagined a dismountable building, alongside a 1700m² cultivated plot including an experimental farm, a community-garden, and a pedagogical garden. The building called Agrolab included a small market, a café, a greenhouse, and educational facilities. The building and the site would function themselves under principles of economic and ecological circuits, and the architecture and spatial organisation were meant to reveal and showcase these circuits, which otherwise would have remained invisible, just as described in J.K. Gibson-Graham's iceberg diagram. These circuits will be part of a network that performs at a local scale, with the idea that it could progressively scale up to the city, and the regional level. We started with the community garden as a way of occupying space with the local community and the first harvest took place before we began to build. For the construction of Agrolab we used recycled materials, trying to showcase the ecological principles on which the strategy was based. From the beginning we had an economic concern about the function of the building, wanting it to host at the same time explicit economic activities (such as the market, or the café), but also other types of collective activities that have to do with more informal social economies, such as skill and knowledge exchange, bartering, and gift economies.

Figure 17.1 Market day, Agrocité, R-URBAN 2015. Copyright atelier d'architecture autogérée.

We also prototyped a number of ecological devices to help the building serve its purposes. For example, we constructed a water-filtration device, self-built with specialist help, the first of its kind in an urban setting. We also tested compost-heating, green walls, and a drip irrigation and a rainwater container to collect and use rainwater. We compiled quite sophisticated studies on watering and cultivation techniques for the poor urban soil we inherited. Urban agriculture in suburban estates is a new field, which explains why many of these techniques and devices needed to be invented.

KG: What it interesting to me about R-URBAN is this living, breathing example of a form of commoning, and what could happen when a local council allowed you to take over a disused space. Commoning involves making and sharing that which supports a community. The practice of commoning is at the same time the practice of becoming community – working out how to access, to use, to care for, to take responsibility for something, and how to distribute its benefits. Commoning can take place on privately owned or on publicly owned properties, and it can be practised around open-access resources, such as the atmosphere or waterways, over which there are no formal rules of ownership. Another aspect of the R-URBAN system is the idea that cities of the future are going to be left with a lot of road space, once we are no longer so dependent on car use. So the other R-URBAN hub, Recyclab, is also a very interesting example of how we might begin to reclaim the public space of roads and recover this commons so as to turn it toward different economic and social purposes.

DP: We installed Recyclab on a road that had been closed some years before, being transformed into an underutilised car park. Recyclab was intended to facilitate the

Figure 17.2 Bee hives, poultry and wormery at Agrocité, R-URBAN 2014. Copyright atelier d'architecture autogérée.

Figure 17.3 Cargo bikes constructed at Recyclab, R-URBAN 2014. Copyright atelier d'architecture autogérée.

recycling and re-using of urban waste, and for providing spaces for its transformation into elements for ecoconstruction. We used containers for the construction of Recyclab because we needed to be able to remove everything if there were problems on the road, or a need to access subterranean services. That's also why other elements, such as the wooden huts, were pre-fabricated. There are workshop spaces on the ground floor in the containers, including a professional and a participatory workshop. On the upper floor there is a co-working space for designers, a kitchen, and also a residence space for artists, designers, and researchers. Both projects provided situations where a number of stakeholders could imagine and set up their own practices and associated economies. The hub hosted recycling workshops run by specialists, eco-design workshops run by designers, but also repair cafés run by the residents themselves. We had a tool bank and there were also coaching sessions to help neighbourhood residents set up their own spaces and enterprises. We set up a local database for materials that could be collected and used.

In the Agrocité hub there was a local market where produce from the garden, objects from Recyclab, and local handicrafts were sold. Local economy and entre-preneurship was actively supported. A good example is that of Yvon, who was supported to set up a worm compost business. He is passionate about worms; he thinks they are good 'companion' workers in our struggle to improve the quality of soil for urban agriculture. We set up a compost farm with him and he produced compost for the garden in exchange of using land for his wormery. He also set up a Compost School, and received accreditation as a compost specialist trainer, and this is how he makes his living now. Many local municipalities need a specialist like Yvon, since organic waste is now processed by the public services. In two years, he has trained 160 compost masters and many of his pupils have also set up compost and related businesses.

It is very important to remember that all of these people are inhabitants of a working-class neighbourhood. Many are unemployed, and some are retired, but they have become the main stakeholders in these projects based on their self-employment or voluntary work. It was quite a challenge to organise a group and explain the economy of a collective undertaking. We had to carefully explain that they would receive individual profit only by participating with a percentage of their time, which would be reinvested in collective activities, in the 'commoning' process. We conceived the details of this process in collaboration with them. Importantly, whatever is the nature of the 'profit', 20 per cent must always be returned to the collective 'pot'. In this way, we produced a complex flow that was both ecological and economic, and circulated between the two units that were built, Agrocité and Recyclab. Unfortunately, the third planned cooperative housing hub was not built because after the local elections in 2014, there was a political change in the municipality, and the new administration blocked the building. This political shift, about which I'll comment more later, raised questions about how to communicate the values being created through the practices supported by R-URBAN. How can these values be taken seriously? How can they become the subject of negotiations that extend from the local neighbourhood scale to the regional scale, and beyond?

KG: What's remarkable about this process is how a need emerged in response to the activities of R-URBAN for achieving the means of governing the commons. There is a whole lot of work required so that a community can make and share a commons. How does a community get constructed? Who are the users, who benefits, who takes the risks, who takes responsibility? Where does the benefit flow? And to some extent, each of these aspects of the R-URBAN project had to forge a new identity and a new way forward for a particular community that was forming around a commons. We've discussed two aspects of the commoning process. One concerns how to acquire the space for a commons, but the second aspect concerns how to build relationships that can be maintained and shared into the future. The work of R-URBAN has also produced ecological repair in a region where much of the land was destitute. There is also a consideration toward other non-human communities – plant species, worms – that were becoming part of the commoning community as well. It is a more-than-human set of communities that is emerging.

DP: Collective governance, as Elinor Ostrom demonstrated so well, is an essential issue for a commoning community.[18] Agreements are needed and a shared concern must be expressed not to destroy, but to support the resources that a community shares. In our case this was initiated through a series of gatherings and talks, some about decision making, others very technical, concerning how ecological loops could work. It was also important to bring external people to these sites; other organisations, institutions, researchers, etc. This meant opening up the co-production process to other than the immediate users. As well as the crucial participation of the local neighbourhood, it is important to know that behind R-URBAN there were many partners and collaborators, both local and international. The local project enabled a trans-local anchoring with the aim of greater sustainability.

KG: There is a complex institutional assemblage behind R-URBAN, and from looking at the number of organisations involved you can imagine that this was a strong network. Nevertheless, key aspects of institutional support were lacking, which made things difficult when the struggle to maintain R-URBAN emerged.

DP: One of the key institutional partners was the municipality; they were effectively the landowner. After the local elections in 2014, everyone involved in the foundation of the project left, and there was a new right-wing municipal goverment with a very ambitious mayor, a woman-mayor with unfortunately no feminist principles at all. She was ideologically against the project and she decided that the municipality would officially stop the former partnership and reclaim the space occupied by the R-URBAN hubs. This demonstrated how dependent a process of 'commoning' is upon political agreements. The project stakeholders refused to leave and the case went to court and the municipality won. A great amount of solidarity was generated amongst the local inhabitants, and amongst professionals, nationally and internationally. We began to overtly act politically, which can be seen as another stage in the co-production process, pointing to the fact that a project which appeared as exclusively economic, ecological, and social was in fact deeply political. Many people signed a petition and we appealed in Cour d'Etat, where we lost again, after some debate. Overall the law betrayed us and we have learned that more generally commons are not legally protected in our capitalist societies. However, all this struggle did have some positive effect, because the municipality adjacent to Colombes offered to host Agrocité and its users. We will keep the social (human) network, but we will lose our more-than-human friends, the worms and the other creatures living there in the garden. Meanwhile, other municipalities have also shown interest and we have commenced R-URBAN Bagneux, where we are currently building a new unit. There is even a R-URBAN unit in London. As a result of our loss in Colombes, rather than disappearing, R-URBAN will multiply. We have also created a R-URBAN Platform that will protect the network, by working with lawyers and securing money for its development. I will conclude on a positive note, by saying that whatever happened, there is hope, and we need to continue to fuel it.

KG: What this demonstrates to me is a different kind of politics – a politics of the assemblage. The assemblage has to be multifaceted. As you have explained to me before, continuing the opposition on site in Colombes was only going to drain more and more energy. That is what is called a moral of resistance politics. Instead you collaboratively manoeuvred in a different way, by increasing the thickness, variety, and diversity of the R-URBAN assemblage, including the institutional support, so that it is now a development agency, a funding body, and other things. There is a valuable message here for the kind of politics that we need to develop and how to instantiate diverse approaches to economies.

Notes

1   While Gibson and Graham's first paper was co-written when they were both graduate students at Clark University in 1978, it was not until 1993 that they published under one name. See J.K. Gibson-Graham, "A Feminist Project of Belonging for the Anthropocene", *Gender, Place and Culture*, Vol. 18, No. 1, February (2011): 1–21, p. 1.

2   See J. K. Gibson-Graham, *Post-Capitalist Politics* (Minneapolis: University of Minnesota Press, 2006); and J. K. Gibson-Graham, *The End of Capitalism (As We Knew It): A Feminist Critique of Political Economy* (Minneapolis: University of Minnesota Press, 2006).

3   Contantin Petcou and Doina Petrescu, "R-URBAN or How to Co-produce a Resilient City" in *Ephemera: Theory and Politics in Organisation*, Volume 15 (1), (2015) p. 250. See www.ephemerajournal. org/contribution/R-URBAN-or-how-co-produce-resilient-city Accessed 27 March 2017. See also http://r-urban.net/en/

4   Doina Petrescu, "Losing Control, Keeping Desire", Peter Blundell Jones, Doina Petrescu, Jeremy Till, eds. *Architecture and Participation* (London: Routledge, 2005), 43–64.

5   Doina Pestrescu, "Altering Practices", Doina Petrescu, ed. *Altering Practices: Feminist Politics and Poetics of Space* (London: Routledge, 2007), p. xvii.

6   But for earlier engagements see S. Watson and K. Gibson, 1995 eds. *Postmodern Cities and Spaces* (Oxford UK and Cambridge USA: Blackwell Publishers), 269.

7   Gibson-Graham, "A Feminist Project of Belonging for the Anthropocene", 2.

8   References to the concepts of Deleuze and Guattari can be found across many of J.K. Gibson-Graham's writings, and key concepts such as Deleuze and Guattari's well known 'rhizome' have been deployed by Petrescu and her studio aaa. See Anne Querrien, Petrescu and Petcou, "Making a Rhizome, or Architecture after Deleuze and Guattari" in Hélène Frichot and Stephen Loo, eds. *Deleuze and Architecture* (Edinburgh: University of Edinburgh Press, 2013), 262–275; Doina Petrescu, "Relationscapes: Mapping agencies of relational practice in architecture", *City, Culture, and Society*, 3, (2012): 135–140.

9   See www.communityeconomies.org and thenextsystem.org/cultivating-community-economies/

10 J.K. Gibson-Graham, Jenny Cameron and Stephen Healy, *Take Back the Economy: An Ethical Guide for Transforming our Communities* (Minneapolis: University of Minnesota Press, 2013).

11 These key concerns are addressed in turn in the chapters of *Take Back the Economy*.

12 Bruno Latour, "From Realpolitik to Dingpolitik, or How to Make Things Public", Bruno Latour and Peter Weibel eds., *Making Things Public: Atmospheres of Democracy* (Cambridge Mass: MIT Press and Karlsruhe: ZKM (Centre for Arts and Media Karlsruhe, 2005), 14–35.

13 See Ethan Miller and J.K. Gibson-Graham, "Thinking With Interdependence: From Economy/ Environment to Ecological Livelihoods", Mary Zournazi and Jill Bennett eds., *Thinking in the World Reader* (London: Bloomsbury Press Academic, 2018), forthcoming.

14 Drawing on Gilles Deleuze and Felix Guattari, *A Thousand Plateaus: Capitalism and Schizophrenia*, Translated by Brian Massumi (Minneapolis: University Of Minnesota Press, 1987) and Bruno Latour, *Reassembling the Social: An Introduction to Actor-Network-Theory* (New York, NY: Oxford University Press, 2005) Ethan Miller and Gibson-Graham define an assemblage as "constituted discursively and materially, produced by various practices of measurement, representation, institution, and discipline, and rendered semi-durable by [its] inculcation as habits of materiality (forms of landscape, tools, etc.) and subjectivity (imagination, desire, etc.)"

15 See J.K. Gibson-Graham, Ann Hill, and Lisa Law, "Re-embedding Economies in Ecologies: Resilience Building in More than Human Communities", *Building Research Information*, 44, (7), (2016): 703–736. Since the publication of this paper we have learnt that the bamboo bridge has been built for the last time in 2017. A small concrete bridge joining Ko Pan and the town of Kampong Cham is nearing completion. Katherine is currently developing a film project that will document events around the last building and watery destruction of the bamboo bridge.

16 For more on the neighbourhood as a key scale for civic resilience see Stevenson F, Petrescu D. (2016) Co-producing neighbourhood resilience *Building Research & Information*, 44(7), 695–702.

17 For more on the commoning aspects of R-URBAN see: D. Petrescu, C. Petcou, C. Baibarac "Co-producing commons-based resilience: lessons from R-URBAN, *Building Research & Information*, 44 (7), (2016): 717–736.

18 E. Ostrom, *Governing the commons: The evolution of institutions for collective action* (New York: Cambridge University Press, 1990).

Work

Chapter 18

Reproductive commons

From within and beyond the kitchen

Julia Wieger

We refuse order as the distinction between noise and music, chatter and knowledge, pain and truth.

Jack Halberstam[1]

In June 2014, I was part of a group that organised a summer school on 'Commoning the City'.[2] The summer school was an early outcome of a research project called 'Spaces of Commoning', conducted by the same group of people from 2014–2016 at the Academy of Fine Arts in Vienna. Over the course of this two-year project, we – a group of artists, architects and social theorists – engaged in research and discussions on urban commons that challenged our working modalities. Inspired by Fred Moten and Stefano Harney's idea of study as a mode of thinking and doing with others, commoning inevitably turned out to be 'the subject as well as the intended means of our study'.[3] The difficulties and contradictions of this approach were palpable during the preparation of the summer school. We discussed at great length how we would provide food for our fifty guests during those nine days of workshops, discussions, tours and talks. We were well aware of how crucial it is to bring reproductive labour into the picture – especially for a project on commoning. But in our preparatory meetings we couldn't help but treat differently the academic and/or artistic work of developing ideas on commoning and the work of meeting the participants' everyday needs. Set within an academic institution, between economies of time and attention, as well as our own expectations, we struggled to hold on to our feminist ideas. Doubtless, our discussions point to the difficulties we face when trying to overcome an existing order, one that ascribes less value to reproductive tasks than those one can list in a résumé.

In recent years, the concept of the commons – the shared resource – has been widely discussed, not least in relation to bottom-up urban practices and alternative forms of living. Our own research on spaces of commoning was founded in the assumption that a commons can only be established by the social practice of commoning; that '[b]eyond shared resources, commoning involves a self-defined community, commoners who are actively engaged in negotiating rules of access and use or the making of social contract'.[4] Spaces of commoning, then, are a set of spatial relations produced by such practices and negotiations. But space is not only a product or an investment for commoning, according to Stavros Stavrides in his recent book *Common Space*, it is 'a means of establishing and expanding commoning practices'.[5]

Many of the discussions on commoning point toward ways of life beyond capitalism. They thoroughly examine everyday practices for possibilities of less exploitative ways of living together. That is also why they so strongly concern the domestic realm, a part of our everyday lives prone to gender inequalities. Describing the struggles of a housing movement in Brazil, Stavrides speaks of the 'politicization of the *oikos*'.[6] But what does the politicization of the *oikos* involve? What power struggles does it address? What are the relations between commoning and reproductive labour?

'Raise our money or we raise hell'[7]

The term *reproductive labour* was introduced in the 1970s by feminist (post-)Marxist thinkers and activists to intervene in their Marxist contemporaries' discussions on class and labour. In their Wages for Housework campaign, writer-activists such as Mariarosa Dalla Costa, Selma James and Silvia Federici used the term to describe the unpaid domestic labour typically carried out by women in private homes. They argued that the (unpaid) work of reproducing the waged workforce is an indispensable part of the capitalist economy. Their theories and activism centred on the gendered division of the working class, between those who get paid for their work and those who do not, criticising traditional Marxist concepts for ignoring the significance of domestic labour. 'They say it is love. We say it is unwaged work', wrote Federici at the beginning of her manifesto *Wages against Housework*,[8] alluding to the mechanisms behind capitalism's devaluation of reproductive labour. In this process, feminist activist of the 1970s deemed that space played an important role: because the work was done at home, it was invisible, not acknowledged as work. Within this domestic space, the ruling ideology was that of the family, which framed domestic labour as being in women's nature, done out of affection or love.[9]

Later, in the 1990s, feminist economist geographers and writing duo J. K. Gibson-Graham argued that the fact that the domestic labour debate of the 1970s followed a rather capital-centric imaginary did not support the search for alternative economies. They recognised the domestic labour debate's important intervention, but they also detected a certain economic determinism. For them, the idea that household labour solely serves the reproduction of the capitalist labour force 'makes it inconceivable at the level of theory to imagine a social dynamic emanating from the household sphere'.[10] In order to be able to rethink such a dynamic in the first place, they present the relation between capitalist and non-capitalist forms of labour as open, and as something yet to be defined. To support this idea of a diverse economy, Gibson-Graham shows how capitalist and non-capitalist economies co-exist – that, in fact, capitalist labour relations only make up the tip of the iceberg of our economy. In their famous illustration *The Economy as an Iceberg* they use the figure of an iceberg to show the disparate perception of capitalist and non-capitalist economies. Even in terms of household labour, they argue that a multiplicity of constellations exist, ranging from exploitative slave and feudal modes to non-exploitative independent (i.e. single) and communal modes. Only the perspective of differentiated household class relations makes it possible to recognise contingencies in labour relations (capitalist and non-capitalist alike) and to imagine post-capitalist worlds.

As a reaction to the social and economic restructuring that globalisation brought about in the 1980s and 1990s involving the destruction of the institutions of the workers' movement and the crumbling of counter-movements, the proponents of the Wages for Housework campaign had to rethink their stance on reproductive labour as well.[11] In her historical research on the rise of the capitalist economy in the fifteenth and sixteenth centuries, Federici draws a direct connection between the emerging exploitation of women's reproductive work (as well as that of colonised land and the slave trade) and the enclosure of the commons.[12] Federici extends the Wages for Housework campaign's critique of a gendered work divide to include the effects of the re-territorialisation of the global work divide. She refers to new enclosures of resources and labour in former colonised countries as an example of an ongoing process of primitive accumulation, but argues that collective forms of reproduction, the reproductive commons, offer ways to resist these processes. They can enable our independence from wage labour and a subordination to capitalist relations.[13]

For the Wages for Housework campaign, the politicisation of the *oikos* meant the unsettling of an exploitative work divide; to make it visible in order to fight against it. Gibson-Graham proposed to look for alternatives beyond the dichotomies of waged/unwaged and productive/reproductive labour and, therefore, also beyond the *oikos* – or, to expand our understanding of the *oikos*, just as Federici proposes to collectivise reproduction to resist capitalist exploitation. Federici's notion of the commons is tightly linked to reproductive labour. She insists (referring to Maria Mies) that 'the production of commons requires first a profound transformation in our everyday life, in order to recombine what the social division of labour in capitalism has separated'.[14]

While our everyday lives are organised, among other things, through their spatial arrangement, and space can be 'a means for commoning practices',[15] how can designs or built spaces address the relations between commoning and reproductive work? How can a design help to oppose established, spatial orders of productive/reproductive labour? Aside from gender inequalities, what other power relations are involved in the organisation of reproductive commons?

Functionalist architecture, kitchens and collectivity

The Heimhof Einküchenhaus was first built as a freestanding three-story apartment building on a former parade ground on the outskirts of Vienna. At the time of its development the area was characterised by patches of new housing projects, allotments and sports facilities. During the first construction phase, from 1921–23, it comprised twenty-four apartments. The Heimhof was a so-called Einküchenhaus, which means 'one-kitchen building'. Its main feature was a central kitchen and a shared dining room that served the tenants of the building. The layout of the individual apartments, though, was reduced to serve basic needs. Furthermore, the building accommodated a shared rooftop terrace, a meeting room and a shared laundry room, as well as a kindergarten.[16]

The Heimhof Einküchenhaus was one of several one-kitchen buildings erected in European cities during the first three decades of the twentieth century. The housing model was widely discussed for different reasons: for the urban middle class, it was a way to save on costs for servants while keeping up their lifestyles, but also to realise reformist ideas of living; while for parts of the socialist feminist movement, the model promised independence for women.[17] In Germany, the social democrat and feminist activist Lily Braun took the view that the centralisation of the domestic economy and its cooperative organisation in one-kitchen buildings was the basis for women's liberation. Her ideas were inspired by the materialist feminist movement in the United States that promoted the rationalisation and collectivisation of household labour through the re-organisation of entire cities.[18]

While such ideas of re-organising housework corresponded well with Functionalist planning ideas, it was the famous Frankfurt kitchen that went on to dominate the layouts of modern housing in Europe. In contrast to the one-kitchen building, its design sought to rationalise the workflow in the kitchen and within the individual apartment. Both ideas, the Frankfurt kitchen and the one-kitchen building, emerged out of the desire for women's emancipation – or at least to reduce the time spent on household labour. Urban theorist Günther Uhlig argues, though, that the typology of the one-kitchen building held potential for more alternatives. This potential lay in its collectivity, as it opened the doors to a much broader range of modes of living than modern mass housing would allow. [19]

But the idea of the one-kitchen building did not prevail. In the opinion of the architect of the Frankfurt kitchen, Margarete Schütte-Lihotzky, the one-kitchen building was simply not affordable for people belonging to the working class.[20] To the bourgeoisie, the model reeked suspiciously of communalism, and it even faced strong resistance among feminist socialists. Feminist socialists were stuck in conflict between micro-political reformist ideas (concerning women's labour) and more sweeping demands for a wholesale revolution – a discussion that echoes today in the arguments that it is vital to pay attention to the contradictions of living autonomously within a capitalist system.[21] However, the example of the one-kitchen building clearly shows that the desire to live differently and change gender relations through design are connected to multiple other struggles. They involve questions such as who can actually afford to organise reproductive labour differently, or arrange life collectively.

In her queer reading of the Heimhof Einküchenhaus, Heidrun Aigner agrees with some of the critique. She observes that for the purpose of women's liberation the building was not especially useful.[22] While the project's objective was to support single or working women, the building did not provide the means to change the gender relations of housework. With its central kitchen, laundry facilities and employees the building had the character of a hotel. While they were paid for their services, it was still women working in the kitchen, cleaning the apartments, doing laundry. Nor did the project tackle oppressive class relations. Only well-off middle-class women and men could afford to live there; meanwhile, their domestic needs were fulfilled by less affluent women.

Nonetheless, Aigner traces other forms of resistance amid the different co-living constellations the building allowed for. Drawing on interviews with witnesses from the project's early years, she discerns a great diversity of living models that diverge from the heteronormative one of the nuclear family. Reports tell about inhabitants appropriating the communal spaces, creating a public situation within the domestic realm that encouraged the development of alternative forms of life together.[23]

Political work, queer households, reproductive commons

The Türkis Rosa Lila Villa is an old two-story building standing on a heavily trafficked street close to the centre of Vienna. It can be easily seen from the nearby subway station. Contrasting with its surroundings, the façade of the Villa is painted violet and pink, and features in large letters the words 'Lesben- und Schwulenhaus' (gay and lesbian house). From time to time there will also be banners hanging from the façade conveying messages such as 'Sichtbar & Selbstbewusst' (visible & self confident), or 'Racism Sexism Homophobia Kill'. The house is an old apartment building that was remodelled to accommodate three shared apartments on each of the upper floors, a counselling centre with a library and a community cafe on the ground floor, as well as a shared space for meetings that is open to the public once a week and a shared courtyard garden.

Türkis Rosa Lila Villa is a self-administered queer co-housing project and community centre for gay, lesbian and trans people. It was founded in 1982 and is still an important address for queer Vienna today. It started out under the name Rosa Lila Villa[24] and its beginnings were embedded in an emerging gay and lesbian movement, as well as in Vienna's squatting scene that opposed rising rents and real estate speculation in the city.[25] Activists squatted an abandoned apartment building owned by the city that was about to be razed. After two years of squatting, the activists successfully negotiated with the municipal government of Vienna the right to use the building for thirty years. In exchange, the activists agreed to renovate the building and offer counselling to gay and lesbian people seeking support.

In her master's thesis on the early years of the Türkis Rosa Lila Villa, Linda Jannach emphasises that in its beginnings the lesbian and gay movement in Vienna had strong connections to the then very active squatting movement there.[26] These overlaps crystallised in the similar strategies within both movements of self-organisation and demands. In Vienna in the 1980s, the establishment of autonomous cultural centres was a frequent goal – be it for gays and lesbians or rebellious youths.[27] The connections to the squatting scene show how important spatial politics were for the emerging lesbian and gay movement in the 1980s. The activists of the Rosa Lila Villa intervened in urban politics as they sought to create a space that countered dominant heteronormative structures of everyday life in the city. But they also used the prominent location of the building to fight discrimination – to make lesbian and gay life as well as the movement's demands visible in the public space of the city – at a time when in Austria it was still punishable by law to publicise same-sex relationships.[28] Simultaneously, and importantly, they wanted to provide a safe space for the inhabitants of the Villa as well as to a larger lesbian and gay community.[29] The activists established a space that allowed for what Gibson-Graham describes as 'the self-cultivation of subjects who can desire and enact other economies and the collaborative pursuit of economic experimentation'. [30]

Even today, this is how political work combines with the everyday life in the Villa. The Villa is an important centre for LGBTQI (Lesbian, Gay, Bisexual, Transgender, Queer, Questioning and Intersex) activism in Vienna. At the same time its activist inhabitants aim to establish politics of daily interaction, habits and routines that support their emancipatory, non-normative ideas. From its beginnings, the project 'was not only a living space, but also a matter of radical, emancipatory politics'.[31] For the Villa, overcoming the heteronormative model of living is closely connected to political work reaching beyond the domestic realm.

Looking back at twenty-five years of activism in the Villa, the activist and writer Marty Huber calls the engagement of the Villa activists 'reproductive work for the community' – the guidance counselling, the energy that goes into self-organisation, the working groups, the learning events for pupils and students, but also the maintenance of and responsibility for the building.[32] While highlighting the Villa's achievements, she warns us that the work brings with it the usual problems of reproductive labour – its draining nature, its invisibility and its lack of acknowledgement, to name but a few concerns.

Over the years, many activist projects have grown out of the Villa – starting there, using its infrastructures and spaces, or being initiated by the activists from the Villa themselves.[33] The most recent project that started at the Villa, which is now an independent (though still very connected) organisation, is Queer Base – a project that supports LGBTQI people who have sought asylum in Austria, who often need specific care during and after lodging their application. Queer Base provides people who have recently fled to Austria contact with a queer community and legal counselling and organises safe housing for them. The project is a good example of what Gibson-Graham describe as a contingency of labour relations. It is a conception of the household where (unpaid) household labour cannot solely be subsumed under capitalist economies. The Villa and its activist projects vividly show other possible economies of household labour which transgress a capitalist realm but also demonstrate that gender relations are 'just one among many – rather than the central – determinant of household class relations'.[34]

Recalling Federici's idea that social movements are only sustainable if they include cooperation and reproduction, I would argue this is what the residents and activists of the Villa bring to the LGBTQI movement of Vienna. They provide a place of support, a backbone maintaining the community's activism and contributing to its agency. As such, it is an experimental ground for establishing reproductive commons, showing that questions of reproduction can go well beyond the designated realm of the kitchen.

Collective housing, forms of support, place

The Frauenwohnprojekt (women's co-housing project) [ro*sa] Kalypso is a newly built five-story building located in a quiet tree-lined street. It is part of the new city development for 3,500 inhabitants in an outer district of Vienna that was opened in the early 2000s. The neighbourhood was developed on the former site of a large cable factory that has shaped the identity of the area over a long period of time. The building is comprised of forty-three apartments, of between 60 and 100m^2, a shared courtyard, a rooftop terrace, and a common room, a laundry room, a workshop and a shared kitchen, all in the vicinity of the terrace. Furthermore, there is a shared office space where individual rooms can be rented.

In this housing project only women can sign a rental contract. The project was initiated in 2003 by the association Frauenwohnprojekt [ro*sa] together with the feminist architect Sabine Pollak. Its residents moved in in 2009, but the project inspired two more women's co-housing projects in Vienna – one completed in the same year and one that will be completed this coming year, in 2017. In an early statement on the plans of the project in the feminist magazine *AUF*, Pollak writes that the scope for women to shape their living environment is rather limited. While this may be true for men as well, she argues, the situation for women is worse because they are being discriminated against: both through the reproductive roles ascribed to them, and by being placed in a financially weaker position in the housing market because they earn less than men. Therefore, she writes, the association [ro*sa] wants to establish a co-housing project that 'in terms of its concepts and contents is organised, realised and managed only by women'.[35]

While less radical in its political demands than the Türkis Rosa Lila Villa, the two projects share the idea that in order to create a self-defined (or autonomous) space one needs to establish, imagine and organise that space collectively. In the planning phase of the project, the group organised numerous workshops to develop key ideas on what a living environment for women could look like.[36] Now living together, the residents meet for assemblies on a regular basis. The project makes it possible for inhabitants to support each other and share reproductive tasks outside of the nuclear family, be it looking after each other's children, or cooking for a larger group in the shared kitchen. The possibility of renting a workspace in the building comes with the intention of making child rearing more compatible with waged labour. Ideas of solidarity and support play an important role, as practices of mutual aid and the collectively facilitated spaces aim to particularly support women in precarious economic situations, such as single mothers.[37]

The women's co-housing project [ro*sa] was subsidised by a housing program of the City of Vienna. It was one of the first projects of what a local advocacy group for collective forms of housing calls a 'Vienna Renaissance of collective housing projects'.[38] Such observations indicate that in Vienna ideas of collective housing have moved toward mainstream (and less radical) discussions of housing politics. While in one way or another questions of solidarity and diversity are addressed in most of these projects, discussions of reproductive labour, gender discrimination, or heteronormativity are conspicuously absent.[39] Even though they are intrinsically connected to housing practices, these topics remain in the domain of 'special' co-housing projects.

In her activism and writing, Federici had come to the conclusion that the 'last three decades have taught us the limits of the wage struggle as the basis for women's liberation'.[40] The fact that the reorganisation of housework on a commercial basis did not eliminate gendered discrimination speaks in favour of a renewed 'collective struggle over reproduction'[41] based on new forms of cooperation outside the logic of the market. She also vehemently reminds us that today the exploitation of reproductive labour is intrinsically connected to an international division of labour and the mechanisms of murderous border regimes. Working against discrimination happening on such macro-political levels appears a considerable challenge, but it is work that must not be neglected within the struggle. Gibson-Graham see potential for struggle in the local. In their pursuit of an economics of possibility, 'place became that which is not fully yoked into a system of meaning; not fully subsumed to and defined within a [global] order. . . . Place is the event in space operating as a dislocation with respect to familiar structures and narratives.'[42]

Notes

1 Jack Halberstam, 'The Wild Beyond: With and For the Undercommons', in *The Undercommons: Fugitive Planning & Black Study*, ed. Stefano Harney and Fred Moten (New York: Minor Compositions, 2013), 9.

2 This text is a reworked and extended version of the essay by Julia Wieger, 'Kitchen Politics', in *Spaces of Commoning: Artistic Research and the Utopia of the Everyday*, ed. Baldauf et al. (Berlin: Sternberg Press, 2016).

3 Anette Baldauf et al., 'Introduction: Having to Make it, without Being Able to', in *Spaces of Commoning: Artistic Research and the Utopia of the Everyday*, ed. Baldauf et al. (Berlin: Sternberg Press, 2016), 25.

4 Ibid., 21.

5 Stavros Stavrides, *Common Space: The City as Commons* (London: Zed Books, 2016), 4.

6 Ibid., 100.

7 'Feminism and Sexual Health', Barnard Center for Research on Women, http://bcrw.barnard.edu/archive/sexualhealth/WagesForHousework.pdf. The slogan is displayed on the pamphlet 'Wages for Housework: From the Government For ALL Women', by the New York Wages for Housework Committee, 1975.

8 Silvia Federici, *Wages against Housework* (Bristol: Power of Women Collective and Falling Wall Press, 1975), 1.

9 Nicole Cox and Silvia Federici, *Counter-Planning from the Kitchen: Wages for Housework, A Perspective on Capital and the Left* (Brooklyn: New York Wages for Housework Committee, 1976).

10 J.K. Gibson-Graham, Esra Erdem and Ceren Özselçuk, 'Thinking with Marx Towards a Feminist Postcapitalist Politics', in *Karl Marx: Perspektiven der Gesellschaftskritik*, ed. Rahel Jaeggi and Daniel Loick (Berlin: Akademieverlag, 2013), 278.

11 Silvia Federici, 'Introduction', in *Revolution at Point Zero: Housework, Reproduction, and Feminist Struggle*, ed. Silvia Federici (Oakland, CA: PM Press, 2012).

12 Silvia Federici, *Caliban and the Witch* (Brooklyn: Autonomedia, 2009).

13 Silvia Federici, 'Feminism and the Politics of the Common in an Era of Primitive Accumulation (2010)', in *Revolution at Point Zero: Housework, Reproduction, and Feminist Struggle*, ed. Silvia Federici (Oakland, CA: PM Press, 2012).

14 Federici, 'Feminism and the Politics of the Common', 144.

15 Stavrides, *Common Space*, 4.

16 Günther Uhlig, *Kollektivmodell 'Einküchenhaus': Wohnreform und Architekturdebatte zwischen Frauenbewegung und Funktionalismus 1900–1933* (Gießen: Anabas-Verlag, 1981).

17 Ibid.

18 Dolores Hayden, *The Grand Domestic Revolution: A History of Feminist Designs for American Homes, Neighborhoods, and Cities* (Cambridge, MA: MIT Press, 1981).

19 Günther Uhlig, 'Kollektivmodell Einküchenhaus: Wirtschaftsgenossenschaften (auch) als kulturelle alternative zum Massenwohnungsbau', *Arch+* 45 (1979): 26–34.

20 Margarete Schütte-Lihotzky, 'Rationalisierung im Haushalt', in *Wien und der Wiener Kreis*, ed. Volker Thurm and Elisabeth Nemeth (Wien: Facultas, 2003), 283.

21 Marina Vishmidt, 'All Shall Be Unicorns: About Commons, Aesthetics and Time', *Open! Platform for Art, Culture & the Public Domain*, 3 September 2014.

22 Heidrun Aigner, 'Das Einküchenhaus Heimhof auf der Schmelz. Zum Potential queer/feministischer Zwischenräume', in *Orts-Erkundungen: Der Stadt auf der Spur*, ed. Alexandra Schwell and Jens Wietschorke (Vienna: Verlag des Instituts für Europäische Ethnologie, 2012).

23 Ibid., 149.

24 The word *Türkis* was added to the project's original name, *Rosa Lila Villa*, in reflection of discussions and the political activism of the villa community that, since its founding, expanded to include trans* activism. See 'Geschichte', in *Die Villa Türkis Rosa Lila*.

25 Marty Huber, 'DO IT! 30 JAHRE ROSA LILA VILLA: UND SIE BEWEGT SICH IMMER NOCH', in *Besetzt!*, ed. Martina Nußbaumer and Werner Michael Schwarz (Vienna: Czernin Verlag, 2012), 208–10.

26 Linda Jannach, 'Entstehungsgeschichte(n) des lesbisch-schwulen Hausprojektes Rosa Lila Villa in Wien. Räumliche Aneignungspraktiken und Widerstand', (Master's thesis, University of Chicago, 2015), 34.

27 Ibid., 50.

28 Marty Huber, '25 Jahre andersrum. Die Rosa Lila Villa an der Linken Wienzeile 102', *Kulturrisse*, no. 2 (2007).

29 Jannach, 'Entstehungsgeschichte(n)', 97.

30 J.K. Gibson-Graham, *A Postcapitalist Politics* (Minneapolis: University of Minnesota Press, 2007), xxiii.

31 'Popolitik', in *Die Villa Türkis Rosa Lila*.

32 Huber, '25 Jahre andersrum'.

33 Florian Anrather, Dani Baumgartner, Jasmin Rilke and Cordula Thym, interview by Julia Wieger and Mara Verlič, Türkis Rosa Lila Villa, Vienna, 14 January 2016.

34 Gibson-Graham, Erdem and Özselçuk, 'Thinking with Marx', 279.

35 Sabine Pollak, 'Das Frauenwohnprojekt [ro*sa] in Wien. Ein selbstorganisiertes Wohnprojekt nach feministischen Grundsätzen', *AUF* no. 122 (2003): 19; the author's translation.

36 Ibid., 20.

37 'Verein', Frauenwohnprojekt [ro*sa] KalYpso.

38 Ernst Gruber, ed., *Gemeinsam Bauen Wohnen in der Praxis. Workshopreihe 2014 über, für und mit Baugruppen in Wien* (Vienna: Verein Initiative für gemeinschaftliches Bauen und Wohnen, 2015), 21.

39 Gruber, *Gemeinsam Bauen Wohnen*; Freya Brandl and Ernst Gruber, 'Gemeinschaftliches Wohnen in Wien. Bedarf und Ausblick', study commissioned by the Vienna City Administration, Unit for Housing Research (MA 50), 2014.

40 Silvia Federici, 'The Unfinished Feminist Revolution', *The Commoner* no. 15 (2012), 187.

41 Ibid., 193.

42 Gibson-Graham, *A Postcapitalist Politics*, xxxii.

Project 7

The kitchen of Praxagora –Turning the private and public inside out

Elin Strand Ruin

Praxagora is the heroine of Aristophanes' *The Power of Women*. In this antique play, Praxagora and her sisters take political control of their city while the men are absent in order to fight in the Trojan War. Moving the kitchens of the city out into its squares, the women in the play turn the private and the public inside out, changing the spatial hierarchy of the city and the conditions for its public life.

I was commissioned by the City of Sundbyberg and the Marabouparken Konsthall (a local art centre within the municipality, which is located on the edge of inner-city Stockholm) to develop, in dialogue with local women of the neighbourhood of Hallonbergen, a permanent intervention in this late modernist suburb. The title of this intervention, with direct reference to the events of Aristophenes' play, was *The Kitchen of Praxagora*. This project formed part of a long-term programme wherein the City worked with artists in order to support local participation in the planning process in Hallonbergen. One of the aims of the programme was to raise the level of safety in the local environment by supporting female presence in the public sphere. The previous four-year-long art project, artist Kerstin Bergendahl's *Park Lek* (literally, "park game" in English), had focused on establishing a close and continuous participatory dialogue in relation to a new zoning plan for Hallonbergen/Ör. Whilst the project was generally regarded as having been incredibly successful, the majority of its participants were men – local women, it was revealed afterwards, had not been involved to the same extent as their male counterparts.

The Kitchen of Praxagora began with a four month pre-study, which I undertook in collaboration with women's groups associated with the local organization Verdandi and the Stella Nova kindergarten starting during the spring of 2016. Based on the story of

Praxagora, our focus was on how we, through our presence, could affect an impact on public space. Initially I had been in contact with Faiza Rebandi at Verdandi, and a crucial connection to an existing local activity was made: The Female Tuesday Soup Lunch that she and her members had hosted for many years. It made the project thoroughly grounded in Hallonbergen and our experiment in the public was partly counted as an extension of their cooking club.

A mobile outdoor kitchen was constructed as a vehicle to investigate how we could "take place" in Hallonbergen. The mobile kitchen made it possible for many to take part in the project, because by simply coming by with their children, people could provide their kids with lunch while at the same time getting to know others and eventually engaging in discussions of needs and visions for the neighbourhood. Five "stops" (in May, June, August, and two in September) were made for the mobile kitchen, creating five novel types of public spaces. Well-known locations in the area – for instance, various impediments, passages, or stairs – were tested and temporarily activated by our domestic presence. The kitchen became a research device, an end in itself, and even an excuse for spending time out in the open.

The mobile kitchen and its journeys constituted a surprising and welcomed feature in the Hallonbergen cityscape, acting as a social magnet for passers-by. People stayed for a meal, helped with the dishes, chatted, and shared a moment together. *The Kitchen of Praxagora* turned out to be a powerful and inclusive activity, and a means to establish a temporary local hub – a new type of temporary public space. Collective cooking and eating changed the micro-morphology of the suburban spaces in which these activities were conducted. The women involved were in charge of the recipes and ingredients used. A world of smells and meals acted as a carrier of diverse cultural heritages and as a natural starting point for conversations: vegetarian Somali-Swedish hash and tea with sugar, cardamom, and clove by Safia was followed by a mild version of Bangladeshi lamb and rice by Shazia; Kurdish *tepsi* by Faiza, which in turn was followed by improvised noodles, with chicken, coconut milk, and homemade curry mix by Dunya. When Shazia Chaudhry, who has worked at the Stella Nova kindergarten for 20 years and knows everyone in the area, cooked in the centre of Hallonbergen on a Sunday afternoon in May, she became a node for those who passed by – for children, parents, grandparents, uncles and aunts, teens, and friends of her family, amongst others. The social network and bonds of friendship and family that Shazia has built up in the neighbourhood for many years became visible in her act of cooking.

Our question, after having carried out this temporary study in advance of a long-term project, was: how could a permanent physical intervention make women's experiences, their labour, their care work, and their networks visible to strengthen their role in the public sphere?

In its permanent form, *The Kitchen of Praxagora* is proposed to take the form of an outdoor kitchen that is cast in concrete, as a replica of two standard kitchen counter-top units. The most ordinary, well-known and beloved kitchen unit is thereby relocated from the private home into the public sphere, and mirrored. The back-to-back placement of the two units – which precisely corresponds to the floor plans of the surrounding housing blocks – gives the effect of "looking into your neighbour's kitchen" and sharing the dinner table with them. The (absent) dividing wall between the flats is shown as a 200 mm gap drawn through the common kitchen table. By creating an outdoor, functioning, collective cooking device which mimics the everyday standard kitchen of the neighbourhoods' most common building typology, I seek to stimulate a re-reading of the private that subversively addresses normalized gender hierarchies, stereotypes of gendered divisions of labour, and traditional family patterns. Cooking and eating together *in a "private" kitchen in public* constitutes an act of taking care of each other, adding, potentially, yet another layer of belonging to Hallonbergen, not only for women but on women's terms.

Acknowledgements

I wish to thank the women involved from Verdandi and Stella Nova in Hallonbergen, the City of Sundbyberg, Stockholm, Sweden: Tabassom Ghulam Farooq, Tima Mehmedovic, Jela Visnjevac, Deko Isashin, Birgitta Runsten, Asmae Saidi, Habiba Evgin, Micaela Santos De Jesus, Shazia Chaudry, Monira Haj Abdalla, Dunia Yosif, Jenny Chen, Rozet Bazer, Anitha Gunnarsson, Tabassom Yousafzai, Patricia Medoza, Micaela Santos, Safia Ahmed, Faiza Rebandi, Michaela Carlsson, Britan Rebandi, Hala Sabo, Heve Hatam, Marie Roze Elias Rut, Michael, Engudai, Karin, Qatra, and plenty of spontaneously involved citizens living in the area.

Project 7 'Cooking in the Public,' May 2016; 'The Kitchen of Praxagora' (film), by Lisa Partby and Elin Strand Ruin, 2017; original apartment plans for Terränglöparen 3, Hallonbergen, by Östin Arkitektkontor, 1973.

Project 7 'The Kitchen of Praxagora' permanent proposal (axonometry), by Studio Elin Strand Ruin, 2016; and mock-up of the permanent kitchen on site, September 2016.

Chapter 19

The critical potential of housework

Catharina Gabrielsson

Cleaning, polishing, dusting, airing, ripping, padding, nailing, drilling, aching, leaking, breathing, sweating, panting . . .[1] In housework, the body of the architect and that of architecture are entangled to a point where borders between object and subject collapse. It is a form of architectural labour, even toil, that deviates from established notions of architectural 'work' which tend to include practices that don't make our hands dirty. If the work of the architect is associated with distance and abstraction, housework implies an opposite mode, defined by intimacy and the concrete. Framing a series of non-representational practices, housework points to architecture as process, submerged in the everyday.[2] Associated with the demeaning and low-paid chores maintaining daily life, however, it is considered of little importance to architecture. Even from a critical feminist approach; turning to 'the people who are women and who work in architecture'; turning to practice as 'the niggling daily activity, the mundane, the bodily, the aspect that always disappoints the metaphoric purity of capital-A architecture' – housework is notably absent.[3] It remains invisible, as work already done, work after hours, work that although it serves as a pre-requisite for architecture goes on unnoticed.

This absence of housework in architectural discourse is only interrupted when established in contrast to architecture 'proper', and then to the effect of comic relief. In *Houselife* (2010) by Ila Bêka and Louise Lemoîne – a documentary film on the housekeeping of Rem Koolhaas/OMA's *House in Bourdeaux* (1998) – the rustic ordinariness of the cleaner and caretaker is juxtaposed with the high-tech aesthetics of modern architecture, making both look ridiculous in a Jacques Tati kind of way. Koolhaas' comment on the film as portraying the *collision* between cleaning and architecture, a clash between 'systems' or 'ideologies', is symptomatic for how the discipline looks upon itself.[4] I would argue that the relationship between housework and architecture is far more complicated than that of a binary opposition. Yet Google 'housework' and you are immediately cast into a world defined by politics, economics and labour kept outside the boundaries of architecture.

My general interests lie in how these conditions structure architecture, and more specifically how housework – both concretely and metaphorically – carries a potential for rethinking a concept infamous for its 'phallocentric effacement of women and femininity'.[5] The aim here is not to discuss 'the complex agency of women in the making of domesticity',[6] nor to set forward ideas on a feminist design for which housework may serve as inspiration [7] – but to show how housework opens up to larger questions of what architecture *is* and what it takes to maintain it. Housework concerns the significance of *work* in at least three capacities: architectural practice (labour), aesthetics (the artwork), and how buildings 'work' (their performance). These significations are enfolded in ways that uncover the limits in how architecture is practiced and generally perceived, and that ultimately concern the production of 'values' in capitalism.

Paying attention

Although dirt and dust have been subjects of interest in architectural theory, they expose issues in need of further exploration. If dust is of relevance for architecture because it 'physically attacks and alters the materials of architecture, while it is, in fact, partly made of architecture's materials, through their wearing, weathering and ruination, from fragments, to debris, to powder',[8] it must also be noted that the additional components of dust – microbes, bacteria, cells and other fragments of living creatures – give further evidence of what is being swept under the carpet. Because if dust 'unsettles regimes of order, propriety, permanence, control, that have otherwise and so far characterized and defined the discipline,' as Teresa Stoppani argues,[9] the multifarious biological components in dust compel us to consider architecture in the midst of ecological relations, transgressing the borders between mind, nature and culture.

In the first instance, then, housework concerns the conditions for keeping these natural elements at bay. While the modern history of domesticity is defined by the rationalisation of housework in tandem with techno-industrial capitalism,[10] the link between housework and biological reproduction affords it a place in the longer history of 'the private'. Hannah Arendt famously situates its origins in the antique household (*oikos*), structurally opposed to (but not separated from) the realm of the public (the Greek city-state or *polis*). Lamenting the collapsing of categories in modern societies, arguing for 'the proper location' of values and activities, Arendt's *The Human Condition* presents a catalogue of spatially defined distinctions that associate the private with necessity rather than freedom; futility rather than permanence; shame rather than honour.[11] For Arendt, the private is a space of darkness and violence, harbouring the secrets of life and death, in distinction from the public where humans attain the ability to transcend these constraints.

The implicit gendering of these distinctions is brought forth in Kathleen McHugh's reflections on the metaphysics of housework. Positing the home as an interstitial space that 'delimits an area in which specific practices create the distinctions between two territories, the natural and the cultural, or the physical and the social', McHugh points to the symbolic function of housework in maintaining this border condition.[12] The female housekeeper becomes an 'agent of a semiotic operation', allocated the task of keeping the house proper: 'surfaces must be kept clean, free from the material that characterizes the outdoors (dirt), from all residue that indicates the work done in the kitchen (food particles), and from the signs of human presence itself (fingerprints and footprints)'.[13] She argues that housework puts women in a dangerous cultural position; someone who gets her hand dirty, who does the dirty work, creating contradictions she must manage and contain within the boundaries of her own body.

We must not forget that it is precisely the allocation of activities to different spheres that serves as a basis for Arendt's distinctions. In an overt critique of Karl Marx,[14] she reserves the term 'labour' for the maintenance of biological life that she locates in the private sphere, which she distinguishes from 'work', that is, the making of durable things whose ontological basis is the market. Here, we must forgo the problems of a phenomenological analysis that criticises Marx while taking capitalism out of the picture. Revising Arendt's categorisations has relevance here, since raising housework to a level of critical awareness – *paying attention* to it – is to resist 'the temptation to separate what must be taken into account and what may be neglected', following the imperative of Isabelle Stengers.[15] If housework is ignored in architecture, it 'creates an obligation to imagine, to check, to envisage, consequences that bring into play connections between what we are in the habit of keeping separate', to confront the separation between 'things that should be shown and things that should be hidden' that Arendt insists on.[16]

Getting our hands dirty

Feminist artists have a long-standing history of paying attention to housework, intertwined with an advanced critique on the identity and legitimacy of the artwork. As noted by Helen Molesworth, however, it is a critique that has constantly been neglected and misrecognised.[17] Pointing to a lacuna in art historiography, she stresses the radicalism of artists such as Martha Rosler who, in the video works *Semiotics of the Kitchen* (1973–74), used novel techniques and strategies of representation to ironically imply that theories of semiotics were unable to account for the role of women as housekeepers. Similarly challenging the conditions and identity of 'work' associated with the art world, Mierle Laderman Ukeles utterly conflated the terms by stating 'MY WORKING WILL BE THE WORK'.[18] In her *Manifesto for Maintenance Art* (1969), Ukeles distinguished between 'development' and 'maintenance', insisting that the former – associated with progress, change and individual creation – was not only dependent on the latter, but leads to a depletion of the Earth's resources.[19] Drawing on her daily work as housekeeper and mother, Ukeles' radical reframing of these practices as 'Art' not only dismantled the borders between public and private but challenged the basis for social *and* artistic distinctions. In a series of performances in the early 70s, Ukeles employed domestic chores (such as dusting and cleaning) to expose the unseen, underpaid and undervalued forms of labour that serve as a prerequisite for 'The White Cube', thereby ensuring art's cultural and monetary value.[20] Drawing from the work of Jackson Pollock – who described his work as 'art of the body', harnessing movement and categorising it as artistic expression – and Marcel Duchamp's 'art of the mind', where he renamed found and previously overlooked objects – Ukeles exposed the rigid confinements of art's valorisation, transposing these strategies into the more radical domain of maintenance.

In setting the scene for such practices, Peggy Phelan points to Yves Klein's first *Anthropometry* performances in Paris 1958. She describes how Klein, dressed in a tuxedo, 'conducted' the composition of the painting by directing three naked women – their bodies sponged with blue paint – to imprint their bodies onto paper according to Klein's rehearsed plan.[21] He later expressed his euphoria in being able to 'dominate' his creation by turning his models into 'living brushes': 'In this way I stayed clean. I no longer dirtied myself with colour, not even the tips of my fingers.'[22] In being distant from such dirtiness, architecture, too, stands at risk in being confronted with housework. Associated with representation and a fundamental distance from its object – the building – architectural practice also relies on the labouring bodies of others.

The home and the house

In its very etymology, housework exposes the complexity of these relations. Straddling between the 'home' and the 'house' – between subjectivity and intimacy, on the one side, and the world of industry and building on the other – housework operates across the categories. The difference in activities associated with these spheres is captured by the Marxian distinction between unproductive and productive labour – not a distinction in terms of their worth, but in relation to the market, the making of profit and surplus value. With the expansion of capitalism, however, the significance of labour and production has undergone a mutation, becoming dislodged from the industrial conditions analysed by Marx. Now at the stage of 'an institutionalised social order' – affecting everything from climate change to 'care deficiencies' to the hollowing out of political power – Nancy Fraser argues that capitalism cannot be grasped from within its own production logic.[23] The multitude of crises in capitalist societies cannot be explained by reference to contradictions *inside* capitalism but in relation to the resources it exploits; its dependence on co-existing 'non-economic' realms that supply what Fraser calls its 'background conditions of possibility'.[24] Alongside the spheres of nature and politics, providing the resources to and enabling capitalist expansion, Fraser highlights the sphere of social reproduction – 'the forms of provisioning, caregiving and interaction that produce and maintain social bonds'– as indispensable for capitalism.[25] She points to activities going on in households, neighbourhoods and public institutions, 'variously called "care", "affective labour" or "subjectivation" ', activities that form 'capitalism's human subjects, sustaining them as embodied natural beings, while also constituting them as social beings, forming their *habitus* and the cultural ethos in which they move'.[26] These environments are deeply implicated by architecture, as architecturally designed, structured and maintained.

The recognition that wage-labour could not exist in the absence of housework has sustained generations of feminist struggles.[27] But if keeping the house clean, cooking and caring for children are freely provided to capitalism, then the production of intimate values associated with the home are equally compromised. The skills of homemaking, as described by Hilde Heynen – 'the caring for things invested with memories or cultural significance, the transmittance of private meanings and values to the next generation, the continuous arranging and rearranging of the necessities of daily life, the performance of family rituals and acts of emotional bonding' – are *habitus* forming skills, partaking in the creation of the human subject in capitalism.[28] Heynen explains how the socio-economic process that shaped the home as separated from the workplace also imbued it with 'subjective' values, giving rise to the 19th-century cult of the home as a refuge for all that was threatened by extinction in modernity.[29] It is a powerful construction that stays with us, feeding imaginaries of home as a protective realm for our personal selves, our memories and close relations. Underpinning Walter Benjamin's seminal reading of the bourgeois interior, however, is how this construction of home is formed by the very powers it purportedly resists.[30]

The tensions in these spatial imaginaries – between home and house, public and private, inside and outside, subjective and objective – are provided with a context by Fraser's analysis. She notes how reproductive (unproductive) labour was *split off* in modernity and relegated to a separate 'private' domestic sphere where its social importance was obscured.[31] The notion of splitting or cleaving off has been conceptualised in terms of *value diremption* (*Wert-Abspaltung*) by feminist Marxist scholar Roswitha Scholz, referring to a process where certain values are allocated as 'Other' to the market. They tend to be coded female, as explained by Scholz:

> Thus, in patriarchal modernity, not only certain activities, but also emotions and character traits (sensuousness, emotionality, weakness of character and mind) are delegated, ascribed and projected towards 'the woman'. The male, enlightened model of subjectivity, which is dominating society, stands for the power of self-assertion (especially in competition), intellect (as implied by an intrinsically capitalist reason), strength of character (yet with respect to the capacity to adapt to capitalist impertinences) amongst others . . . [32]

The imaginaries of home (and what Benjamin called its phantasmagoria) can thus be seen as formed through a process of 'splitting off' values from the world of industry and commerce: not as a resistance to capitalism but as inherently *structured* by it. Although the gendered division has mutated again in what is allegedly post-industrial capitalism, fused by financialisation and affect-driven consumption, what Scholz points to is the formative logic in capitalism's distribution of values. The 'non-economic' spheres that Nancy addresses cannot be conceived of as 'other' to the market, but are 'part and parcel of capitalist society, historically co-constituted in tandem with its economy, and marked by their symbiosis with it.'[33] Thoroughly undermining the categorisation of Hannah

Arendt, by this thinking it also becomes clear that the home cannot serve as a locus for critique or as a site for resistance.[34] Rather, it is by exposing the multi-stranded connections and contradictions between different spheres – what Fraser calls their 'boundary struggles' – a more complex critique becomes possible; on and from within capitalist society.

From the outlook of capitalism, the distinction between 'home' and 'house' is now merely a turn of phrase. The process that began with the rationalisation of housework, powered by technology and its 'objects of desire', has now led to the commodification of the imaginary of home as such. With accompanying identities and lifestyles, notions of 'home' are driving everything from real estate speculations and home-food deliveries to Airbnb. This is because the logic of capitalism is totalising, and for continuous growth, there must be an increase of relations in the market.

Housework and maintenance

Yet housework points to an ethics of care that is fundamentally at odds with capitalist accumulation. As neoliberalism commodifies the values, services and properties associated with the home, it sets off a longer chain of exploitation that destabilises and ultimately destroys the assets on which capitalist society depends. For, as Fraser notes, 'no society that systematically undermines social reproduction can endure for long'.[35] Arguing for a systemic understanding of processes operating across the categories, Fraser's recent work shows the enduring relevance of Mierle Laderman Ukeles' *Manifesto*. Locating maintenance in the personal, the general and the Earth, Ukeles showed how domestic work, service work and caring for the environment were intimately connected. As a permanent artist-in-residence at the New York Sanitation Department, Ukeles' practice evolved towards installations and choreographies involving landfills, refuse and garbage, exposing the mountains of waste produced by consumerist society. Today, as informed by Isabelle Stengers, we could say that Ukele's *Maintenance Art* series was an 'intrusion of Gaia'; not an assertion of a 'nurturing mother' that keeps us all safe, but a forceful reminder of the assemblage of relations that, inert to our wishes and needs, form the basis for human existence.[36]

The implications of housework thus cannot be limited to domesticity, nor is keeping the house merely a private concern. In *Maintenance Architecture* (2016), however, Hilary Sample argues that maintenance is of importance for architecture in being a *public* activity. Requiring 'formal organisation and teams of skilled workers . . . dedicated to safeguarding the holistic image of an architectural work', she distinguishes it from cleaning which is associated with the domestic, therefore private and individual, 'engaging only with parts of buildings'.[37] In ensuring the longevity of buildings and their 'enduring beauty', Sample identifies how maintenance raises a range of concerns – professional hierarchies and social divides, building performance and decay, issues to do with post-occupancy, and the visual regimes in architecture – summed up as 'a range of imperfections'.[38] Sample's book is an annotated collection of artworks that explore different aspects of maintenance, yet she completely misunderstands the criticality of these practices in assuming public and private as part of a fixed and natural order. Indeed, her insisting on the difference between maintenance and cleaning (albeit inconsistently argued and described) falls back on this assumption, serving as an implicit justification for why maintenance should be an architectural concern. Unable to see the intrinsic connections between 'value-productive' maintenance work and the 'unproductive' activities of the household, Sample's reading is devoid of criticality, despite the many unsettling aspects of maintenance brought up by the book. Thereby, as a concept and a form of practice, the status quo of architecture is paradoxically preserved.

The way I see it, housework carries a potential to go beyond this narrow conception of architecture and allows us to challenge the assumptions built into its disciplinary logic. For this to become possible, we must understand both maintenance and cleaning as care-taking practices engaged with buildings as dynamic matter, shifting and transformed through occupancy and decay, partaking in the production of subjectivities, drawing on and subjected to resources and forces that go far beyond the physical boundaries of walls. Framed in terms of 'housework', these care-taking practices call on a wider assemblage of relations, activities, spaces and temporalities that, although hidden and ignored in architecture, constitute its background conditions of possibility. Consider, for instance, the undervalued yet necessary tasks that serve as a requisite for architectural production. As a commercial practice, architectural labour relies on resources, activities and relations that aren't (yet) on the market or that aren't attributed with monetary value. It might involve working overtime with competitions, participating in public debate, sustaining contacts, keeping track of products, protocols, and codes and engaging with the process at the building site; activities that although they are necessary for the quality of the final 'product' are not formally productive. Although some of these activities fall into other categories and are funded as investments, the amount of unpaid labour necessary for maintaining an architectural practice is a widely shared concern. In academia, the countless additional tasks of administration, management and social bonding that fill up the 'extra hours' – tasks that don't guarantee an academic career but are necessary for keeping things running – readily map as housework. The steady increase of these tasks, integral to the managerial turn of university administration, exposes a strange correlation between a tightened monetary logic and added burdens of housework.

Issues of time are important here, and linger behind the distinctions of human activities proposed by Hannah Arendt. Whereas 'labour' is written into the repetitive, cyclical movement defined by necessity and animal life, 'work' concerns the fabrication of durable products that, unlike labour, has a defined beginning and end.[39] But shifting the context for these activities transforms their temporalities completely. By *paying attention* to housework, Ukeles' performances operated as interventions or ruptures that significantly expanded the field of how art was conceptualised and practiced. Identifying the contradictions and fallacies inherent to Western ideals of progress, she saw maintenance as 'the proper sustenance of change'. In much the same way, housework operates as a lens to question 'development' in architecture, associated with the linearity of the project and the 'thinglike' quality of its commodified object. From an architectural point of view, the distinction between cyclic and linear time is entirely questionable. Cleaning the house and painting it are actions that make it new: alterations can radically transform the significance of architecture. Projects are postponed, repeated, dismantled and resumed as drawn into the repetitious crises of capitalism. Indeed, as argued by Runting and Torisson, the architectural project must now be understood as a producer for 'anticipatory affect', dislocated from a temporality of future execution.[40]

Maintaining architecture

Housework essentially works on the domesticity of architecture. Rather than serving to confirm divisions between nature and culture, public and private, cyclic or linear time, it attains a critical potential by making transversal connections across these divides. Expanding on the context for how architecture is normally perceived, housework unsettles notions that form the nexus of the discipline. Structured by modernity and capitalism, as two parallel and entwined historical processes, architecture draws its identity and legitimacy from the values of the building as object, precariously balancing between its commodified value and those 'split off' as art. We must forego the complex dialectics in this relationship, and the schizophrenic contradictions it contains – signalled (for instance) between the detrimental 'spectacle' and sacrosanct 'experience' frequently encountered in architectural phenomenology. Sufficient to note that from August Schmarsow onwards, as informed by 19th-century German aesthetics on empathy, form and space, the legitimacy of architecture as a form of art is founded on spatial experience. It is therefore interesting to note what remains hidden and ignored in this conception, for instance, as stated by Le Corbusier, distinguishing architecture from ordinary building and from the works of the engineer: 'the purpose of construction is to make things hold together; of architecture to move us.'[41] Not only does this statement expose how architecture is more closely associated to how buildings are *sensed* than with ensuring their permanence and reliability, it also raises questions concerning the wider implications of this 'movement'. If aesthetics in architecture is reduced to the subjective experience of space, linked to properties in purportedly fixed and immovable objects, it means to ignore the vagaries of taste, the social distinctions inherent to judgement, the shifting of semiotics and cultural codes, and the implications of unforeseeable affects.

Reduced to the 'wow-factor' of buildings, the power of architecture to 'move us' is perhaps its strongest remaining asset in neoliberal capitalism. The point is that within this register, keeping the house clean and ensuring its keeping, are essentially architectural practices. Disconnected from the social codex that certifies architecture as an art form – reliant on, as Rancière says, 'a specific gaze and a form of thought to identify with it'– architectural aesthetics essentially concerns the experience of the sensible milieu 'in which the distinction between those things that belong to art and those that belong to life are blurred'.[42] In setting the conditions for this experience – curating the experience of space, maintaining the object (whether along with or counter to the intentions of its author) – the low and denigrated chores of housework are not 'Other' to architecture, but provide the basis for its 'Art'. The omission of housework from architectural discourse exposes the fragile, yet enduring imaginations of authorship, progress and control that structure the discipline. Housework confronts us with what it really takes to keep architecture pure and proper, and the broader field of exploitations kept out of the equation. Making housework central to a re-evaluation of architecture is therefore to maintain the discipline, and to preserve a caring ethos to practice – which in the current realm of capitalism is necessarily hard and dirty work.

Notes

1 This chapter draws on my previous essay, 'Housework' (*Nordic Journal of Architecture* 3:2:2012), and reuses the first few sections from that text. The list of activities alludes to Richard Serra's *Verb List Compilation: Actions to Relate to Oneself* (1967–68) – 'to roll', 'to crease', 'to fold' etc. – related to his sculptural practice at a time when the identity of the artwork and the role of the artist underwent foundational reformulations.

2 While my understanding of practice has similarities with what Nishat Awat, Tatjana Schneider and Jeremy Till propose as 'spatial agency', unlike them, I regard aesthetics as a crucial element for and in any reconfiguration of architecture. See their rejection of aesthetics as linked to 'static properties', following a critique on architecture identified with the 'building as object', Awat et al., 2011: 27.

3 *The Architect: Reconstructing her Practice*, The MIT Press, Cambridge Massachusetts, London England, 1996: xii.

4 Excerpt from an interview with Koolhaas. See: 'KOOLHAAS HOUSELIFE – Bêka & Lemoine's film on Bordeaux House by Rem Koolhaas – Trailer 3'. YouTube video, 32 seconds. Posted Sep 30, 2009. https://www.youtube.com/watch?v= W_uQYZO2MOk.

5 Elizabeth Grosz quoted in Debra Coleman, 'Introduction', in D. Coleman, E. Danze and C. Henderson (eds.) *Architecture and Feminism.* New York: Princeton Architectural Press, 1996: xiii.

6 Gülsüm Baydar, 'Figures of wo/man in contemporary architectural discourse', in H. Heynen and G. Baydar (eds.) *Negotiating Domesticity*, London and New York: Routledge, 2005: 32.

7 Elizabeth Diller, 'Bad press" in Hughes, 1998.

8 Ben Campkin and Paul Dobraszczyk, 'Architecture and dirt: introduction', *The Journal of Architecture* 12:4, 2007: 350.

9 Teresa Stoppani, 'Dust revolutions: dust, *informe*, architecture (notes for a reading of dust in Bataille)', *The Journal of Architecture* 12:4, 2007: 437

10 Hilde Heynen, 'Modernity and domesticity: tensions and contradictions', in H. Heynen and G. Baydar (eds.) *Negotiating Domesticity*, London and New York: Routledge, 2005

11 Hannah Arendt, *The Human Condition*, Chicago and London: University of Chicago Press, 2nd ed., 1998: 73.

12 Katheleen Anne McHugh, 'The Metaphysics of Housework: Patricia Gruben's *The Central Character*' in A. Ballantyne (ed.) *What is Architecture?* London and New York: Routledge, 2002: 102.

13 Ibid., 107.

14 On the significance of Karl Marx in Arendt's work, 'the absent authority' who is 'appropriated in silence', see Tama Weisman, *Hannah Arendt and Karl Marx: on Totalisation and the tradition of western political thought*, Plymouth: Lexington books, 2014.

15 Isabelle Stengers, *In Catastrophic Times: Resisting the Coming Barbarism*, Translated by A. Goffey. Open Humanities Press in collaboration with meson press, 2015: 62

16 Ibid., 62; Arendt 1998: 72.

17 Helen Molesworth, 'House Work and Art Work', *October* Vol. 92, 2000: 81–82.

18 Mierle Laderman Ukeles, from *Manifesto for Maintenance Art, 1969. Proposal for an Exhibition: 'Care'.* Quoted in Helena Reckitt, *Art and Feminism*, London and New York: Phaidon Press, 2001: 93.

19 Ibid., 198.

20 Molesworth 2000: 78, Phillips 2017.

21 Peggy Phelan, 'Survey' in H. Reckitt (ed.) *Art and Feminism*, London: Phaidon 2001: 28.

22 Ibid.

23 Nancy Fraser, 'Behind Marx's Hidden Abode: For an Expanded Conception of Capitalism', *New Left Review* 86, 2014: 67.

24 Ibid., 60.

25 Ibid., 61 .

26 Nancy Fraser, 'Contradictions of Capital and Care', *New Left Review* 100, 2016: 101.

27 Most notably through the Wages for Housework movement, discussed by Silvia Federici in *Revolution at Point Zero: Housework, Reproduction and Feminist Struggle*, New York, Common Notions, 2012.

28 Heynen 2005: 20.

29 Heynen 2005: 7–9.

30 Walter Benjamin, 'IV. Louis-Philippe, or the Interior' in 'Paris, the Capital of the Nineteenth Century', *The Arcades Project*, trans. Howard Eiland and Kevin McLaughlin, Cambridge, Massachuseets, and London, England, The Belknap Press of Harvard University Press, 2002, 8–9.

31 Fraser 2016: 102.
32 Roswitha Scholz, quoted in Elmer Flatschart, 'The commodity and its Other', *Culture and Organization*, Vol. 18 Issue 5, 2012: 409.
33 Fraser 2014, 70.
34 Fedirici 2012: 2.
35 Fraser 2016: 99.
36 Stengers 2016: 43–50.
37 Hilary Sample, *Maintenance Architecture,* Cambridge, Massachusetts, London, England: The MIT Press, 2016: 7.
38 Ibid., 20.
39 Arendt 198: 144.
40 Helen Runting and Fredrik Torisson, 'Managing the Not-Yet: The Architectural Project under Semio-Capitalism', *Architecture & Culture*, Vol. 5 Issue 2, forthcoming 2017
41 Le Corbusier, *Towards a New Architecture*, trans. Fredrick Etchell, New York: Dover Publications, 1986: 19. French original: 'La Construction, c'est pour faire tenir; l'Architecture, c'est pour émouvoir', *Vers une Architecture* (1924).
42 Jacques Rancière, *Aesthetics and its Discontents.* Trans. G. Rockhill. London: Polity Press, 2009: 5, 6.

Chapter 20

The garage

Maintenance and gender

Janek Oźmin

The suburban garage, arguably one of modernity's most prolific reflexive inventions, has received little attention in terms of critical discourse in architecture. Contemporary Marxist feminism has been utilised in architectural theory to illustrate a series of binary conditions related to the home, including hidden forms of labour, paid and unpaid work, productive and reproductive spheres, public and private, sex and gender. Through this discourse, the subject of maintenance (which includes physical repairs and renovation, housework and homemaking) is broadly accepted as a means of producing and inhabiting architectural space. This innovation has been key in determining alternative forms of architectural practice that contest and intervene in dominant patriarchal images and descriptions of the home. The garage is uniquely situated between public and private realms, house and infrastructure, store and facilitator, place of work and labour, and has often been utilised as a free and reprogrammable space in close proximity to the home. This image of liminality is expressed in a variety of media including advertising and film, where the garage situates ambiguous forms of masculinity by connecting gendered forms of maintenance to images of technology and consumption. The suburban garage as reflexive invention initially responded to the need to house an automobile, but later it becomes a site of continual reimagining, responding not only to the collective subjectivity of the household but also to practices that cannot be contained within the programme of the house. By questioning the binary applications of gender and maintenance theory, it may be possible to understand how capitalism operates to produce new forms of masculine domesticities and domestic masculinities.

The garage has had a specific relationship with masculinity and domesticity since its inception in the early nineteenth century. Early examples of the garage typology were based on carriage houses and often contained equipment for animal husbandry and vehicle care. Blacksmith workshops stood next to mechanical workshops and battery storage. Manure boxes and hay feeders were within range of oil and petrol drainage infrastructure. The early cars required chauffeurs and, in turn, accommodation for these emerging professionals, part engineer, part gentleman.[1] Accordingly they were usually housed in special apartments above the storage space of the garage or, in the case of Le Corbusier's Villa Savoye (1928), in a specially designed apartment on the ground floor with its own front door and clearly separated from the maids' rooms. Le Corbusier claimed that these types of servant spaces were doomed in the age of the machine, and that with their disappearance the dark and poorly ventilated attic spaces would also vanish.[2] The morphology of the garage and the American home is well documented by Folke T. Kihlstedt, who describes in detail how mass produced commercial garage designs developed from an off-the-shelf kit to become a necessary programmatic inclusion for keen real estate developers.[3]

It took close to thirty years before the garage found a fixed location for itself, meandering from back garden to alongside the road in front, and finally becoming attached to the house. On one side of a fireproof wall was a highly engineered and scientifically planned workspace for domestic productivity in the form of a kitchen, on the other side was an open unplanned room big enough to hold the family car. Early cars were peculiar commodities in the sense that the models were sold as unstable machines requiring a variety of inputs from owners in exchange for mobility in the social and business (work) worlds. However, with the arrival of Fordism the car reached a level of mechanical stability, and this changed the nature of the garage. As a result, the garage came to be used not only as a space for the storage of the car but to include a workbench for home repairs and maintenance, storage for the materials required to maintain the house, including gardening equipment and space for the overflow of unused household commodities.[4] The workshop bench and its associated power tools and material working machines were associated with masculine identity, while feminine identity was structured around household appliances associated with housekeeping and homemaking. Nevertheless, the activity of mechanical repair was not limited to men, and American colleges of the 1920s included a variety of courses in mechanical maintenance designed to provide women with the necessary skills to repair the house.[5] Critics of patriarchy might reflect on the irony of this set-up, wherein the domestic prisoner is required to mend her own cell – particularly in a context where women had access to training in repair skills, but were denied access to engineering courses.[6]

The politicising of gender, property, maintenance and unpaid-labour power was key to the feminist discourse of the 1970s. Drawing on Marxist theories and a critique of class structures, Silvia Federici's influential essay of 1975, 'Wages for Housework', discussed the hidden economics of domestic maintenance in relation to capitalism.[7] The origins of this structure date back to the Greek *oikos* (home), where the household and its material properties, including slaves, women and children, had an economic and ecological relation to the collective city. In classical terms, the household naturally constructs the ground for discourse on labour and work as it involves the organisation and maintenance of a household's material wealth. Economy (oik-onomia) contributes to the reproduction of the internal and external environment of the home, or the Ecology (oik-logia). As maintenance of the home is embedded in these economic and ecological conditions, the politics of household property and the terms of its reproduction can be taken as a key site for intersectional discourse.

From this position, housework is part of a performance of maintenance invisibly propping up what Federici identifies as a 'system of control'. Amidst her Marxist critique of the hidden relations of labour-power, Federici's description of 'Housework' utilises social science categorisations of sex roles. The prevalent patriarchal logic, Federici was contending, is represented in such publications as Parsons and Bales' *Family Socialization and Interaction Process* (1956), where the family structure is organised around socially normalised 'feminine' and 'masculine' character traits. 'Expressive' aspects of gender are described by the authors as relating to the feminine (women) providing 'care and love'; the 'Instrumental' is associated with the masculine (male) 'breadwinner'.[8] 'The husband-father, in holding an acceptable job and earning an income from it, is performing an essential function or set of functions for his family (which of course includes himself in one set of roles) as a system.'[9] In this sociological system masculinity is represented as the (male) 'internalised' sex role, allowing for social change.[10]

Federici inverts the logic of Parsons and Bales' description of what they posit as naturally feminine jobs, such as 'nurses, maids, teachers, secretaries'[11] which are intimately connected to the expressive characteristics of gender, in order to reveal the grip of patriarchal society on the feminine. R. W. Connell proposes that it was 'the political complacency of this framework, rather than the sex role concept itself, that was disrupted by feminism in the 1970s'.[12] What remains prominent in terms of discourse on the home is that expressive maintenance work situates itself at a juncture between sex role theory and the modern physical apparatus of the household, which is normally discussed in reference to Taylorism and the kitchen. Rather than qualify acts of maintenance according to distinct sex roles, it may be possible to consider how the home itself structures forms of maintenance around gender. In order to develop this line of thinking, it is important to take into account developments in masculine domesticities since the early period of Fordism. Changes in masculine domesticities have occurred most notably since the emergence of Generation X.

Generation X is broadly defined as those subjects who were born in Western developed nations roughly between the late 1960s and the early 1980s. This transformation can be understood through the reciprocal formulae of Masculine Domesticities and Domestic Masculinities.[13] The former describes the way in which the home is transformed through the actions of the male subject, and the latter the way in which the male subject changes in relation to the home. Masculinities are understood to be 'culturally constructed in relation to femininities' and both should be considered to hold a 'diverse and contested set of identities,' which differ relative to time and place.[14] The suburban garage is a unique domestic space in the sense that it is inherited as a peripheral and unfinished room which requires an act of intervention to transform it beyond a storage space for a car. This act has the capacity to transform the home through its articulation as an infrastructure of maintenance while simultaneously reflecting responses to identities structured within the home.

To clarify what I mean by this reciprocal formula, I will discuss film and television depictions involving garages and Generation X men: *Ferris Bueller's Day Off* (1986),[15] and *American Beauty* (1999),[16] *Homeland* (2011)[17] and *I Love You Man* (2009).[18] The selected media will be brought into the discussion drawing on a psychoanalytical film critique following a sociological description of maintenance and the garage. These two forms of critique – the sociological and the psychoanalytical – work to reveal hidden systems of power and governance by revealing how the subject is positioned within a patriarchal system. While Federici concentrates on a socio-political approach to revealing systems of power, the film theorist Laura Mulvey adopts a psycho-political reading to reveal the apparatus of cinema.[19] Although spread out over a period of thirty-five years, the depictions of the masculine subject in these examples of the garage rely on a suspension of normalised labour conditions: a day off; unemployment; transitioning to civilian life; freedom from the family through bachelorhood. The characters embody what Mulvey describes as passive feminine qualities such as deviance from the norm and lack of individual trajectory, or are directly involved in raising children in a patriarchal symbolic order that contradicts their own subjectivity. Peter Lehman argues that while Mulvey's theoretical assessment of the patriarchal system that organises visual pleasure is fundamental in terms of understanding how capitalism operates through the objectification of the female body, the male body is also objectified and sexualised in cinema.[20] The issue at stake in relation to the garage is understanding not only how the male body is represented within the home but how the combination of body and space is used in relation to commodification of masculine domesticities.

Stephen Graham and Nigel Thrift propose that maintenance relates to the world in three vital ways: First, by revealing that the world is in a constant state of decay and transformation; second, that maintenance and repair constitute a 'vital source of variation, improvisation and innovation' and finally, that it requires a considerable amount of economic activity to perform a system when it breaks . . . '[21] It is in this space between breakdown and restoration of the practical equilibrium . . . that repair and maintenance makes its bid for significance.[22] That is to say, Graham and Thrift propose – drawing on Heidegger's tool analysis – that much of the sociotechnical infrastructure of the world remains invisible until it ceases to work, losing its 'ready-at-hand' qualities. In disclosure the tools and process required to remake the world become visible opening up new sets of relations and subjectivities. The garage is a space that not only holds dormant things, brought to life in processes of maintenance and repair, but also provides space for the creation of subjectivities that assist in the stabilisation of the home. 'Things only come into visible focus as things when they become inoperable – they break or stutter and they then become the object of attention.'[23] Steven J. Jackson furthers this concern by discussing 'broken world thinking' as both 'normative and ontological'.[24]

In this context, the tool is situated in a larger scale of infrastructural articulation. Taking the car as an apt example for this chapter, the shelter, maintenance and repair of a car operates within a Large Technical System that includes, car, road, petrol, oil, passengers, drivers, signalling, road rules, etc. Stephen Graham and Simon Marvin

explain with respect to Large Technical Systems, 'that much of the "urban" is infrastructure; that most infrastructure actually constitutes the very physical and sociotechnical
fabric of cities; and that the cities and infrastructure are seamlessly coproduced, and
co-evolve, together within contemporary society'.[25]

Throughout its history the suburban garage is identified as a specific place in the
structuring of masculinities, as it provides a space where men can contribute to domestic
labour without compromising socially defined gender roles. Steven Gelber explains that
self-investment in the home during the 1920s transcended class more effectively than it
did gender.[26] Do-it-yourself (DIY) culture was originally associated with blue-collar workers
whose performance of DIY labour in the home was a way of contributing to the upkeep
and maintenance of the family, especially where this work added monetary value,
perceived or real, to the home. DIY culture also developed in white-collar workers who
were looking 'to recapture the pride that went along with doing a task from start to finish
with one's own hands.'[27]

This mixture of conditions allows a series of subjectivities to be embedded
within masculine maintenance and housework. Within the new regulated working week
the father and husband was expected to spend time with his children and support his wife
while maintaining a sense of masculine identity. Maintenance from a masculine perspective
was not a chore; rather, it was used to reinforce an image of homogeneous masculinity,
'permitting men, depending on their circumstances, to rationalise it [labour] as money-
saving, trouble-saving, useful, psychologically fulfilling, creative, or compensatory'.[28]

These practices can be understood as forms of Productive Consumption
deeply rooted in DIY culture. In this context, 'productive consumption' involves acquiring
material and equipment via waged labour for the purpose of adding value or maintaining
the value of household property. Importantly, the work is carried out outside the directly
mediated market wage and is produced through unpaid labour power. This also establishes a hierarchy of unpaid labour in relation to the gender-roles. While masculine maintenance and repair activities have been traditionally constructed around perceived and
real profit, value and experience, feminine maintenance has been associated with the
interior image of the home and unrelated to the formal economy. The garage that holds
a workshop, material and equipment inevitably mediates the practices of maintenance
between the interior and exterior realms of the home; between private apparatus for
living and public infrastructure.

Differences between productive consumption as leisure and productive
consumption as necessity are also reflected in the processes and techniques used in the
practice of maintenance. For the enthusiast who treats maintenance as a leisure pursuit,
a job doesn't need to be finished; those who carry out maintenance out of necessity are
organising their practice around completing a task within as short a time span as
possible.[29] As Moisio, Arnould and Gentry describe in a contemporary study 'Productive
Consumption in the Class- Mediated Construction of Domestic Masculinity', there are
two distinct forms of practice. On the one hand there is the high-cultural-capital subject
(HCC), the 'suburban-craftsman'; and on the other hand there is the low-cultural-capital
subject (LCC), the 'family-handyman'. The family-handyman relates to the home as a
workplace and views productive consumption as a form of 'compensatory masculinity'[30]

identified with specific domestic gender roles which are further articulated in relationships where the breadwinner role as described in the 1950s has been inverted.[31] In the performance of maintenance the suburban-craftsman has the time and the finances to focus on 'competence, skills and process', utilising the activity as both a 'therapeutic class tourism' and a way of competitively differentiating themselves from other males.[32]

This presents two completely different sets of conditions for the consumption of products and materials: HCC men seek out high quality precision power tools, and LCC men favour a larger quantity of equipment at a lower price.[33] Entering the garage to carry out maintenance work has fundamentally different connotations depending on context. Referring specifically to unemployment during the depression of the 1930s, Gelber points out the importance of masculine identity in relation to maintenance when he proposes that you can't lose a job if you're working for yourself.[34] There is an important link between the contexts that require self-sufficiency and those that relate to maintenance as therapeutic activities and class-tourism. These are reflected in the forms of consumption and infrastructures required to support them. The garage as a space of maintenance comes into view not only, as Graham and Thrift suggest, when something is broken[35] but also through consumptive and compensatory gender practices.

A monument to free time and the garage as a site of commodity fetishism

The garage as a setting for the complexities and effects of masculine identity and maintenance appears in *Ferris Bueller's Day Off* (1986).[36] The film's supporting character, Cameron Frye, confronts his relationship with his father, Morris, in the garage through the vandalisation and then destruction of his father's restored Ferrari. The garage itself can be described as a hollowed-out iteration of the Glass House designed by Philip Johnson. In the film the totalising glass container, an architecture of impossible appropriation, has been completely cleared of any domestic equipment. Within it, three restored vintage sports cars stand, including a special edition Ferrari 250 GT California Spyder. Frye's character, indecisive, neurotic, lacking in confidence, is set in distinction from Ferris's character, charming and rebellious at the same time. Frye explains to Ferris that the Ferrari, the number plate of which reads NRVOUS, was reconstructed by his father in his spare time. However, the glass lined garage-as-showcase is not suited to the difficult disassembly and construction work required to spread out the components of a vehicle and then reassemble them. One imagines that this happens off site, either with the help of professionals, or by being relocated for periods of time away from the household. Wherever the maintenance and reconstruction work has taken place, it is not a place Frye has ever been to, alluding to a complex relationship between father and son of neglect imposed through maintenance as a form of commodity fetishism.

After being appropriated by Ferris to assist in breaking Sloane, the ambiguous love interest of Ferris and Frye, out of school, the car is returned to the garage and placed on a jack with the engine stuck in reverse, in an attempt to wind the odometer backwards, thus hiding the crime of its use. This plan ultimately fails, and Frye pours his frustration into the Ferrari's front grill, literally kicking it through the glass enclosure into a wooded valley below the house. The scene ends with Frye realising a second catastrophic collision is imminent as his actions have now put him on course to confront his absent father. The restored car, both a monument to his father's spare time and hand-crafted precision Italian engineering, now sits in a crumpled heap at the bottom of a valley.

If one imagines Ferris Bueller in his forties, he could be walking straight into the postmodern life illustrated in the film *American Beauty*,[37] in which a forty-year-old Lester Burnham comes to terms with his masculinity as a resident in well-to-do suburban America. Following a commute to work, Lester wakes to find himself sitting in front of a computer screen trapped behind the prison bars of sales data. Inside the home is no better, where Lester finds himself rejected by Carolyn, his wife, and teenage daughter, Jane. Carolyn, a realtor, is emancipated from the role of a stay-at-home suburban mother through waged labour. The only image of Carolyn attending to the house has her in the garden pruning highly cultivated roses as a hobby. For Carolyn, housework is performed only at the workplace, where she is seen scrubbing empty houses before potential clients arrive.

Lester ultimately finds himself in the garage rummaging through abandoned artefacts, pulling out a set of weights before stripping his clothes off in front of the side window. If the computer screen and work in marketing had almost killed him, it is the garage that will save him. However, by contrast with the masculine home-enthusiasts of the past, the project isn't to repair a door, paint the fence, reconstruct a Ferrari or build a chesterfield stool; it is to rebuild the subject from the body outwards. Lester starts to convert the interior of the garage from a household junk space and tool workbench to include wicker chairs and a music system in what could be described as a man cave – 'the perfect masculine identity project where men can take control and produce a personalised space for themselves'.[38] The garage frames two confrontational scenes: first between Lester and Carolyn, where she confronts his abandonment of the traditional instrumental role as man of the house; and second with his neighbour Colonel Fitts. Following years of self-repression, the colonel comes out in an awkward encounter, mistaking Lester's transformation. The colonel visits him late one evening in the pouring rain, and as Lester pops the garage door open with a hand clicker the colonel makes his move for a tender embrace and confession. Lester's masculine transformation is pulled back by Hollywood, left incomplete; he rejects the colonel, sending him back out through the garage door into the pouring rain, confirming the heterosexual status quo: that 'hegemonic masculinity is constructed as a gender position that is as much "not gay" as it is "not female".[39]

The homoerotic tension that is played out in *I Love You Man*,[40] a film that describes a fledgling 'bromance', can be read against the concept of the 'buddy movie' which 'the active homosexual eroticism of the central male figures can carry the story without distraction'.[41] The garage here plays an important part in the seduction of the feminine lead protagonist into the world of the masculine bachelor. This is achieved through the accumulation of commodities into a constructed space of heterosexual masculine pleasure, including references to masturbation, porn, music, drugs and all-male gatherings. The film suggests a flattening out and smoothing of the garage as free space holding alternative forms of labour into one of leisurely consumption. Alternatively, the image depicted in the television series *Homeland*, a political thriller set in the destabilised post-9/11 America shows Brody, a returned war veteran and suspected turned agent, subvert his family garage into a space of prayer and espionage.[42] Without irony, the garage is the only space in the home that has not had video surveillance installed, leaving Carrie, a CIA counterterrorism agent, with a blind spot in the family home. The garage is key to understanding that Brody is not suffering from post-traumatic stress syndrome but is in a process of estrangement from his wife and family. Brody literally turns his back on the world of commodities and memories of suburban life held within the garage in order to pray facing a crack of light emanating from the underneath of a roller shutter door.

To conclude, this essay has attempted to illustrate how the garage operates as a performative space, activated through practices of maintenance, which contributes to the production of masculine domesticities and domestic masculinities. By situating the garage within a structure of sociological and psychoanalytical critique, it is possible to understand how the garage operates as a reflexive space in constant transformation with the subjects who inhabit and construct it. Additionally, the garage can be understood as belonging to a world of sociotechnical infrastructure, which becomes activated through acts of maintenance contributing to the structuring of gender identity within the household. This condition is also present in the cinematic representation of the garage which, through visual narrative, brings the subject into direct contact with processes of gendered commodification. This includes the representation of the garage as a space of retreat from the collective household into a private and commodified masculine sphere. In order to explore this condition further, and to broaden the possibilities of domestic architecture, an approach to understanding maintenance as a contrasexual or intersexual spatial practice could be developed. This is a difficult proposition for architecture to consider, as it situates spatial practice at an intersecting point between sociotechnical infrastructure and the commodification of gender which is co-produced by the household through the practice of maintenance.

Notes

1   Alfred Harmsworth Northcliffe, *Motors and Motor-Driving*, 2nd ed., The Badminton Library of Sports and Pastimes (London: Longmans, Green). p. 65.
2   Jacques Sbriglio, *Le Corbusier: La Villa Savoye*, Guides Le Corbusier (Paris Basel; Boston: Fondation Le Corbusier; Birkhäuser). p. 50.
3   D.L. Lewis and L. Goldstein, *The Automobile and American Culture* (University of Michigan Press, 1983). p. 167.
4   Leslie G. Goat, "Housing the Horseless Carriage: America's Early Private Garages," *Perspectives in Vernacular Architecture* 3. p. 67.
5   Amy Bix, "Creating 'Chicks Who Fix': Women, Tool Knowledge, and Home Repair, 1920–2007," *Women's Studies Quarterly* 37, no. 1/2 (2009). p. 40.
6   Ibid. p. 40.
7   S. Federici, *Revolution at Point Zero: Housework, Reproduction, and Feminist Struggle* (PM Press, 2012). Wages for Housework.
8   T. Parsons and R.F. Bales, *Family Socialization and Interaction Process* (Routledge, 1956).
9   Ibid. p. 13.
10 R.W. Connell, *Masculinities* (Polity Press, 2005). p. 23.
11 Federici, p.20 and Parsons and Bales, p.15.
12 Connell, p. 23.

13   Andrew Gorman-Murray, "Masculinity and the Home: A Critical Review and Conceptual Framework," *Australian Geographer* 39, no. 3.

14   Ibid. p. 368.

15   John Hughes, "Ferris Bueller's Day Off," (Hollywood, California: Paramount Home Entertainment, 1986).

16   Sam Mendes, "American Beauty," (Universal City, California: DreamWorks Home Entertainment, 1999).

17   Jeffrey Nachmanoff "Homeland," in *Semper I, Season 01 Episode 04*, ed. Alex Gansa and Howard Gordon (USA: Showtime Networks, 2011).

18   John Hamburg, "I Love You Man," (USA: Dreamworks Distribution LLC (2009) (USA) (theatrical), 2009).

19   Mulvey, Laura. "Visual Pleasure and Narrative Cinema," *Screen* 16, no. 3 (1975): 6–18.

20   Peter Lehman, *Running Scared : Masculinity and the Representation of the Male Body*, Culture and the Moving Image (Philadelphia: Temple University Press, 1993). p. 6.

21   Stephen Graham and Nigel Thrift, "Out of Order," *Theory, Culture & Society* 24, no. 3. p.5–7.

22   Ibid. p. 3.

23   Ibid. p. 2.

24   Steven J. Jackson, "Rethinking Repair," in *Media Technologies: Essays on Communication, Materiality, and Society*, eds., T. Gillespie, P.J. Boczkowski, and K.A. Foot (MIT Press, 2014). p. 221 and further elaborated on p. 231.

25   Stephen Graham and Simon Marvin, *Splintering Urbanism: Networked Infrastructures, Technological Mobilities and the Urban Condition* (London: Routledge, 2001). p. 179.

26   Steven M. Gelber, "Do-It-Yourself: Constructing, Repairing and Maintaining Domestic Masculinity," *American Quarterly* 49, no. 1 (1997). p. 82.

27   Ibid. p. 68.

28   Ibid. p. 83.

29   Risto Moisio, Eric J. Arnould, and James W. Gentry, "Productive Consumption in the Class-Mediated Construction of Domestic Masculinity: Do-It-Yourself (Diy) Home Improvement in Men's Identity Work," *Journal of Consumer Research* 40, no. 2 (2013).

30   Ibid. p.303 quoting Karen D. Pyke, "Class-Based Masculinities: The Interdependence of Gender, Class, and Interpersonal Power," *Gender and Society* 10, no. 5 (1996).

31   Moisio, Arnould, and Gentry, p. 308.

32   Ibid. p. 303.

33   Ibid. p. 309.

34   Gelber.

35   Graham and Thrift.

36   Hughes.

37   Mendes.

38   Östberg, Jacob, "Masculine Self-Presentation," in *The Routledge Companion to Identity and Consumption* (Routledge, 2012). p. 129.

39   Rachel Jewkes et al., "Hegemonic Masculinity: Combining Theory and Practice in Gender Interventions," *Culture, Health & Sexuality* 17, no. 2.

40   Hamburg.

41   Laura Mulvey, "Visual Pleasure and Narrative Cinema," *Screen* 16, no. 3 (1975). Referring to Molly Haskell, *From Reverence to Rape: The Treatment of Women in the Movies*, 1st ed. (New York,: Holt, 1974), p. 362.

42   Michael Cuesta, "Homeland," in *Grace, Season 01 Episode 02*, eds., Alex Gansa and Howard Gordon (USA: Showtime Networks, 2011).

Project 8

Fatima's shop:
A kind of homeplace

Huda Tayob

1. A kind of space

For Mary Douglas, home is a 'kind of space'. It is a domestic space and a non-profit space. It is not necessarily a fixed space yet it contains a regularity of practices, people and things, which create an embryonic community. It has an orientation: it is aesthetic, moral, and controlled. It has a capacity for storage and responds to external pressures. It is divided, differentiated, and parceled out for different uses. It is in 'real time'.[1]

Fatima's shop has an orientation: it too is controlled space. The heavy metal door and padlocks are a direct response to memories of violence both within and beyond South Africa's borders. Fatima is a Somali refugee. The capacity for storage is prominent: it reflects planning for the future based on memories of displacement in the past. This is a space for regular visits from friends and family, prayers throughout the day, feeding children, preparing food, and after-school homework.

2. A Homeplace

For bell hooks, home is a multiplicity of places for different groups. It is a site of radical potential, regardless of material scarcities. It may be fragile or materially scarce; a space of poverty, deprivation, and hardship. Yet it is also a space of dignified subjects, safe, caring, and nurturing. 'This task of making someplace was not simply a matter of black women providing service; it was about the construction of a safe place where black people could affirm one another'.[2] It is a space that has to be constructed, serviced, and labored on. A *Homeplace* is a space of work.

Fatima's shop is a trading space and her primary source of income. It is a precarious space, and materially limited. On approach, you are faced with an abundance of things, most of them small, and most for sale. Every surface, corner, wall, and most of the floor are covered in goods, things, and objects. Some of these are familiar and ordinary, such as leather sandals, belts, caps, pairs of jeans, shirts, and t-shirts. Others are not so familiar; Fatima told me these are groceries for Somali food. Various packets of spices, stocks, and different types of oils are stored in shelves; clothes are hung from the walls and ceiling on hooks and hangers.

A wooden-veneer counter holds her accounting book, a tin of small change, an old laptop, a kettle, a thermal flask with Somali tea, a packed breakfast and lunch, and her son's food. In the center of the space is her 1-year-old son's cot, where he sleeps and plays throughout the day.

3. A kind of *Homeplace*

Fatima's shop is in a Somali mall in a northern suburb of Cape Town. It is a small rectangular space around 2.5 square meters in size. A corrugated iron roof leans out about 2 m beyond the space, extending into the walkway. Three walls frame the space; the fourth is the shop front. There is a clear orientation outwards. This front elevation has a pull-down steel shutter which opens or closes the entire surface. When closed, it is padlocked to the ground, securing the space. It is a safe space. When open, it is the shop front and entrance. It was only closed twice when I visited; once when Fatima was sick, and a second time when she had an interview with the UN. As a result of the long hours she spent here (12 hours most days) it was not uncommon to visit her while she was cutting meat, vegetables, or onions, preparing to cook her evening meal. The days were punctuated by regular prayer intervals and with guests dropping by, bringing news of violence in the surrounding townships, events in Kenya—from Eastleigh or Dadaa—or Somalia, or the latest update or rumor about resettlement cases from the UN. Plastic chairs and boxes act as both seats and storage, and are arranged and rearranged throughout the day to accommodate guests arriving and leaving.

There is no kitchen, no stove, no beds (apart from the cot). Her shop is one space, there is no separate living room. It is a family space and a trading space. It is a safe space. It is a space that is constructed by Black female work. As a trading space, it marks the limits of archival and ethnographic recognition of the female refugee as subaltern.[3] Drawing out the spaces suggests that it is a *kind of Homeplace*.

Notes

1   Mary Douglas, 'The Idea of a Home: A Kind of Space', *Social Research* 58, no.1 (1991): 287–307.
2   bell hooks, 'Homeplace: A Site of Resistance,' in *Yearning: Race, Gender, and Cultural Politics* (Boston, MA: South End Press, 1990), 42.
3   Gayatri Chakravorty Spivak, 'Can the Subaltern Speak?' in *Marxism and the Interpretation of Culture*, edited by C.Nelson and L.Grossberg (Basingstoke: Macmillan Education, 1988), 271–313; Ananya Roy, 'Slumdog Cities: Rethinking Subaltern Urbanism', *International Journal of Urban and Regional Research* Volume 35.2 (2011): 223–38.

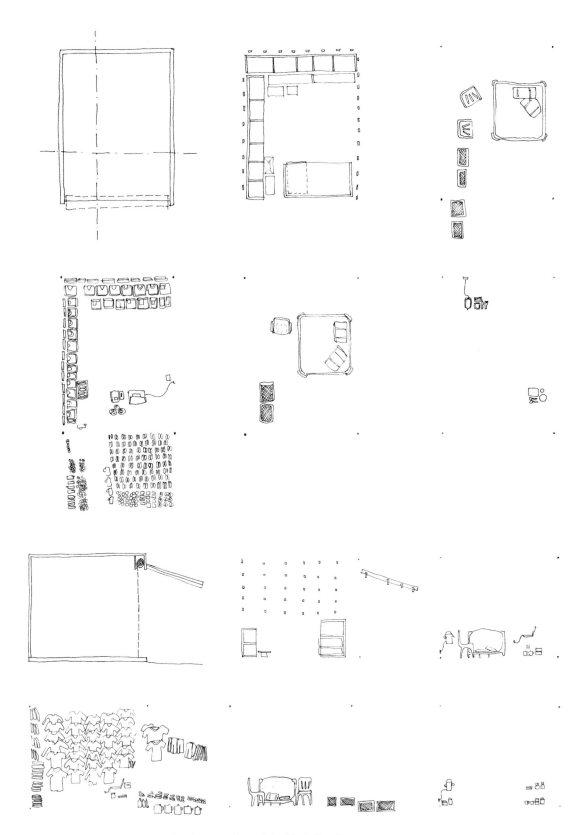

Project 8 Drawings by Huda Tayob, 2016. Copyright Huda Tayob.

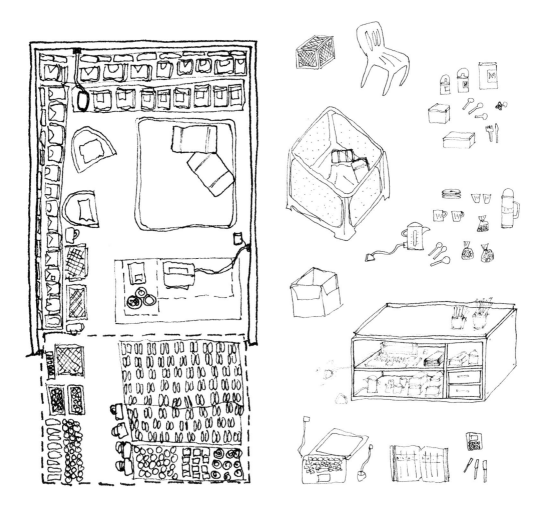

Chapter 21

Invisibility work?

How starting from dis/ability challenges normative social, spatial and material practices

Jos Boys

Introduction

The research outlined here expanded exponentially from a simple question: why is disability not critically examined, like gender, sexuality or race in architecture? Why has disability somehow remained consistently stuck in a non-historical and atheoretical relationship to building design theories and practices? It is invisible in both avant-garde and mainstream architectural theories and discourses, just as it is a persistent absence in critical and cultural theory more generally.[1] Within the discipline of architecture disability remains predominantly framed by design guidance and building regulations on the one hand, and by a 'common sense' language of accessibility and inclusive/universal design on the other. Neither of these approaches is wrong; but they act to locate disability as a concept, and disabled people as a constituency, as completely separate from social or cultural politics. Unlike gender, sexuality or race – and the feminist, queer, critical race and post-colonial studies that underpin associated scholarship and debate – it seems we assume 'disability' to be unable to bring any kind of criticality or creativity to architecture.

So, how then, does feminism and architecture in its already diverse variations and positions currently take notice of disability? Because a similar question has to be asked – why does feminism within architecture and the built environment not often pay attention to disability, even whilst it is deeply concerned with social justice and inclusion? This is *not* because there is no theory, critique or activism to engage with. Second wave western/global north feminism from the 1970s and 1980s included many disabled feminist theorists and activists who explored interconnections between and across gender and disabled identities, and between personal narratives of impairment and social analyses of disability.[2] There has also been a strongly emerging seam of theoretical and critical thought in disability studies – sometimes explicitly feminist, often integrative across and between identities – with much that examines accessibility, inclusion and built space.[3] But this fantastically rich and provocative work has had almost no impact on architectural and related discourses, or on architectural feminisms, a huge gap for the subject.[4]

Here, I want to outline some ways in which disability studies, disability arts practice and disability activism are directly relevant and crucial to our understandings of how built space works, and how we can unravel the everyday social, spatial and material practices through which space is made and re-made (as well as challenged and contested) as 'normal'. As many disability studies scholars have noted, 'centralizing dis/ability as a major concept of agency . . . disrupts, questions and alters the common modes of spatial ordering'.[5] To do this the chapter will be framed around exploring three, interconnected, notions of *work*. This is first, the often unnoticed – and differential – work involved in negotiating our built surroundings: paying attention to how this operates relationally at the intersections of different kinds of bodies, minds and material space. Second, it is about the commonsense 'ordinary' work of making and re-making particular social, spatial and material practices through our everyday attitudes, talk and actions. That is, how do particular kinds of 'normal' become routinised and so ordinary as to be invisible? Finally I will explore the work involved in perpetuating and/or contesting unequal and normative practices through architectural, artistic, political and personal interventions.

Throughout I will focus on how architecture-related practices can act to 'forget' the complexity of bodies, and to favour particular kinds of bodies over others. And I will argue that this requires investigating both *what* bodies matter and what matters *about* bodies in the attitudes and approaches that frame both 'normal' architectural practices, and feminist engagements with them. This requires a focus on how ordinary routines across social, design, educative, research and professional trajectories are perpetuated and/or contested.[6] As Sacks (1984) argues, 'being ordinary' takes effort.[7] Not noticing things and making assumptions is actually an ongoing, socially achieved activity. I call this *invisibility work*. This concerns both the amount of unnoticed effort that goes into making disability as a concept and disabled people as a constituency invisible; and the very invisibility of abled-ness that allows 'normal' bodies to be seem as nothing much, as not worth talking about. This covers, for instance, the work of avoiding discomfort (of privileging the non-disabled person's feelings of 'not knowing what to do' when meeting a disabled person over actually seeing that person); of persistently naming disabled peoples' lives in particular ways (as tragic, pitiful and/or inspiring); of simplistically perpetuating a binary opposition between disability and able-bodiedness, so as to give only the latter agency and value; of seeing disabled people as separate and as a 'problem' for architectural design, that can be left to design guidance and legal requirements; and of assuming thoughtlessly (that is, without thought) that design theories and methods do not need to critically or creatively engage with their own normativity.

Unencumbered subjects 'versus' unruly bodies

Central to what I am arguing here is that the non-disabled body-mind can ignore its own embodiment. In negotiating built space with ease, it can forget the vulnerabilities of corporeality and mental competency (just as, within a masculinist and class society it can 'forget' the differential and inequitable effects of gender, sexuality, race or poverty). As Titchkosky writes:

> language recommends that we conceive of the able-body as something that just comes along 'naturally' as people go about their daily existence. People just jump into the shower, run to the store, see what others mean while keeping an eye on the kids . . . All of this glosses the body that comes along while, at the same time, brings it along metaphorically. Speaking of 'normal bodies' as movement and metaphor maps them as if they are a natural possession, as if they are not mapped at all.[8]

What is this often unnoticed – and often differential – work involved in negotiating everyday life in all its materiality? It is an entangled mixture of the practical (dressing, washing, cooking, cleaning, journeying); of our personal and social encounters with each other, artefacts and spaces; and of the everyday intersections between ourselves and the wider societies, cultures, economies and politics within which we locate ourselves and are located. These kinds of work are precisely the means through which the making and remaking of commonsense everyday attitudes and actions is achieved.

What then, is the invisibility work that enables architecture – which is so centrally about occupation and use – to avoid bodily, mental and social difference? This is most immediately about how disability *and* ability are framed in relationship to each other, perpetuated as a certain kind of 'obvious' commonsense. Buildings and spaces are first designed for the abled. Disabled people become a clearly bounded and separate category who now constitute a problem since they do not fit this norm; whose 'special needs' must now be met by adding extras onto what is already designed. Jay Dolmage calls this retro-fitting:

> To retrofit is to add a component or accessory to something that has already been manufactured or built. This retrofit does not necessarily make the product function, does not necessarily fix a faulty product, but it acts as a sort of correction.[9]

Retro-fitting 'solutions' are inherently reactive. They operate in a technical and legal space, not a creative or generative one. Then, when as a result spaces and services are not accessible, it becomes the individual problem of the 'misfitting' person to try and resolve.[10] By keeping disability separate as a clearly bounded category that can be dealt with *after* 'normal' design is done, bodies – that is abled bodies – are assumed non-problematic, unmarked and unencumbered. But what if we do not see bodies in this way, but instead recognise that disability and ability are relational and ambiguous and that bodies are never 'free' from the material spaces they occupy, or the activities they are undertaking? [11] What if we try instead to open up what it is to have a body – or rather what Price calls a bodymind – that has everyday effects; is potentially fragile; is interesting for its differences not its averages; and is embodied, both in the sense of sheer corporeality and of social identities and labeling (Figure 21.1)? [12]

Figure 21.1 tentatively tries to chart what it is to have a bodymind-in-space. Rather than technical guidance that attempts to pin down the functional differences of

Having a body	Examples of personal, social, material and spatial intersections	Some social norms about space
Keeping your balance	Gravity. Slippery and uneven surfaces. Confusing reflections. Carrying or pushing loads. Scanning for things to hold onto. Dealing with exhaustion and weakness.	Assumption of uninterrupted and fast motion, autonomous, independent and unimpeded by others or by built surroundings.
Negotiating obstacles and hazards	Heights, widths, steps, shadows, unexpected items. Confusing visual information. Judging distances and gaps. Planning accessible and doable routes. Needing help. Watching out for others.	Assumption of continuous visual, physical and mental agility; with high-speed, instinctive and independent processing of, and responses to, immediate experiences and changing circumstances.
Maintaining energy	Deciding journey length and time. Looking for places to rest. Pausing stops. Slowness and unevenness of progress.	Assumption of own unnoticed and boundless fatigue-free energy. Imperviousness to others and/or frustration as others' perceived slowness.
Thinking ahead	Pre-planning. Scanning spaces for needed resources and facilities. Navigating via environmental clues. Managing orientation and disorientation. Needing to ask for help. Interdependence.	Assumption of lack of external need, based on self-containment and adequate personal resources. No need of recourse to support.
Dealing with sensory overload	Negotiating crowds, noise, bright or flashing lights. Managing complex and multiple data inputs.	Assumption of ability to retrieve required data seamlessly and to be able to block out non-relevant data
Managing encounters with others	Staring, or unwanted interactions. Not matching communication norms. Social policing such as 'gaslighting' and micro-aggressions. Out-of-placeness and misfitting. Feelings of exposure.	Assumption that face-to-face encounters are non-problematic. Ability to handle unspoken social rules as obvious, unnoticed and straightforward.
Managing resources	Organising access to resources (money, transport, goods etc.,) required to support mobility and use of relevant facilities. Effort required to access resources and support. Lack of resources.	Assumption of adequate personal resources to negotiate built environment easily; and assumption of personal fault if such resources are not available.

Figure 21.1 Some implications of having a body. Adapted from Boys 2017: 149. Copyright: Jos Boys.

different impairments, the kinds of statement offered here suggest more hybrid and complex intersections. Whilst not avoiding the real effects that different impairments can have on accessing built space, such a framework hopes to embed the inseparability of experience from social stereotyping and assumptions. It also begins to show how having a body (what a body can do/is expected to do/ is noticed as doing) is entangled simultaneously with space and with gender, sexuality, race and class as well as disability. Maybe such descriptions of interconnectedness can help rethink design processes beyond the normal or average body.

Going beyond such ableist assumptions also suggests recognising what Partington-Sollinger calls disabled peoples' 'particular prowess for "reading space"', or as Tobin Siebers puts it: [13]

> . . . disabled people have to be ingenious to live in societies that are by their design inaccessible and by their inclination prejudiced against disability. It requires a great deal of artfulness and creativity to figure out how to make it through the day when you are disabled, given the condition of our society. [14]

Disabled people are not passive users of services who need things 'done' for them, but rather *experts* in negotiating material space. As I have written elsewhere, there are already a considerable amount of narratives and critiques from diverse disabled people, that open up perceptions and experiences of both the material world and everyday social encounters; as well as many interesting projects by disabled artists and others that explore non-normal embodiment. [15] Disabled artists in particular have dealt with issues that include the fragility of bodies, the powerful and powerless qualities of being an outsider, strangeness and normality, diversity and difference, communalities and interdependencies, isolation and independence, all of which offer potential new forms of architectural thinking and doing at the intersections of bodies, artefacts, encounters and material spaces.

The work of (not) including

The writings of disability studies scholars Tanya Titchkosky and Rod Michalko offer a powerful investigation of how disability and disabled people come to be treated differently. In 'To Pee or Not to Pee?' (2008) and *The Question of Access: Disability, Space, Meaning* (2011), for example, Titchkosky is particularly interested in what it is possible (ordinary, normal) to say about making changes to the built environment that can improve the everyday experiences of disabled people. She examined her own workplace (a Canadian university) and its intentions around, and implementation of, inclusive building design – particularly accessible toilets. Her research shows that the common-sense view of many of her colleagues towards disabled people is that whilst 'anyone' will be aware of disability, they are willing to treat it as a marginal issue, and to see failures to provide access as *understandable mistakes*. The fact that the lack of an accessible toilet prevents many disabled people from easily using the building was just something that happened. It did not make non-disabled people angry or determined to make a change. The problem, then, was not articulated around the unacceptability of disabled people being discriminated against, but as the (unfortunate) result of many difficulties. This, Titchkosky suggests, persistently locates disabled people as 'included as excludable'.[16] Such comments are not merely well intentioned. They are the justificatory narratives that maintain a particular shape to everyday social and spatial practices:

> The interpretive act of justification is intimately tied to collective understandings of the meaning of what is. As an interpretive social act, justification is not merely second order to the fact of exclusion . . . it is how we do exclusion as well as generate its everyday sensibility.[17]

Using concepts such as 'included as excludable', as well as unraveling the everyday talk that makes and remakes social and spatial practices in particular ways and not others, helps makes visible the invisibility work that puts disability in its place. These ideas can also help us interrogate shifts in the contemporary gendering of space.[18] Other authors have examined how these processes of including but not including operate institutionally – for example, through 'diversity' policies that work only at the level of appearances, as Sara Ahmed eloquently describes in her book *On Being Included*.[19]

How, then, do different kinds of bodyminds intersect in particular ways and not others across architectural theory and practice? Elsewhere I have investigated how different architectural theories and approaches assume particular bodies.[20] This is not about complaining that such architects do not take account of accessibility. It is to unravel what kinds of bodies are being imagined, and what it is that matters about these bodies. Of course, the assumed rational and functional body/user of modernism has been critiqued and there is now considerable interest in the sensual and feeling body, sometimes through an emphasis on the experiential, elsewhere around bodily augmentation and cyborgian robotics.[21] But these still start from completely abled bodies. In fact, a current persistent problem for architects is that the very unmarked nature of being able-bodied means that material space is *not* noticed. This may suggest a recognition of the problem Titchkosky highlights , but I suggest that in architectural theory and practice something else usually happens. Titchkosky (and disability studies scholars more generally) are looking for a form of practice that interrogates differences between bodies and reveals their inequitable spatialisation. Contemporary design theories and methods, on the other hand, concentrate on how able-bodied occupants can be persuaded to pay attention to – to revel in – their specific surroundings. In cultural theory as well as architecture, for example, enthusiasm for cyborgian forms and augmented bodies becomes about playing only with the *abled* body.[22] As Davis writes:

> The disabled body is a nightmare for the fashionable discourse of theory because that discourse has been limited by the very predilection of the dominant, ableist culture. The body is seen as a site of 'jouissance' that defies reason, that takes dominant culture and its rigid, power-laden vision of the body to task . . . The nightmare of the (disabled) body is one that is deformed,

maimed . . . Rather than face this ragged image, the critic turns to the fluids of sexuality, the gloss of lubrication . . . But almost never to the body of the differently abled.[23]

Being Other becomes no longer a threat or a problem but a freely chosen position by theorists who can then claim their radical 'transgression' (and ignore both their own privilege and abledness) by deliberately appearing to place themselves 'on the margins', outside of everyday conventions and stereotypes. But this is a peculiar kind of Otherness, which values specific qualities – unproblematically imbued with autonomy, mobility and agency – whilst in fact obscuring the realities of diverse kinds of embodiment, and the persistent marginalisation of specific groups. Again, then, we need to unravel the kind of work that is going on to better understand what it is that persistently matters about bodies within architecture and what the effects are on bodies as a concept, and on the perceptions and experiences of diverse bodies in built space itself.

Going beyond invisibility work

There are many writings and projects that start from disability and difference, which can inform architectural feminisms, as well as architecture more generally. These also constitute work; the work of perpetuating and/or contesting unequal and normative practices through architectural, artistic, political and personal interventions. I have illustrated many examples elsewhere, and there remain many more to be captured and shared (Figure 21.3).

Here though, in conclusion, I want to explore a particular case of disabled people being 'included as excludable' and the justificatory narratives that accompanied it. I want to raise questions about how non-disabled feminists (including myself) can pay attention to, challenge and transform their own unthinking invisibility work in 'forgetting' about disability discrimination, even whilst engaging critically and creatively with gender. This is because feminism – as with disability studies – has a central tenet that research and practice must be more than an academic endeavour: it must also aim to improve the position of disadvantaged groups in society.[24]

In January 2017 the feminist philosopher Judith Butler briefly arrived in London to give a public lecture at University College London (UCL) in the UK. At the last minute the venue was changed to accommodate the large demand for tickets. The new lecture hall is inaccessible, and when a physically disabled student complained, she was merely told by the university that yes indeed, this was the case – the hall was not accessible to people using wheelchairs. In response the student, Naomi Jacobs, organised a protest letter signed by 66 disabled and non-disabled academics and students, and Butler was contacted about the situation; whilst Jacobs reported on the ongoing situation on her blog.[25] UCL's answer this time was that she could watch the lecture remotely, via live streaming, their suggested retro-fitting. Jacobs then proposed a boycott, one taken up by other disabled people and their friends. No non-disabled people – including those who signed the letter – participated in the boycott, or shared with her the relegation to watching the lecture remotely via a screen.

Figure 21.2 Interior Architecture students from Westminster University London explore different perspectives on space. Tilted Horizons workshop co-created by disabled artist Liz Crow and design tutor Julia Dwyer as part of Arts Council funded Disabled Artists Making Dis/Ordinary Spaces (DAMD/OS) Project. Staircase, Bartlett School of Architecture UCL, UK. May 2017. Photograph by Jos Boys.

Throughout UCL made no apologies, rather giving the kinds of justificatory narratives that Titchkosky met in Canada; that it is just one instance, that such a situation could not be helped, that of course they wished the lecture theatre was accessible, that they would try and do better next time, that it was a rational decision based on health and safety, that it is okay that some people who were included just happen to be now excluded. And after the lecture, UCL managers asked Jacobs to help them make more events accessible. As she notes:

> I'm a professional equality trainer, but like many disabled people, I'm often asked for my expertise and emotional labour to 'help' institutions discriminate less, *without pay*.[26]

Here, disabled people's expertise in negotiating the built environment becomes something that is their responsibility to share on a voluntary basis. Abled-bodied people need helping out of their ignorance – an ignorance that is 'not the result of a benign gap in our knowledge, but [of] deliberate choices to pursue certain kinds of knowledge while ignoring others'.[27] This 'solution to difficulties' looks to a disabled individual to do the work; both the actual work of advice, but also the work of *representation* – to stand for both their own category of impairment, and for disability as a whole. As Jacobs goes on to say, expecting this work is the normal experience of disabled people – 'fighting disablism and barriers, are full-time jobs in themselves, on top of our other work.'

This is the endless, unnoticed work of being disabled in an ableist society. Again, we have to ask; what is the invisibility work going on in framing lack of access and inclusion as an individualised problem only for those who face its consequences? In the UCL case, Judith Butler has promised to refuse to lecture in inaccessible venues in the future. Jacobs also recognises that she had some support from non-disabled people; but that this did not go as far as a boycott. Anger at inequality did not affect or change the desire to see Butler 'in the flesh' even whilst some disabled colleagues had to watch her remotely. What would it take, Jacobs asks, for all non-disabled academics to refuse to speak in inaccessible venues? It took the disabled artist Ryan Gander's refusal to speak at the Architectural Association in London before they finally got design students to create a decent – even if temporary – ramp.

Interestingly, disability studies scholars and activists have often focused on the university and it's framing of 'normal' academic life.[28] This work mixes theory with practice; it explores both how to theorise what is happening, and to intervene through the creation of alternatives For Mia Mingus, as for others, this centres on collective access – moving beyond merely individualised logistical requirements to the creation of other kinds of social-material spaces. For example:

> I got to spend over a week creating collective access with a group of twenty-three disabled folks and our non-disabled comrades. I got to spend eight days getting a glimpse into a different world and experiencing a kind of interdependency that let me loosen my shoulders; that let me breathe.
>
> . . . This was about being very clear that we wanted to shift the individualized and independent understanding of access and queer it and color it interdependent. This was about building crip solidarity. We wanted to create a liberated space. We would pool our resources: body and ability, financial, material and more. We would not just think about disability as separate from class, age, race, queerness, family, children, gender, citizenship, violence, but we would understand it as intimately connected.[29]

Making such collective spaces is, I would argue, both feminist and inclusive. What, then, are the ways feminist architectures can engage with dis/ability? This suggests taking notice of disabled peoples' various perceptions and experiences; as well as recognising the ambiguity and complexity of categories around both disability and ability, and resisting stereotypes. It means considering the everyday work for dis/abled people in living our multiple lives, in our diverse and differential intersections with built space; paying attention to the unnoticed assumptions of being abled; opening up to view what constitutes 'normal' social and spatial practices and creatively intervening towards enabling rather than disabling effects. Finally, it means challenging the lack of engagement with dis/ability in architectural theories and practices; starting from the richness and variety that bodily difference and unruly bodies can bring to design and related practices and discourses; and working towards conceptual frameworks and methods that embed better understandings of how bodily difference and the spatial-material are entangled.

Notes

1 Leonard J. Davis, *Enforcing Normalcy: Disability, Deafness, and the Body*, (London: Verso 1995) and *Bending Over Backwards. Disability, Dismodernism and Other Difficult Positions* (New York: NYU Press 2002).
    Jos Boys, *Doing Disability Differently: An Alternative Handbook on Architecture, Dis/ability and Designing for Everyday Life* (London and New York: Routledge 2014) and *Architecture, Space, Architecture: A Reader*, (ed.) (London and New York: Routledge 2017).
2 e.g. Nancy Mairs, *Waist-High in the World: A Life Among the Nondisabled*, (Boston, MA: Beacon Press 1996); Jenny Morris, (ed.) *Encounters with Strangers: Feminism and Disability* (London: The Women's Press 1996); Susan Wendell, *The Rejected Body: Feminist philosophical reflections on disability* (London: Routledge 1996); Margaret Shildrick, *Leaky Bodies and Boundaries: Feminism, Postmodernism and (Bio)ethics* (London: Routledge 1997); Mairian Corker and Sally French, (eds.) *Disability Discourse* (Buckingham: Open University Press 1999); Carol Thomas, *Female Forms: Experiencing and Understanding Disability* (Buckingham: Open University Press 1999); Ellen Samuels, 'Critical Divides: Judith Butler's Body Theory and the Question of Disability', *National Women's Studies Association Journal*, 14 (3), (Fall 2002); Sally B. Minter, *Unruly Bodies: Life writing by women with disabilities* (Chapel Hill, NC: University of North Carolina Press 2007).
3 Rod Michalko, *The Difference that Disability Makes* (Philadelphia, PA: Temple University Press 2002); Tobin Seibers, *Disability Theory* (Ann Arbor, MI: University of Michigan Press 2008) and *Disability Aesthetics* (Ann Arbor, MI: University of Michigan Press 2010a); Tanya Titchkosky, *The Question of Access: Disability, Space, Meaning* (Toronto: University of Toronto Press 2011); Margaret Price, *Mad At School: Rhetorics of Mental Disability and Academic Life* (Ann Arbor, MI: University Of Michigan Press 2011); Jay Dolmage, *Disability Rhetoric* (Syracuse, NY: Syracuse University Press 2013); Aimi Hamraie, 'Designing Collective Access: A Feminist Disability Theory of Universal Design' *Disability Studies Quarterly* 33, no. 4 (2013).
4 Jos Boys, (ed.) *Architecture, Space, Architecture: A Reader* (London and New York: Routledge 2017).
5 Michael Schillmeier, *Rethinking Disability; Bodies, Senses and Things*, (London: Routledge 2010) 116.
6 Judith Butler, *Bodies that Matter: on the Discursive Limits of Sex* (London and New York: Routledge 2011).
7 Harvey Sacks, 'On doing "being ordinary"', in J.M. Atkinson and J. Heritage (eds.) *Structures of Social Action: Studies in Conversation Analysis* (Cambridge: Cambridge University Press 1984).
8 Tanya Titchkosky, 'To Pee or not to Pee? Extraordinary Exceptions in a University Environment', *Canadian Journal of Sociology* 3, no. 1 (2008): 103.
9 Jay Dolmage, 'Mapping Composition: Inviting Disability in the Front Door' in Lewiecki-Wilson, Cynthia and Brenda Jo Brueggemann, (eds.) with Jay Dolmage, *Disability and the Teaching of Writing* (Boston: Bedford/St. Martin's, 2008).
10 Rosemarie Garland Thomson, 'Misfits: A Feminist Materialist Disability Concept', *Hypatia* 26, no. 3 (Summer, 2011): 591–609.
11 Boys, *Doing Disability Differently*, 2014.
12 Margaret Price, 'Un/shared space: the dilemma of inclusive architecture' in Boys, J. (ed.) *Disability, Space, Architecture: A Reader* (London and New York: Routledge 2017).
13 Zoe Partington-Sollinger, *Naked Space*, CABE Scholarship report. Unpublished. 2008.
14 Tobin Siebers, 'The Art Of Disability: An Interview With Tobin Siebers by Mike Levin', *Disability Studies Quarterly* 30, no. 2 (2010).
15 Boys, *Doing Disability Differently*, 2014.
16 Titchkosky, *The Question of Access*, 2011.
17 Titchkosky, 'To Pee or not to Pee?', 2008, 41.
18 Angela McRobbie, *The aftermath of feminism: gender culture and social change* (Los Angeles and London: Sage 2009); Lisa Baraitser, *Maternal Encounters: The Ethics of Interruption* (New York and London: Routledge 2009).
19 Sara Ahmed, *On Being Included: Racism and Diversity in Institutional Life* (Durham and London: Duke University Press 2012). See also Dolmage, 'From steep steps to retrofit', 2017, and Price, 'Un/shared space', 2017.
20 Jos Boys, 'Architecture, place and the "care-full" design of everyday life,' in Bates, C., Imrie, R., Kullman, K. (eds.) *Care and Design: Bodies, Buildings, Cities* (Hoboken, NJ: Wiley-Blackwell 2016a) and 'Diagramming for a dis/ordinary architecture' in Boys, Jos. (2017) (ed.) *Architecture, Space, Architecture: A Reader* (London and New York: Routledge 2016a) 135–154.

21 Rob Imrie, 'The Body, Disability and Le Corbusier's Conception of the Radiant Environment' in R. Butler and H. Parr (eds.) *Mind and Body Spaces: Geographies of Disability, Illness and Impairment* (London and New York: Routledge 1999). 25–45 and 'Architects' conceptions of the human body', *Environment and Planning D: Society and Space*, 21 (1), 2003, 47–65. Jonathan Hill, (ed.) *Occupying Architecture: between the architect and the user* (London: Routledge 1998) and *Actions of Architecture: architects and creative users* (London: Routledge 2003).

22 Vivian Sobchack, 'A Leg to Stand On: Prosthetics, Metaphor, and Materiality' in M. Smith and J. Morra (eds.) *The Prosthetic Impulse: from a Posthuman Present to a Biocultural Future* (Cambridge, MA: MIT Press 2006).

23 Davis, *Enforcing Normalcy*, 1995: 5.

24 Sara Ahmed, Sara *Living a Feminist Life*, (Durham and London: Duke University Press 2017).

25 Naomi Jacobs, 'Theory: Judith Butler and the UCL lecture' February 11, available at: https://butlighthouse. wordpress.com/2017/02/11/why-we-have-to-fight-for-access-to-theory-judith-butler-and-the-ucl-lecture/

26 Ibid.

27 Aimi Hamraie, 'Designing Collective Access', 2013.

28 Hamraie ibid., and *Building Access: Disability, Universal Design, and the Politics of Knowing-Making* (Minneapolis, MN: University of Minnesota Press 2017); Price, 'Mad at School' 2011 and 'Un/shared Space', 2017; Dolmage, *Disability Rhetoric*, 2013.

29 Mia Mingus, 'Reflections on an Opening: Disability Justice and Creating Collective Access in Detroit', August 23, 2010 available at: https://leavingevidence.wordpress.com/2010/08/23/reflections-on-an-opening-disability-justice-and-creating-collective-access-in-detroit/.

Chapter 22

On the critiques

Abortion clinics

Lori A. Brown

To examine the explicitly politicised space of the abortion clinic, and to do so in the context of United States, is to immediately call into question the relationship between public space and the right to freedom of speech as guaranteed by the First Amendment of the Constitution. As divisive as abortion continues to be in the more conservative areas of the United States – and with the new administration's anti-choice position becoming ever clearer – 'abortion provides an interesting platform to think through complex relationships of space, a woman's body, varying degrees of federal and state control, the fluid and ever-shifting terrain of reproductive healthcare access, potentials of design thinking in transforming spatial relationships and ways to radically rethink these issues to provoke change'.[1] Seeking architecturally specific intersections,[2] I ask: What can the architecture discipline learn from examining spaces such as abortion clinics? What can architects contribute to these everyday spaces? How can design engage with the broader concerns of public space in zones like abortion clinics and what can our role as designers become in such spaces? How can spatial thinking imagine access to reproductive healthcare more creatively and broadly?

Design research examines the multiple and complex issues influencing how space and spatial relationships are created, as I have discussed in my earlier book *Feminist Practices*.[3] Focusing on the politics of space, and how such politics shape our environments, moves the discipline, as architect Murray Fraser suggests, beyond rather internalised discourse focused on form and object fixation.[4] To be involved within current social and cultural issues expands architecture's engagement with the every day and future of our world.

Although not all clinics provide medical services beyond abortion care, most do. That they remain unfairly targeted is a concern for all who are invested in access to women's healthcare. We must become even more vigilant, and pay particularly careful attention to what the current administration will attempt to do. This chapter expands upon earlier research conducted for *Contested Spaces* in order to discuss how the process of research shapes ideas and creates opportunities for action and activism. Here, I present two research tangents, which I use as examples in order to discuss, more broadly, how action-oriented research influences the discipline and expands the role that architecture and architects play in the pertinent issues of our time. Architecture, I argue, is ever more necessary in the sociopolitical environment we currently find ourselves in.

Introducing reproductive healthcare insurance

In 2010, President Obama signed the Affordable Care Act (ACA), a law that expanded women's healthcare coverage. This was three years prior to the publication of *Contested Spaces*. The ACA provided that women will not be required to cover out-of-pocket expenses for wellness examinations, preventative or maternity care, or contraception coverage. No longer would coverage cost more for women than men because of blatant gender discrimination, as it once did.[5] Since the passage of the ACA, Republicans in Congress have worked to dismantle and overturn it – attempting to repeal the ACA every year for the six years between 2011 and 2016. As a new United States administration took office in January 2017, securing an entirely Republican-dominated federal government, these questions become ever more relevant and critical to consider. It comes as no surprise that one of the first agenda items for the Republican-controlled 2017 Congress led by a Republican President is to repeal the ACA, and although thus far the repeal has been unsuccessful, many questions are left unanswered about the future of healthcare coverage for the millions of people who received insurance under the ACA. More specifically for the considerations of this chapter, the paramount question is what will access to women's reproductive healthcare look like? Will women's coverage be drastically reduced? Will the US reinstate pre-2010 obstacles to care and access? The effects of dismantling the ACA would greatly affect women, specifically poor women of colour. This will in turn place greater pressure on access to reproductive care for those who have so few remaining options.

Another Republican tactic has been to attempt to defund Planned Parenthood (PP). Despite the fact that in December 2016, right before leaving office, the Obama administration acted to prevent such actions from taking place,[6] according to mainstream media soundbites, this is still more possible than ever before – several states have in fact attempted to prevent federal funding for PP through restrictions on federal family planning funding accessed at the state level before the Obama intervention.[7] Although out of all the services that PP provides only 3 per cent are abortion, the majority of their care is centred on contraception (31 per cent) and testing and treatment (45 per cent). Therefore, PP is a primary access point for broader healthcare by women across the country. PP provides basic gynaecological care, prenatal care, testing for sexually transmitted diseases, HIV, and cancer screening.[8] If the Republicans succeed in eliminating funding for PP, basic healthcare for millions of women and teens will either disappear or become too expensive to access. The ramifications of defunding PP are therefore enormous and will have devastating effects.

Upon closer examination, however, it does appear that defunding PP may prove far more difficult than is being reported. According to National Public Radio, it will be difficult to remove federal support by virtue of the diversity of government funding streams supporting PP, which form a complex financial web. Federal law would have to be rewritten to change the federal Medicaid guarantee of patient provider choice. Additionally, if the defunding efforts were successful, an overall increase in government spending would result, due to the removal of contraceptive coverage and the resulting increase in births.[9]

Research – action

In examining spaces that are inherently and undeniably politicised, architecture is clearly required to engage and respond politically. As feminist geographer Pamela Moss writes, '[t]heory, as a combination of both conceptualisations of phenomena and an explanation of how phenomena work, exist, or articulate, and praxis, as a politically active way to live in the world, are undeniably linked. Understanding one as integrally wrapped up within the other creates an environment where there cannot be any act that is not political.'[10]

Engagement with such fraught spaces can be imagined in terms of the use of both disciplinary and interdisciplinary methods. Disciplinary strategies can be exemplified by the mapping and spatial analysis of influences, both visible and invisible, that directly shape the built environment. Interdisciplinary methods, as I learned from my feminist colleagues in geography, can include broader feminist methodological conceptualisations and approaches that impact on how research is framed from the outset, how data is collected and circulated, and how relations are constructed between all those involved in a project. As Moss states, '[m]aking a methodology "feminist" implies politicizing a methodology *through* feminism.'[11] Further, as a feminist architect, it is critical for me that design methodology reflects research methodology: in the case of my engagement with abortion clinics, both aim to be collaborative and co-produced. Once again, this is an approach inspired by feminist geographers. Heidi Gottfried writes that '[p]articipatory research exemplifies one of the most radical and activist elements of feminist methodology by enlisting a community's participation and collaboration in social change projects.'[12]

Tangent 1: Law into architecture

In my work on *Contested Spaces* and subsequent research into abortion clinics, visiting independent providers' clinics and interviewing clinic owners and directors provided invaluable insights into the on-the-ground spatial concerns they had to contend with.

Direct interaction with these providers became an obvious requirement to more accurately represent the issues they were encountering. It was only after such visits that I was ready to speculate upon the potential of design as a conceptual tool for understanding the influences on the built environment and its materialisation.

Literally being able to enter abortion clinics – which of course was required each time such a visit was made – is not as clear-cut as one would imagine (even if in theory, access is available to all). Free speech curtails access whenever there is a concern that speech is being too heavily curtailed. Public space is a mechanism to curtail abortion access through concerns about the constraint of free speech and protestors' rights, which are at times placed over and above a woman's right to access a clinic. Historically, courts weigh the importance of free speech more heavily than the right to access.

Architectural visualisation strategies are able to make legible a myriad of state restrictions and Supreme Court decisions, which define proximities between bodies, buildings, public space and protestors. In *Contested Spaces*, I therefore examined and visually translated factors that exert powerful effects on how places are built and, by extension, how and who accesses reproductive healthcare; I visualised state restrictions, transportation costs in terms of time and money, poverty rates, building codes, and cultural and social local norms. Ideas to expand access serve as a mechanism of provocation. For example, if we consider alternative access points – through pharmacies who stock and sell emergency contraception, hospitals that would be required to once again provide abortions, or even shopping malls or high school medical clinics already frequented by a larger segment of the target population – availability exponentially increases. 'New' access points such as these would dramatically increase access across a state.

Other influences that benefit from being visualised relate to religious and cultural factors in states where both legislative chambers are anti-choice. In southern and mid-western states, there are an extraordinary number of religious institutions. Mapping these reveals not only the number of institutions per city, but also how pervasive such institutions are across a state. Although the US was founded with an explicit separation between church and state, many state governments (and the policies they enact) are directly influenced by religious beliefs. Many lawmakers openly and publicly state this. Just this past election cycle, the Vice President expressed the following sentiments on the campaign trail: '[I] couldn't be more proud to stand with a pro-life candidate.'[13] He has also become the only sitting Vice President to speak at the anti-abortion, religiously associated, 'March for Life' rally in Washington DC, in its forty-four-year history.[14] This is a direct indication that a separation between church and state is not being maintained.

Space affects access: space was found to be politically manipulated by those against abortion in order to produce difficulties for those seeking abortion care. In the most literal of terms, these anti-choice tactics created (and continue to create) difficulties in reaching a clinic's front door, which were experienced most often by poor women of colour. Such tactics create uneven access across the country. Women of means will never have the same impediments to access as poor women of colour. After visiting many clinics and interviewing providers across the United States, avenues for engagement that can translate into action include, I would argue: providing design ideas for clinics, analysing building code changes, and (via spatial analysis and spatial inquiry) formulating proposed interventions that positively impact these everyday spaces.

Tangent 2: Architecture into law

The US is a federal republic, wherein federal law establishes certain broader legal frameworks that states must follow. Yet, due to the way that the Constitution grants the states rights, and depending upon how federal law has been written (for example, whether issues are clearly defined or if legislation is less explicit and allows variations in oversight from state to state), states have the ability to legislate and control various aspects of governance. Certain states have proven quite adept in undermining federal guarantees if the state governing bodies are in disagreement with federal law. These strategies have become especially successful in regards to reproductive healthcare, sexual education, and women's ability to access contraception and abortion. Although these rights have been hard won over decades, they are also subject to ongoing attempts at dismantlement.

The US Supreme Court's 1973 *Roe v. Wade* decision finally gave women the federal right to terminate a pregnancy. However, as I discuss in a forthcoming co-authored essay, the decision considered the 'potential regulatory authority of the states as distinct from Congress, given that the federal government is one of limited and enumerated powers, with minimal authority over abortion'.[15] Because of the decision's trimester approach to regulating abortion, states have a more vested interest later into the pregnancy's term. This begins in the second trimester with their concern over the health of the mother and manifests in the third trimester as the state's interest in the potential of life, banning abortion except to protect the life of the pregnant woman.[16] The federal right to terminate a pregnancy has been gradually diminished by incremental reductions in access to abortion through a variety of legislation, which has been allowed by the Supreme Court in acknowledgement of a state's interest in possible life.[17] An opening is thus provided for states to exert more of their own legislative control in their stance on abortion. In 1992, this opening was significantly expanded by *Planned Parenthood of Southeastern Pennsylvania v. Casey*, a decision that extended state interest beyond the trimester approach as long as a woman does not encounter an 'undue burden' exerted through state restrictions.[18] Thus although there is a federal guarantee of a right to abortion for women in the United States, states have slowly and carefully chipped away at this right, so much so that women who are the most economically vulnerable are in certain states essentially unable to access the procedure.

The second opportunity for feminist architectural research, beyond visualising access, presented itself in the possibility of providing architectural expertise for lawyers who represent clinics. As one lawyer, who was working on representing clinics in Pennsylvania, mentioned to me, she had not been able to find a single feminist architect to consult to help her decipher the language of building codes. As a result, she had difficulty preparing her arguments to specifically address the architectural language of the codes, as this was outside her area of expertise. This was clearly an opportunity for applied architectural knowledge. I analysed and diagrammed building codes in states where the clinic buildings were reclassified from constituting 'medical facilities' to conforming to the more restrictive category of 'ambulatory surgical centres'. These code changes precipitated the closure of many clinics in states where abortion risked being unavailable to the most economically disadvantaged. Architectural analytical skills and the use of diagramming and simple axonometric drawings were employed to convey 'before and after' code changes and the impacts these changes would have for clinics in certain states.

Cases: Texas and Virginia

Texas and Virginia provide important case studies that exemplify the on-the-ground impact of states seeking to limit, if not eliminate, access to one of the safest known medical procedures. In past years, both states have been at the forefront of curtailing reproductive healthcare access, and have used state laws and building codes as political means to do so. These surreptitious anti-choice efforts have had differing rates of success in Texas and Virginia.[19]

Although their history exceeds the scope of this chapter, it is sufficient to say that both states have a contentious relationship to reproductive healthcare access. It is important to note that in June 2016, the Supreme Court's *Whole Woman's Health et al. v. Hellerstedt* decision ruled unconstitutional state laws that required clinics be held to surgical centre building code requirements, and doctors to have hospital admitting privileges, declaring this regulation created an 'undue burden'. The court found that: 'neither of these provisions offers medical benefits sufficient to justify the burdens upon access that each imposes. Each places a substantial obstacle in the path of women seeking a previability abortion, each constitutes an undue burden on abortion access.'[20]

The dramatic increase in state restrictions, both in the lead up to and following the Supreme Court's 2016 decision, has had a devastating effect on the ability of clinics to remain open. The most extreme example is Texas, one of the geographically largest and most populated states in the country. As a result of the draconian laws passed by the Texas legislature since 2013, Texas has gone from a state with forty clinics to having only nineteen at the time of the Supreme Court hearing,[21] and even as few as eight clinics in 2014.[22]

During this period, I analysed the changes in state building code requirements addressing clinics, in order to help make clear why these changes were not improving lives or the safety of abortion healthcare, but instead being used solely as a political tool. This activism provided a mechanism for architecture to engage with real world issues and be politically responsive. Together with research assistants, I created a before-and-after set of diagrams for Texas and Virginia. These included how the layout of a hypothetical clinic would need to be adapted in response to the code changes (see Figure 22.1).

I also served as an expert witness through letters I wrote for the ACLU Reproductive Freedom Project, whose legal efforts were instrumental in preventing these changes from taking effect in Virginia. In my letter I made the argument that:

> [D]esign and construction codes were originally created to protect the life and safety of those who occupy buildings, including all building scales and all

Texas Abortion Facility Requirements (2012)

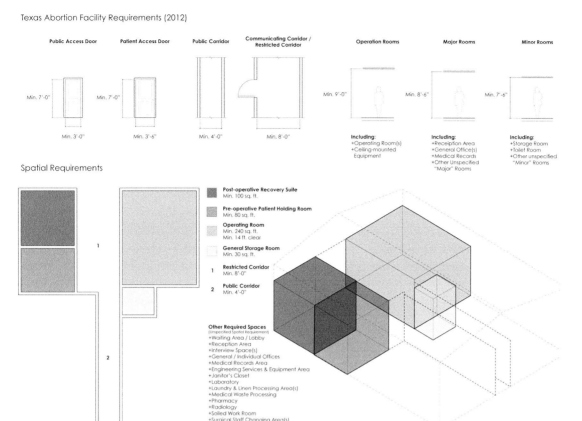

See Title 25 Texas Administrative Code, Part 1 §135.52 (2009).

Figure 22.1 Texas Building Code analysis example. Texas Abortion Facility requirements including change in door height, corridor widths, room dimensions and spatial adjacencies. Copyright Lori A. Brown, 2016.

building types. Design and construction codes are meant to ensure such issues as egress requirements, occupancy loads, wall construction to prevent the spread of fire, minimum room sizes and pertinent concerns for the welfare of building occupants to name just a few ... These new requirements are not medically necessary or appropriate for the healthcare and reproductive services that abortion clinics provide. There are other medical facilities that perform far more invasive procedures, even requiring sedation, that are not held to the same level of building code requirements. Several that come to mind include dental and plastic surgery facilities, birthing centers, and places performing colonoscopies ... From a design and construction code perspective, abortion clinic spatial uses are not the same nor should be equated to hospital code requirements, or regulated similarly to the surgical requirements hospitals must adhere to ... The design and construction requirements for abortion clinics should be the same requirements used for medical offices. These cover the life and safety standards appropriate for the level of care being provided.[23]

Since the Supreme Court ruling, these concerns are no longer an issue; however, for the years prior to the decision, the research was useful for lawyers arguing before courts and the state boards of health commissions.

The second action I will highlight is the ongoing design work for the only remaining clinic in Jackson, Mississippi. This project began as a collaboration with Kimberly Tate and ArchiteXX, a women and architecture group based in New York City. Interested in challenging the architecture competition structure where winners for 'best' design are selected, we organised the 'Private Choices Public Spaces' call for ideas as an open public call asking for only a single postcard to be submitted during the summer of 2014. All submittals were exhibited that fall in a show designed and curated by ArchiteXX at The Sheila C. Johnson Design Center, within the Arnold and Sheila Aronson Galleries at Parson's The New School for Design. We organised public programming to engage with the broadest and most diverse audiences possible, including a roundtable discussion with an interdisciplinary group of New School faculty, a screening of a documentary about the Jackson clinic followed by a discussion with a lawyer from the Center for Reproductive Rights and the owner and director of the Jackson clinic, as well as an

Figure 22.2 'Private Choices Public Spaces' installation at The Sheila C. Johnson Design Center Arnold and Sheila Aronson Galleries at Parson's The New School for Design. Photograph by Ashley Simone, 2014.

open and public design charrette generating yet more postcard design ideas, which were added to the exhibition.

This structure allowed us to do several things simultaneously. First, we wanted to use this platform to raise broader awareness about the role and critical importance of design in all public space, especially in such contested spaces as women's healthcare clinics. To quote directly from our design call:

> Design is a powerful, effective, and often under-utilised tool in addressing the complexities of contested spaces. ArchiteXX calls you to collaborate with us in a practice of active citizenship through design. We believe design must engage challenging social and political dimensions of the built environment, such as access to reproductive health care, in order to make improvements at all scales for all people. Knee-jerk reactions to these issues are prevalent in mainstream media. We invite the public to think more broadly and deeply about the role design can play in dialogue with such complicated and multi-layered issues. The public-private threshold of an abortion clinic is a highly-nuanced interface of strong personal sentiments. Our design action takes the discomfort head-on, illuminating the spatial implications of access to reproductive health care and the role design can play in expanding the conversation.
>
> ArchiteXX initiated this design action to put our values regarding the profession of architecture into practice. Critical of the exploitative nature of conventional design competitions, the project is framed as an open-collaborative think-tank. The design action promotes dialogue and collaboration rather than competition to execute its goal. Through this mode of activism, we hope to transform the profession. It is an iterative and lived practice outside the norms of the conventional office. 'Private Choices, Public Spaces' is our first attempt, and we want to invite you to work with us.[24]

Our prompt asked for participants to consider the following:

> How can design enable dialogue in contested public spaces?
> How can a safe space be created within zones of protest?
> How can one's personal experience inform design in socially and politically charged spaces?
> How much space is needed for the personal, social, and public zones of access to reproductive healthcare?
> How should the separation between the public and private spaces of an abortion clinic be physically defined?

Second, we saw this design call, exhibition, and public programming as instrumental in practising engaged design research based on action and activism grounded in research undertaken for my book *Contested Spaces*. It brought architecture out into a much broader context. This is a critically important aspect of broadening architecture's engagement with current issues and thus expanding architecture's potential for working with others. Third, these particular design questions foreground and hopefully mainstream an explicitly female experience as the focal point of a design call – something that is not typically the case within architecture. Fourth, collaborative engagement has produced another tangent where we are now working with a team from one of the submittals to move the postcard idea forward into a detailed proposal to enable fundraising events to support eventual construction.

Conclusion

Action-based design research affects the built environment. As Katja Grillner writes, participatory action research works toward bringing about systemic change.[25] For me, this includes affecting power relations within the academy, and with respect to the discipline of architecture's perceived boundaries of engagement in the world. I acknowledge that I work from a position of privilege within the academy, which provides me with the financial stability to be able to do this sort of work. This is one of the reasons I left conventional practice: I sought a way to practise that would allow me, or even require me, to use design to improve the lives of the less privileged, who might not be aware of what architects do.

With the new US administration in place, it is unclear what is going to happen with respect to access to healthcare in general, and to women's reproductive healthcare specifically. It appears that this research is not yet concluded. As long as there are opportunities for architectural interdisciplinary involvement, architects are able to engage, to take action, and help foster agency. In this, we can follow Patricia Maguire who argues for a broader 'commitment to a liberatory, transformational project that is essential to any definition of feminism and feminist scholarships. At its core, feminism and its scholarship is a political movement for social, structural, and personal transformation.'[26] Citing Michelle Russell, 'the point is to challenge the world, not only study it'.[27]

Notes

1 Lori A. Brown, *Contested Spaces: Abortion Clinics, Women's Shelters and Hospitals* (Farnham: Ashgate Publishing, 2013), 2.
2 As I have written in the introduction to *Contested Spaces: Abortion Clinics, Women's Shelters and Hospitals*, this research has been a result of my personal frustration with the discipline's perceived lack of political engagement. My work continues to be activated by and engaged with examining such overlooked and under examined spaces, questioning and expanding architecture's spatial agency at an array of scales, and through the intersection between architecture and contested spatial relationships. The work is part of a larger collective of practices 'calling into question or critically dismantling power dynamics, . . . giving voice and representation to those who are often silenced or not represented, . . . helping to bring communities into action through collaborative design processes and . . . revealing the deeply embedded sociopolitical relationships structuring our spaces. See: Brown, *Contested Spaces*, 3.
3 See Lori A. Brown, ed., *Feminist Practices: Interdisciplinary Approaches to Women in Architecture* (Farnham: Ashgate Publishing, 2011) for other examples of design research at various scales.
4 Murray Fraser, '"A Two-Fold Movement": Design Research as Dialectical Critical Practice', in *Design Research in Architecture An Overview*, ed. Murray Fraser (Farnham: Ashgate Publishing, 2013), 217–18.
5 'ObamaCare and Women: ObamaCare Women's Health Service', in *Obamacare Facts*, http://obamacarefacts.com/obamacare-womens-health-services/.
6 Jackie Calmes, 'Obama Bars States From Denying Federal Money to Planned Parenthood,' *The New York Times*, 14 December 2016.

7   Julie Rovner, 'That Vow to Defund Planned Parenthood: Easy to Say, Hard to Do,' Policy-ish *NPR*, 15 January 2017.

8   Planned Parenthood, "Planned Parenthood Federation of American Annual Report 2014–2015" (2015), www.plannedparenthood.org/files/2114/5089/0863/2014-2015_PPFA_Annual_Report_.pdf.

9   Rovner, 'That Vow to Defund Planned Parenthood'.

10 Pamela Moss, 'Taking on, Thinking about, and Doing Feminist Research in Geography', in *Feminist Geography in Practice Research and Methods*, ed. Pamela Moss (Oxford: Blackwell Publishers, 2002), 13.

11 Ibid., 12.

12 Heidi Gottfried, 'Engaging Women's Communities: Dilemmas and Contradictions in Feminist Research' in *Feminism and Social Change: Bridging Theory and Practice*, ed. Heidi Gottfried (Urbana: University of Illinois Press, 1996), 10.

13 'Abortion Rights and Trump's Supreme Court Nominee', *On Point with Tom Ashbrook*, 30 January 2017.

14 'Mike Pence to Speak at Anti-Abortion Rally in First for Sitting Vice President', *Democracy Now*, 27 January 2017.

15 Lori Brown, Shoshanna Ehrlich, and Colleen MacQuarrie, 'Subverting the Constitution: Anti-Abortion Policies and Activism in the United States and Canada' in *Canadian Abortion Politics: Twenty-Five Years After Morgentaler*, ed. Tracy Penny Light and Shannon Stettner, forthcoming 2017.

16 Ibid.

17 Ibid.

18 Ibid.

19 To provide insight into reproductive healthcare access in the US, one needs to be aware of the scope of state restrictions that have been passed. Listed below are some of the state restrictions common to both Texas and Virginia.

   • Physician-only restriction; state prohibits certain qualified health care professionals from performing abortions
   • State restricts young women's access to abortion with mandatory parental notice and consent requirements
   • State allows certain entities to refuse specific reproductive health services, information, or referrals
   • Women subjected to biased counselling requirements and mandatory delays
   • State prohibits certain state employees or organizations from receiving state funds for counselling or referring women to abortion services
   • State restricts insurance coverage of abortion
   • Certain state employees/organisations are prohibited from receiving state funds for advocating or promoting abortion services
   • State refers women to crisis pregnancy centres (these often state-supported centres are anti-choice and established to convince women not to have an abortion; they provide an ultrasound but no medical care)
   • Building codes requiring clinic to meet ambulatory surgical centre facility requirements
   • Law provides for a 'Choose Life' licence-plate program that funnels money into anti-choice organisations.

20 'Texas Abortion Providers: Expansions & Restrictions Abortion Providers: Restrictions', *NARAL Pro-Choice America*, www.prochoiceamerica.org/government-and-you/state-governments/state-laws/tx-abortion-providers-expansions-restrictions.html (accessed January 16, 2017). *Whole Woman's Health et al. v. Hellerstedt, Commissioner, Texas Department of State Health Services, et al.,* Case No. 15–274, Certiorari to the United States Court of Appeals for the Fifth Circuit. (S. Ct. 2016).

21 Alexa Ura et al., 'Here Are the Texas Abortion Clinics That Have Closed Since 2013', *The Texas Tribune*, 28 June 2016.

22 'Tracking Texas Abortion Access Map', *Rewire*, 15 June 2016.

23 Author's letter to Virginia State Board Health Commissioner and Members of the Virginia Board of Health, 9 February 2015.

24 'Design Action 2014: Private Choices, Public Spaces'.

25 Katja Grillner, 'Design Research and Critical Transformations: Situating Thought; Projecting Action,' in *Design Research in Architecture: An Overview*, ed. Murray Fraser (Farnham: Ashgate Publishing, 2013), 89.

26 Patricia Maguire, 'Uneven Ground: Feminisms and Action Research' in *Handbook of Action Research*, ed. Peter Reason and Hilary Bradbury (London: Sage Publications, 2006), 61.

27 Ibid.

Chapter 23

The entrepreneurial self

Claudia Dutson

In 2000, management guru Tom Peters presented a millennial subjectivity for the dotcom age: 'Icon Woman' would be ' . . . turned on by her work! The work matters! The work is cool! She is in your face! She is an adventurer! She is the CEO of her life! . . . She is determined to make a difference!'[1]

Recognising that the discipline of architecture has become entangled with – and compromised by – the political and economic power shifts of the last forty years, architects and academics have responded with calls for strategies of engagement with some of the major actors in neoliberal capitalism in order to affect change. It is a concept with a number of different nuances: Rem Koolhaas' cynical engagement with Silicon Valley,[2] Keller Easterling's subversive 'playing with the rules of the game, manipulating things from within,'[3] and Sam Jacob's call for architects to embrace the skills of 'communications agencies, advertising and design' and 'fulfil the core disciplinary remit of making the world a better place.'[4]

While the tactics and standpoints differ, they all point to the limitations of oppositional politics and the marginalisation of the architect as a political agent, proposing instead new strategic performances with which architects can 'expand [their] repertoires of political activism,'[5] and the enactment of subjectivities and skillsets commonly found in the tech industry. These subjectivities will either leverage the effects of 'disrupting the mechanisms of capitalism'[6] through day-to-day activity, or aim to take a seat at tables of power. The argument for getting engaged at the table is that architectural academics and practitioners can be more influential than they would be if their engagement is antagonist to 'direct capitalism into more responsible enterprise.'[7]

The logic behind the argument is, in part, a recognition that we are firmly implicated in the processes of neoliberal capitalism: there is no longer an 'outside' from which to launch a critique or resistance. It is also the celebration of an agent derived from the neoliberal model of the entrepreneur – the archetype of which is the knowledge worker of the tech industry – an inventive and autonomous tactician which, it is hoped, holds potential to outdo capitalism on its own terms. However, this subjectivity has an ambiguous status: it is a trope, celebrated by McKinsey consultants like Peters, based on a pervasive myth about the potentials of disruption,[8] and it also echoes a Marxist political concept which hopes to locate within the contradictions of capitalism a possibility of emancipatory change or collapse of the system.

One of the most fully realised proposals that both acknowledges, and to some degree struggles with, the immanent difficulties of deploying a covertly subversive and disruptive subjectivity that can 'play in the system, but use it to their own ends'[9] is Peggy Deamer's ongoing work on architectural labour. Whilst Deamer invites us to see the valences of the knowledge worker as a subjectivity that can be advantageously occupied without resorting to power structures that monetise it, she nonetheless warns that the entrepreneur is neoliberalism's 'dream child' and the 'pretty face' of 'precarity, hyper-individualism, competition, and the inability to identify as a class in need of common security.'[10]

Drawing on a line of thought from the *Autonomia* movement in Italy that identifies the worker in post-Fordist economies of the knowledge industry as having a new agency, the knowledge worker suggests a possibility for autonomous 'self-actualisation' and consciousness. Deamer's hope is that in recognising their roles as labourers, specifically as immaterial labourers, there is a 'potential for mining the advantages of capitalism's new focus on production for architectural labour, value and relevance while also having a more fulfilling, less passive, and more disruptive role in capitalism.'[11]

As Deamer makes clear, architects are late to theorise their work as labour and, as a result, have underdeveloped strategies to address the nature of the economic and political conditions of neoliberal capitalism – this inability to identify as workers, she argues, means that 'we fail to politically position ourselves to combat capitalism's neoliberal turn.'[12] While some of her proposals are aimed towards immediate, pragmatic concerns about the specific labour conditions of architecture (the culture of unpaid interning, unpaid overtime, the apprentice system and exploitation) Deamer proposes that aligning architectural labour with the most radical elements of theories of immaterial labour can enable it to evade 'neoliberalism's grasp.'[13]

It is necessary, if unwieldy, to run through a set of definitions and characterisations of concepts of labour – immaterial labour, knowledge work and emotional labour – in order to assess this subjectivity and to consider what the implications are for women who take on the role of the entrepreneur. First, by focusing on Deamer's work, I will assess the perceived autonomy of the entrepreneur through critiques of immaterial labour in the creative industries, and ethnographies of knowledge work. Second, I will consider the formation of a passionate and entrepreneurial subjectivity – who in 'getting engaged' uses her affects to induce in another party a particular disposition and change in values – through Arlie Russell Hochschild's concept of emotional labour.[14]

I foreground feminist debates on the nature of contemporary work, supported by ethnographies of knowledge work and emotional labour, over Maurizio Lazzarato's thesis on immaterial labour, since the former are grounded in empirical study and reveal a far more precarious subjectivity than is hoped. The work of Hochschild, and Angela McRobbie, cautions us against underestimating the private and personal costs of entrepreneurial work, whilst Gideon Kunda, Catherine Casey and Yiannis Gabriel signal that we may overestimate the agency of the entrepreneurial subject.

However, I also want to propose that the political premises of Deamer's consideration of architectural work as labour,[15] and indeed Easterling's investigation of the operational modes of the institutions and corporations and dominant power players in the built environment, are timely and valuable.[16] Drawing on Rosi Braidotti's encouragement that we make 'adequate cartographies of our real-life conditions,'[17] I suggest that their work provides us with the basis from which to develop our practices.

Immaterial labour and knowledge work

Immaterial labour is defined by Lazzarato as the 'labour that produces the informational and cultural content of the commodity.'[18] It refers in the first instance to the work of abstracting and translating processes of production into computer networks, algorithms and data flows, and in the second to 'the kinds of activities that are not normally recognised as "work". It is the implications of these affective processes, 'defining and fixing cultural and artistic standards, fashions, tastes, consumer norms, and, more strategically, public opinion',[19] that I will elaborate on.

In 1959, the management consultant Peter Drucker introduced the term 'knowledge worker' to describe an increasing number of people who 'think for a living'. This includes doctors, teachers, finance workers, engineers – and indeed architects – those who work in the creative industries and information technologies, applying existing knowledge to solve complex problems, creating new knowledge or transferring knowledge into new domains.[20] The outputs of knowledge work are often 'innovative' and non-standard: they can be products or designs, patents, intellectual property, software, artworks. The value of knowledge work is not primarily the material worth of the physical product but its immaterial and abstract qualities.

The concepts of immaterial labour and knowledge work are closely connected, yet there are assumptions about the possibilities of the former that are contradicted by the history of knowledge work. Lazzarato has identified 'polymorphous self-employed autonomous work' as the most pervasive form of labour in neoliberal capitalism, and the intellectual worker as an entrepreneur who is 'inserted within a market that is constantly shifting and within networks that are changeable in time and space.'[21] While this implies that management has had to reactively cultivate this potent new force of labour, ethnographies of knowledge work instead describe these exact same practices as constitutive: they produce the subjectivities of knowledge work.

The concept of autonomy rests on the worker's investment in her own cognitive capital, signalling the ownership of both the means of production and the product – and is thus a key step in the identification of subjectivity as a potential for political trans-formation. However, the central processes at work in forming an entrepreneurial subjec-tivity, while documented extensively in management theory, are not fully elaborated in Lazzarato's political critique of work. In theories that develop Lazzarato's immaterial labour thesis, there is an overemphasis on the idea that the worker can 'achieve fulfilment through work' and 'find in her brain her own unalienated means of production.'[22] Deamer draws on this articulation of the worker as preceding his/her 'insertion into a labour context'[23] as a subject that industry does not itself create 'but simply takes it on board and adapts it'[24] and therefore distinguishes knowledge work as 'that which capitalism chews on easily' from immaterial labour as 'that which it can't easily digest.'[25] Yet Angela McRobbie calls attention to the 'aggressive neo-liberal underpinning of immaterial labour and the forms of biopower which shape up amenable kinds of subjectivities, giving rise to a new kind of society of control.'[26]

The possibility of a 'radical autonomy' where the architectural worker is able to use capitalism to her own ends is pre-empted by the formation and re-formation of subjectivity *through* work, as elucidated by Kunda's case study of the tech industry.[27] The knowledge industry is indeed characterised by an emphasis on autonomy – certainly relative to administrative fields and factory work – and the shift of top-down management to self-management, since the knowledge worker is expected to take on the responsibility for their own continuing development and acquisition of new knowledge. This entrepre-neurial subjectivity has its roots in the high-tech industries that arose in post-war America. West-Coast technology companies – particularly Varian and Hewlett Packard – sought to challenge the top-down hierarchical management styles of corporate America through innovative working practices. The new management style focused on the individual; celebrating an entrepreneurial spirit in their employees it encouraged risk-taking and, crucially, recognised that employees sought purposeful work. A necessity arose to foster a sense of shared objective between the company and the employee. These objectives, often vague and hyperbolic, downplayed the profit-making aspirations of a company in favour of 'making a difference' and 'changing the world' thus incorporating an employee's need for personal growth and desire to do meaningful work with a bigger shared goal.[28]

This is achieved through what Kunda describes as 'culture',[29] a feature of manage-ment that is not merely responding to the needs of a cognitively and affectively engaged workforce, but one that takes an active constitutive role in the formation of those workers. Kunda outlines the processes of eliciting affective states, especially positive ones such as passion and enthusiasm: specifically the way the motivations and values of its workers were operated on by 'controlling the underlying experiences, thoughts, and feelings that guide [an employee's] actions.'[30] Kunda explains that the aim of culture is towards organi-sational interest and self-interest becoming the same thing.[31] Specifically highlighting the worker's entanglement of the 'real self' with the employee's need for self-actualisation and a yearning to realise positive change in wider society, the ideal candidate in Kunda's study is the 'self-starter' – an entrepreneurial subjectivity elicited by 'behavioural rules [that] are vague: be creative, take initiative, take risks, "push at the system", and, ultimately, "do what's right".'[32] The resulting entrepreneur-employee is thus 'driven by internal commitment, strong identification with company goals, and intrinsic satisfaction from work.'[33]

It is important to note that the entrepreneur is not necessarily the CEO of a business, nor self-employed, but anybody who has taken on an entrepreneurial (that is risk-taking and self-driven) role within their own employment. And whilst the company cultures that are the basis of my argument address employees embedded in large corporations, the salient features of such cultures are no longer confined to any one organisation and their employees. As the *Autonomia* movement noted: worker relations left the factory and are now diffuse within society.[34]

Academics from across the creative industries have noted that 'artists, new media workers and other cultural labourers are hailed as 'model entrepreneurs' by industry and government figures.'[35] The work of 'creatives' mirrors the political economy of post-Fordist work, not simply because it is precarious, but in its being 'reliant on affective and cognitive work processes like communication, teamwork, improvisation, self-management and the performing body.'[36] Opening up discussions about the biopolitics of immaterial labour, specifically in relation to gender, Elyssa Livergent connects the defining conditions of employment: precarity, competition and 'reliance on informal networks and communities to access work' with the fundamentally affective dimension of immaterial labour. The entrepreneur-performer 'seeks to develop abilities and communities that will support her in innovating and risking with her body, her ideas and her relationships' as she matches 'capitalism's aspirations for an ideal passionate, socialized and productive, post-Fordist worker.'[37]

The concept of passionate work:[38] the exuberant commitment demanded of 'self-reliant' (although already in debt) women, and romanticising of the all-nighter to 'complete a fashion collection, or to wrap up a film edit', expose what McRobbie calls a 'gender effect' which is missing in debates of immaterial labour.[39] She is adamant that any political potential of the 'entrepreneur' in neoliberal economies 'is decisively pre-empted by the intense forms of biopolitical governmentality which constantly address women and their bodies' in ways that connect personal satisfactions with consumer culture, and individualises the negative affects of a woman's desire to become the CEO of her life. For McRobbie, there is an imperative to 'explore the actual points of tension – the levels of anxiety, the new realms of pain and injury – which accrue from the excessive demands of these multi-tasking careers'[40] as entrepreneurs in the creative sectors.

While this appears to trouble Deamer's ideas, it might also help us to reconcile her timely work with a feminist position of situated ethics. Isabelle Stengers' warning that the entrepreneur is a 'person of "opportunity", deaf and blind to the question of the world that their efforts contribute towards constructing'[41] guides us to pay attention to the broader contexts that Deamer has been interrogating. For Rosi Braidotti 'a subject's ethical core is not his/her moral intentionality, as much as the effects of the power . . . her actions are likely to have upon the world' thus re-inscribing historical accounts of activism, and ongoing accounts of present activity (in evidence in the 2016 AHRA Architecture and Feminisms conference in Stockholm) with an updated urgency.[42] These existing practices in architecture,[43] in particular those that foreground the desire to 'enter into modes of relation with multiple others'[44] by bringing numerous stakeholders and disciplines into a discussion, enter into an ethical account of the consequences of actions taken.

As well as revealing relational models of agency that are not based on an individual's entrepreneurial autonomy and disruptive potential, they also highlight the imperative to counter the hyper-individualism that underlies the proposal to get engaged entrepreneurially with communities of care. The grounding of Jane Rendell's Ethics in the Built Environment project in situated feminist practices, for instance, brought a pressing need for her to account for the sequence of events that led to her 'standing down' as Dean of Research, and to speak frankly about the affective costs for the individual who takes a stand.[45]

Making a transversal connection between the work of activism and Deamer's proposition allows us to consider both taking a stand and taking a seat as a form of labour. Can we explore the 'actual points of tension' of the work of activism and interrogate the entrepreneurial subjectivity who takes her 'seat at the table' to influence or steer capitalism towards better ends? If we take an engagement to also be an attempt on the part of the political agent to affect the beliefs, values and actions of businesses, corporations and institutions, can 'getting engaged' and 'playing in the system' be considered a kind of affective and emotional labour?

Emotional labour

To this discussion I bring the concept of emotional labour, first proposed by sociologist Arlie Russell Hochschild in her book *The Managed Heart*, as the management of a worker's states of being (their emotions, attitudes and beliefs) in order to affect the states of being of another (usually their customers).[46] It includes the work of flight attendants, call-centre workers and waiting staff (typically sectors endorsing service-with-a-smile) but can refer to any work where an emotional disposition is a requirement of the job, for instance doctors, teachers, academics, and – as noted by McRobbie and Livergent – creative workers.

An example from Hochschild is the management of the specific emotions in the airline industry – cheerfulness and anger. The smile in service-with-a-smile is expected by paying customers, but must at the same time appear genuinely offered. Anger, on the other hand, is an emotion that must be managed in the passenger, as well as in the flight attendants themselves as they are patronised, sexually harassed and on the receiving end of passenger ire. Employees are 'not just required to see and think as they like and required to only show feeling (surface acting) in institutionally approved ways'[47] but must endeavour to really feel it – this is called 'deep acting'. Hochschild's attention is focused on how employees are expected to draw on personal emotional reserves, a company expects the 'authentic' self to be at work and 'hopes to make this private resource a company asset.' At the same time, sophisticated techniques of 'deep acting' are deployed by the company who 'suggest how to imagine and thus how to feel'.[48]

Hochschild draws out the reciprocal and negative effects of deep acting on the sense of self, where managing affective states through a kind of acting is not centred on the contrivance of outward effects, but on the production of authentic emotions that are felt internally. Hochschild challenges the idea that a distinction can be maintained between 'real' emotions and those elicited by the company, asking whose emotions are being performed by an employee as they reconcile their private feelings with those expected at work:[49]

> The worker may lose touch with her feelings, as in burnout, or she may have to struggle with the company interpretation of what they mean.[50]

The labour of emotional labour is both the requirement 'to induce or supress feeling in order to sustain the outward countenance that produces the proper state of mind in others'[51] as well as the process of reclaiming her own feelings. The flight attendants in Hochschild's study are left to devise ways, both at work and at home, to set the boundaries of their own emotions themselves. Such an ambivalence is also the 'most pervasive and manifest effect of the experience of working in the new culture'[52] of the knowledge industry. Kunda writes that it is common for employees to simultaneously hold an adherence to a company culture and its contradictory cynicism:

> While the culture is . . . founded on self-awareness, [there is a] deeply ingrained ambiguity. Where an overarching morality is preached, there is also opportunistic cynicism; and where fervent commitment is demanded, there is pervasive irony.[53]

These ethnographies support McRobbie's suggestion that the subjectivities of post-Fordist work are neither robust nor fully-formed. Both Kunda and Hochschild report on individualised subjectivities that are vulnerable to burnout,[54] exhaustion and confusion: 'the subject is 'an ambivalent, fluctuating, ironic self, at war with itself and with its internalised images of self and other.'[55]

Hochschild's work on the consequences of emotional labour correlates with Kunda's findings on the management of affects – such as cheerfulness, passion and motivation – in strong company cultures within the knowledge and creative industries, and, by extension, any work where the manipulation of emotions and affect become part of labour. While neither Deamer nor Easterling have presented the entrepreneur as specifically gendered, I suggest that viewing the entrepreneur as someone who takes her seat at the table in order to affect change through her influence, puts focus upon the emotional labour of influencing the values, beliefs and actions of systemic or institutional bodies – be they corporations, institutions or industry professionals.

This strongly suggests that the proposal to engage with institutions, companies and practices that one sees as ethically problematic by 'taking a seat at the table' in order to promote more responsible courses of action, and in the hope of 'making a difference' is falsely premised. In showing that entrepreneurial subjectivity is itself constituted through the elicitation and production of affects, values, behaviours, experiences and desires that align with the company's values, Hochschild and Kunda present a subject that is far more conflicted and compromised than Easterling and Deamer would hope, and also one that is unlikely to be radically autonomous.

'Believe that together we can do anything'[56]

The problem for the political project of radical autonomy (that is, a subject that precedes its insertion into work) is that in the entrepreneur all the moments that signify her autonomy are identified in ethnographies of work as moments where subjectivity is at its most precarious. Identifying the 'the deeply constitutive effects' and 'specific performativity of emotional labour' where the employee must go beyond 'seeming to be but . . . coming to be,'[57] Kathi Weeks affirms the findings of ethnographies of knowledge work, where management solicits shared objectives and channels (vague) behavioural rules in the course of realising a new employee subjectivity. These processes call into question the possibility of enacting a subversive subjectivity, and the possibility that such subjectivities can move the values, actions and beliefs of 'capitalism' into better modes.

McRobbie highlights the costs of enacting entrepreneurial subjectivities that have become privatised and individualised and warns that interstices that present themselves as the potential emergence of a political resistance are momentary and fleeting in the 'landscape of capitalist domination, which entails new levels and forms of submission.'[58] Further, she queries the celebration of the 'vitality and apparent proto-communism of contemporary economic forms'[59] in the political landscapes of the US, UK and Europe, where individual responsibility for health, work, and economic wellbeing takes precedence. For McRobbie meaningful work and a more autonomous, participatory and intelligent role in the workplace does not mean that we are 'better able to re-imagine solidaristic forms of mutual support and co-operation.'[60] It is rather a remuneration for the losses of the welfare state; the dismantling of unions; and for the undermining of the power of solidarities in feminist and anti-racist activism, and this remuneration simultaneously restructures society through a complex biopolitics.[61] These shifts run counter to solidarity since they inaugurate what McRobbie calls a 'powerful regime which inculcates cynicism and opportunism manifest in the context of . . . network sociality.'[62]

Indeed, for Yiannis Gabriel, cynicism itself disables any critical standpoint from which a critique of an organisation can be made. Cynicism, he says, is based on an individual's acknowledgement of an instrumental dependence on the organisation and a simultaneous denial of psychological attachment to it. Thus, 'the cynic's core fantasy is the belief that they can remain "unpolluted" – untouched by the organisation's iniquities, even as they profit from its bounty.'[63]

Parallels can be drawn here with the architect-activist who hopes to engage with corporate or institutional entities in order to affect change, whilst resisting being affected by it, even as they benefit from that position. Cynicism, as described by Gabriel, is not so much an internal lack of sincerity in the subject, but a conflict between dependency and denial of attachment. Taking a seat at the table entails some degree of instrumental dependence on the protocols to secure that place: in order to get a seat in the first place one must enact a subjectivity that has to at least appear to have internalised of a set of values, beliefs and motivations that are counter to what one holds. The denial of attachment is the belief that the worker will remain unaffected by their engagement, or their failure to recognise that any position of influence is contingent – up until the moment that they speak up and disclose their true position.

In conclusion I want to return to another possibility within Deamer's proposal, one that I find more hopeful. Whilst I propose that the subjectivities created and elicited by management itself, in line with its own culture, are not the location for enacting sustainability, resistance or situating ethical or subversive movements – the recognition that we are within the system that we intend to critique is an important step.

For Braidotti, a feminist immanent position 'assumes the humility of saying "we are a part of capitalism"' and counters the tendency to try to locate the specific break points of capitalism. Reminding us that capitalism 'doesn't break, it bends – it enfolds and unfolds',[64] Braidotti's centre-staging of the biopolitical aspects of this enfolding can be addressed by bringing ethnographies, case studies and specific empirical research into dialogue with architecture. The work of Deamer and Easterling could therefore be seen as a forensic account of the contemporary architecture sector in which, as architectural practitioners and academics, we now work. They both provide excellent analysis of the conditions of neoliberal capitalism in relation to architecture and in bringing the discourses of immaterial labour into the pragmatics and realities of architectural work, Deamer has instigated a long-overdue project.

By connecting these discourses of subjectivity within the context of work, with feminist activist practices in the built environment, there is a potential to develop positions of critical practice that do not rely on the individualised, privatised management of affect in disruptive, tactical or subversive ways. Current academic practices in architecture that are negotiating their engagements with ethically questionable institutions, and with the real-world effects of neoliberal economic policies, reveal not only the necessity for, but the possibilities and positive effects of structuring ethical relations.

In working to create supportive frameworks we need to ensure that our attempts to make a difference mean that we neither merely shift or reproduce the exploitations of a system onto another group of people, nor leave those who do speak out open to vulnerability and institutional bullying. Whether we take a stand, or take a seat at the table, we must not ignore the costs of performing in this new economy.

Notes

1 Tom Peters, 'What Will We Do for Work?', *TIME*, 155.21 (2000) 68–71.
2 See for instance, Pooja Bhatia, 'Rem Koolhaas Takes Silicon Valley', in *OXY*, (28 December 2014) http://www.ozy.com/provocateurs/rem-koolhaas-takes-silicon-valley/36643
3 Keller Easterling, 'Forging Rules: Glass Bead in Conversation with Keller Easterling and Benedict Singleton', *Glass Bead*, www.glass-bead.org/journal/site-0-castalia-the-game-of-ends-and-means/?lang=enview
4 Sam Jacob, 'Architecture might have to become less architectural', Dezeen.com https://www.dezeen.com/2014/01/16/opinion-sam-jacob-how-architecture-can-regain-social-significance/
5 Summary of *Extrastatecraft* on *KellerEasterling.com*, http://kellereasterling.com/books/extrastatecraft-the-power-of-infrastructure-space
6 Peggy Deamer, 'Architectural Work: Immaterial Labour', in *Industries of Architecture*, ed. by Katie Lloyd Thomas, Tilo Amhoff, Nick Beech (Abingdon, Oxon: Routledge, 2015) 147.
7 Deamer, 'Architectural Work: Immaterial Labour', 146.
8 Disruptive talent refers to individuals who 'see the world differently.' This term was introduced to me by Katie Lloyd Thomas, and the concepts of 'disruption' and 'disruptive innovation' come from Clayton Christensen's 1997 book, *The Innovator's Dilemma* and has been heavily criticised for a lack of credible basis. Jill Lepore, 'The Disruption Machine', *The New Yorker*, www.newyorker.com/magazine/2014/06/23/the-disruption-machine; A psychometric testing company based in Cambridge,

UK claim to have originated the term and the BBC describe Richard Branson as an example of a disruptive talent. www.cambridgenetwork.co.uk/news/assessing-disruptive-talent-going-beyond-psychometrics/

9   Deamer, 'Architectural Work: Immaterial Labour', 144.

10 Peggy Deamer, 'The Architect as Activist', *Culture Matters*, http://culturematters.org.uk/index.php/itemlist/user/721-peggydeamer and Peggy Deamer, Quilian Riano and Manuel Shvartzberg, 'Identifying the Designer as Worker', *MasContext.com*, www.mascontext.com/tag/manuel-shvartzberg/

11 Deamer, 'Architectural Work: Immaterial Labour', 146.

12 Deamer, 146.

13 Deamer, 144.

14 Arlie Russell Hochschild, *The Managed Heart: Commercialization of Human Feeling* (Berkeley, CA: University of California Press, 2003), 6–7.

15 See also Peggy Deamer, 'Globalization and the Fate of Theory', in *Global Perspectives on Critical Architecture*, ed. Gevork Hartoonian, (Abingdon, Oxon: Routledge, 2015); and Peggy Deamer, 'Practising Practice', in *Perspecta: The Yale Architecture Journal*, Vol. 44, (2011).

16 Keller Easterling, *Extrastatecraft: The Power of Infrastructure Space* (London: Verso, 2014).

17 Rosi Braidotti, 'On Putting the Active Back into Activism', *New Formations*, Number 68, Spring 2010, 42–57, 56.

18 Maurizio Lazzarato, 'Immaterial Labour', in *Radical thought in Italy: A Potential Politics*, ed. by Paolo Virno, Michael Hardt (Minneapolis: University of Minnesota Press, 1996), 133–47, 133.

19 Lazzarato, 'Immaterial Labour', 142.

20 Peter F. Drucker, *Landmarks of Tomorrow: A Report on the New Post Modern World*, (London: Heinemann, 1959).

21 Lazzarato, 'Immaterial Labour', 149.

22 Tiziana Terranova, 'Free Labor: Producing Culture for the Digital Economy', in *Social Text*, 63 Volume 18, Number 2, (Summer 2000), 33–58, 37.

23 Deamer, 'Architectural Work: Immaterial Labour', 144.

24 Deamer, 144.

25 Deamer, 144.

26 Angela McRobbie, 'Reflections on Feminism, Immaterial Labour and the Post-Fordist Regime', in *New Formations*, 70, (2011) 60–76, 69.

27 Gideon Kunda, *Engineering Culture: Control and Commitment in a High-Tech Corporation*, (Philadelphia: Temple University Press, 2009).

28 They also have a strong connection with counter-culture movements such as the Human Potential Movement which drew on Abraham Maslow's ideas and Douglas McGregor's concept of Theory X & Theory Y.

29 Kunda, *Engineering Culture,* 4–11.

30 Kunda, 11.

31 Kunda, 91.

32 Kunda, 90.

33 Kunda, 11.

34 McRobbie, 'Reflections on Feminism', 69.

35 Rosalind Gill and Andy Pratt, 'Precarity and Cultural Work in the Social Factory? Immaterial Labour, Precariousness and Cultural Work', in *Theory, Culture & Society*, Volume 25 No. 7–8, (December 2008) 1–30, 1.

36 Elyssa Livergant, 'The Passion Players', *New Left Project,* http://www.newleftproject.org/index.php/site/article_comments/the_passion_players (accessed 27th June 2016).

37 Livergant, 'The Passion Players'.

38 Angela McRobbie, 'Is Passionate Work a Neoliberal Delusion?', *openDemocracy,* https://www.opendemocracy.net/transformation/angela-mcrobbie/is-passionate-work-neoliberal-delusion (accessed 5th April 2017).

39 McRobbie, 'Is Passionate Work a Neoliberal Delusion?'; Peggy Deamer has also challenged the naturalisation of the all-night culture in architecture and its association with 'passion' and status, she actively prevents her students from working this way. https://www.datumdiscourse.org/blog/2017/1/2/peggy-deamer-interview-with-datum

40 McRobbie, 'Reflections on Feminism', 75.

41 Isabelle Stengers, 'The Cosmopolitical Proposal', in *Making Things Public: Atmospheres of Democracy,* ed. Bruno Latour & Peter Weibel (Cambridge, Mass.: MIT Press, 2005) 994–1003, 998.

42 It is impossible to name all of these since they were the rule, rather than the exception at the conference, but I refer especially to Peg Rawes and Douglas Spencer, Igea Troiani, Katherine Gibson and Doina Petrescu, Jos Boys and Lori Brown, in this volume.

43 In the United Kingdom Peg Rawes' work on ethics, biopolitics and relational practices, and Jane Rendell's situated ethical engagement with divestment in fossil fuels at UCL, and her Ethics in the Built Environment project are key examples.

44 Rosi Braidotti, 'On Putting the Active Back into Activism', 45.

45   Jane Rendell, 'Giving an Account of Oneself: Architecturally', *Journal of Visual Culture* Volume 15:3, (4 October 2016) 334–348.

46   Arlie Russell Hochschild, *The Managed Heart*, 6–7.

47   Hochschild, *The Managed Heart*, 49.

48   Hochschild, 49.

49   Hochschild, 197.

50   Ibid., 197.

51   Hochschild, 7.

52   Catherine Casey, '"Come, Join Our Family": Discipline and Integration in Corporate Organisational Culture'. *Human Relations*, 52:.2, (1999) 155–178, 169.

53   Kunda, 222.

54   Hochschild, 186–188.

55   Kunda, 222.

56   Rule eleven of Carly Fiorina's 'Rules of the Garage' for Hewlett Packard. John C. Abell, 'Rules of the Garage, and Then Some', *Wired*, (2009) https://www.wired.com/2009/01/rules-of-the-ga/ (accessed 3 October 2015).

57   Kathi Weeks suggests that Hochschild's work proves invaluable in forming a position on the critical immanent subjectivity, since it 'enables some crucial insights into the significance of the rise of immaterial forms of labour.' Specifically 'that "active emotional labour" is first, a skilful activity, and second, a practice with constitutive effects.' Kathi Weeks, 'Life Within and Against Work: Affective Labor, Feminist Critique, and Post-Fordist Politics', *Ephemera*: *Theory & Politics in Organization*, 7.1. (2007) 233–249, 241.

58   McRobbie, 70.

59   McRobbie, 69.

60   McRobbie, 64.

61   McRobbie, 63.

62   McRobbie, 65.

63   Yiannis Gabriel, 'Beyond Happy Families: A Critical Reevaluation of the Control-Resistance-Identity Triangle', *Human Relations*, 52.2 (1999) 179–203, 191.

64   Heather Davis and Rosi Braidotti, 'Thinking with Zoe: An Interview with Rosi Braidotti', *AModern,net* http://amodern.net/article/amoderns-thinking-zoe/

Index

Page numbers in italics refer to figures.

Index